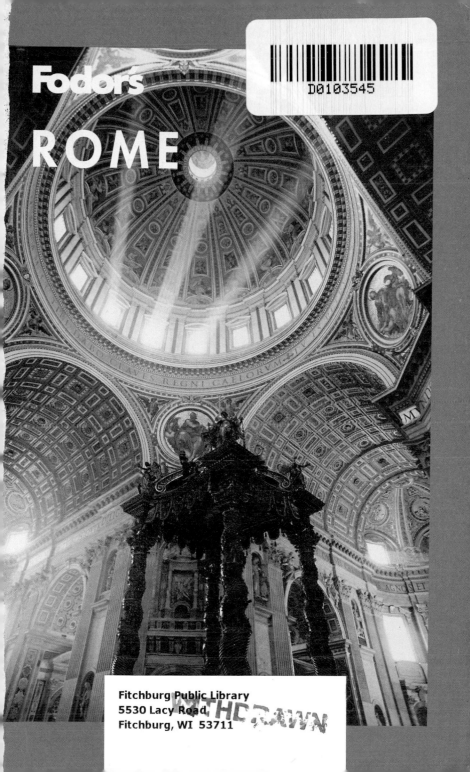

Fodor's

ROME

D0103545

WELCOME TO ROME

Italy's vibrant capital lives in the present, but no other city on earth evokes its past so powerfully. For over 2,500 years, emperors, popes, artists, and common citizens have left their mark here. Archaeological remains from ancient Rome, art-stuffed churches, and the treasures of Vatican City vie for your attention, but Rome is also a wonderful place to practice the Italian-perfected *il dolce far niente,* the sweet art of idleness. Your most memorable experiences may include sitting at a caffè in the Campo de' Fiori or strolling in a beguiling piazza.

TOP REASONS TO GO

★ **History:** The Colosseum and the Forum are just two amazing archaeological musts.

★ **Food:** From pasta and pizza to innovative fare, great meals at trattorias or enotecas.

★ **Art:** Works by Michelangelo, Raphael, Bernini, and Caravaggio dazzle around the city.

★ **Churches:** Places of worship from the Byzantine to baroque eras hold artistic bounty.

★ **Landmarks:** The Pantheon, St. Peter's Basilica, the Spanish Steps—to name only a few.

★ **Shopping:** Chic boutiques around Piazza di Spagna, flea-market finds in Trastevere.

Fodor's ROME

Design: Tina Malaney, *Associate Art Director*; Erica Cuoco, *Production Designer*

Photography: Jennifer Arnow, *Senior Photo Editor*

Maps: Rebecca Baer, *Senior Map Editor*; Mark Stroud, Henry Colomb (Moon Street Cartography); David Lindroth, *Cartographers*

Production: Angela L. McLean, *Senior Production Manager*; Jennifer DePrima, *Editorial Production Manager*

Sales: Jacqueline Lebow, *Sales Director*

Business & Operations: Chuck Hoover, *Chief Marketing Officer*; Joy Lai, *Vice President and General Manager*; Stephen Horowitz, *Head of Business Development and Partnerships*

Writers: Ariston Anderson, Nicole Arriaga, Agnes Crawford, Maria Pasquale

Editors: Amanda Sadlowski, Caroline Trefler, Alexis Kelly, Anuja Madar

Production Editor: Carrie Parker

11th Edition

ISBN 978-0-14-754672-2

ISSN 0276–2560

All details in this book are based on information supplied to us at press time. Always confirm information when it matters, especially if you're making a detour to visit a specific place. Fodor's expressly disclaims any liability, loss, or risk, personal or otherwise, that is incurred as a consequence of the use of any of the contents of this book.

SPECIAL SALES

This book is available at special discounts for bulk purchases for sales promotions or premiums. For more information, e-mail specialmarkets@penguinrandomhouse.com.

PRINTED IN THE UNITED STATES OF AMERICA

10 9 8 7 6 5 4 3 2 1

CONTENTS

CONTENTS

ABOUT
THIS GUIDE

Fodor's Ratings

Everything in this guide is worth doing—we don't cover what isn't—but exceptional sights, hotels, and restaurants are recognized with additional accolades. **Fodor's Choice** ★ indicates our top recommendations; highlights places we deem highly recommended; and **Best Bets** call attention to notable hotels and restaurants in various categories. Care to nominate a new place? Visit Fodors.com/contact-us.

Trip Costs

We list prices wherever possible to help you budget well. Hotel and restaurant price categories from **$** to **$$$$** are noted alongside each recommendation. For hotels, we include the lowest cost of a standard double room in high season. For restaurants, we cite the average price of a main course at dinner or, if dinner isn't served, at lunch. For attractions, we always list adult admission fees; discounts are usually available for children, students, and senior citizens.

Hotels

Our local writers vet every hotel to recommend the best overnights in each price category, from budget to expensive. Unless otherwise specified, you can expect private bath, phone, and TV in your room. For expanded hotel reviews, visit Fodors.com.

Top Picks	Hotels &
★ **Fodor's** Choice	**Restaurants**
	⊡ Hotel
Listings	⟲ Number of
⊠ Address	rooms
✉ Branch address	❍ Meal plans
☎ Telephone	W Restaurant
🖷 Fax	⟲ Reservations
⊕ Website	🏛 Dress code
✎ E-mail	▭ No credit cards
▧ Admission fee	$ Price
☺ Open/closed	
times	**Other**
Ⓜ Subway	⇨ See also
✛ Directions or	☞ Take note
Map coordinates	⅄ Golf facilities

Restaurants

Unless we state otherwise, restaurants are open for lunch and dinner daily. We mention dress code only when there's a specific requirement and reservations only when they're essential or not accepted.

Credit Cards

The hotels and restaurants in this guide typically accept credit cards. If not, we'll say so.

EUGENE FODOR

Hungarian-born Eugene Fodor (1905–91) began his travel career as an interpreter on a French cruise ship. The experience inspired him to write *On the Continent* (1936), the first guidebook to receive annual updates and discuss a country's way of life as well as its sights. Fodor later joined the U.S. Army and worked for the OSS in World War II. After the war, he kept up his intelligence work while expanding his guidebook series. During the Cold War, many guides were written by fellow agents who understood the value of insider information. Today's guides continue Fodor's legacy by providing travelers with timely coverage, insider tips, and cultural context.

EXPERIENCE ROME

ROME TODAY

Rome, the Eternal City, is 25 centuries old and yet is still constantly reinventing itself. The glories of Ancient Rome, the pomp of the Renaissance Papacy, and the futuristic architecture of the 20th and 21st centuries all blend miraculously into a harmonious whole here. The fact that you can get Wi-Fi in the shadow of 2,000-year-old ruins sort of sums things up, and it's this fusion of old and new and the casual way that Romans live with their weighty history that make this city so unique.

The 21st Century

Rome has changed a lot, relatively speaking, since the millennium. Much of the *centro storico* (historic center) has been pedestrianized or has had its access limited to residents, public transport, and taxis, so you can now stroll around landmarks like the Pantheon, the Trevi Fountain, and the Spanish Steps without having to dodge a constant stream of traffic. One radical change for Italy is that smoking is banned in all public places, including restaurants and pubs. And central areas such as Monti, Testaccio, and San Lorenzo have become gentrified or arty-chic, so you can extend your sightseeing range to spots tourists wouldn't have dreamed of visiting back in the 1980s or '90s.

Multiculturalism

While nowhere near as diverse as cities such as London and Paris, spend a day in Rome's Esquilino neighborhood, for instance, and you'll see that the Eternal City is slowly becoming more cosmopolitan. Once famous for its fruit and vegetable market at Piazza Vittorio, Esquilino has fast become a multiethnic stomping ground, with a vast array of Chinese, Indian, African, and Middle Eastern restaurants. The now world-famous Orchestra di Piazza Vittorio, made up of 16 musicians from North Africa, South America, the Caribbean, Eastern Europe, and Italy, got their start in this ramshackle district just steps from Rome's Termini station and now perform at festivals around the world. It's worth noting, too, that Rome, the stronghold of Roman Catholicism is also home to Europe's largest mosque. Located near the elegant Parioli district, north of the city, its doors opened in 1995 and welcomes visitors of all faiths.

WHAT'S NEW

Over morning cappuccinos Romans love especially to talk about two things: sports and politics. As a sort of ritual greeting, Romans discuss the latest news about the city's two soccer teams and the latest political scandal.

In the world of sports, Roma and Lazio supporters are bitter enemies. Hostilities between fans of these two teams peak twice a year, during the "derby," the direct matches between the two teams. If you happen to be in Rome at this time, you'll witness surreal and unusual silences periodically overtaking the city, only to be broken by thunderous screaming and shouting when a goal is scored.

Politics-wise, after the controversial era of Silvio Berlusconi, Roman first embraced the young prime

New Architecture

Rome may be firmly anchored in the distant past, but that's never been an obstacle to its journey into the new millennium. Just look at some of the architectural marvels that have emerged in the last 20 years: the Auditorium Parco della Musica (Renzo Piano, 2002), the new Jubilee Church (formerly Chiesa di Dio Padre Misericordioso; Richard Meier, 2003), the Museo dell'Ara Pacis (Richard Meier, 2006), and the MAXXI—Museo Nazionale delle Arti del XXI Secolo (Zaha Hadid, 2010). In 2011, Rome also built a new bridge: the grandiose Ponte della Musica over the Tiber River. The eco-friendly bridge, which looks like two giant white harps rising from the ground, can be used only by pedestrians and cyclists. Other more modern projects are in the works too, including the Massimiliano Fuksas–designed New Congress Center, nicknamed "La Nuvola" for its futuristic suspended cloud shape, which finally opened in October 2016.

New Transportation Lines

Romans are anxiously awaiting the completion of the new Metro Linea C, which will cut through the city center at Piazza Venezia and link with both the A and B lines at Ottaviano for St. Peter's and the Colosseum, respectively. Expected to considerably ease surface-traffic congestion, progress on the new line has gone slowly, because every time a shaft is sunk in Roman ground, it reveals some new important archaeological site and all work halts for the ensuing excavation. The entire Metro station planned for Piazza Torre Argentina had to be canceled, in fact, due to the wealth of material uncovered. Currently only the peripheral section of line C is running, from Lodi eastward.

In addition, Italo, Italy's first private railway, now gives travelers an alternative to the high-speed Frecciarossa service offered by state-run Trenitalia. Both Italo and Trenitalia trains leave from Termini and the newly restructured Tiburtino station, connecting Rome with most of Italy's other major cities. Journey times are roughly the same, but Italo is usually cheaper, especially when booking in advance online. Trenitalia's high-speed Frecciarossa trains are fancier, especially in business class and above, and amenities include leather seats by furniture designer Poltrona Frau and free (although rather spotty) on-board Wi-Fi.

minister, Matteo Renzi when he gained power in 2014. The 39-year-old center-left politician was the youngest head of government Italy has ever had. But the recent tide of populism spreading through Europe reached Italy in late 2016, when a constitutional referendum to amend parts of the Italian Constitution was overwhelmingly defeated by voters and Renzi stepped down in response to what he saw as a vote against his government. Eyes are currently on President Sergio Mattarella to see what happens next; either a temporary government will form from the current Parliament or there will be a round of early elections for the PM spot.

WHAT'S WHERE

The following numbers refer to chapters in the book.

3 Ancient Rome. No other archaeological park in the world has so compact a nucleus of fabled sights.

4 The Vatican. An independent sovereign state, the Pope's residence draws millions to St. Peter's Basilica and the Vatican Museums. Borgo and Prati are the neighborhoods right outside the Vatican.

5 Piazza Navona, Campo de' Fiori, and the Jewish Ghetto. The Piazza Navona and Campo de' Fiori are busy meeting points, surrounded by restaurants and caffè, with the Pantheon nearby. The Jewish Ghetto is the historic center of Jewish life in Rome, and still home to Rome's main synagogue.

6 Piazza di Spagna. The Spanish Steps are iconic, and the surrounding area is the place to window shop, thanks to upscale fashion boutiques. The Trevi Fountain is a short walk away.

7 Repubblica and Quirinale. These areas bustle with government offices during the day, but are also home to several churches and sights, including the Bernini's Baroque Sant'Andrea al Quirinale.

8 Villa Borghese and Piazza del Popolo. The Villa Borghese, Rome's vast city park, is home to dazzling museums while nearby Piazza del Popolo is prime people-watching territory.

9 Trastevere. This picturesque neighborhood attracts locals and visitors to its restaurants and wine bars. The Janiculum Hill has incomparable views.

10 Aventino and Testaccio. These neighborhoods are off the usual tourist track but have the vibrancy of true Rome. Aventino is an elegant residential area, while Testaccio is traditionally working-class, although rapidly gentrifying, and has a hip nightlife scene.

11 Monti, Esquilino, Celio, San Lorenzo, San Giovanni, Pigneto, and the Via Appia Antica. These are some of Rome's least touristy and most beloved neighborhoods, with plenty of ancient sights and spectacular churches, as well as Monti's artisanal shops, restaurants, bars, and high-end boutiques. The verdant Via Appia Antica leads past the landmark church of Domine Quo Vadis to the catacombs and beyond.

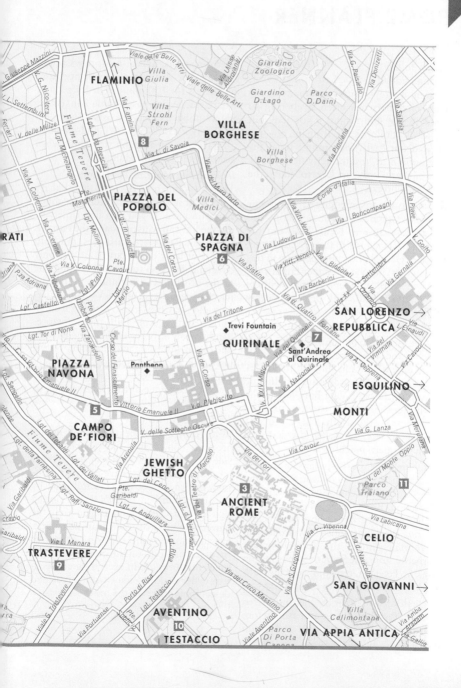

ROME PLANNER

When to Go

Spring and fall are the best times to visit, with mild temperatures and many sunny days. Summers are often sweltering so come in July and August if you like, but we advise doing as the Romans do—get up and out early, seek refuge from the afternoon heat, resume activities in early evening, and stay up late to enjoy the nighttime breeze.

Most attractions are closed on major holidays. Come August, many shops and restaurants close as locals head out for vacation. Remember that air-conditioning is still a relatively rare phenomenon in this city, so carrying a small paper fan in your bag can work wonders. Roman winters are relatively mild, with persistent rainy spells.

Getting Around

The centro storico of Rome comprises that which stood inside the 3rd-century walls of the city; it contains most of the major tourist sights. The borders are roughly the Vatican to the east, Villa Borghese to the north, Termini station to west, and the Colosseum to the south. This large area is easier to navigate when divided into smaller modern neighborhoods.

Fortunately for tourists, many of Rome's main attractions are concentrated in the centro storico and can be covered on foot. In addition, Rome has a good network of public transport, both above and below ground. The Metro Linea A will take you to Termini station, the Trevi Fountain (Barberini stop), the Spanish Steps (Spagna stop), St. Peter's (Ottaviano), and the Vatican Museums (Cipro), to name a few.

Single tickets (BIT) for the bus and Metro cost €1.50 and must be purchased before boarding. They are available at Termini station, from automatic ticket machines in Metro stations, and at most newsstands. These tickets can be used on all city buses and trams for 100 minutes or for a single Metro ride. A day pass (Roma 24h) covering all public transport costs €7, while a weekly ticket (CIS) is €24. Children under 10 travel free on all public transport when accompanied by an adult.

Making the Most of Your Time

There's so much to do in Rome that it's hard to fit it all in, no matter how much time you have. If you're a first-time visitor, the Vatican Museums and the remains of ancient Rome are must-sees, but both require at least half a day, so if you only have one day, you're best-off picking one or the other. Save time and skip lines by purchasing tickets for the Vatican Museums and the Colosseum (with the Roman Forum and Palatine Hill) online beforehand. If you have more than one day, do one on one morning and the other on the next. If you're planning to visit the Galleria Borghese, tickets can sell out days (or weeks) in advance during high season, so make sure to book early.

Addresses in Rome

In the centro storico, most street names are posted on ceramic-like plaques on the side of buildings, which can make them hard to see. Addresses are fairly straightforward: the street name is followed by the street number, but it's worth noting that Roman street numbering, even in the newer outskirts of town, can be erratic. Usually numbers are even on one side of the street and odd on the other, but sometimes numbers are in ascending consecutive order on one side of the street and descending order on the other side.

Hop-On, Hop-Off Bus

Rome has multiple hop-on, hop-off sightseeing-bus tours, with competing operators aggressively trying to lure you with flyers, though City Sightseeing runs the ones you'll see most frequently. Note that Rome is actually not ideally served by bus tours, as most of the main sights are close together and on small streets not accessible by bus. You may find walking between sights easier than getting on and off buses constantly.

City Sightseeing. Hop-on, hop-off buses leave every 15–20 minutes daily, beginning at 9 am from Via Marsala (beside Termini station), on a 100-minute loop, which passes the Colosseum and St. Peter's, and makes stops close to the Trevi Fountain and Piazza Navona. ⊕ *www.city-sightseeing.com* ✉ *from €25.*

Etiquette

Although you may find Rome much more informal then many other European cities, Romans will nevertheless appreciate attempts to abide by local etiquette. When entering an establishment, the key words to know are: *buongiorno* (good morning), *buona sera* (good evening), and *buon pomeriggio* (good afternoon). These words can also double as a good-bye upon exit. Remember to avoid short hemlines and sleeveless or low-cut tops in churches. It is common practice (but not obligatory) to leave a tip in a restaurant: usually between 5% and 10% will be appreciated, or just round up. Taxi drivers don't expect tips, but if you round up the tab they will be grateful. Even in bars, leave a small coin for your cappuccino.

Street Smarts

As in most big cities, use common sense with your valuables. If you carry a purse, keep a firm grip on it, and don't leave it unattended or on the back of a chair, and be especially aware of pickpockets at major tourist sights and train stations. It's never a bad idea to look at menu prices before ordering and check your bill when leaving. Be careful when crossing streets, as Roman motorists have a rather carefree attitude toward traffic lights.

Discounts and Deals

In addition to single- and multiday transit passes, a three-day Roma Pass (€36 ⊕ *www.romapass.it*) covers unlimited use of buses, trams, and the Metro, plus free admission to two museums or archaeological sites of your choice and discounted entrance to others. A two-day pass is €28 and includes one museum.

Roman Hours

On Sunday, Rome virtually shuts down, and on Monday, most state museums and exhibition halls, plus many restaurants are closed. Daily food shop hours generally run 10 am–1 pm and 4 pm–7:30 pm or 8 pm; but other stores in the center usually observe continuous opening hours. Pharmacies tend to close for a lunch break and keep night hours (*ora rio notturno*) in rotation. As for churches, most open at 8 or 9 in the morning, close noon–3 or 4, then reopen until 6:30 or 7. St. Peter's, however, has continuous hours 7 am–7 pm (until 6 pm in the fall and winter); and the Vatican Museums are open Monday but closed Sunday (except for the last Sunday of the month).

Tourist Information

The Department of Tourism in Rome, called Roma Capitale, staffs green information kiosks (with multilingual personnel) near important sights, as well as at Termini station and Leonardo da Vinci Airport.

ROME
TOP ATTRACTIONS

Roman Forum
(A) This fabled labyrinth of ruins variously served as a political playground, a center of commerce, and a place where justice was dispensed during the days of the Roman Republic and Empire (500 BC–AD 500). Today, the Forum is a silent ruin: *Sic transit gloria mundi* (So passes away the glory of the world).

The Colosseum
(B) Legend has it that as long as the Colosseum stands, Rome will stand; and when Rome falls, so will the world. One of the Seven Wonders of the World, the mammoth amphitheater was begun by Emperor Vespasian and inaugurated by Titus in the year AD 80.

The Pantheon
(C) Constructed to honor all pagan gods, this best-preserved temple of ancient Rome was rebuilt in the 2nd century AD by Emperor Hadrian, and has survived intact because it was consecrated as a Christian church. Its dome is still considered an architectural marvel.

Piazza Navona
(D) You couldn't concoct a more Roman street scene: crowded caffè tables at street level, wrought-iron balconies above, and, at the center of this urban "living room," Bernini's spectacular Fountain of the Four Rivers and Borromini's super-theatrical Sant'Agnese.

Vatican City
Though its population numbers only in the hundreds, the Vatican—home base for the Catholic Church and the papacy—makes up for it with the millions who visit each year.

St. Peter's Basilica
(E) Every year, millions of pilgrims flock to the world's most important Catholic church to visit the site of the martyrdom and burial of St. Peter, marvel at Michelangelo's cupola, the *Pietà*, and Bernini's papal altar.

The Spanish Steps

(F)Byron, Shelley, and Keats all drew inspiration from this magnificent *scalinata*, constructed in 1723. Connecting the ritzy shops at the bottom with the ritzy hotels at the top, this is one of Rome's liveliest spots, with tourists and locals congregating on the steps and around the fountain at their base. The steps face west, so sunsets offer great photo ops.

Trastevere

(G)Located just across the Tiber River, this time-stained, charming, village-like neighborhood is a maze of jumbled alleyways, traditional Roman trattorias, cobblestone streets, and medieval houses. The area also has one of the oldest churches in Rome—Santa Maria in Trastevere.

Trevi Fountain

(H)One of the few fountains in Rome that's actually more absorbing than the people crowding around it, the Fontana di Trevi was designed by Nicola Salvi in 1732—and immortalized in *La Dolce Vita*. This granddaddy of all fountains may be your ticket back to Rome—that is, if you throw a coin into it.

Galleria Borghese

(I)Only the best could satisfy the aesthetic taste of Cardinal Scipione Borghese, whose holdings evoke the essence of Baroque Rome. Spectacularly painted ceilings and colored marble frame great Bernini sculptures and paintings by Caravaggio, Titian, and Raphael, among others.

ROME MUSEUMS, AN OVERVIEW

The city of Rome is, itself, a museum, with a breathtaking amount of sculpture on the city's streets; but there are also endless treasures filling the palaces and galleries.

Major Museums

At the top of a visitor's priority list, the **Musei Vaticani (Vatican Museums)** include the Borgia papal apartments and the frescoed Raphael Rooms; legendary works by Leonardo, Raphael, and Caravaggio; and of course Michelangelo's sublime *Last Judgment* and Sistine Chapel ceiling. Rome's second most popular museum is the **Galleria Borghese**, in the Villa Borghese Park: it has some of Bernini's most famous sculpture groups, as well as works by Raphael and Titian. The **Palazzo dei Conservatori** has some of the classical world's most famous sculptures, while the **Museo Nazionale Etrusco di Villa Giulia** contains the most important collection of Etruscan art and antiquities in Italy.

Museums of Antiquities

The two **Musei Capitolini** (including the Palazzo dei Conservatori) stand atop the Capitoline Hill. The City of Rome has gathered so much stuff over the centuries that it needs four separate museums to house it all: **Palazzo Altemps**, **Palazzo Massimo alle Terme**, **Terme di Diocleziano**, and **Crypta Balbi**, collectively known as the **Musei Nazionale Romano**. The **Museo dei Fori Imperiali**, inside the ruins of Mercati di Traiano, offers a privileged view of the Colonna Traiana. Crowning the Palatine hill, the **Museo Palatino** incorporates the rooms of the surprisingly humble House of Augustus. For something unusual, visit the **Centrale Montemartini**, where 400 ancient Roman statues stand among the machinery of a historic electric power station.

Great Art Collections

Palazzo Barberini houses Raphael's *La Fornarina*, the baker's daughter who was the artist's mistress and perhaps his secret wife. The same lovely girl modeled for his frescos in **Villa Farnesina**, commissioned by millionaire banker Agostino Chigi. Palazzo Corsini belonged to Pope Clement XII's nephew, who put together a huge collection of old masters. The magnificent 17th-century **Palazzo Doria Pamphilj**, still owned by the original family, has one of the most important collections of old masters in Rome. Enjoy the optical illusion in **Palazzo Spada**, where Borromini created a trompe-l'oeil gallery. **Villa Torlonia** has three museums, including a collection of rare Art Nouveau stained glass. **Palazzo Venezia** has medieval and Renaissance artifacts.

Modern and Contemporary Art Galleries

Rome's top contemporary art museum is the **MAXXI**, while late 19th and 20th century art is found at the **Galleria Nazionale d'Arte Moderna**. The **MACRO** contemporary art museum is in two locations: a former Peroni brewery and a former slaughterhouse. American art dealer Larry Gagosian's **Gagosian Gallery** has a branch in Rome with standout temporary exhibitions.

House Museums

The **Museo Atelier Canova Tadolini** is crammed with plaster casts and prep models of the artists' work. In the townhouse of Napoléon's niece, the **Napoleonic Museum** has a charming collection of Empire-style memorabilia. The tiny exhibition at the **Keats-Shelley House** offers insight into the last months of English Romantic poet John Keats's life.

TOP CHURCHES IN ROME

Many of Rome's churches double as places of worship and museums, full of amazing works of art and objects of high craftsmanship.

The Tiber Trail

St. Peter's Basilica, the world's largest church and a treasure trove of art, tops most visitors' lists for Michelangelo's *Pietà* and Bernini's high altar. One of Rome's oldest churches, **Santa Maria in Trastevere**, dedicated to the Virgin Mary, is said to have been built on the place where a stream of pure oil miraculously started to gush from the ground foretelling Jesus' birth—visit to see the glittering 12th-century mosaics. Make like Audrey Hepburn in *Roman Holiday* and stick your hand in the mouth of the Bocca della Verità, regarded as a lie detector since the Middle Ages, at the 12th-century Romanesque church of **Santa Maria in Cosmedin**. Legend says that if you tell a lie with your hand in the face's mouth, it'll be bitten off.

Baroque Splendor

Many of Rome's most interesting churches are in the Baroque center of the city, near the Pantheon and Piazza Navona. This is where you'll find Borromini's **Sant'Agnese in Agone**; the Jesuit church **Sant'Ignazio**, with its stunning trompe-l'oeil dome painted by Andrea Pozzo (the ceiling is considered almost as resplendent as the Sistine Chapel); and Rome's only Gothic church, **Santa Maria sopra Minerva**, with Michelangelo's *Risen Christ*. Just behind Piazza Navona, **Santa Maria della Pace** is another example of Baroque architecture. The semicircular facade was designed by Pietro da Cortona; inside is Raphael's celebrated fresco *Sibilla*. The elaborate **Sant'Andrea della Valle** is also a Baroque heavy-hitter, with a collection of paintings from the 17th century and one of the most impressive domes in Rome. **Santa Maria del Popolo** contains works by Raphael, Carracci, Caravaggio, and Bernini.

Layers of History

Many of the buildings you'll see while walking through the centro storico of Rome are built over other buildings, which, in turn, are often layered on top of even older buildings. **San Giovanni in Laterano**, first built by Constantine, is now the Cathedral Church of Rome and the mother church of the Catholic world. The present 12th-century church of **San Clemente** is built over a 4th-century church—one of the first Christian basilicas in the Roman Empire—underneath which are the remains of a pagan Temple to Mithras. Similarly, under the **San Bartolomeo all'Isola** church on Tiber Island lies the ruins of the 3rd-century-BC Temple of Aesculapius, the Greek god of medicine and healing. **Santa Maria in Aracoeli** now occupies the spot where the Temple of Juno Moneta once crowned the summit of the Capitoline Hill.

And Even More Churches

Santa Maria della Vittoria holds Bernini's masterpiece, *The Ecstasy of Saint Teresa*. Michelangelo's colossal *Moses* is housed in **San Pietro in Vincoli**. Caravaggio's celebrated frescoes depicting the life of St. Matthew are in **San Luigi dei Francesi**. The 4th-century **Santa Maria Maggiore** is one of the four great basilicas of Rome, often referred to as Our Lady of the Snows. According to legend, the Virgin Mary appeared in a vision to a wealthy couple without heirs. At the height of the Roman summer, snow fell during the night on the summit of the Esquiline Hill, and they chose this spot to dedicate their church.

ROME FESTIVALS

The City of Eternal Festivals, Rome has a bevy of internationally recognized festivals. In the fall and spring especially, you can see local and international talent in some of the city's most beautiful venues, outside and in.

Film

Festival Internazionale del Film di Roma. In the fall, cinephiles head to Rome for the International Festival of Film, two packed weeks of cinema celebration and celebrity spotting. The festival showcases Hollywood hits, Italian indie and experimental films, art-house films and shorts, and conversations with global cinema icons. ⊠ *Viale Pietro De Coubertin 10, Flaminio* ⊕ *www.romacinemafest.it.*

Venezia e Locarno a Roma Festival. Immediately following the finale of the Venice Film Festival in September, Rome's cinemas host Da Venezia a Roma, a two-week screening of Locarno's and Venice's competition films. Films are screened in their original languages with Italian subtitles when necessary. ⊠ *Rome* ⊕ *www.agisanec.lazio.it.*

Fine Art and Theater

RomaEuropa. For six weeks in early fall, the RomaEuropa festival ignites stages and theaters as a collective, multivenue avant-garde performing and visual arts program, showcasing international artists, installations, film, and performance. ⊠ *Rome* ☎ *06/45553050* ⊕ *www.romaeuropa.net.*

Music

Estate Romana. A summer-long, city-sponsored cultural series, many of these events are free and take place outdoors along the Tiber River and in piazzas all around the city. Look for cinema events, art programs, theater, book fairs, and guided tours of some of Rome's monuments by night. ⊠ *Rome* ⊕ *www.estateromana.comune.roma.it.*

I Concerti nel Parco. This beautiful evening-concert series is held under the stars in Rome's largest park, Villa Doria Pamphilj. From June through August, the concerts are held at sunset and last late into the evening, showcasing a variety of musical genres from classical to contemporary. There are some winter events, including Christmas concerts, as well. ⊠ *Via di S. Pancrazio, Trastevere* ⊕ *www.iconcertinelparco.it.*

Il Tempietto. This series of unforgettable concerts takes place throughout the year in otherwise inaccessible sites, like the 1st-century Teatro di Marcello. Music runs the gamut from classical to contemporary. ⊠ *Via del Teatro di Marcello, Jewish Ghetto* ☎ *06/45615180* ⊕ *www.tempietto.it.*

Rock in Roma. June through August, the Ippodromo, the Stadio Olimpico, and other stages become the heart of rock "n' roll. ⊠ *Ippodromo delle Capannelle, Via Appia Nuova 1255, Via Appia Antica* ⊕ *www.rockinroma.com.*

Roma Incontra il Mondo. World-class headliners as well as its beautiful location in Villa Ada, a former monarch's residence, make Roma Incontra il Mondo one of Europe's most impressive world-music festivals. The summer concert series is held in the middle of the park and begins at 10 pm, followed by dancing until 2 am. ⊠ *Laghetto di Villa Ada, Parioli* ⊕ *www.villaada.org.*

ROME LIKE A LOCAL

"When in Rome, do as the Romans do." The phrase may be clichéd, but it's advice worth taking: Romans know how to live life to the fullest, indulging in the simplest pleasures and doing so with style. Put yourself in their shoes (Fendi, preferably) and be a Roman for a day.

Il Mercato

If you're looking to rub shoulders with real Romans, there's no better place to do it than at the local open-air food market, where vendors turn the practice of selling the region's freshest produce into a grand theatrical performance. The most popular market is the Campo de' Fiori, Rome's oldest food market. Nowadays, you'll find craft and clothing stands among the food stalls, as well as pricey gastronomic specialties. For a more authentic experience, head to the Piazza Vittorio Market, where people come from all over the world to hawk fresh produce and meat at bargain prices.

La Piazza

For Italians young and old, *la piazza* serves as a meeting place—for making dinner plans, people-watching, and catching up with friends. The Campo de' Fiori is a bustling marketplace by day; by night, the piazza turns into a popular hangout for Romans and foreigners lured by its pubs, cheap eateries, and street caffè. The Piazza Navona and the Piazza del Rotonda, in front of the Pantheon, are also excellent hangouts. The Piazza di Spagna, at the bottom of the Spanish Steps, is generally overrun by hawkers selling fake Prada bags and selfie sticks and is less fun for congregating.

L'Aperitivo

The Milanese invented it, but the Romans perfected *l'aperitivo*. Similar to "happy hour" (but without the drink specials), this is a time to meet up with friends and colleagues for drinks after work or on weekends. Hours are usually 7–9 pm. The aperitif experience can sometimes be an economic alternative to dinner, as it often includes an all-you-can-eat appetizer buffet of finger foods, sandwiches, and pasta salads, all for the price of one drink.

Il Caffè

If there's something Romans certainly can't live without, it's *il caffè* (espresso), and there is no shortage of coffee bars to satisfy the craving. Real Italian espresso is a thimble-full of aromatic black liquid, prepared by a barista—you can have it *ristretto* (concentrated), *doppio* (double), *americano* (hot water added), *macchiato* (with a drop of milk foam), *marocchino* (with a drop of cream and a sprinkling of cocoa), or even sinfully *corretto* (with a splash of grappa). A cappuccino is espresso with steamed milk and foam. In summer, order a *caffè shakerato* (freshly made espresso shaken briskly with sugar and ice, to form a froth when poured) or a *caffè freddo* (iced espresso).

La Passeggiata

A favorite Roman pastime is *la passeggiata* (literally, "the promenade"). Especially on weekends in the late afternoon and early evening, couples, families, and packs of teenagers stroll up and down Rome's main streets and piazze. It's a ritual of exchanging news and gossip, window-shopping, flirting, and gelato eating that adds up to a uniquely Italian experience. One top promenade is the Via del Corso.

GREAT ITINERARIES

Rome is jam-packed with things to do and see. These are some of our suggested itineraries. Make sure to leave yourself time to just wander and get the feel of the city as well.

Rome 101

Rome wasn't built in a day, but if that's all you have to see it, take a deep breath, strap on some stylish-but-comfy sneakers, and grab a cappuccino to help you get an early start. Get ready for a spectacular sunrise-to-sunset tour of the Ancient City.

Begin by getting a coffee at the bar of the Caffè Sant'Eustachio right when it opens at 9 am. Close by are two opulently over-the-top monuments that show off Rome at its Baroque best: the church of Sant'Ignazio, with its stunning painted ceiling, and the princely Palazzo Doria Pamphilj, packed with great old master paintings. Midmorning, head west a few blocks to find the fabled Pantheon, still looking like Emperor Hadrian might arrive shortly. A few blocks north is San Luigi dei Francesi, home to Caravaggio's earliest major commissions.

Just before lunch, saunter a block or so westward into the gorgeous Piazza Navona, studded with Bernini fountains. Then take Via Cucagna (at the piazza's south end) and continue several blocks toward Campo de' Fiori's open-air food market. This is a great place to stop for lunch.

Two more blocks toward the Tiber brings you to one of the most romantic streets of Rome—Via Giulia—laid out by Pope Julius II in the early 16th century. Walk past 10 blocks of Renaissance palazzi and ivy-draped antiques shops to take a bus (from the stop near the Tiber) over to the Vatican.

Gape at St. Peter's Basilica, then hit the treasure-filled Musei Vaticani (for the Sistine Chapel) in the early afternoon. During lunch, the crowds thin out some, but you can avoid lines entirely if you book online at ⊕ *biglietteriamusei.vatican.va* (the €4 service fee is well worth the time saved). Wander for about two hours and then head for the Ottaviano stop near the museum and Metro your way to the Colosseo stop.

Climb up into the Colosseum and picture it full of screaming toga-clad citizens enjoying the spectacle of gladiators in mortal combat. Follow Via dei Fori Imperiali to the entrance of the Roman Forum. Photograph yourself giving a "Friends, Romans, Countrymen" oration (complete with upraised hand) by a crumbling column. At sunset, the Forum closes and the floodlights come on.

March down the Forum's ancient Via Sacra and back out into Via dei Fori Imperiali where you will head around "the wedding cake," the looming Vittorio Emanuele Monument (Il Vittoriano), to the Campidoglio. Here, on the Capitoline Hill, tour the great ancient Roman art treasures of the Musei Capitolini, and admire the view over the Forum from the Tabularium and toward St. Peter's from the terrace by the museum's caffè. If you're not entering the museum, there is a spectacular view over the Forum from the Capitoline Hill (at the top of via Monte Tarpeo).

After dinner, hail a cab—or take a long passeggiata walk down *La Dolce Vita* memory lane—to the Trevi Fountain, a gorgeous sight at night. Don't forget to toss a coin in over your shoulder to ensure a trip back to Rome.

Temples Through Time: Religious Rome

Making a trip to Rome and not going to see the Vatican Museums or St. Peter's Basilica is almost like breaking one of the Ten Commandments. Get an early start at the the Musei Vaticani, where one of the world's grandest and most comprehensive collections of artwork is stored. As above, book tickets online at ⊕ *biglietteriamusei.vatican.va* beforehand to skip the lines. Once you've conquered both, take the Metro from Ottaviano to Piazza del Popolo (Metro stop: Flaminio), where Santa Maria del Popolo is not to be missed for its famous chapels decorated by Raphael and Caravaggio.

Head south along the Via del Corso for about 10 blocks toward Sant'Ignazio, an eye-popping example of Baroque Rome, with its amazing, "Oh, I can't believe my eyes" optical illusion of a dome. Take Via Sant'Ignazio to Via Piè di Marmo, which will lead you to Piazza della Minerva, where Bernini's elephant obelisk monument lies in wait. Take in the adjacent Gothic-style Santa Maria sopra Minerva, best known for Michelangelo's *Risen Christ*.

Then make your way south to Corso Vittorio Emanuele and the bus piazza at Largo Argentina, where you'll take Tram No. 8 to picturesque Trastevere, one of Rome's loveliest areas. Make your way through a series of winding cobblestoned alleyways and piazze toward the famed Piazza Santa Maria in Trastevere, where one of Rome's oldest churches—Santa Maria in Trastevere—stands. Dedicated to the Virgin Mary, the church has a fine display of glimmering gilded mosaics covering what is one of Rome's most spectacular naves.

Retail Therapy: Shop-'Til-You-Drop Rome

For luxury shopping, there's no better place to treat yourself to some retail therapy than the network of elegant streets at the Spanish Steps. If money is no question, Rome's Via dei Condotti is *paradiso*. To continue the shopping spree, head down Via del Babuino for fabled antique furniture and fine jewelry, and Via Frattina for exclusive boutiques. Even if you're a penny-pincher, window-shopping can be just as fun as you make your way down to the more affordable Via del Corso. Department store–style shopping can be done in the Galleria Alberto Sordi halfway along the Corso, or at COIN in Termini station.

If vintage is your thing, head toward Piazza Navona and down Via del Governo Vecchio, where an assortment of vintage shops showcase high-end clothing, handbags, and accessories. Via del Boschetto in Monti has some of the best consignment shops in the city.

Now that you've blown your shopping budget, it's time for real bargain-shopping, Roman-style. For rock-bottom bargains try the city's open-air and flea markets. Rome's largest and most famous are markets on Via Sannio in San Giovanni (Monday–Saturday) and the Porta Portese market (Sunday) in Trastevere. The market on Via Sannio specializes in new and used clothing, shoes, and accessories. The Porta Portese market sells everything but the kitchen sink: clothes, souvenirs, antiques, housewares, and knick-knacks galore, although there's a lot of junk too.

ROME WITH KIDS

There are plenty of ways to keep the younger set occupied in Rome—with the added bonus that getting them to eat isn't usually a problem, with pizza, pasta, and gelato on the menus.

Archaeology

If your kids are into archaeology or gladiators, traipsing the ruins of ancient Rome can provide hours of entertainment. Who can resist climbing the giant steps of the **Colosseum?** For the true enthusiast, the Roman Gladiator School offers group and private lessons in which your little one (or big one) can dress up like Spartacus and learn sword-fighting techniques and a bit about the lives of these warriors.

Roman Gladiator School. Two-hour lessons in how to be a gladiator include clothing to dress up in as well as "weapons" and shields—it's great fun and a great way to get some history lessons. The instructors are top-quality, and experienced at dealing with participants of varying levels. There's a viewing platform for those who prefer to observe their friends and family. ⊕ *www.viator.com/tours/Rome/ Roman-Gladiator-School-Learn-How-to- Become-a-Gladiator/d511-2466GLAD* 🖾 *From €55.*

Explore the Parks

Take little ones to see the Teatrino Pulcinella's open-air **puppet show** weekdays on the Janiculum hill, where you can also enjoy a great view of the city, or to the San Carlino puppet theater weekends on the Pincio Terrace in **Villa Borghese Park.** (Tips for the puppeteers are greatly appreciated.) Villa Borghese is also home to other kid-oriented attractions such as the **Bioparco** (zoo), with over 1,000 animals in peaceful landscaped surroundings. Rent a bike (on the Pincio at Viale dell'Orologio or at Piazzale M. Cervantes near the zoo)

and explore the vast Borghese estate. Or take a rowboat out on the Laghetto di Villa Borghese. At only €3 per person for 20 minutes, it's one of the best ways to explore the park's incredible sculptures, temples, and natural beauty.

Creepy Stuff

Rome's catacombs (underground cemeteries) are intriguing enough to wipe the boredom off most teenagers' faces, and the best is the **Catacombe di San Callisto** on the Via Appia Antica. It's hard not to be impressed by the labyrinth of dark corridors and grisly tales of Christian martyrs. The **Capuchin Crypt** under Santa Maria della Concezione is gruesomely mesmerizing, with the skulls and bones of 3,700 friars arranged on the walls and ceiling in fanciful patterns. Take the kids to the Bocca della Verità (Mouth of Truth) at **Santa Maria in Cosmedin,** and warn them that it bites off liars' hands!

Water Fountains

The public water fountains in Rome are free (and perfectly safe) to drink from; the only problem is figuring out how to do it without getting wet. A good trick is to block a hole under the spout with your finger to create a fountain, or bring bottles to fill up.

FREE AND CHEAP

Rome may be on the fast track to becoming one of the most expensive cities in Europe, but there are still a slew of free and inexpensive things to do in the *Città Eterna*. For a quick look at a range of low-cost activities, check out the Comune di Roma's tourism website (⊕ *www.turismoroma.it*).

Art and Archaeological Sites

Roman churches are the ultimate destinations for art viewing, with works by such masters as Caravaggio, Tintoretto, Michelangelo, and Raphael on view for free. Nor does it cost anything to see the celebrated Roman fountains or enter the Pantheon to gaze at the famous dome and pay homage at Raphael's tomb. On the first Sunday of each month, public museums, monuments, and archaeological sites are free for all visitors, but it's best to avoid the massive crowds at places like the Colosseum and take advantage of less famous sites. During the *Settimana della Cultura,* or Cultural Week (usually in spring), many of the major archaeological sites and museums in and around Rome waive their entrance fees as well. Check ⊕ *www.beniculturali.it* for exact dates and listings. The Musei Vaticani are free on the last Sunday of every month—open only until 12:30, though, and there's usually a huge line.

Music and Performances

Rome's summer season has a vast program of free or low-cost events June–mid-September, including open-air concerts ranging from pop to classical. Rome's parks, the Tiber Island, and many major piazze become impromptu venues for street artists, cinema under the stars, food festivals, and musical and theatrical performances—many of which are free. Throughout the year, many of Rome's historic churches host free recitals and chamber music concerts that are not widely advertised. Look out for flyers in hotels, on caffè counters, or stuck to lampposts. Check the website ⊕ *www. turismoroma.it* or phone ☎ *06/0608* for information. *Wanted in Rome* magazine (online and in print) is a good source of information about events in English. If hearing the organs of St. Peter and getting a glimpse of the Pope in person are tempting thoughts, it's always free to go to papal Mass. Get your tickets from the Swiss Guards at the Bronze Door and prepare to arrive at least a few hours early to get a good seat. Tickets for holiday Masses can be requested using the online form at ⊕ *www.papalaudience. org/papal-mass.*

Unofficial Sightseeing

For a cheap version of the hop-on, hop-off bus tour, board Tram No. 3, which trundles through Trastevere and Aventino, past the Colosseum and San Giovanni, and arrives at the museums of the Belle Arti in the Villa Borghese. You get 100 minutes of travel for a mere €1.50, not to mention the added bonus of free people-watching. And of course, for the price of an espresso, you can always sit for hours outdoors at a piazza caffè.

ITALIAN ART 101

With so much wonderful art to see in Rome, it's useful to have a cheat sheet listing a few of the major artists whose names come up often.

Gian Lorenzo Bernini (1598–1680) ushered in the Italian Baroque; you'll see his work—especially sculpture but also architecture—everywhere you turn, from the colonnade of St. Peter's to the stupendous Fountain of the Four Rivers in Piazza Navona. He was the first to succeed in capturing the softness of flesh in marble: see the goddess struggle desperately with the grim God of the Underworld in *The Rape of Proserpina*, in Galleria Borghese. His masterpiece, *The Ecstasy of Saint Teresa*, is at the church of Santa Maria della Vittoria. Many of the more conservative members of the clergy were shocked when this work was unveiled, and it is not hard to see why.

Francesco Borromini (1599–1667), a leading Baroque architect, was Bernini's eternal rival. The two started their working lives together as assistants to Carlo Maderno. When Maderno died, Borromini, who was introverted and depressive, expected to take over as chief architect of St. Peter's, but the Pope gave the job to the personable, charming Bernini instead. Borromini's personal masterpiece is the Church of San Carlo alle Quattro Fontane. Borromini eventually killed himself, consumed with frustration and jealousy because Bernini's Fountain of the Four Rivers in Piazza Navona had totally overshadowed his own work on the facade of the Church of Sant'Agnese in Agone, just opposite.

Caravaggio (1571–1610), known as "the Damned" because of his mutinous and dissolute character, was an innovator who changed the concept of painting, introducing the effects of *chiaroscuro* (light and dark) to create atmosphere and convey moods. Some of his most famous works are three masterpieces dedicated to St. Matthew, in the Church of San Luigi dei Francesi near Piazza Navona; many of his other celebrated paintings can be found in Galleria Borghese. Caravaggio incurred the wrath of the establishment because he portrayed the saints as ordinary people with careworn faces, dirty feet, and ragged clothing, as in *The Crucifixion of St. Peter* in the Church of Santa Maria del Popolo.

Michelangelo (1475–1564) is the uncontested giant of the Renaissance, celebrated in his lifetime and regarded with awe and reverence today. He saw himself as a sculptor but (unwillingly) turned his hand to the colossal job of frescoing the Sistine Chapel ceiling, achieving one of the world's greatest masterpieces, equaled only by his *Last Judgment*. To appreciate his genius as a sculptor, see his powerful *Moses* in the church of San Pietro in Vincoli, a total contrast to his delicate and sensitive *Pietà* in St. Peter's.

Raphael (1483–1520), a master of the High Renaissance known during his brief lifetime as the "Divine Raphael," is considered to have achieved levels of perfection seldom approached by other artists. His depictions of Madonna are infused with spirituality and calm; his compositions are models of balance and harmony. He was 25 when he began painting the four rooms in the Vatican Palace that are now known by his name. Perhaps his most famous portrait, however, is *La Fornarina*, featuring the baker's daughter who was his lover (and perhaps his wife), on view in Palazzo Barberini.

ROME'S BEST WALKS

Updated
by Ariston
Anderson

With more masterpieces per square foot than any other city in the world, Rome presents a particular challenge for visitors: just as they are beginning to feel hopelessly smitten by the spell of the city, they realize they don't have the time—let alone the stamina—to see more than a fraction of its treasures. Rome was not built in a day, and neither can it be seen in one day, or even two or three. As the Italian author Silvio Negro once put it: *Roma, non basta una vita* ("Rome, a lifetime is not enough").

For this reason, it can be wise to have a focused itinerary. To provide just that, here are three strolls that introduce you to especially evocative stretches of the city: The Centro Storico, where Rome's bravura Baroque style sets the city's tone; the cobbled streets of Trastevere and the picturesque Tiber Island; and the Roman Forum, where the glory that was (and is) Rome is best captured.

Along the way, terra-cotta-hued *palazzi* (palaces), Baroque squares, and time-stained ruins will present an unfolding panorama of color upon color—an endlessly varied palette that makes Rome one of Europe's most enjoyable cities for walking. Forget about deadly earnest treks through marble miles of museum corridors and get ready to immerse yourself in some of Italy's best "street theater." Just be sure to pack flat shoes, as Rome's uneven, often-neglected cobblestone streets are brutal on anything with a heel.

In addition, these three tours of clustered sightseeing capture quintessential Rome while allowing roamers to make minidiscoveries of their own. Use these itineraries as suggestions to keep you on track as you explore both the famous sights and those off the beaten path. Remember that people who stop for a *caffè* (coffee) will enjoy the day more than those who breathlessly try to make every second count.

A STROLL THROUGH THE BAROQUE QUARTER

The most important clue to the Romans is their Baroque art—not its artistic technicalities, but its spirit. When you understand that, you'll no longer be a stranger in Rome. Flagrantly emotional, heavily expressive, and sensuously visual, the 17th-century artistic movement known as the Baroque was born in Rome, the creation of four geniuses, Gian Lorenzo Bernini, Francesco Borromini, Annibale Caracci, and Caravaggio. Ranging from the austere drama found in Caravaggio's painted altarpieces to the jewel-encrusted, gold-on-gold decoration of 17th-century Roman palace decoration, the Baroque sought to both shock and delight by upsetting the placid, "correct" rules of the Renaissance masters. By appealing to the emotions, it became a powerful weapon in the hands of the Counter-Reformation. Although this walk passes such sights as the Pantheon—ancient Rome's most perfectly preserved building—it's mainly an excursion into the 16th and 17th centuries, when Baroque art triumphed in Rome.

We wend our way through one of Rome's most beautiful districts—Vecchia Roma (Old Rome), a romantic nickname given to the areas around Piazza Navona and the Campo de' Fiori. Thick with narrow streets with curious names, airy Baroque piazzas, and picturesque courtyards, and occupying the horn of land that pushes the Tiber westward toward the Vatican, this has been an integral part of the city since ancient times. For centuries, artisans and shopkeepers toiled in the shadow of the huge palaces built to consolidate the power and prestige of the leading figures in the papal court who lived and worked here. The greatest artists flocked here to get commissions. Street names still reflect the celebrated crafts, such as Via dei Chiavari for the keymakers or Via dei Cartari for the papermakers. Today, artisans still live hereabouts, but their numbers are diminishing as the district has become one of Rome's ritziest.

FROM EARTHLY TO HEAVENLY GLORY

We begin just off the main thoroughfare of Rome, the Via del Corso, about four blocks northwest of Piazza Venezia's traffic hub. Heading up the Corso, make a left turn down tiny Via Montecatini to emerge into the delightful proportions of the ocher and stone **Piazza di Sant'Ignazio.** Any lack in size of this square is made up for in theatricality. Indeed, a Rococo theater set was exactly what its architect, Filippo Raguzzini, had in mind when he designed it in 1727. The exits and entrances these days, however, are by Carabinieri, not actors, the main building "backstage" being a police station. With perfectly matching concave facades, two other buildings make up "the wings." It's a rare example of the *barocchetto*—that is, the "cute" Baroque—a term that demonstrates how Italian art critics have a name for everything.

At one time the chapel of the gigantic Collegio Romano, the church of **Sant'Ignazio**—on your left—was Rome's largest Jesuit church. Honoring the order's founding saint, it is famous for its over-the-top Baroque spectacle—few churches are as gilt-encrusted, jewel-studded, or stupendously stuccoed. This is the 17th-century Counter-Reformation pulling out all the stops: religion as supreme theater.

Walk down the vast nave and position yourself on the yellow marble disc on the floor and prepare to be transported heavenward. Soaring above you, courtesy of painter-priest Fra Andrea Pozzo, is a frescoed *Allegory of the Missionary Work of the Jesuits* (1691–94). While an angel holds the Jesuit emblem IHS (*In Hoc Signo Vinces*)—"In this sign we conquer"—just below, upward, ever upward, soars Saint Ignatius in triumph, trailed by a cast of thousands. A masterly use of perspective opens giddying vistas where clouds and humans interact until the forces of gravity seem to flounder. *Diavolerie*—"fiendish tricks"—a commentator of the time called such wonders.

Looking back toward the entrance door, notice how the painted columns—continuations more or less of their real marble equivalents below—seem to rise straight into heaven. Now walk 20 yards back toward the door, and gaze again. And experience an optical earthquake: Those straight columns have tilted 60 degrees. Believe it or not, the whole towering edifice of classic arches, columns, and cornices from the windows upward is entirely flat.

Time to walk down the nave and admire the massive dome—although it is anything but. Dome, windows, the golden light, they're all illusion—all that majestic space is in reality flat as the top of a drum, mere paint masterfully applied across a round canvas 17 meters in diameter in trompe l'oeil fashion. Funds for a real dome ran out, so Pozzo created the less costly but arguably no less marvelous "flat" version here. Another disc set in the marble floor marks the spot where his deception takes maximum effect.

GOD'S LITTLE MASCOT

Head out of the church, turning left to find Via Saint Ignazio, then left again to Via Pie' di Marmo, which leads into Piazza Santa Caterina di Siena and the Piazza della Minerva. Here stands Santa Maria sopra Minerva, the only major church in Rome built in Gothic style, and famous as the home of Michelangelo's *Risen Christ*. But the object of our delight is right on the piazza: the **Obelisk of Santa Maria sopra Minerva**, one of 13 old obelisks still present in Rome, an astounding conceit of an obelisk astride an elephant, masterfully designed by Gian Lorenzo Bernini. The obelisk is a soaring emblem for theology and the vertiginous weight of knowledge, the beast beneath embodying that which is needed to support it—a mind that is both humble and robust, and never, thank heaven, beyond a jest, even when at its own expense. After a Dominican adviser of the Pope criticized Bernini's work during the process, he made sure to have the elephant's behind pointing toward the nearby Dominican convent, with the elephant looking behind him sneeringly. Romans have affectionately nicknamed the place the *Piazza dell'Elefantino* (Square of the baby elephant).

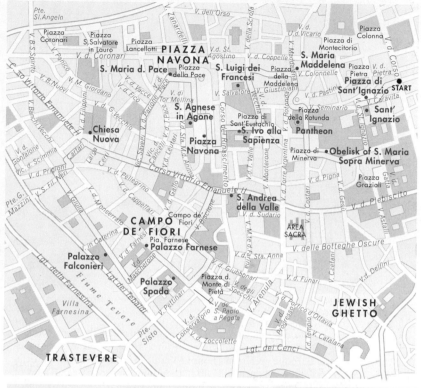

Why Go?:	Rome gave birth to the Baroque—the lavish, eye-popping style that revolutionized Europe in the 17th century—and this walk shows off Rome's Baroque at its best.
Good in the 'Hood:	Marveling at Bernini fountains, time-traveling back to the 17th century, watching the world pass by on Piazza Navona, and Rome's best cup of coffee.
Highlights:	Caravaggio paintings at San Luigi dei Francesi, Sant'Ignazio, Via Giulia, Palazzo Farnese, and Piazza Navona.
Where to Start:	Piazza di Sant'Ignazio, a few blocks north of Piazza Venezia (turn left off the Corso on Via Montecatina to access the piazza); take Bus 40 or 64 to Piazza Venezia or Bus No. 122 down the Corso to get here.
Where to Stop:	For a caffeine fix, make a stop at Sant'Eustachio il Caffè—regarded by many as serving up the best coffee in Rome—just around the corner from the Pantheon at Piazza di Sant'Eustachio 82. Unless you want to pay the somewhat exorbitant fees for sitting at one of the outdoor tables, common for cafés in the center, take your coffee as the Romans do—at the bar inside.
Time:	Four to six hours, depending on your pace.
Best Time to Go:	Get an early start, around 9 am, and you'll be able to visit most of the churches before they close for their midday siesta at noon.
Worst Time to Go:	If the weather is inclement or gray, wait for a sunnier day.

No need to pack bottled Pellegrino on your walks—just savor the refreshing water from city fountains along the way, as Romans have done for centuries.

Straight ahead is the curving, brick-bound mass of the **Pantheon,** the most complete building surviving from antiquity, and a great influence on Baroque architects. Follow Via della Minerva to Piazza della Rotonda and go to the north end of the square to get an overall view of the temple's columned portico: it once bore two Baroque bell towers of Bernini's design but, after being ridiculed for their similarity to "donkey's ears," they were demolished. Enjoy the piazza and side streets, where you will find a busy caffè and shopping scene.

Returning to the Piazza della Rotunda, continue northward on Via della Maddalena and proceed into Piazza della Maddelena. In the corner is the excellent Gelateria San Crispino. Using only high quality ingredients (with prices to match), its specialty meringues come in three different variants: chocolate, hazelnut and caramel. Meanwhile, in front is the Rococo facade of the church of **Saint Maria Maddalena,** its curly and concave stone appearing as malleable as the ice cream that you may have just eaten, a gelato for the eyes. Inside the church observe how the late-17th-century Baroque twists and meanders into the 18th-century Rococo style. Marble work was seldom given such ornate or sumptuous treatment, and here it is often gilded as well, as is the magnificent organ loft.

Head to Via Pozzo delle Cornacchia, directly opposite the church facade, and turn right on Via della Scrofa. Immediately turn left and you'll find the church of Sant'Agostino, and the first Caravaggio of the day, *The Madonna of Loreto* inside the Cavalletti Chapel. Also known as the *Pilgrim's Madonna*, it depicts the barefoot Virgin and Child while two peasants kneel before them in adoration. The painting caused an uproar at the time, as the barefoot woman with her thin halo could be interpreted as any woman emerging from the night, standing in a decripit doorway.

Continue south two blocks on Via della Scrofa to the looming church across the square, **San Luigi dei Francesi**—the church of Rome's French community. In the left-side chapel closest to the altar are the masterpieces painted by Caravaggio on the calling, receiving of the gospel and martyrdom of Saint Matthew—these three gigantic paintings had the same effect on 17th-century art that Picasso's *Demoiselles d'Avignon* had on 20th-century artists. Illuminated in Caravaggio's landmark chiaroscuro (light and shadow) style, these are works unrivaled for emotional spectacle. The artist's warts-and-all drama was a deeply original response to the Counter-Reformation writings by St. Carlo Borromeo and the result is Baroque at its sublime best.

THE STING OF WISDOM

Continue south on Via della Dogana Vecchia to Piazza di Sant'Eustachio. As culture-vulture exhaustion may be setting in, it's time for a coffee. There's no better place than Il Caffè, which, a true Roman will tell you, serves the best coffee in Rome, if not the universe. Inside the bar an espresso costs €1.20; outside, the price triples, but then, up on your left, the best available view of Saint Ivo's dome is thrown in. **Sant'Ivo alla Sapienza** is considered by many to be Francesco Borromini's most astounding building. To get another look at the bizarre pinnacle crowning its dome (the church's rear entrance is on Piazza Sant'Eustachio), head down Via del Salvatore and turn left on Corso del Rinascimento to No. 40. Here a grand courtyard view of the church reveals Borromini—Bernini's great rival—at the dizzying top of his form.

Admire the church's concave facade and follow your gaze upward to see how Borromini mixes concave and convex shapes like a conjurer in stone. This performance is topped first with the many-niched lantern, and then the spiraling so-called *puntiglione,* or giant stinger. Some suggest Borromini was inspired by that ziggurat of ziggurats—the Tower of Babel, featured in many paintings of the time. A more popular theory cites the sting of a bee, and indeed the nickname means just that. This would also square with the building having been begun under Pope Urban VIII of the Barberini family, whose three-bee'd crest is stamped throughout Rome. Neatly enough, the bee is also a symbol of wisdom, and this palace of Sapienza was once the decadent home of the University of Rome.

THE QUEEN OF PIAZZAS

Leaving the courtyard, follow all the crowds one block to reach that showstopper of Baroque Rome, **Piazza Navona**. The crown jewel of the *centro storico* (historical center), this showcases Bernini's extravagant Fontana dei Quattro Fiumi, whose statues represent the four corners

of the earth and, in turn, the world's great rivers. Emperor Domitian's stadium once stood on this site, hence the piazza's unusual oval shape. Before someone figured out that the piazza's church of **Sant'Agnese in Agone** was designed prior to the fountain, common belief held that Bernini's fountain-figures were poised as if looking in horror at the inferior creation of Borromini, Bernini's rival. For lunch, grab a ringside caffè seat and take in the piazza spectacle—this is some of the most delicious scenery on view in Europe. Prices here are outrageous, but remember that you're paying for the theater.

After lunch, escape the maddening crowds by exiting the piazza on the little *vicolo* (alleyway) to the right of the church complex, Via di Tor Millina, to turn right on Via di S. Maria dell'Anima. Continue to the soaring bell tower of the church of Saint Maria dell'Anima, then make a sharp left up a narrow alley to emerge on pretty Piazza della Pace. The centerpiece of one of the city's cutest streetscapes is the church of **Santa Maria della Pace,** commissioned by the great Chigi-family art patron, Pope Alexander VII. Although there are two great Renaissance treasures inside—Raphael's *Sibyls* and Bramante's cloister—the Baroque masterstroke here is the church facade, designed in 1657 by Pietro da Cortona to fit into the tiny *piazzina*, created to accommodate the 18th-century carriages of fashionable parishioners.

GRAND PALAZZOS COME IN THREES

Take the street leading to the church, Via della Pace (past the always chic Antico Caffè delle Pace), and continue a few blocks south down to the big avenue, Corso Vittorio Emmanuele II. Turn right a couple of blocks to reach the **Chiesa Nuova,** another of Rome's great Counter-Reformation churches (with magnificent Rubens paintings inside), and, directly to the left, Borromini's Oratorio dei Filippini. Head across the Corso another two blocks toward the Tiber along Via dei Cartari and turn left on Via Giulia, often called Rome's most beautiful street. While laid out—as a ruler-straight processional to St. Peter's—by Michelangelo's patron, Pope Julius II, it is lined with numerous Baroque palaces (Palazzo Sachetti, at No. 66, is still home to one of Rome's princeliest families). At No. 1 is **Palazzo Falconieri,** probably Borromini's most regal palace and now home to the Hungarian academy—note the architect's rooftop belvedere adorned with the family "falcons."

Looming over everything else is the massive **Palazzo Farnese,** a Renaissance masterpiece. You can tour the palace (today the French Embassy) in English on Wednesday at 5 pm, if booked well in advance on ⊕ *inventerrome.com*. Inside is the fabled Galleria, with frescoes painted by Annibale Carracci. These florid depictions of gods and goddesses were among the first painted in the Baroque style and were staggeringly influential. Due to ongoing renovation work, the gallery may not be accessible at your time of visit.

If you can't get into the Farnese, no problem. Just a block to the south is the grand **Palazzo Spada.** The rich exterior trim of painted frescoes on the top story hint at the splendors within: grand salons nearly wall-papered with old master paintings capture the opulent, 17th-century version of *Lifestyles of the Rich and Famous.*

But don't miss the *colonnato prospettico* in the small courtyard between the library and the palace cortile. While the colonnaded tunnel, with a mythological figure in marble at the far end, seems to extend for 50 feet, it is actually only one-third that length.

Due to anamorphic deformation used as a trick by the designer, once thought to be Borromini himself (now seen as the work of Giovanni Maria da Bitono), the columns at the far end are only two feet high!

PUCCINI'S CHOICE

For the grand finale, head four blocks northward along Via Biscione back to the Corso Vittorio Emmanuele. Landmarking the famous Baroque church of **Sant'Andrea della Valle** is the highest dome in Rome (after St. Peter's).

Designed by Carlo Maderno, the nave is adorned with 17th-century frescoes by Lanfranco, making this one of the earliest ceilings in full Baroque figure.

Richly marbled chapels flank the nave, the setting Puccini chose for Act I of his opera *Tosca.* The arias sung by Floria Tosca and her lover Cavaradossi (load it on your iPod) strike exactly the right note to con-clude this tour of Rome.

TRASTEVERE: THE VILLAGE WITHIN THE CITY

Charming, cobblestoned Trastevere is often considered the stomping grounds of real Rome locals. Staunchly resisting the tides of change for centuries, millionaires and real estate agents started to arrive at this off-the-beaten path district over a decade ago. It's heavily populated by *romani di Roma*—those born and bred in the Eternal City for at least seven generations—who call themselves the only true Romans. To brook no arguments, they named their charming July fete the *Festa de Noantri*, or the "Festival of We Others," as the people of Trastevere pugnaciously labeled themselves so as to be distinguished from "Voiantri," the "you others" of the rest of Rome or anywhere else.

In fact, the Trasteverini have always been proud and combative, a breed apart. Dating back to Republican times when it hosted both Jewish and Syriac communities as well as assorted slaves and sailors, the area was only incorporated into the "Urbs" (or city proper) by Emperor Augustus in 7 BC. By the Middle Ages, Trastevere still wasn't considered truly part of Rome, and the "foreigners" who populated its maze of alleys and piazzas fought bitterly to obtain recognition for the neighborhood as a *rione (district),* or official district of the city. In the 14th century the Trasteverini won out and became full-fledged Romans, while stoutly maintaining their separate identity.

It's been the case ever since. Trastevere has always attracted "outsiders," and those have included celebrated artists and artisans. Raphael's model and mistress, the dark-eyed Fornarina (literally, "the baker's daughter"), is believed to have been a Trasteverina. The artist reportedly took time off from painting the *Galatea* in the nearby Villa Farnesina to woo the winsome girl at the tavern now occupied by a popular trattoria, Da Romolo. Long cocooned from "the strange disease of modern life," the district these days has been colonized with trendy boutiques and discos. Today, it's newly hip with actors and alternative thinkers, as well as legions of American students studying at John Cabot University. Tourists love the place, with good reason, but it's far less crowded than other central areas and retains a sleepy village feel mid-week. Trastevere remains a delight for dialecticians, biscuit eaters, winebibbers, and book browsers alike.

TIBER ISLAND

The best gateway to Trastevere turns out to be one of Rome's most picturesque: the Ponte Fabricio over the **Isola Tiberina,** the island wedged between Trastevere and the Campo area. As you stride over Rome's oldest bridge, let's not forget that Trastevere, literally translated, means "across the Tiber."

In Rome every stone worth its weight has a story attached. The one behind the Tiber Island, writes ancient historian Livy, is that Etruscan leader Tarquin, on his banishment, left behind a crop of grain in the Campo Marzio. For various superstitious reasons this was uprooted, put in baskets, and thrown into the Tiber for good riddance. Mud and sediment did the rest. The resulting island was eventually walled in the shape of a ship, ready to take on board another myth: allegedly this is where Aesculapius, god of medicine, landed from Greece (or his serpent double did). Whichever, the medical tradition continues to this day in the Hospital of Fratebenefratelli, the large building to your right. For one of Rome's most unique ancient survivals, head (in the opposite direction) down the embankment to the island's southern tip to the **ancient "stone prow,"** which was once part of the base of a temple. The surviving fragment is carved with the serpent of Aesculapius, god of health and medicine. Visit the church of **San Bartolomeo,** built above Aesculapius's Temple which dates back to the 10th century. Off to the right is one of the world's most beautiful movie theaters, the open-air Cinema d'Isola di Tiberina (which operates during the summer festival of Estate Romana). Cross the second bridge—the Ponte Cestio (dated 26 BC)—to get to Trastevere proper.

MEDIEVAL NOOKS AND CRANNIES

You're now on the Lungotevere riverside road but cross over and down the stairs to hit the pretty **Piazza in Piscinula** (from *piscina,* pool, referring to the ancient thermal baths once located here), home to **Saint Benedetto in Piscinula,** a 17th-century church with a much earlier campanile, one of the smallest and cutest in Rome, housing two original Medieval bells. Here St. Benedict, the founder of Western monasticism, once had a cell. The church has recently been restored by the Brazilian "Heralds of the Gospel" who, in resplendent uniform, are there on Sunday to greet visitors and worshippers alike. The multicolor 12th-century floor is a wonder in itself. On the opposite flank of the square is the 14th-century **Casa dei Mattei,** replete with cross-mullioned windows and loggias.

History nestles quietly in every nook and cranny off the square, but opt for the charming incline at the northern end, the **Via dell'Arco dei Tolomei,** graced with a medieval house built over an arch. One block north, let history take a rest in Via della Luce at a bakeshop par excellence—just look for the sign "Biscotti." The shop has been managed for generations by the Innocenti family, offering charming and courteous service often rare in Rome. Several blocks farther north, the "Middle-Aged" want to detour up to Piazza Belli, where they'll find one of the largest medieval structures in Trastevere, the **Torre degli Anguillara,** a much-restored mini-fortress whose main tower dates from the 13th century.

Back under the Tolomei arch, this street leads into the Via dei Salumi and one block leftward brings you to **Via dell'Atleta,** with a number of picturesque medieval houses. Via dell'Atleta runs into **Via dei Genovesi,** which commemorates the Genovese sailors who thronged Trastevere when it was the papal harbor in the 15th century. These gents roomed in the vicinity of the 15th-century church of San Giovanni Battista dei Genovesi, which has an extraordinary cloister. Whether Christopher Columbus ever stayed here is not recorded, but the dates would fit. Meanwhile, at a ring of the bell (at No. 12 Via Anicia), the cloister is still visitable, by donation, every afternoon 3–6, except during the month of August.

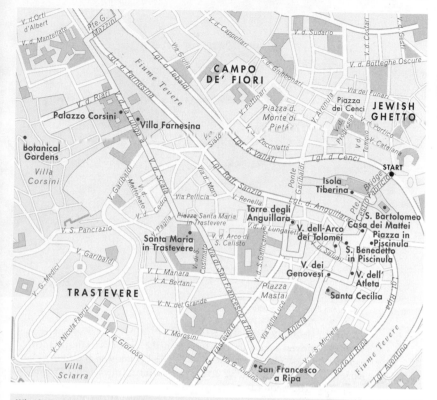

Why Go?:	Frozen-in-amber, this enchanting little nook of Rome has the city's best neighborhood vibe.
Good in the 'Hood:	Chilling out in Piazza Santa Maria in Trastevere, walking in Raphael's footsteps, roaming historical alleyways, lunching on Romolo's gorgeous terrace.
Highlights:	Mosaic splendor at Santa Maria in Trastevere, tiny Piazza in Piscinula, picturesque Isola Tiberina, Bernini's Blessed Ludovica Albertoni.
Where to Start:	Isola Tiberina (Tiber Island), accessed via tram from Largo Torre Argentina—get off near the Jewish Ghetto area, a few blocks from the Isola.
Where to Stop:	Just around the corner from the Piazza Maria you'll find the Bar San Calisto. Don't be deceived by its shabby 60s appearance. This stuck-in-time bar is a real institution, animated by young and old who come here to relax. Try to snag an outdoor table for a well-deserved coffee break. Make a gelato stop at Via della Lungaretta, where I Fior di Luna, a local institution, serves up scoops made using only the freshest, best-quality ingredients. Via della Lungara heads north to the Principe Amadeo bridge, where you can take No. 64 bus back to the city center.
Time:	Three to five hours, depending on your pace.
Best Time to Go:	The afternoon light here is best, but some churches, including almost all of Rome's smaller ones, close from about noon to 4 pm.
Worst Time to Go:	As the sun sets, hipster crowds arrive—Trastevere has a completely different vibe at night.

The Ponte Cestio connects the Isola Tiberina with Trastevere.

SAINTLY PORTRAITS IN STONE

Via dei Genovesi leads directly to one of the district's majestic medieval landmarks, the church of **Santa Cecilia**, which was built atop the Roman house of this martyr and patron saint of music. In 1599, her body was exhumed at the Catacombs of St. Callixtus and found to be miraculously intact. Sculptor Stefano Maderno was summoned to attest in stone to what he saw, and sketched before decomposition set in. In a robe-turned-shroud the saint lies on her side, head turned away, across her neck a deep gash, which she's supposed to have survived for three days after suffocation in a steam bath had left her not only unscathed but singing (all this sent Marquis de Sade into rather dubious raptures). With its almost mystically white marble, the work has a haunting quality that few statues can match. But the greatest treasure can be seen only if you exit and ring the bell on the left: for a donation (suggested €3) a nun will show you to an elevator that ascends to a *Christ in Judgment* by Pietro Cavallini, a contemporary of Giotto. Painted in 1293, the frescoes are remarkably intact.

Leaving the church, turn left and walk down Via Anicia several blocks to Piazza San Francesco d'Assisi and **San Francesco a Ripa**. The fourth chapel on the left features Bernini's eye-knocking statue of the *Blessed Ludovica Albertoni,* a Franciscan nun whose body is buried beneath the altar. It has been remarked that the Baroque, at its most effective, served not just to educate but to sweep you off your feet. Here's an example. Marble pillow, folds, and drapery in abundance, all set off the deathbed agony and ecstasy of the nun—her provocative gesture of clutching at her breast is actually an allusion to the "milk of charity."

MAJESTIC SANTA MARIA

We now set off for the walk's northern half by heading up Via di San Francesco a Ripa, one of Trastevere's main shopping strips. But this dreary stretch actually enhances the delight at finding, at the end of the street, **Santa Maria in Trastevere**, famously set on one of Rome's dreamiest piazzas. Noted for its fountain and caffè, it is the photogenic heart of the rione. Fellini evidently thought the same, making it a supporting star of his film *Roma*.

Staring down at you from the 12th-century church façade are the famed medieval frescoes of the Wise and Foolish Virgins. Dramatically spotlit at night, these young ladies refer to the "miraculous" discovery of oil here in 39 BC. In the mosaic, the Virgin is set between the wise virgins and two foolish ones—the latters' crownless heads bowed with shame at having left their lamps empty, the flame extinguished. In the church's presbytery the *fons olii* marks the spot from whence the oil originally flowed.

Thanks to its gilded ceiling, shimmering mosaics, and vast dimensions, the church nave echoes the spectacle of an ancient Roman basilica—the columns and other structural elements are said to have come from the Baths of Caracalla. The church's main wonder, however, must be the golden mosaics behind the altar. The famous mosaics of Pietro Cavallini depict episodes in the life of the Virgin so often revisited during the Renaissance. With its use of perspective, the work—completed in 1297—is seen as something of a watershed between the old, static Byzantine style and the more modern techniques soon to be taken up by Giotto. This is the very dawn of Western art.

The piazza outside is the very heart of the Trastevere rione. With its elegant raised fountain and sidewalk caffè, this is one of Rome's most beloved outdoor "living rooms," open to all comers. Through innumerable generations, this piazza has seen the comings and goings of tourists and travelers, intellectuals and artists, who lounge on the steps of the fountain or lunch at Sabatini's, whose food has seen much better days but whose real estate, with its tables set up directly in front of the fountain, is among Rome's most coveted. Here the paths of Trastevere's residents intersect repeatedly during the day; they pause, gathering in clusters to talk animatedly in the broad accent of Rome or in a score of foreign languages. At night, it's the center of Trastevere's action, with street festivals, musicians, and gamboling dogs vying for attention from the throngs of people taking the evening air.

RAPHAEL WAS HERE

Directly north of the church is Piazza Sant'Egidio (the small but piquant Museo di Trastevere is here) and then you enter Via della Lungara, where, several blocks along on the right, the **Villa Farnesina** stands (hours are 9–2 daily, except Sunday). Originally built by papal banker and high-roller Agostino "Il Magnifico" Chigi, this is Rome at its High Renaissance best.

Pull up a caffè seat and settle down to enjoy the daily spectacle that is the Piazza di Santa Maria in Trastevere—one of Rome's favorite "living rooms."

Enter the Loggia di Galatea to find, across the ceiling, Peruzzi's 1511 horoscope of the papal banker, presumably not foretelling the family's eventual bankruptcy and the selling off of the same property (and horoscope) to the wealthy Farnese family. Off left, next to the wall, sits Sebastiano di Piombo's depiction of one-eyed giant *Polyphemus* with staff and giant panpipes; this is what, just next door, Raphael's *Galatea* is listening to in her shell-chassis, paddle-wheeled chariot. With the countermovement of its iconic putti, nymphs, sea gods, and dolphins, this legendary image became a hallmark of Renaissance harmony.

In the next room, also—or at least mostly—decorated by Raphael, is the *Marriage of Cupid and Psyche*. After provoking the jealousy of Venus, Psyche has to overcome a number of trials before being deemed fit to drink the cup of immortality and marry Cupid. Here, of course, is an alter ego for Agostino Chigi. The paintings are made still more wonderful by Giovanni da Udine's depictions of flower and fruit separating one from the other as if it were a giant *pergolato* (or arbor)—gods float at every angle while ornithologists will delight in spotting Raphael's repertoire of bird species. Climbing upstairs one passes through Peruzzi's Hall of Perspectives to Chigi's private rooms. Here, in Il Sodoma's *Alexander's Wedding*, Roxanna is being lovingly undressed by a bevy of cupids. Note the one so overexcited he attempts a somersault like a footballer after a winning goal. Tours in English are held Saturdays at 10 am.

QUEEN CHRISTINA AT HOME

Directly across the street from the Villa Farnesina is the **Palazzo Corsini** (*Tues.–Sun., 8:30–2*), entered via a gigantic stone staircase right out of a Piranesi print. This was formerly the palazzo of pipe-smoking Christina of Sweden, immortalized by Greta Garbo on the silver screen and to whom history, that old gossip, attaches the label, "Queen without a realm, Christian without a faith, and a woman without shame." Her artistic taste is indisputable.

The second room alone contains a magnificent Rubens, Van Dyck's *Madonna of the Straw,* an Andrea del Sarto, and then, courtesy of Hans Hoffman, surely the hare of all hares. Worth the price of admission alone is Caravaggio's *John the Baptist.* In other rooms, for aficionados of high-class gore, there's Salvator Rosa's *Prometheus,* the vulture *in flagrante* and on Prometheus's face a scream to rival Munch. A visit to the **Botanical Gardens** that stretch behind the galleria is well worth a visit, if just to restore a sense of calm after all that Baroque bloodletting.

To get back to central Rome, walk to Piazza Trilussa and cross over the pedestrian Ponte Sisto.

ROME OF THE EMPERORS: A ROMAN FORUM WALK

Taking in the famous vista of the Roman Forum from the terraces of the *Campidoglio* (Capitoline Hill), you have probably already cast your eyes down and across two millennia of history in a single glance. Here, in one fabled panorama, are the world's most striking and significant concentrations of historic remains. From this hilltop aerie, however, the erstwhile heart of ancient Rome looks like one gigantic jigsaw puzzle, the last piece being the Colosseum, looming in the distance. Excavations only began in earnest in the late 19th century, and then the very heart of the ancient Roman Empire began to be unearthed. While it is fine to just let your mind contemplate the scattered pieces of the once-impressive whole, it is even better to go exploring to decipher the significance of the Forum's noble fragments. This walk does precisely that.

WORLD'S MIGHTIEST HEIRLOOM

To kick things off, we start just south of the Forum at ancient Rome's hallmark monument, the **Colosseum** (with its handy Colosseo Metro stop). Be wary of the dozens of tour guides outside the monument. Real-deal guides will have an official city license identifying their skills. Official guides must take a rigorous test to earn one of the city's few coveted licenses. Others are well-meaning students who can legally only accept a tip as fee. And many more are scam artists on the search for their latest prey, including the beefy men dressed up as gladiators. If you must have a souvenir photo with them to take home, negotiate the price ahead of time (maximum a few euros to take a picture with your own camera).

Convincingly austere, the Colosseum is the Eternal City's yardstick of eternity. A special road having been built to transport the Travertine stone from nearby Tivoli—these quarries are still there to this day—the building was begun under the emperor Titus Flavius Vespasianus (aka Vespasian), and it was named the Flavian Amphitheater after his family. His son Titus, according to his father's will, inherited the task of finishing it in AD 80 while his other son, Domitian, built the gladiatorial schools on the adjacent Colle Oppio.

The new building was to erase memories of Nero, who had privatized a vast swath of land near the public Forum for his private palace; in fact, the Colosseum was positioned directly over a (drained) former lake in Nero's gardens. Close by stood a 120-foot high statue in gilded bronze, which had once represented Nero himself as the sun god. After Nero's death, the features of the statue were modified and it was simply a representation of the sun god. The size of the statue was such that it was known as the Colossus, which would subsequently give the nearby building its nickname.

A typical day at the Colosseum would begin with a wild-beast hunt, then a pause for lunch, during which the sparse crowd was entertained with tamer displays by jugglers, magicians, and acrobats, along with much less tame criminal punishments. The main event followed: the gladiators, fighting one another in elaborate costumes and amid stage

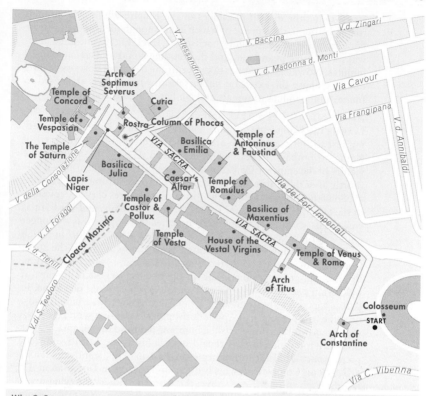

Why Go?:	Ancient Rome's "Times Square," this Forum was the civic core of the city and is the best place to experience the ageless romance of the Eternal City.
Good in the 'Hood:	Walking in the footsteps of Julius Caesar, Mark Antony, St. Paul, and Nero; visiting the peaceful gardens of the Palatine, home of the emperors.
Highlights:	Arches of Septimus Severus, Titus, and Constantine; the Colosseum; the Via Sacra; the Roman Forum.
Where to Start:	Piazza del Colosseo, with its handy Colosseo Metro stop.
Where to Stop:	Inside the archaeological ruins, there are drinking fountains and a couple of vending machines (on the Palatine and the via Nova in the Forum) for hot days. Just a five-minute walk from the Colosseum on Via di San Giovanni in Laterano 40, fresh and creamy gelato and homemade Sicilian specialties await you at the genuine Cremeria Don Pepe.
Time:	Two to five hours, depending on your pace and how detailed you wish the visit to be.
Best Time to Go:	To avoid the harsh midday sun start your tour of the Forum early or in the late afternoon.
Worst Time to Go:	Midday in high summer, when the sun is high and merciless in the Forum, particularly in the summertime—remember, there are no roofs and few trees to shelter under at these archaeological sites. The Palatine has more shade (and a small air-conditioned museum). Crowds are at their thickest after 10 am.

sets evoking the distant provinces of the Empire while wild animals roamed around, the smaller of which came though the trapdoors in the floor from the underground "backstage" level. Eighty entrance archways fed people in and out, and the building could be evacuated in 10 minutes. Nowadays, you can take one of the elevators upstairs to level one to glimpse the extensive subterranean passageways that used to funnel all the unlucky animals and gladiators into the arena.

ANCIENT ARCHES TELL THE TALE

Leaving the Colosseum behind, admire the **Arch of Constantine,** standing just to the north of the arena. The largest and best preserved of Rome's triumphal arches, it was erected in AD 315 to celebrate the victory of the emperor Constantine (280–337) over Maxentius—it was shortly after this battle that Constantine converted Rome to Christianity. Something of an amalgam historically, it features carved depictions of the triumphs of emperors Trajan, Marcus Aurelius, and Hadrian as well, a cost-cutting recycling that indicates the empire was no longer quite what it once was. You have to walk down Via dei Fori Imperiali to the only Forum entrance, located about halfway down the street from the Colosseum and across from Via Cavour, to enter the Forum. From there, you can take a left up the ancient Via Sacra to start at the Forum's southwestern point with the **Temple of Venus and Roma.** In part it was proudly designed by would-be architect Hadrian—at least until the true professional Apollodurus pointed out that with Hadrian's measurements the goddess risked bumping her head on the apse, a piece of advice for which he was repaid with banishment. Off to your left, on the spur of hillside jutting from the Palatine Hill, stands the famed **Arch of Titus.** Completed by his brother, and successor, Domitian in AD 81, the arch in one frieze shows the Roman soldiery carrying away booty—the golden menorah, the silver trumpets, an altar table—from the destruction of the Temple in Jerusalem 10 years earlier. On the other side there is Titus on the same Via Sacra, in this case being charioted toward the Capitol after the campaign in Palestine begun by his father Vespasian. Through the arch, photograph the great vista of the entire Forum as it stretches toward the distant Capitoline Hill.

MASSIVE MAXENTIUS

After doubling back down the Via Sacra, make sure to take in the massive **Basilica of Maxentius,** or the third of it left standing. Heavily damaged during Alaric's sack of Rome in 410, it had been founded by Maxentius in 306–10, then completed by Constantine the Great, Maxentius's archenemy, at the battle of the Milvian Bridge. The three remaining side vaults give an idea of the building's scale; also to how, through their use of brick and barrel vaulting, the Romans had freed themselves from the tyranny of gravity. Here once stood—or sat rather—the surrealistically large head and other body fragments of Constantine (now in the outside courtyard of the Palazzo dei Conservatori), the first Christian emperor. Rome's first Christian basilica, San Giovanni in Laterano, originated many of the features used in the basilica here. Not surprisingly this most majestic of ruins was much admired and studied by the great Renaissance architects and painters alike—in Raphael's *School of Athens* the background edifice is surely a depiction of what you are seeing here. Today, the basilica is the site of wonderful concerts in summer and the occasional dramatized trial of this or that emperor (e.g., Nero and Tiberius).

TEMPLES STILL STANDING TALL

Resuming your walk back toward the Capitoline Hill, the next building is the **Temple of Romulus.** The Romulus here is not Rome's founder but the son of Emperor Maxentius. Apart from the Pantheon, this is the only Roman temple to remain entirely intact—so intact even the lock in the original bronze doors is said to still function. This is due to its having subsequently been used, at least until the late 19th century, as the atrium of a Christian church above. The stonework across the lintel is as perfect as when it was made, as are the two porphyry pillars. For an inside view of the same temple and, until a century ago, the attached church atrium, enter the Church of Cosma and Damiano from the Via dei Fori Imperiali side and peer through the glass at the end of the main chapel.

Proof of how deeply buried the Forum was throughout Medieval times can be seen in the wonderful pillars of the next building down, the **Temple of Antoninus and Faustina,** his wife. Those stains reaching halfway up are in fact centuries-old soil marks. Further evidence of the sinking Forum are the doors of the 13th-century church above—note how they seem to hang almost in midair. Now a full 30 feet above the temple's rebuilt steps, originally they would, of course, have been at ground level. Here we see an example of the Christian world not so much supplanting the pagan world as growing out of it. Meanwhile, there against the blue, read the words "Divo Antonino" and "Diva Faustina," proclaiming the couple's self-ordained "divination."

A CAESAR AMONG CAESARS

Continue your walk toward the Capitoline Hill by strolling by the largely vanished **Basilica Emilia.** To the left, however, is the Temple of Caesar, sometimes referred to as **Caesar's Altar,** where, after his assassination from 23 knife wounds, Caesar's body was brought hotfoot for cremation. Peep behind the low wall and now in Caesar's honor there are flowers instead of flames. Now look up and head over, just across the road known as the Vicus Tuscus, to the three wonderfully white pillars of the **Temple of Castor and Pollux.** This was reconstructed by Augustus to pay homage to the twin sons of Jupiter and Leda, who helped the Roman army to victory back in the 5th century BC. The emperor Caligula, says Suetonius, "had part of the temple incorporated into his palace as his own vestibule. Often he would stand between the divine brothers displaying himself for worship by those visiting the temple."

To this temple's right sits the **Basilica Julia.** After the death of Julius Caesar, all chaos broke loose in Rome and preluded another long bout of civil war. This ended with the victory of Augustus who, ever the dutiful stepson, had this massive basilica completed in his father's honor. Pitted with column marks, a rectangular piece of the ground remains. As with other Roman basilicas, the place was more judicial in nature, swarming, according to Pliny, with 180 judges and a plague of lawyers. Look carefully at the flooring and you might still spy a chessboard carved into the marble, perhaps by a bored litigant.

HAUNT OF THE VESTAL VIRGINS

Backtrack a bit along the Via Sacra past the Temple of Castor and Pollux to the circular **Temple of Vesta**. In a tradition going back to an age when fire was a precious commodity, the famous vestal virgins kept the fire of Rome burning here. Of the original 20 columns only three remain, behind which stretch the vast remains of the **House of the Vestal Virgins**. Privileged in many ways—they had front-row seats in the Colosseum and rights of deciding life and death for poor gladiators, for example—they were also under a 30-year-long vow of chastity. As everyone knows, the notorious punishment for breaking their vow was being buried alive. But it is time to turn back and press on with our walk. Crossing the central square and walking back toward the towering Capitoline Hill, you are now entering the midsection of the open area of the Forum proper; you can see to your left the **Column of Phocas**. The last monument to be built on the by now largely abandoned Forum was this column, erected by an otherwise forgotten Byzantine emperor. In 1813, on the orders of Pope Pius VII, the area was excavated, with the assumption that the column belonged to the Temple of Jove Custode. Then, at the base, surfaced the inscription, describing how it had been erected in 608 to the Christian emperor from the east on his bequeathing the Pantheon to the Roman Church.

A BURIAL TOO SOON

The long stone platform presiding over this area is the famous **Rostra**. *Forum* comes from an old Latin word meaning "to meet," and it was from here that Rome's political elite would address the people. Indeed, this is where, with some help from Shakespeare, Mark Antony would have pronounced his rabble-rousing "I come to bury Caesar, not to praise him." The name Rostra dates to the custom of adorning the platform with prows of captured ships following an early naval victory off Antium/Anzio in 338 BC.

Going back even farther is, on the other side of the Via Sacra, the so-called **Lapis Niger**, or Black Stone, which marks the site of a Temple to Romulus. The small sanctuary underneath goes back to the 6th century BC, as does a strange column with the oldest Latin inscription yet known, cursing all those who profaned the place—irreverent archaeologists take note!

Altogether mightier in scale is the **Curia**—the Senate house of ancient Rome—nearby. Not the building of the earlier republican period, this is a version rebuilt by Diocletian and in turn rebuilt in 1937. Here sat the 300 members of Senate, then rendered largely powerless by Diocletian. Originally decorating the nearby rostra, the two friezes show the much earlier emperor Trajan. Meanwhile the porphyry statue without a head has been attributed to Trajan also. But there is a neater theory: with the turnover in emperors reaching to as many as six per year and porphyry being almost priceless, the head was replaceable by whatever emperor happened to be in power.

See you later, gladiator: the Colosseum hosted gladiatorial combats for centuries and up to 30,000 may have tragically perished in its arena.

HEADS AND TALES

Continue back down the Via Sacra, where towers one of the Forum's extant spectaculars, the **Arch of Septimus Severus.** Built by his sons, it celebrates Septimus's campaign against the Parthians and the ensuing influx into Rome of booty and slaves. A number of these, their hands tied behind them, are depicted. Also on view is the murderous Caracalla, son number two, though the head of his elder brother Gaeta has, Stalin-fashion, been erased. Sadly, many other heads have also had a Caracalla done on them by the erosive fumes of Roman traffic.

Continuing left and up the Via Sacra, you reach the base of the celebrated **Temple of Saturn.** Now the name of a planet, Saturn was then as close to the earth as you can get, the word originating from *sero*—"to sow." Saturn was originally a corn god, first worshipped in Magna Grecia, then allowed, so goes the patriotic myth, to settle in Rome by the city's presiding deity, Janus. That Saturn was the God of Plenty in more than an agricultural sense is also attested to by the fact that beneath the floor was kept the wealth of the Roman treasury.

Position yourself below the easternmost two of the eight columns of Egyptian marble and peer upward as they reach higher than a rocket at Cape Canaveral and are every bit as majestic.

HAIL AND FAREWELL

Meanwhile, up ahead ascends the last stretch of the Via Sacra—the so-called Clivus Capitolinus. On the left is the **Temple of Vespasian.**

Bowing to the powerful nature of time, now only three splendid columns remain. Next door once stood the **Temple of Concord.**

Built back in republican times, it celebrated the peace between the oft-warring patricians and plebs, the two cardinal elements in the winning formula of SPQR—in other words the patrician Senate (S) and the people (PQ). A few stones mark the spot—and the last piece in the Forum's monumental jigsaw.

For a better sense of the whole area—a sort of archaeological gestalt—climb onto the Palatine (the stairs are very steep; easier access is up the path by the Arch of Titus) to the terrace at the Horti Farnesiani Gardens for a breathtaking view to put your walking into panoramic context. While here, you can't help but ponder on the truth of *sic transit gloria mundi* ("thus passes the glory of the world")—a similar view by moonlight inspired Edward Gibbon to embark on his epic *Decline and Fall of the Roman Empire*.

ANCIENT ROME

Getting Oriented

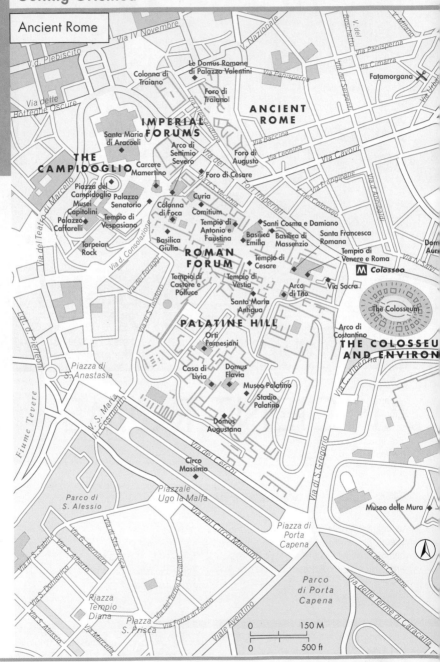

Ancient Rome

Via IV Novembre
V.d. Plebiscito
Via delle Botteghe Oscure
Colonna di Traiano
Le Domus Romane di Palazzo Valentini
Foro di Traiano
Via Panisperna
Via Cimarra
Fatamorgana

ANCIENT ROME

IMPERIAL FORUMS
Santa Maria di Aracoeli
Arco di Settimio Severo
Foro di Augusto
Via Leonina
Via Cavour

THE CAMPIDOGLIO
Carcere Mamertino
Foro di Cesare

Piazza del Campidoglio
Palazzo Senatorio
Musei Capitolini
Curia
Colonna di Foca
Comitium
Palazzo Caffarelli
Tempio di Vespasiano
Tempio di Antonio e Faustina
Santi Cosma e Damiano
Santa Francesca Romana
Tarpeian Rock
Basilica Giulia
Basilica Emilia
Basilica di Massenzio
Tempio di Venere e Roma
ROMAN FORUM
Tempio di Cesare
Dom Aur
M Colosseo

Tempio di Castore e Polluce
Tempio di Vestia
Arco di Tito
Via Sacra
Santa Maria Antigua
The Colosseum

PALATINE HILL
Orti Farnesiani
Arco di Costantino
THE COLOSSEU AND ENVIRON

Piazza di S. Anastasia
Casa di Livia
Domus Flavia
Museo Palatino
Stadio Palatina
Domus Augustana

Fiume Tevere
Circo Massimo
Via dei Cerchi

Parco di S. Alessio
Piazzale Ugo la Malfa
Piazza di Porta Capena
Museo delle Mura

Piazza Tempio Diana
Piazza S. Prisca
Parco di Porta Capena
Via delle Terme di Caracalla

| 0 | | 150 M |
| 0 | | 500 ft |

TOP REASONS TO GO

The Colosseum: Clamber up the stands to the emperor's box and imagine the gory games as Trajan saw them.

The Roman Forum: Walk through crumbling, romantic ruins—a trip back 2,000 years—to the heart of one of the greatest empires the world has ever seen.

The Campidoglio: Watch the sun go down over ancient and Renaissance Rome from the back of the Campidoglio, the best view in town.

Capitoline Museums: See eye-to-eye with the ancients—the busts of emperors and philosophers are more real than ideal.

Caffè Capitolino: Sip prosecco on the terrace of the Palazzo Caffarelli—part of the Musei Capitolini complex—while you take in a Cinerama scene of Roman rooftops.

MAKING THE MOST OF YOUR TIME

This area is relatively compact, but it's rich with history. Serious history buffs should give themselves a full day to see all of it, including an hour in the Colosseum, an hour or more in the Forum, and two hours in the Musei Capitolini. Even for ancient Rome experts, taking a tour can be helpful, as a good guide can bring the piles of rubble and ruins to life in a way that no written explanation can, but book a guide in advance instead of picking up one of those trying to shill their expertise on-site.

The longest line in Rome, aside from the one at the Vatican Museums, is at the Colosseum, so go either immediately when it opens (at 8:30 am) or later in the afternoon, when many tour buses have started to depart. There is little to no shade in the Forum, so it gets very hot and dusty in summertime—another reason to either go early or start late.

GETTING HERE

The Colosseo Metro station is right across from the Colosseum and a short walk from both the Roman and Imperial forums, as well as the Palatine Hill. Walking from the very heart of the historic center will take about 20 minutes, much of it along the wide Via dei Fori Imperiali. The little electric Bus No. 117 from the center or No. 175 from Termini will also deliver you to the Colosseum's doorstep. Any of the following buses will take you to or near the Roman Forum: Nos. 60, 75, 85, 95, and 175.

QUICK BITES

Fatamorgana. A short walk from the Roman Forum, this small Roman chain serves excellent gelato, including familiar favorites and adventurous flavors such as gorgonzola, olive, and tobacco. A bench outside offers relief after a day of walking. ⊠ *Piazza degli Zingari 5* ☎ *06/48906855* ⊕ *www.gelateriafatamorgana. com* Ⓜ *Cavour.*

3

Sightseeing
★★★★★
Nightlife
★★
Dining
★★
Lodging
★★★
Shopping
★

Updated
by Agnes
Crawford

If you ever wanted to feel like the Caesars—with all of ancient Rome (literally) at your feet—simply head to Michelangelo's famed Piazza del Campidoglio. There, make a beeline for the terrace flanking the side of the center building, the Palazzo Senatorio, Rome's ceremonial city hall. From this balcony atop the Capitoline Hill you can take in a breathtaking panorama.

Looming before you is the entire Roman Forum, the *caput mundi*—the capital of the known world—for centuries, and where many of the world's most important events in the past 2,500 years happened. Here, all Rome shouted as one, "Caesar has been murdered," and crowded to hear Mark Antony's eulogy for the fallen leader. Here, legend has it that St. Paul traversed the Forum en route to his audience with Nero. Here, Roman law and powerful armies were created, keeping the barbarian world at bay for a millennium. And here the Roman emperors staged the biggest blow-out extravaganzas ever mounted for the entire population of a city, outdoing even Elizabeth Taylor's entrance in *Cleopatra*.

But after a more than 27-century-long parade of pageantry, you'll find that much has changed in this area. The marble fragments scattered over the Forum area makes all but students of archaeology ask: is this the grandeur that was Rome? It's not surprising that Shelley and Gibbon once reflected, on the sense that *sic transit gloria mundi*—"thus passes the glory of the world." Yet spectacular monuments—the Arch of Septimius Severus, the Palatine Hill, and the Colosseum (looming in the background), among them—remind us that this was indeed the birthplace of much of Western civilization.

Before the Christian era, before the Emperors, before the powerful Republic that ruled the Mediterranean, Rome was founded on seven hills. Two of them, the Capitoline and the Palatine, surround the Roman Forum, where the Romans of the later Republican and Imperial ages worshipped deities, debated politics, and wheeled and dealed. It's all history now, but this remains one of the world's most striking and significant concentrations of ancient remains: an emphatic reminder of the genius and power that made Rome the fountainhead of the Western world.

THE CAMPIDOGLIO

Your first taste of ancient Rome should start from a point that embodies some of Rome's earliest and greatest moments: the Campidoglio. Here, on the Capitoline Hill (which towers over the traffic hub of Piazza Venezia), a meditative Edward Gibbon was inspired to write his 1764 tome, *The History of the Decline and Fall of the Roman Empire.* Of Rome's famous seven hills, the Capitoline is the smallest and the most sacred. It has always been the seat of Rome's government, and its Latin name echoes in the designation of the national and state capitol buildings of every country in the world.

TOP ATTRACTIONS

Fodor's Choice
★

Le Domus Romane di Palazzo Valentini. If you find your imagination stretching to picture Rome as it was two millennia ago, make sure to check out this "new" ancient site just a stone's throw from Piazza Venezia. As was common practice in Renaissance-era Rome, 16th-century builders simply filled in ancient structures with landfill, using them as part of the foundation for Palazzo Valentini. In doing so, the builders also unwittingly preserved the ruins beneath, which archaeologists rediscovered during excavations in 2007. It took another three years for the two opulent, imperial-era *domus* (upscale urban houses) to open to the public on a regular basis.

Descending below Palazzo Valentini is like walking into another world. Not only are the houses luxurious and well-preserved, still retaining their beautiful mosaics, inlaid marble floors, and staircases, but the ruins have been made to "come alive" through multimedia. Sophisticated light shows re-create what it all would have looked like, while a dramatic, automated voiceover accompanies you as you walk through the rooms, pointing out cool finds (the heating system for the private baths, the mysterious fragment of a statue, the porcelain left here when part of the site became a dump during the Renaissance) and evidence of tragedy (the burned layer from a fire that ripped through the home). If it sounds corny, hold your skepticism: it's an effective, excellent way to actually "experience" the houses as ancient Romans would have—and to learn a lot about ancient Rome in the process. A multimedia presentation halfway through also shows you what central Rome would have looked like 2,000 years ago.

The multimedia tour takes about an hour. There are limited spots, so book in advance over the phone, online, or in person; make sure you book one of the three daily English tours (at 1:30, 2, and 2:30 pm). The tour should be enjoyable for older children, but little ones might be afraid of how dark the rooms can be. ⊠ *Via Foro Traiano 85, Piazza Venezia* ☎ *06/32810,* ⊕ *www.palazzovalentini.it* 🎫*€13.50, including booking fee* ☾ *Closed Tues.* Ⓜ *Colosseo.*

THE CAMPIDOGLIO

✉ *Piazza dei Campidoglio, including the Palazzo Senatorio and the Musei Capitolini, the Palazzo Nuovo, and the Palazzo dei Conservatori, Piazza Venezia* Ⓜ *Colosseo.*

TIPS

■ The piazza centerpiece is the legendary equestrian statue of Emperor Marcus Aurelius, but in 1999 a copy replaced the 2nd-century-AD original, which moved to a new wing of the surrounding Musei Capitolini. The Sala Marco Aurelio and its glass room also protect a gold-plated Hercules along with more massive body parts, this time bronze, of what might be Constantine or that of his son Constans II (archaeologists are yet undecided).

■ While there are great views of the Roman Forum from the terrace balconies to either side of the Palazzo Senatorio, the best view may be from the Tabularium, the arcade balcony below the Senatorio building, accessible with admission to the Musei Capitolini. The museum also has the Terrazza Caffarelli, featuring a restaurant with a magical view toward Trastevere and St. Peter's.

Spectacularly transformed by Michelangelo's late-Renaissance designs, the Campidoglio was once the epicenter of the Roman Empire, the place where the city's first shrines stood, including its most sacred, the Temple of Jupiter. The Capitoline Hill originally consisted of two peaks: the Capitolium and the Arx (where Santa Maria in Aracoeli now stands). The hollow between them was known as the Asylum. Here, prospective settlers once came to seek the protection of Romulus, legendary first king of Rome—hence the term "asylum." Later, during the Republic, in 78 BC, the Tabularium, or Hall of Records, was erected here.

By the Middle Ages, however, the Capitoline had become an unkempt hill strewn with ancient rubble. In preparation for the impending visit of Charles V in 1536, triumphant after the empire's victory over the Moors, his host, Pope Paul III Farnese, decided that the Holy Roman Emperor should follow the route of the emperors, finishing triumphantly at the Campidoglio. The pope was embarrassed by the decrepit goat pasture the hill had become and so commissioned Michelangelo to restore the site to glory. The resulting design added a third palace along with Renaissance-style facades and a grand paved piazza. Newly excavated ancient sculptures, designed to impress the visiting emperor, were installed in the palaces, and the piazza was ornamented with the giant stone figures of the Discouri and the ancient Roman equestrian statue of Emperor Marcus Aurelius (the original now housed in the Musei Capitolini).

Fodor's Choice   **Musei Capitolini.** Surpassed in size and richness only by the Musei Vati-
★   cani, this immense collection was the world's first public museum. A
greatest-hits collection of Roman art through the ages, from the ancients
to the Baroque, it's housed in the twin Museo Capitolino and Palazzo
dei Conservatori that bookend Michelangelo's famous piazza. Although
some pieces in the collection—which was first assembled by Sixtus IV
(1414–84), one of the earliest of the Renaissance popes—may excite
only archaeologists and art historians, others are unforgettable, including the original bronze statue of Marcus Aurelius whose copy sits in
the piazza.

Buy your ticket and enter the Palazzo dei Conservatori where, in the
first courtyard, you'll see the giant head, foot, elbow, and imperially
raised finger of the fabled seated statue of Constantine, which once filled
the Basilica of Maxentius, his defeated rival. Upstairs is the resplendent
Salone dei Orazi e Curiazi (Salon of Horatii and Curatii), decorated
with a magnificent gilt ceiling, carved wooden doors, and 16th-century
frescoes depicting the history of ancient Rome. At both ends of the hall
are statues of the Baroque era's most charismatic popes, Urban VIII
and Innocent X.

The heart of the museum is the **Exedra of Marcus Aurelius** (Sala Marco
Aurelio), which showcases the spectacular original bronze statue of the
Roman emperor whose copy sits in the piazza below. To the right, the
room segues into the area of the Temple of Jupiter, with its original
ruins rising organically into the museum space. A reconstruction of
the temple and Capitoline Hill from the Bronze Age to the present day
makes for a fascinating glimpse through the ages.

On the top floor, the museum's *pinacoteca,* or painting gallery, has some
noted Baroque masterpieces, including Caravaggio's *The Fortune Teller*
and *St. John the Baptist.* Also on the top floor (but on the other side
of the Palazzo dei Conservatori), the Caffè Capitolino (daily 9–7) has
spectacular views over Rome in the direction of St. Peter's.

To get to the Palazzo Nuovo, take the stairs or elevator to the basement
of the Palazzo dei Conservatori, where the corridor uniting the two
contains the Epigraphic Collection, a poignant collection of ancient
gravestones. Halfway along the corridor, and before going up into the
Palazzo Nuovo, be sure to take the detour to the right to the Tabularium
Gallery and its unparalleled view over the Forum.

On the stairs inside the Palazzo Nuovo, you'll be immediately dwarfed
by Mars in full military rig and lion-topped sandals. Upstairs is the
noted **Sala degli Imperatori,** lined with busts of Roman emperors, and
the **Sala dei Filosofi,** where busts of philosophers sit in judgment—a
fascinating who's who of the ancient world. Within these serried ranks
are 48 Roman emperors, ranging from Augustus to Theodosius. Nearby
are rooms filled with masterpieces, including the legendary Dying Gaul,
the Red Faun from Hadrian's Villa, and a Cupid and Psyche. ⊠ *Piazza
del Campidoglio, Piazza Venezia* ☎ *06/0608* ⊕ *www.museicapitolini.
org* ⊠ *€13 (€15 with exhibitions); audio guide €6* Ⓜ *Colosseo; Bus Nos.
44, 63, 64, 81, 95, 85, and 492.*

Santa Maria di Aracoeli. Sitting atop its 124 steps, Santa Maria di Aracoeli perches on the north slope of the Capitoline Hill. The church rests on the site of the temple of Juno Moneta (Admonishing Juno), which also housed the Roman mint (hence the origin of the word "money"). According to legend, it was here that the Sibyl, a prophetess, predicted to Augustus the coming of a Redeemer. He in turn responded by erecting an altar, the Ara Coeli (Altar of Heaven). This was eventually replaced by a Benedictine monastery, and then a church, which was passed in 1250 to the Franciscans, who restored and enlarged it in Romanesque-Gothic style. Today, the Aracoeli is best known for the **Santo Bambino,** a much-revered olivewood figure of the Christ Child (today a copy of the 15th-century original that was stolen in 1994). At Christmas, everyone pays homage to the "Bambinello" as children recite poems from a miniature pulpit. In true Roman style, the church interior is a historical hodgepodge: classical columns and large marble fragments from pagan buildings, as well as a 13th-century Cosmatesque pavement. The richly gilded Renaissance ceiling commemorates the naval victory at Lepanto in 1571 over the Turks. The first chapel on the right is noteworthy for Pinturicchio's frescoes of San Bernardino of Siena (1486). ⊠ *Via del Teatro di Marcello, at top of steep stairway, Piazza Venezia* ☎ *06/69763838* Ⓜ *Colosseo; Bus Nos. 44, 160, 170, 175, and 186.*

WORTH NOTING

Carcere Mamertino (*Mamertine Prison*). The state prison of the Middle Ages has two subterranean cells where Rome's enemies, most famously the Goth, Jugurtha, and the indomitable Gaul, Vercingetorix, were imprisoned and died of either starvation or strangulation. Legend has it that in the lower cell saints Peter and Paul were imprisoned under Nero, and a miraculous spring of water appeared with which they baptized their jailers. A church, San Giuseppe dei Falegnami, now stands over the prison. The multimedia tour has received mixed reviews: it focuses on the Christian history of the site, and the audio is more fluffy than historical. ⊠ *Via del Tulliano, Piazza Venezia* ☎ *06/698961* 💶 *€10* 🕙 *Closed Mon., Wed., and Fri.* Ⓜ *Colosseo.*

Palazzo Senatorio. During the Middle Ages, this city hall looked like those you might see in Tuscan hill towns: part fortress and part assembly hall. The building was entirely rebuilt in the 1500s as part of Michelangelo's revamping of the Campidoglio for Pope Paul III; the master's design was adapted by later architects, who wisely left the front staircase as the focus of the facade. The ancient statue of Minerva at the center was renamed the Goddess Rome, and the river gods (the River Tigris remodeled to symbolize the Tiber, to the right, and the Nile, to the left) were hauled over from the Terme di Costantino on the Quirinal Hill. Today, it is the regional seat of Rome's Comune administration and is not open to the public. ⊠ *Piazza del Campidoglio, Piazza Venezia* Ⓜ *Colosseo.*

Tarpeian Rock. In ancient Rome, traitors were hurled to their deaths from here. In the 18th and 19th centuries, the Tarpeian Rock became a popular stop for people making the Grand Tour because of the view it gave of the Palatine Hill. Today, the Belvedere viewing point has been

An Emperor Cheat Sheet

OCTAVIAN, or Caesar Augustus, was Rome's first emperor (27 BC–AD 14). While it upended the republic once and for all, his rule began a period of prosperity and peace known as the Pax Romana.

The name of **NERO** (AD 54–68) lives in infamy as a violent persecutor of Christians and as the murderer of his wife, his mother, and countless others. Although it's not certain whether he actually it played the fiddle (as legend has it) as Rome burned in AD 64, he was well known as an actor.

DOMITIAN (AD 81–96) declared himself "Dominus et Deus"—Lord and God. He stripped away power from the Senate, and as a result, after his death, he suffered "Damnatio Memoriae": the Senate had his name and image erased from all public records.

TRAJAN (AD 98–117), the first Roman emperor to be born outside Italy (in southern Spain), enlarged the empire's boundaries to include modern-day Romania, Armenia, and Upper Mesopotamia.

HADRIAN (AD 117–138) designed one rebuilding of the Pantheon, constructed a majestic villa at Tivoli, and initiated myriad other constructions, including the famed wall across Britain.

MARCUS AURELIUS (AD 161–180) is remembered as a humanitarian emperor, a Stoic philosopher whose *Meditations* are still read today. Nonetheless, he was an aggressive leader of the empire and devoted to expansion.

CONSTANTINE I (AD 306–337) made his mark by legalizing Christianity, an act that changed the course of history by legitimizing the once-banned religion and paving the way for the papacy in Rome.

long shuttered for restoration, but you can proceed a short walk down to Via di Monte Tarpeo, where the view is spectacular enough. It was on this rock that, in the 7th century BC, Tarpeia betrayed the Roman citadel to the early Romans' sworn enemies, the Sabines, only asking in return to be given the heavy gold bracelets the Sabines wore on their left arm. The scornful Sabines did indeed shower her with their gold, and added the crushing weight of their heavy shields, also carried on their left arms. ⊠ *Via del Tempio di Giove, Piazza Venezia* Ⓜ *Colosseo.*

THE ROMAN FORUM

Fodor's Choice ★ **The Roman Forum.** From the main entrance on Via dei Fori Imperiali, descend into the extraordinary archaeological complex that is the Foro Romano, once the very heart of the Roman world. The Forum began life as a marshy valley between the Capitoline and Palatine hills—a valley crossed by a mud track and used as a cemetery by Iron Age settlers. Over the years a market center and some huts were established here, and after the land was drained in the 6th century BC, the site eventually became a political, religious, and commercial center: the Forum.

Hundreds of years of plunder reduced the Forum to its current desolate state. But this enormous area was once Rome's pulsating hub, filled with stately and extravagant temples, palaces, and shops, and crowded with people from all corners of the empire. Adding to today's confusion is the fact that the Forum developed over many centuries; what you see today are not the ruins from just one period but from a span of almost 900 years, from about 500 BC to AD 400. Nonetheless, the enduring romance of the place, with its lonely columns and great broken fragments of sculpted marble and stone, makes for a quintessential Roman experience.

There is always a line at the Colosseum ticket office for the combined Colosseum/Palatine/Forum ticket, but in high season, lines sometimes also form at the Forum and Palatine entrances. Those who don't want to risk waiting in line can book their tickets online in advance, for a €2 surcharge, at www.coopculture.it. Choose the print-at-home option and avoid the line to pick up tickets. ⊠ *Entrance at Via dei Fori Imperiali, Monti* ☎ *06/39967700* ⊕ *www.coopculture.it* ✆ *€12 (combined ticket with the Colosseum and Palatine Hill, if used within 2 days); audio guide €5* Ⓜ *Colosseo.*

TOP ATTRACTIONS

Fodor's Choice ★   **Arco di Settimio Severo** (*Arch of Septimius Severus*). One of the grandest triumphal arches erected by a Roman emperor, this richly decorated monument was built in AD 203 to celebrate Severus's victory over the Parthians. It was once topped by a bronze statuary group depicting a chariot drawn by four (or perhaps as many as six) life-size horses. Masterpieces of Roman statuary, the stone reliefs on the arch were probably based on huge painted panels depicting the event, a kind of visual report on his foreign campaigns that would have been displayed during the emperor's triumphal parade in Rome to impress his subjects (and, like much statuary then, were originally painted in florid, lifelike colors). ⊠ *West end of Foro Romano, Monti* Ⓜ *Colosseo.*

Arco di Tito (*Arch of Titus*). Standing at the northern approach to the Palatine Hill on the Via Sacra, this triumphal arch was erected in AD 81 to celebrate the sack of Jerusalem 10 years earlier, after the First Jewish–Roman War. The superb view of the Colosseum from the arch

THE RISE AND FALL OF ANCIENT ROME

ca. 800 BC	Rise of Etruscan city-states.
510	Foundation of the Roman Republic; expulsion of Etruscans from Roman territory.
343	Roman conquest of Greek colonies in Campania.
264–241	First Punic War (with Carthage): increased naval power helps Rome gain control of southern Italy and then Sicily.
218–200	Second Punic War: Hannibal's attempted conquest of Italy, using elephants, is eventually crushed.

reminds us that it was the emperor Titus who helped finish the vast amphitheater, begun earlier by his father, Vespasian. Under the arch are two great sculpted reliefs, both showing scenes from Titus's triumphal parade along this very Via Sacra. You still can make out the spoils of war plundered from Herod's Temple, including a gigantic seven-branched candelabrum (menorah) and silver trumpets. During his sacking of Jerusalem, Titus killed or deported most of the Jewish population, thus initiating the Jewish diaspora—an event that would have far-reaching historical consequences. ⊠ *East end of Via Sacra, Monti* Ⓜ *Colosseo.*

Basilica di Massenzio (*Basilica of Maxentius*). Only about one-third of the original of this gigantic basilica (in the sense of a Roman courthouse and meeting hall) remains, so you can imagine what a wonder this building was when first erected. Today, its great arched vaults still dominate the north side of the Via Sacra. Begun under the emperor Maxentius about AD 306, the edifice was a center of judicial and commercial activity, the last of its kind to be built in Rome. Over the centuries, like so many Roman monuments, it was exploited as a quarry for building materials and was stripped of its sumptuous marble and stucco decorations. Its coffered vaults, like that of the Pantheon's dome, were later copied by many Renaissance artists and architects. ⊠ *Via Sacra, Monti* Ⓜ *Colosseo.*

Comitium. The open space in front of the Curia was the political hub of ancient Rome. Julius Caesar had rearranged the Comitium, moving the Curia to its current site and transferring the imperial **Rostra,** the podium from which orators spoke to the people (decorated originally with the prows of captured ships, or *rostra,* the source for the term "rostrum"), to a spot just south of where the Arch of Septimius Severus would be built. It was from this location that Mark Antony delivered his funeral oration in Caesar's honor. On the left of the Rostra stands what remains of the **Tempio di Saturno,** which served as ancient Rome's state treasury. The area of the Comitium has been under excavation for several years and is currently not open to visitors. ⊠ *West end of Foro Romano, Monti* Ⓜ *Colosseo.*

Curia. This large brick structure next to the Arch of Septimius Severus, restored during Diocletian's reign in the late 3rd century AD, is the

150 BC	Roman Forum begins to take shape as the principal civic center in Italy.
146	Third Punic War: Rome razes city of Carthage and emerges as the dominant Mediterranean force.
133	Rome rules entire Mediterranean Basin except Egypt.
49	Julius Caesar conquers Gaul.
44	Julius Caesar is assassinated.
27	Rome's Imperial Age begins; Octavian (now named Augustus) becomes the first emperor and is later deified. The Augustan Age is celebrated in the works of Virgil (70 BC–AD 19), Ovid (43 BC–AD 17), Livy (59 BC–AD 17), and Horace (65–8 BC).

Forum's best-preserved building—thanks largely to having been turned into a church in the 7th century. By the time the Curia was built, the Senate, which met here, had lost practically all of the power and prestige that it had possessed during the Republican era. Still, the Curia appears much as the original Senate house would have looked. Today, the Curia generally is open only when hosting an exhibition. Definitely peek inside if it's open, and don't miss the intricately inlaid 3rd-century floor of marble and porphyry, a method called *opus sectile*. ⊠ *Via Sacra, northwest corner of Foro Romano, Monti* Ⓜ *Colosseo.*

Tempio di Castore e Polluce. The sole three remaining Corinthian columns of this temple beautifully evoke the former grandeur and elegance of the Forum. This temple was dedicated in 484 BC to Castor and Pollux, the twin brothers of Helen of Troy, who carried to Rome the news of victory at Lake Regillus, southeast of Rome—the definitive defeat of the deposed Tarquin dynasty. The twins flew on their fabulous white steeds 20 km (12 miles) to the city to bring the news to the people before mortal messengers could arrive. Rebuilt over the centuries before Christ, the temple suffered a major fire and was reconstructed by the future Emperor Tiberius in 12 BC, the date of the three standing columns. ⊠ *West of Casa delle Vestali, Monti* Ⓜ *Colosseo.*

Tempio di Vesta. Although it's just a fragment of the original building, the remnant of this temple conveys the sophisticated elegance architecture achieved in the later Roman Empire. Set off by florid Corinthian columns, the circular *tholos* was rebuilt by Emperor Septimius Severus when he restored this temple around AD 205. Dedicated to Vesta, the goddess of the hearth, the highly privileged Vestal virgins kept the sacred flame alive. Next to the temple, the **Casa delle Vestali** gives you a glimpse of the splendor in which these women lived out their 30-year vows of chastity. Marble statues of the Vestals and fragments of mosaic pavement line the garden courtyard, which once would have been surrounded by lofty colonnades and at least 50 rooms. Chosen when they were between 6 and 10 years old, the six Vestal virgins dedicated the next 30 years of their lives to keeping the sacred fire burning, a tradition that dated back to the very earliest days of Rome, when guarding the community's precious fire was essential to its well-being. Their standing in Rome was considerable: among women, they were second in rank

43 AD	Rome invades Britain.
50	Rome is the largest city in the world, with a population of a million.
65	Emperor Nero begins the persecution of Christians in the Empire; Saints Peter and Paul are executed.
70–80	Vespasian builds the Colosseum.
98–117	Trajan's military successes are celebrated with his Baths (98), Forum (110), and Column (113); the Roman Empire reaches its apogee.

only to the Empress. Their intercession could save a condemned man, and they did, in fact, rescue Julius Caesar from the lethal vengeance of his enemy Sulla. The virgins were handsomely maintained by the state, but if they allowed the sacred fire to go out, they were scourged by the high priest, and if they broke their vows of celibacy, they were buried alive (a punishment doled out only a handful of times throughout the cult's 1,000-year history). The Vestal virgins were one of the last of ancient Rome's institutions to die out, enduring until the end of the 4th century AD—even after Rome's emperors had become Christian. ✉ *South side of Via Sacra, Monti* Ⓜ *Colosseo.*

Via Sacra. The celebrated "Sacred Way," paved with local volcanic rock, runs through the Roman Forum, lined with temples and shrines. It was also the traditional route of religious and triumphal processions. Pick your way across the paving stones, some rutted with the ironclad wheels of Roman wagons, to walk in the footsteps of Julius Caesar and Marc Antony. ✉ *Monti* Ⓜ *Colosseo.*

WORTH NOTING

Basilica Emilia. Once a great colonnaded hall, this served as a meeting place for merchants and as a court house from the 2nd century BC; it was rebuilt by Augustus in the 1st century AD. A spot on one of the basilica's preserved pieces of floor, immediately to the right as you enter the Forum, testifies to one of Rome's more harrowing moments—and to the hall's purpose. That's where bronze coins melted, leaving behind green stains, when Rome was sacked and the basilica was burned by the Visigoths in 410 AD. The term "basilica" refers here to the particular architectural form developed by the Romans: a rectangular hall flanked by colonnades, it could serve as a court of law or a center for business and commerce. The basilica would later become the building type adopted for the first official places of Christian worship in the city. ✉ *On right as you descend into Roman Forum from Via dei Fori Imperiali entrance, Monti* Ⓜ *Colosseo.*

Basilica Giulia. The Basilica Giulia owes its name to Julius Caesar, who ordered its construction; it was later completed by his adopted heir Augustus. One of several such basilicas in the center of Rome, it was where the Centumviri, the hundred-or-so judges forming the civil court,

238 AD	The first wave of Germanic invasions penetrates Italy.
293	Diocletian reorganizes the Empire into West and East.
330	Constantine founds a new Imperial capital (Constantinople) in the East.
410	Rome is sacked by Visigoths.
476	The last Roman emperor, Romulus Augustus, is deposed. The western Roman Empire falls.

met to hear cases. The open space between the Basilica Emilia and this basilica was the heart of the Forum proper—the prototype of Italy's famous piazzas, and the center of civic and social activity in ancient Rome. ⊠ *Via Sacra, Monti* Ⓜ *Colosseo.*

Colonna di Foca (*Column of Phocas*). The last monument to be added to the Forum was erected in AD 608 in honor of the Byzantine emperor Phocas who had donated the Pantheon to Pope Boniface IV. It stands 44 feet high and remains in good condition. ⊠ *West end of Foro Romano, Monti* Ⓜ *Colosseo.*

Santa Francesca Romana. This church, a 10th-century edifice with a Renaissance facade, is dedicated to the patron saint of motorists. On her feast day, March 9, cars and taxis crowd the Via dei Fori Imperiali below for a special blessing—a cardinal and *carabinieri* (Italian military) on hand, plus a special siren to start off the ceremony. The incomparable setting continues to be a favorite for weddings. ⊠ *Piazza di Santa Francesca Romana, next to Colosseum, Monti* Ⓜ *Colosseo.*

Santa Maria Antiqua. The earliest Christian site in the Forum was originally part of an imperial structure at the foot of Palatine Hill before it was converted into a church sometime in the late 5th century. Within it are some exceptional frescoes dating from the 6th to the 9th centuries. Buried by a 9th-century earthquake, the church was abandoned and a replacement was eventually built on top in the 17th century. This newer church was knocked down in 1900 during excavation work on the Forum, which revealed the early medieval church beneath. ⊠ *South of Tempio di Castore and Polluce, at foot of Palatine Hill, Monti* Ⓜ *Colosseo.*

Tempio di Antonino e Faustina. Erected by the Senate in honor of Faustina, deified wife of Emperor Antoninus Pius (AD 138–161), Hadrian's successor, this temple was rededicated to the emperor as well upon his death. Because it was transformed into a church (San Lorenzo in Miranda), it's one of the best-preserved ancient structures in the Forum. ⊠ *North of Via Sacra, Monti* Ⓜ *Colosseo.*

Tempio di Cesare. Built by Augustus, Julius Caesar's successor, what survives of the base of the temple stands over the spot where Caesar's body was cremated. A pyre was improvised by grief-crazed citizens who kept the flames going with their own possessions. ⊠ *Via Sacra, opposite the Tempio di Antonino e Faustina, Monti* Ⓜ *Colosseo.*

Tempio di Venere e Roma. Once Rome's largest and possibly cleverest temple (it was dedicated to Venus and Rome or, in Latin, to "Venere" and "Roma"), it was begun by Hadrian in AD 121. The temple is accessible from the end of the Forum near the Arco di Tito, and offers a great view of the Colosseum. ⊠ *East of Arco di Tito, Monti* Ⓜ *Colosseo.*

Tempio di Vespasiano. All that remains of Vespasian's temple are three graceful Corinthian columns. They marked the site of the Forum through the centuries while the rest was hidden beneath overgrown rubble. Nearby is the ruined platform that was the **Tempio di Concordia.** ⊠ *West end of Foro Romano, Monti* Ⓜ *Colosseo.*

The "Bel Air" of ancient Rome, the Palatine Hill was the address of choice of Cicero, Agrippa, and the emperors Tiberius, Caligula, and Domitian.

THE PALATINE HILL

Fodors Choice
★

Palatine Hill. Just beyond the Arco di Tito, the Clivus Palatinus—the road connecting the Forum and the Palatine Hill—gently rises to the heights of the Colle Palatino (Palatine Hill), the oldest inhabited site in Rome. Now charmingly bucolic, with pines and olive trees to provide shade in summer, this is where Romulus is said to have founded the city that bears his name, and despite its location overlooking the Forum's traffic and attendant noise, the Palatine was the most coveted address for ancient Rome's rich and famous. During the Roman Republic it was home to wealthy patrician families—Cicero, Catiline, Crassus, and Agrippa all had homes here—and when Augustus (who had himself been born on the hill) came to power, declaring himself to be the new Romulus, it would thereafter become the home of emperors. (Indeed, the very word "palace" comes from the name of the hill.) Not all of the emperors lived here peacefully: Caligula, for example, was murdered in the still-standing and unnerving (even today) tunnel, the Cryptoporticus. After Augustus's relatively modest residence, Tiberius extended the palace and other structures followed, notably the gigantic extravaganza constructed for Emperor Domitian. ⊠ *Entrances at Piazza del Colosseo and Via di San Gregorio 30, Monti* ☎ *06/39967700* ⊕ *www. coopculture.it* ✉ *€12 combined ticket, includes single entry to Palatine Hill–Forum site and single entry to Colosseum (if used within 2 days)* Ⓜ *Colosseo.*

Continued on page 78

RE-CREATING THE ANCIENT CITY

Time has reduced ancient Rome to fields of silent ruins, but the powerful impact of what happened here, of the genius and power that made Rome the center of the Western world, echoes across the millennia. In this one compact area of the city, you can step back into the Rome of Cicero, Julius Caesar, and Virgil. You can walk along the streets they knew, cool off in the shade of the Colosseum that loomed over the city, and see the sculptures poised over their piazzas.

Today, this part of Rome, more than any other, is a perfect example of the layering of historic eras, the overlapping of ages, of religions, of a past that is very much a part of the present.

Although it has been the capital of the Republic of Italy only since 1946, Rome has been the capital of *something* for more than 2,500 years, and it shows. The magnificent ruins of the Palatine Hill, the ancient complexity of the Forum, the Renaissance harmony of the Campidoglio—all are part of Rome's identity as one of the world's most enduring seats of government.

This is not to say that it's been an easy 2½ millennia. The Vandal hordes of the 3rd century, the Goth sacks of the Middle Ages, the excavations of a modern-day Mussolini, and today's modern citizens—all played a part in transforming Rome into a city of fragments. Semi-preserved ruins of ancient forums, basilicas, stadiums, baths, and temples are strewn across the city like remnants of some Cecil B. DeMille movie set. Even if you walk into the Termini McDonalds, you'll find three chunks of the 4th century BC Servian Wall. No wonder first-time visitors feel that the only thing more intimidating than crossing a Roman intersection at rush hour is trying to make sense of the layout of ancient Rome.

The following pages detail how the new Rome overlaps the old, showing how the modern city is crammed with details of all the city's ageless walls and ancient sites, even though some of them now lie hidden underneath the earth. Written in these rocks is the story of the emperors, the city's greatest builders. Thanks in large part to their dreams of glory—combined with their architectural megalomania—Imperial Rome became the fountainhead of Western civilization.

Colosseum; (top) Head of Emperor Constantine, Musei Capitolini

THE WAY ROME WAS

Circus Maximus: Atop the Palatine Hill, the emperor's royal box looked down on the races and games of this vast stadium— most Early Christians met their untimely end here, not in the Colosseum.

Capitoline Hill (Campidoglio): Most important of Rome's original seven hills, and home to the Temple of Jupiter, the "capital" hill was strategically located high above the Tiber and became the hub of the Roman Republic.

Palatine Hill (Palatino): The birthplace of Rome, settled by Romulus and Remus, the Palatine ultimately became Rome's

Theater of Pompey

Circus of Domitian

Pantheon

CAMPUS MARTIUS

Isola Tiberina

Theater of Marcellus

Temple of Jupiter

CAMPIDOGLIO

Campus Borum

TRASTEVERE

House of Augustus

PALATINO

AVENTINO

Circus Maximus

Rome in the Year 300 AD

"Beverly Hills" for it was home to Cicero, Julius Caesar, and a dozen Emperors.

Roman Forum: Downtown ancient Rome, this was the political heart of the Republic and

Empire—the place for processions, tribunals, law courts, and orations, and it was here that Mark Antony buried Caesar and Cleopatra made her triumphant entry.

Colosseum: Gladiators fought for the chance to live another day on the floor before 50,000 spectators in this giant arena, built in a mere eight years and inaugurated in AD 80.

Domus Aurea: Nero's "Golden House," a sprawling example of the excesses of Imperial Rome, once comprised 150 rooms, some shimmering with gold.

THEY CAME, THEY SAW, THEY BUILT

Remember the triumphal scene in the 2000 film *Gladiator?* Awesome expanses of pristine marble, a cast of thousands in gold-lavished costumes, and close-ups of Joaquin Phoenix (playing Emperor Commodus) on his way to the Colosseum: Rome à la Hollywood. But behind all the marble splendor seen in the film lies an eight-centuries-long trail that extends back from Imperial Rome to a tiny village of mud huts along the Tiber river.

Museo della Civiltà Romana's model of Imperial Rome

ROMULUS GOES TO TOWN

Legend has it that Rome was founded by Romulus and Remus, twin sons of the god Mars. Upon being abandoned in infancy by a wicked uncle, they were taken up and suckled by a she-wolf living on a bank of the Tiber. (Ancient gossip says the wolf was actually a woman nicknamed Lupa for her multiple infidelities to her shepherd husband.)

As young men, Romulus and Remus returned in 753 BC to the hallowed spot to found a city but came to blows during its building, ending in the death of Remus—which is how the city became Roma, not Rema.

Where myth ends, archaeology takes over. In 2007, Roman excavators uncovered a cavernous sanctuary dedicated to the brothers situated in the valley between the Palatine and Capitoline (Campidoglio) hills in central Rome. Often transformed into "islands" when the Tiber river overflowed, these two hills soon famously expanded to include seven hills, including the Esquiline, Viminale, Celian, Quirinale, and Aventine.

SIMPLY MARBLE-LOUS

Up to 510 BC, the style of the fledging city had been set by the fun-loving, sophisticated Etruscans—Rome was to adopt their vestal virgins, household gods, and gladiatorial games. Later, when the Republic took over the city (509 BC–27 BC), the austere values promulgated by its democratic Senate eventually fell to the power-mad triumvirate of Crassus, Pompey, and Julius Caesar, who waved away any detractors—including Rome's main power-players, the patrician Senators and the populist Tribunes—by invoking the godlike sovereignty of emperorship.

Republican Rome's city was badly planned, in fact not planned at all, and the great contribution of the Emperor Augustus—who took over when his stepfather Caesar was assassinated in 43 BC—was to commence serious town planning, with results far surpassing even his own claim that he "found Rome brick and left it marble." Which was only fitting, as floridly colored marbles began to flow into Rome from all of the Mediterranean provinces he had conquered (including obelisks transported from Egypt to flaunt his victory over Cleopatra).

Via Sacra in the Roman Forum with the Temple of Saturn in the foreground and the Basilica Julia on the right.

A FUNNY THING HAPPENED ON THE WAY TO THE ROMAN FORUM

It was during Augustus's 40-year long peaceful reign that Rome began its transition from glorified provincial capital into great city. While excavations have shown that the area of the Roman Forum was in use as a burial ground as far back as the 10th century BC, the importance of the Forum area as the political, commercial, and social center of Rome and, by extension, of the whole ancient world, grew immeasurably during Imperial times. The majestic ruins still extant are remnants of the massive complex of markets, civic buildings, and temples that dominated the city center in its heyday.

After Rome gained "empire" status, however, the original Forum was inadequate to handle the burden of the many trials and meetings required to run Western civilization, so Julius Caesar built a new forum. This apparently started a trend, as over the next 200-plus years (43 BC–AD 180), four different emperors—Augustus, Domitian, Vespasian, and Trajan—did the same. Oddly enough, the Roman Forum became four different Forums. They grew, in part, thanks to the Great Fire of AD 64, which Nero did not set but for which he took credit for laying waste to shabbier districts to build new ones.

For half a millennium, the Roman Forum area became the heart and soul of a worldwide empire, which eventually extended from Britain to Constantinople. Unfortunately, another thousand years of looting, sacking, and decay means you have to use your vivid imagination to see the glory that once was.

■TIP→ For a step-by-step tour of the Roman Forum, see the "Rome's Best Walks" chapter.

WHERE ALL ROADS LEAD

Even if you don't dig ruins, a visit to the archaeological ruins in and around the Roman Forum is a must. Rome's foundation as a world capital and crossroads of culture are to be found here, literally. Overlapped with Rome's current streets, this map shows the main monuments of the Roman Forum (in tan) as they originally stood.

Via IV Novembre

Via C. Battisti

Trajan's Column

V. Alessandrina

TRAJAN'S FORUM

CAMPIDOGLIO

Via del Teatro di Marcello

Tabularium

Palazzo Senatorio

Carcere Mamertino

Arch of Septimus Severus

Curia

Umbilcus Urbis Romae

The Rostra

TEMPLE OF JUPITER

V. L. Petroselli

Temple of Vespasian

Roman Forum

Basilica Julia

Tarpeian Rock

Temple of Saturn

Temple of Castor and Pollux

V. C. Jugario

V. della Consolazione

V. d. Foraggi

V. d. Fienili

V. d. S. Teodoro

Cloaca Maxima

TIBERIAN PALACE

MONTE

House of Livia

V. del Velabro

Circus Maximus

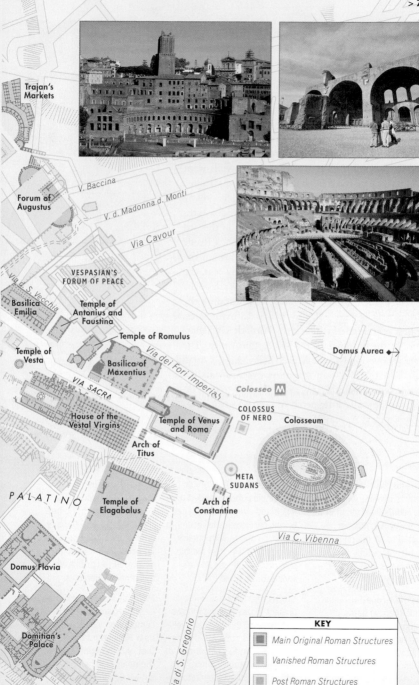

Trajan's Markets

V. Baccina

V. d. Madonna d. Monti

Via Cavour

Forum of Augustus

VESPASIAN'S FORUM OF PEACE

Via d. S. Vecchia

Basilica Emilia

Temple of Antonius and Faustina

Temple of Romulus

Temple of Vesta

Basilica of Maxentius

Via dei Fori Imperiali

Domus Aurea ◆→

Colosseo Ⓜ

COLOSSUS OF NERO

Colosseum

VIA SACRA

House of the Vestal Virgins

Temple of Venus and Roma

Arch of Titus

META SUDANS

PALATINO

Temple of Elagabalus

Arch of Constantine

Via C. Vibenna

Domus Flavia

Via di S. Gregorio

Domitian's Palace

KEY

◼ Main Original Roman Structures

◼ Vanished Roman Structures

◼ Post Roman Structures

URBIS ROMÆ: THE EXPANDING CITY

Today's Campitelli district—the historic area comprising the Forums and the Colosseum—was, in fact, a relatively small part of the ancient city. From the center around the Forum, the old city dramatically grew outwards and in AD 7, the emperor Augustus organized ancient Rome into 14 *regiones,* administrative divisions that were the forerunners of today's historic *rioni* (districts). Rome's first city walls went up in the 6th century BC when King Servius Tullius built an eight-mile ring. As the city's borders greatly expanded, however, the outlaying areas needed extra protection. This became a dire necessity in the 3rd century when Germanic tribes arrived to sack Rome while Emperor Aurelian was fighting wars on the southern border of the empire. Fueled by fear, the emperor commissioned an 11-mile bulwark to be built of brick between 271 and 275. Studding the Aurelian Walls were 380 towers and 18 main gates, the best preserved of which is the Porta di San Sebastiano, at the entrance to the Via Appia Antica. The Porta is now home to the Museo delle Mura, a small but fascinating museum that allows you to walk the ancient ramparts today; take Bus No. 118 to the Porta. From the walls' lofty perch you can see great vistas of the timeless Appian Way.

KEY

Archeological area of Rome

Hills

Mausoleum of Hadrian (Castel S. Angelo)

CAMPUS MARTIUS

Circus of Domitian (Piazza Navona)

Fiume Tevere

Theater of Pompey (Campo de' Fiori)

TRASTEVERE

Pantheon: Built in 27 BC by Augustus's general Agrippa and totally rebuilt by Hadrian in the 2nd century AD, this temple, dedicated to all the pagan gods, was topped by the largest dome ever built (until the 20th century).

Baths of Caracalla: These gigantic thermal baths, a stunning example of ancient Roman architecture, were more than just a place to bathe— they functioned somewhat like today's swank athletic clubs.

Isola Tiberina: The Temple of Aesculapius once presided over this island—which was shaped by ancient Romans to resemble a ship, complete with obelisk mast and (still visible) marble ship prow—and was Rome's shrine to medicine.

Circus of Domitian: Rome's present Piazza Navona follows the shape of this ancient oval stadium built in 96 AD—houses now stand on top of the *cavea*, the original stone seating, which held 30,000 spectators.

Campus Borum: Today's Piazza della Bocca della Verità was ancient Rome's cattle market and the site of two beautifully preserved 2nd century BC temples, one dedicated to Fortuna Virilis, the other to Hercules.

Porta di San Sebastiano: The largest extant gate of the 3rd-century Aurelian Walls, located near the ancient aqueduct that once brought water to the nearby Baths of Caracalla, showcases the most beautiful stretch of Rome's ancient walls.

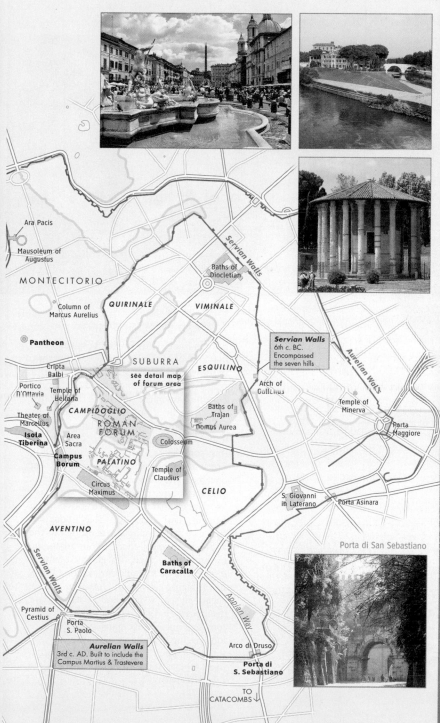

Ara Pacis

Mausoleum of Augustus

MONTECITORIO

Column of Marcus Aurelius

QUIRINALE

Pantheon

Cripta Balbi

Portico D'Ottavia

Temple of Bellona

Theater of Marcellus

Isola Tiberina

CAMPIDOGLIO

Area Sacra

Campus Borum

ROMAN FORUM

PALATINO

Circus Maximus

AVENTINO

Servian Walls

Pyramid of Cestius

Porta S. Paolo

Aurelian Walls
3rd c. AD. Built to include the Campus Martius & Trastevere

SUBURRA

see detail map of forum area

Baths of Diocletian

VIMINALE

Servian Walls

ESQUILINO

Arch of Gallienus

Baths of Trajan

Domus Aurea

Colosseum

Temple of Claudius

CELIO

Servian Walls
6th c. BC. Encompassed the seven hills

Temple of Minerva

Aurelian Walls

Porta Maggiore

S. Giovanni in Laterano

Porta Asinara

Porta di San Sebastiano

Baths of Caracalla

Appian Way

Arco di Druso

Porta di S. Sebastiano

TO CATACOMBS↓

BUILDING BLOCKS OF THE EMPERORS

The oft quoted remark of Augustus, that he found Rome brick and left it marble, omits a vital ingredient of Roman building: concrete. The sheer size and spectacle of ancient Rome's most famous buildings owe everything to this humble building block. Its use was one of the Romans' greatest contributions to the history of architecture, for it ennabled them not only to create vast arches, domes, and vaults—undreamed of before— but also to build at a scale and size never before attempted. The fall of the Roman empire ultimately arrived, but great architectural monuments remain to remind us of its glory.

THE ARCH
VESPASIAN'S COLOSSEUM

Born in Riete, Titus Flavius Vespasian was the first of the new, military emperors. A down-to-earth countryman, with a realistic sense of humor, his dying words "I think I am in the process of becoming a god" have lived on. Along with generally restoring the city, which had burned down under Nero, he started the Colosseum, (his son, Titus, finished it, in AD 80). Erected upon the swampy marsh that once held the *stagnum*, or lake, of Nero's Golden House, the Colosseum was vast; its dimensions underscored how much Romans had come to value audacious size. The main architectural motif was the arch—hundreds of them in four ascending birthday tiers, each tier adorned with a different style of column: Doric, Ionic, Corinthian, Corinthian pilaster. Inside each arch was a statue (all of which have disappeared). Under these arches, called *fornices,* ancient Romans were fond of looking for bedfellows (so famously said the great poet Ovid), so much so that these arches gave a new word to the English language.

THE VAULT
NERO'S DOMUS AUREA

Most notorious of the emperors, but by no means the worst, Nero had domestic and foreign policies that were popular at first. However, his increasing megalomania was apparent in the size of his Domus Aurea, the "Golden House," so huge that the cry went up "All Rome has become a villa." Taking advantage of the Great Fire of AD 64, Nero wanted to re-create his seaside villa at Baia (outside Naples) right in the middle of Rome, building a vast palace of polychrome marble with a dining room with perforated ivory ceilings so that diners could be showered with flowers and perfume (designed by Fabullus, Nero's decorator). But the masterstrokes were the gigantic vaulted rooms—the Room of the Owls and the octagonal-shaped center room—designed by Nero's architects, Severus and Celer. Greek post-and-lintel architecture was banished for these highly dramatic spaces created by soaring vaults. You can still tour the ruins of Nero's "villa" but his 120-foot-high colossal bronze statue gave way to make room for the Colosseum.

THE DOME
HADRIAN'S PANTHEON

The concrete Roman dome at its most impressive can be seen in the Pantheon (around AD 125), a massive construction 111 feet across. It is a fascinating feat of both design and engineering, for it is modeled on a sphere, the height of the supporting walls being equal to the radius of the dome. Larger than Saint Peter's, this dome of domes was constructed by the greatest Imperial builder of them all, the Emperor Hadrian. Poised on top of the dome's mighty concrete ring, the five levels of trapezoid-shaped coffers represent the course of the five then-known planets and their concentric spheres. Then, ruling over them, comes the sun, represented symbolically and literally by the so-called oculus—the giant "eye" open to the sky at the top. The heavenly symmetry is further paralleled by the coffers themselves: 28 to each row, the number of lunar cycles. In the center of each would have shone a small bronze star. All of the dome's famous gilt trim was stripped away by the Barberini popes in the 17th century, who melted it down to decorate the Vatican.

TOP ATTRACTIONS

Casa di Augustus. First discovered in the 1970s and opened only in 2006, this was the residence of the great emperor Augustus (27 BC–14 AD) before he became great. (Archaeologists have recently found two court-yards rather than one, though, in the style of Rome's ancient Greek kings, suggesting Augustus maintained this house after his ascension to prominence.) The house here dates to the time when Augustus was known merely as Octavian, before the death of, and Octavian's adoption by, his great uncle Julius Caesar. Four rooms have exquisite examples of Roman wall decorative frescoes (so precious that only five people at a time are admitted): startlingly vivid and detailed are the depictions of a narrow stage with side doors, as well as some striking comic theater masks. Note that access to the site is available only on a guided tour. ⊠ *Northwest crest of Palatine Hill, Monti* ☏ *06/39967700* ⊕ *www.coopculture.it* Ⓜ *Colosseo.*

Casa di Livia (*House of Livia*). First excavated in 1839, this house was identifiable from the name inscribed on a lead pipe, Iulia Augusta. In other words, it belonged to the notorious Livia who—according to Robert Graves's *I, Claudius*—made a career of dispatching half of the Roman imperial family. (There's actually very little evidence for such claims.) She was the wife of Rome's first, and possibly greatest, emperor, Augustus. He married Livia when she was six months pregnant by her previous husband, whom Augustus "encouraged" to get a divorce. As empress, Livia became a role model for Roman women, serving her husband faithfully, shunning excessive displays of wealth, and managing her household. But she also had real influence: As well as playing politics behind the scenes, she even had the rare honor (for a woman) of being in charge of her own finances. Here, atop the Palatine, is where she made her private retreat and living quarters. The delicate, delightful frescoes reflect the sophisticated taste of wealthy Romans, whose love of beauty and theatrical conception of nature were revived by their descendants in the Renaissance Age. Access to the site is available only via guided tour. ⊠ *Northwest crest of Palatino, Monti* ☏ *06/39967700* ⊕ *www.coopculture.it* Ⓜ *Colosseo.*

Circo Massimo (*Circus Maximus*). From the belvedere of the Domus Flavia, you can see the Circus Maximus, the giant arena where 300,000 spectators watched chariot races while the emperor looked on. Ancient Rome's oldest and largest racetrack lies in a natural hollow between two hills. The oval course stretches about 650 yards from end to end; on certain occasions, there were as many as 24 chariot races a day and competitions could last for 15 days. The charioteers could amass fortunes rather like the sports stars of today. (The Portuguese Diocles is said to have totted up winnings of 35 million sestertii.) The noise and the excitement of the crowd must have reached astonishing levels as the charioteers competed in teams, each with their own colors—the Reds, the Blues, etc. Betting also provided Rome's majority of unemployed with a potentially lucrative occupation. The central ridge was the site of two Egyptian obelisks (now in Piazza del Popolo and Piazza San Giovanni in Laterano). Picture the great chariot race scene from

MGM's *Ben-Hur* and you have an inkling of what this all looked like. ✉ *Between Palatine and Aventine hills, Aventino* Ⓜ *Circo Massimo*.

Domus Augustana. In the Imperial palace complex, this area, named in the 19th century for the "Augustuses" (a generic term used for emperors, in honor of Augustus himself), consisted of private apartments for Emperor Domitian and his family. Here Domitian—"Dominus et Deus," as he liked to be called—would retire to dismember flies (at least, according to Suetonius). ✉ *Southern crest of Palatine Hill, Monti* Ⓜ *Circo Massimo*.

Domus Flavia. Domitian used this area of the Imperial palace complex for official functions and ceremonies. It included a basilica where the emperor could hold judiciary hearings. There was also a large audience hall, a *peristyle* (a columned courtyard), and the imperial *triclinium* (dining room)—some of its mosaic floors and stone banquettes are still in place. According to Suetonius, Domitian had the walls and courtyards of this and the adjoining Domus Augustana covered with the shiniest marble to act as mirrors to alert him to any knife pointed at his back. They failed in their purpose: he died in a palace plot, engineered, some say, by his wife Domitia. ✉ *Southern crest of Palatine Hill, Monti* Ⓜ *Circo Massimo*.

WORTH NOTING

Museo Palatino. The Palatine Museum charts the history of the hill from Archaic times, with quaint models of early villages (on the ground floor), to Roman times (on the ground and upper floors). There is a good video reconstruction of the hill in Room V on the ground floor, and a collection of colored stones used in the decorations of the palace, with a map showing the distant Imperial regions whence they came. Upstairs, the room dedicated to Augustus houses painted terra-cotta moldings and sculptural decorations from various temples—notably the Temple of Apollo Actiacus, whose name derives from the god to whom Octavian attributed his victory at Actium (the severed heads of the Medusa in the terra-cotta panels symbolize the defeated Queen of Egypt). There is also a selection of imperial portraits on the upper floor, including a rare surviving image of Nero. ✉ *Northwest crest of Palatine Hill, Monti* ⊕ *www.museopalatino.com* ✉ *€12 combined ticket, includes single entry to Palatine Hill–Forum site and single entry to Colosseum (if used within 2 days)* Ⓜ *Colosseo*.

Orti Farnesiani. Alessandro Farnese, a nephew of Pope Paul III, commissioned the 16th-century architect Vignola to lay out this archetypal Italian garden over the ruins of the Palace of Tiberius, up a few steps from the House of Livia. This was yet another example of the Renaissance renewing an ancient Roman tradition. To paraphrase the poet Martial, the statue-studded gardens of the Flavian Palace were such as to make even an Egyptian potentate turn green with envy. ✉ *Palatine Hill, Monti* Ⓜ *Colosseo*.

Stadio Palatino. Built by Domitian and erroneously referred to since the 19th century as the "stadium," this was in fact a sunken garden that created a terrace on the slopes of the hill. It may also have been used to stage games (but not chariot races) and other amusements for the emperor's benefit. ⊠ *Southeast crest of Palatine Hill, Monti* Ⓜ *Circo Massimo.*

THE IMPERIAL FORUMS

Imperial Forums. A complex of five grandly conceived complexes flanked with colonnades, the Fori Imperiali contain monuments of triumph, law courts, and temples. The complexes were tacked on to the Roman Forum, from the time of Julius Caesar in the 1st century BC until Trajan in the very early 2nd century AD, to accommodate the ever-growing need for buildings of administration and grand monuments.

From Piazza del Colosseo, head northwest on Via dei Fori Imperiali toward Piazza Venezia. Now that the road has been closed to private traffic, it's more pleasant for pedestrians (it's closed to all traffic on Sunday). On the walls to your left, maps in marble and bronze, put up by Benito Mussolini, show the extent of the Roman Republic and Empire (at the time of writing, these were partially obstructed by work on Rome's new subway line, Metro C). The dictator's own dreams of empire led him to construct this avenue, cutting brutally through the Fori Imperiali, and the medieval and Renaissance buildings that had grown upon the ruins, so that he would have a suitable venue for parades celebrating his expected military triumphs. Among the Fori Imperiali along the avenue, you can see the Foro di Cesare (Forum of Caesar) and the Foro di Augusto (Forum of Augustus). The grandest was the Foro di Traiano (Forum of Trajan), with its huge semicircular Mercati di Traiano and the Colonna Traiana (Trajan's Column). You can walk through part of Trajan's Markets on the Via Alessandrina and visit the Museo dei Fori Imperiali, which presents the Imperial Forums and shows how they would have been used through ancient fragments, artifacts, and modern multimedia. ⊠ *Via dei Fori Imperiali, Monti* ☎ *06/0608* ⊕ *www.mercatiditraiano.it* ▣ *Museum €14* Ⓜ *Colosseo.*

TOP ATTRACTIONS

Colonna di Traiano (*Trajan's Column*). The remarkable series of reliefs spiraling up this column celebrate the emperor's victories over the Dacians in today's Romania. It has stood in this spot since AD 113. The scenes on the column are an important primary source for information on the Roman army and its tactics. An inscription on the base declares that the column was erected in Trajan's honor and that its height corresponds to the height of the hill that was razed to create a level area for the grandiose Foro di Traiano. The emperor's ashes, no longer here, were kept in a golden urn in a chamber at the column's base; his statue stood atop the column until 1587, when the pope had it replaced with a statue of St. Peter. ⊠ *Via del Foro di Traiano, Monti* Ⓜ *Caveur.*

Foro di Traiano (*Forum of Trajan*). Of all the Fori Imperiali, Trajan's was the grandest and most imposing, a veritable city unto itself. Designed by architect Apollodorus of Damascus, it comprised a vast basilica (at the time of writing, closed for restoration), two libraries, and a colonnade laid out around the square—all at one time covered with rich marble ornamentation. Adjoining the forum were the **Mercati di Traiano** (Trajan's Markets), a huge, multilevel brick complex of shops, taverns, walkways, and terraces, as well as administrative offices involved in the mammoth task of feeding the city. The **Museo dei Fori Imperiali** (Imperial Forums Museum) opened in 2007, taking advantage of the Forum's soaring vaulted spaces to showcase archaeological fragments and sculptures while presenting a video re-creation of the original complex. In addition, the series of terraced rooms offers an impressive overview of the entire forum. A pedestrian-only walkway, the Via Alessandrina, also allows for an excellent (and free) view of Trajan's Forum.

To build a complex of this magnitude, Apollodorus and his patrons clearly had great confidence, not to mention almost unlimited means and cheap labor at their disposal (readily provided by slaves captured in Trajan's Dacian wars). They also contained two semicircular lecture halls, one at either end, which are thought to have been associated with the libraries in Trajan's Forum. The markets' architectural centerpiece is the enormous curved wall, or *exhedra,* that shores up the side of the Quirinal Hill excavated by Apollodorus's gangs of laborers. Covered galleries and streets were constructed at various levels, following the exhedra's curves and giving the complex a strikingly modern appearance.

As you enter the markets, a large, vaulted hall stands in front of you. Two stories of shops or offices rise up on either side. Head for the flight of steps at the far end that leads down to Via Biberatica. (*Bibere* is Latin for "to drink," and the shops that open onto the street are believed to have been taverns.) Then head back to the three tiers of shops and offices that line the upper levels of the great exhedra and look out over the remains of the Forum. Empty and bare today, the cubicles were once ancient Rome's busiest market stalls. Though it seems to be part of the market, the **Torre delle Milizie** (Tower of the Militia), the tall brick tower that is a prominent feature of Rome's skyline, was actually built in the early 1200s. ⊠ *Via IV Novembre 94, Monti* ☎ *06/0608* ⊕ *www.mercatiditraiano.it* ⊠ *€14* Ⓜ *Caveur; Bus Nos. 85, 175, 186, 810, 850, H, 64, and 70.*

Fodor'sChoice ★ **Santi Cosma e Damiano.** Home to one of the most striking early Christian mosaics, this church was adapted in the 6th century from two ancient buildings: the library in Vespasian's Forum of Peace and a hall of the Temple of Romulus (dedicated to the son of Maxentius who had been named for Rome's founder). In the apse is the famous AD 530 mosaic of Christ in Glory. It reveals how popes at the time strove to re-create the splendor of imperial audience halls into Christian churches: Christ wears a gold, Roman-style toga, and his pose recalls that of an emperor addressing his subjects. He floats on a blue sky streaked with a flaming sunset—a miracle of tesserae mosaic-work. To his side are the figures of Saint Peter and Saint Paul, who represent Cosmas and Damian (patron saints of doctors), two Syrian benefactors whose charity was such that they were branded Christians and condemned to death. Beneath this

Hollywood got it wrong, historians got it right: plenty of gladiators died in the Colosseum, but early Christians only met their tragic fate in the nearby Circus Maximus arena.

awe-inspiring work is an enchanting mosaic frieze of holy lambs. ⊠ *Via in Miranda 11, Monti* ☎ *06/6920441* Ⓜ *Colosseo; Bus Nos. 85, 850, 87, and 571.*

WORTH NOTING

Foro di Augusto (*Forum of Augustus*). These ruins, along with those of the **Foro di Nerva,** on the northeast side of Via dei Fori Imperiali, give only a hint of what must have been impressive edifices. The three columns are all that remain of the Temple of Mars Ultor. ⊠ *Via dei Fori Imperiali, Monti* Ⓜ *Colosseo.*

Foro di Cesare (*Forum of Caesar*). In an attempt to rival the Roman Forum, Julius Caesar had this extension built in the middle of the 1st century BC. Each year without fail, on the Ides of March, flowers are laid at the foot of Caesar's statue. ⊠ *Via dei Fori Imperiali, Monti* ☎ *06/0608* Ⓜ *Colosseo.*

THE COLOSSEUM AND ENVIRONS

Legend has it that as long as the Colosseum stands, Rome will stand—and when Rome falls, so will the world. No visit to Rome is complete without a trip to the obstinate oval that has been the iconic symbol of the city for centuries. Looming over a group of the Roman Empire's most magnificent monuments to imperial wealth and power, the Colosseum was the gigantic sports arena built by Vespasian and Titus. To its west stands the Arco di Constantino, a majestic, ornate triumphal arch, built solely as a tribute to the emperor Constantine; victorious armies purportedly marched under it on their return from war. To the east of the Colosseum, hidden under the Colle Oppio, is Nero's opulent Domus Aurea, a palace that stands as testimony to the lavish lifestyles of the emperors—it is occasionally accessible by joining a guided tour. Check ⊕ *www.coopculture.it* for details and reservations.

TOP ATTRACTIONS

Arco di Costantino (*Arch of Constantine*). This majestic arch was erected in AD 315 to commemorate Constantine's victory over Maxentius at the Milvian Bridge. It was just before this battle, in AD 312, that Constantine—the emperor who converted Rome to Christianity—legendarily had a vision of a cross and heard the words, "In this sign thou shalt conquer." Many of the rich marble decorations for the arch were scavenged from earlier monuments, both saving money and placing Constantine in line with the great emperors of the past. It is easy to picture ranks of Roman centurions marching under the great barrel vault. ⊠ *Piazza del Colosseo, Monti* Ⓜ *Colosseo.*

Fodor's Choice
★

The Colosseum. The most spectacular extant edifice of ancient Rome, the Colosseum has a history that is half gore, half glory. Here, before 50,000 spectators, gladiators would salute the emperor and cry *Ave, imperator, morituri te salutant* ("Hail, emperor, men soon to die salute thee").

Senators had marble seats up front and the Vestal Virgins took the ringside position, while the plebs sat in wooden tiers at the back, then the masses above on the top tier. Over all was the amazing velarium, an ingenious system of sail-like awnings rigged on ropes and maneuvered by sailors from the imperial fleet, who would unfurl them to protect the arena's occupants from sun or rain.

From the second floor, you can get a bird's-eye view of the hypogeum: the subterranean passageways that were the architectural engine rooms that made the slaughter above proceed like clockwork (visitable via prebooked tour). In a scene prefiguring something from Dante's *Inferno*, hundreds of beasts would wait to be eventually launched via a series of slave-powered hoists and lifts into the bloodthirsty sand of the arena above.

Designed by order of the Flavian emperor Vespasian in AD 72, the arena has a circumference of 573 yards and was faced with travertine from nearby Tivoli. Its construction was a remarkable feat of engineering, for it stands on marshy terrain reclaimed by draining an artificial lake on the grounds of Nero's Domus Aurea. Originally known as the Flavian amphitheater, it came to be called the Colosseo because the Colossus of Nero, a 115-foot-tall gilded bronze statue of the emperor, once stood nearby.

Legend has it that as long as the Colosseum stands, Rome will stand; and when Rome falls, so will the world... not that the prophecy deterred Renaissance princes (and even a pope) from using the Colosseum as a quarry. In the 19th century, poets came to view the arena by moonlight; today, mellow golden spotlights make the arena a spectacular sight at night.

Are there ways to beat the ticket lines at the Colosseum? First off, if you go to the Roman Forum, a couple of hundred yards down Via dei Fori Imperiali on your left, or to the Palatine, down Via di San Gregorio, the €12 ticket you purchase there includes admission to the Colosseum and, even better, lets you jump to the head of the long line. Another way is to buy the Romapass (*www.romapass.it*) ticket, which includes the Colosseo. You can also book a ticket in advance through *www. coopculture.it* (for a €2 surcharge). Or you can book a tour online with a company (do your research to make sure it's reputable) that lets you skip the line. Avoid the tours sold on-the-spot around the Colosseum; although you can skip the lines, the tour guides tend to be dry, the tour groups huge, and the tour itself rushed. ⊠ *Piazza del Colosseo, Monti* ☎ *06/39967700* ⊕ *www.coopculture.it* ≊*€12 (combined ticket with the Roman Forum and Palatine Hill, one entry for either site if used within 2 days)* Ⓜ *Colosseo; Bus 117, 75, 81, 673, 175, 204.*

WORTH NOTING

Domus Aurea (*Golden House of Nero*). Legend has it that Nero famously fiddled while Rome burned. Fancying himself a great actor and poet, he played, as it turns out, his harp to accompany his recital of "The Destruction of Troy" while gazing at the flames of Rome's catastrophic fire of AD 64. Anti-Neronian historians propagandized that Nero, in fact, had set the Great Fire to clear out a vast tract of the city center to build his new palace. Today's historians discount this as historical folderol (going so far as to point to the fact that there was a full moon on the evening of July 19, hardly the propitious occasion to commit arson). But legend or not, Nero did get to build his new palace, the extravagant Domus Aurea (Golden House)—a vast "suburban villa" that was inspired by the emperor's pleasure palace at Baia on the Bay of Naples. His new digs were huge and sumptuous, with a facade of pure gold, seawater piped into the baths, decorations of mother-of-pearl, fretted ivory, and other precious materials, and vast gardens. It was said that after completing this gigantic house, Nero exclaimed, "Now I can live like a human being!" Note that access to the site is exclusively via guided tours, and currently only on weekends. ⊠ *Via della Domus Aurea, Monti* ☎ *06/39967700 booking information* ⊕ *www.coopculture.it* Ⓜ *Colosseo.*

Museo delle Mura. Rome's first walls were erected in the 6th century BC, but the ancient city greatly expanded over the next few centuries. In the 3rd century AD, Emperor Aurelian commissioned an 11-mile wall to protect the southern border of the empire. Studding the Aurelian Walls were 380 towers and 18 main gates, the best-preserved of which is the Porta di San Sebastiano at the entrance to the Via Appia Antica. That gate is also home to a small museum that allows visitors to walk a section of the ancient ramparts, from which there are wonderful views of the Appian Way. ⊠ *Via di Porta San Sebastiano, Via Appia Antica* ☎ *06/060608* ⊕ *www.museodellemuraroma.it* ⊘ *Closed Mon.* Ⓜ *Bus No. 118.*

THE VATICAN

Getting Oriented

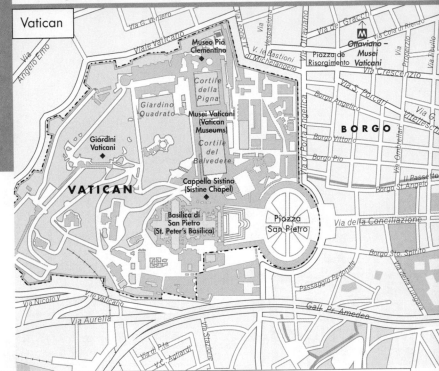

GETTING HERE

Metro stops Cipro or Ottaviano will get you within about a 10-minute walk of the entrance to the Musei Vaticani. Or, from Termini station, Bus No. 40 Express or the famously crowded No. 64 will take you to Piazza San Pietro. Both routes swing past Largo Argentina, where you can also get Bus No. 571 or 46.

A leisurely meander from the *centro storico,* (historic center) across the exquisite Ponte Sant'Angelo, will take about a half hour.

HOW TO BEAT THOSE LONG LINES

Home to the Sistine Chapel and the Raphael rooms, the Musei Vaticani are among the most congested of all Rome's attractions, drawing up to 30,000 visitors per day in high season.

For years, people thought the best way to get a jump on the crowds was to be at the front entrance when it opened at 9 am, particularly on the last Sunday of the month, when admission is free (the museums are otherwise closed on Sunday). The problem was, everyone else had the same idea. Result: Rome's version of the Calgary Stampede.

Instead, the best way to avoid long lines is to make reservations for an extra €4 (⊕ *biglietteriamusei.vatican.va/ musei/tickets/do*). Although reservations do minimize your wait time, it can still be extremely busy once you're inside, though afternoons are usually less busy. The free Sunday is best avoided altogether, unless you're feeling very brave and patient.

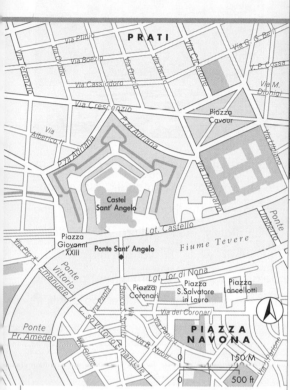

TOP REASONS TO GO

Michelangelo's Sistine Ceiling: The most sublime example of artistry in the world, this 10,000-square-foot fresco took the artist four long, neck-craning years to finish.

St. Peter's Dome: Climb the twisting Renaissance stairs to the top for a well-earned view (the elevator to the right of the main church portico goes up to the base of the dome, but there are still a lot of stairs afterwards).

Papal Blessing: Join the singing, flag-waving throngs from around the world at the Wednesday general audience on St. Peter's Square (usually September–June, weather permitting).

Musei Vaticani: Savor one of the Western world's best art collections—from the Apollo Belvedere to Raphael's *Transfiguration*. It can be overwhelming though, so don't plan to see everything.

St. Peter's Basilica: Stand in awe of the largest church in the world.

Another good idea is to schedule your visit during the Wednesday General Audience, held in the piazza of St. Peter's or at Aula Paolo VI, usually at 10:30 am (and usually suspended during July and August). To see the pope's calendar, visit ⊕ *www.vatican.va*.

Finally, you might book a tour, either with the Musei Vaticani directly or with a private agency that guarantees that you'll skip the line. The Vatican's own guided tour of the museums and Sistine Chapel, which can be booked online, costs €32 and lasts two hours.

Hours for the Vatican Museums are now 9–6 (last entrance at 4:20). The last Sunday of the month, when entrance is free, hours are 9–2 (last entrance at 12:30). The museums close the first three Sundays of every month; other dates of closures include January 1 and 6, February 11, March 19, Easter and Easter Monday, May 1, June 29, August 14 and 15, November 1, and December 8, 25, and 26.

Sightseeing
★★★★★
Nightlife
★★
Dining
★★★
Lodging
★★★
Shopping
★★

For many, a visit to the Vatican is one of the top reasons to visit Rome, and it is a vast and majestic place, jam-packed with things to see. The Borgo and Prati are the neighborhoods immediately surrounding the Vatican, and it's worth noting that, while the Vatican may well be a priority, these neighborhoods are not the best places to choose a hotel, as they're quite far from other top sights in the city.

THE VATICAN

Updated
by Agnes
Crawford

Climbing the steps to St. Peter's Basilica feels monumental, like a journey that has reached its climactic end. Suddenly, all is cool and dark … and you are dwarfed by the gargantuan nave and its magnificence. Above is a ceiling so high it must lead to heaven itself. Great, shining marble figures of saints frozen mid-whirl loom from niches and corners. And at the end, a throne for an unseen king whose greatness, it is implied, must mirror the greatness of his palace. For this basilica is a palace, the dazzling center of power for a king and a place of supplication for his subjects. Whether his kingdom is earthly or otherwise may lie in the eye of the beholder.

For good Catholics and sinners alike, the Vatican is an exercise in spirituality, requiring patience but delivering joy. Some come here for a transcendent glimpse of a heavenly Michelangelo fresco; others come in search of a direct connection with the divine. But what all visitors share, for a few hours, is an awe-inspiring landscape that offers a famous sight for every taste: rooms decorated by Raphael, antique sculptures like the Apollo Belvedere, famous paintings by Giotto and Bellini, and, perhaps most of all, the Sistine Chapel—for the lover of beauty, few places are as historically important as this epitome of faith and grandeur.

The story of this area's importance dates back to the 1st century, when St. Peter, the first Roman Catholic pope, was buried here. The first basilica in his honor rose on this spot some 250 years later under Emperor Constantine, who legitimized Christianity. It wasn't until the early 15th century, however, that the papacy decided to make this area not only a major spiritual center but the spot from which they would wield temporal power as well. Today, it's difficult not to be reminded of that worldly power when you take in the massive Renaissance walls surrounding Vatican City—the international boundary of an independent sovereign state, established by the Lateran Treaty of 1929 between the Holy See and Mussolini's government.

Vatican City covers 108 acres on a hill west of the Tiber and is separated from the city on all sides, except at Piazza di San Pietro, by high walls. Within the walls, about 1,000 people are permanent residents. The Vatican has its own daily newspaper (*L'Osservatore Romano*), issues its own stamps, mints its own coins, and has its own postal system (run by the Swiss). Within its territory are administrative and foreign offices, a pharmacy, banks, an astronomical observatory, a print shop, a mosaic school and art restoration institute, a tiny train station, a supermarket, a small department store, and several gas stations. The sovereign of the world's smallest state is the pope, Francis, elected in March 2013 after his predecessor, Benedict XVI, stepped down (the first time a pope has "resigned" from office since 1415). His main role is as spiritual leader to the world's Catholic community.

Today, there are two principal reasons for sightseeing at the Vatican. One is to visit the Basilica di San Pietro, the most overwhelming architectural achievement of the Renaissance; the other is to visit the Musei Vaticani, which contain collections of staggering richness and diversity, from ancient Etruscan treasures and Egyptian mummies and an actual piece of the Moon.

Inside the basilica—breathtaking both for its sheer size and for its extravagant interior—are artistic masterpieces including Michelangelo's *Pietà* and Bernini's great bronze *baldacchino* (canopy) over the main altar. The Musei Vaticani, their entrance a 10-minute walk from the piazza, hold endless collections of many of the greatest works of Western art. The Laocoön, Leonardo's *St. Jerome*, and Raphael's *Transfiguration* are all here. The Sistine Chapel, accessible only through these museums, is Michelangelo's magnificent artistic legacy, and his ceiling is the High Renaissance in excelsis in more ways than one.

TOP ATTRACTIONS

Fodor's Choice ★ **Basilica di San Pietro.** The world's largest church, built over the tomb of Saint Peter, is the most imposing and breathtaking architectural achievement of the Renaissance (although much of the lavish interior dates to the Baroque). It covers 18,000 square yards, runs 212 yards in length, and is surmounted by a dome that rises 435 feet and measures 138 feet across its base. Five of Italy's greatest artists—Bramante, Raphael, Peruzzi, Antonio Sangallo the Younger, and Michelangelo—died while striving to build it.

The history of the original St. Peter's goes back to AD 326, when the emperor Constantine completed a basilica over the site of the tomb of

Vatican City

Via R. Fiore

V. Marcantonio Bragadin

Via Meloria

Via Angelo Emo

Via F. Sivori

Via D. Millelire

Via Angelo Emo

Via V. Pisani

V.le Vaticano

Museo Missionario Etnologico

Serre

V.le Benedetto

Sta. Maria Mediatrice

Viale Centrale del Bosco

Giardini Vaticani

Viale dei Giardini Quadrati

V.le Vaticano

Clivo delle Mura Vaticane

Entrance to the Gardens

V.le d'Utzi

V.le dell'Osservatorio

Collegio Etiopico

Via del Seminario Etiopico

Via Vaticana

Sto. Marta

Sto. Stefano

Palazzo di Giustizia

Scuola d'Arte Mosaica

Via del Mosaico

V.le Vaticano

V.le Pio XII

V.le Vaticano

V.le Vaticano

Via Aurelia

Via Nicolo V

Via S.t Antonino

Via Benedetto XIV

Via Aurelia

0   200 feet

0   200 m

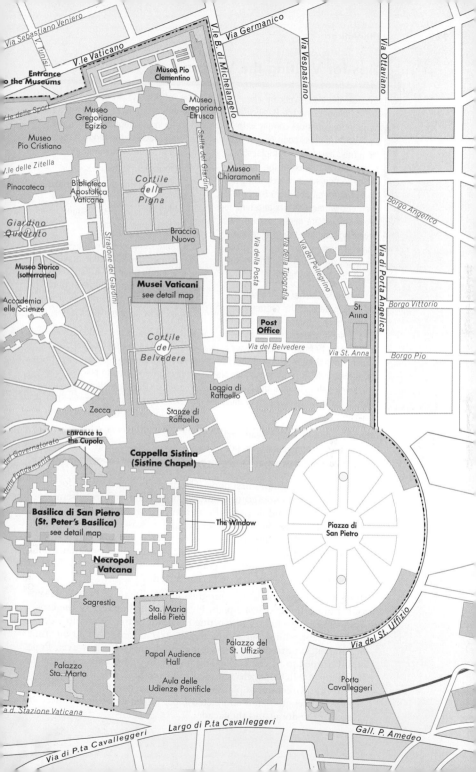

Tips for Visiting the Vatican

To enter the Musei Vaticani, the Sistine Chapel, and the Basilica di San Pietro, you must comply with the Vatican's dress code or you may be turned away by the implacable custodians stationed at the doors. (Also: no penknives, which will show up in the metal detector.) For both men and women, shorts and tank tops are taboo, as are miniskirts and other revealing clothing. Wear a jacket or shawl over sleeveless tops, and avoid T-shirts with writing or pictures that could risk giving offense.

If you opt to start at the Musei Vaticani, note that the entrance on Viale Vaticano (there's a separate exit on the same street) can be reached by Bus No. 49 from Piazza Cavour, which stops right in front; on foot from Piazza del Risorgimento (Bus No. 81 or Tram No. 19); or a brief walk from the Via Cipro–Musei Vaticani stop on Metro Linea A.

The collections of the museums are immense, covering about 7 km (4½

miles) of displays. To economize on time and effort, once you've seen the frescoes in the Raphael rooms, you can skip much of the modern religious art in good conscience and get on with your tour.

You can rent a somewhat dry audio guide in English explaining the museums, including the Sistine Chapel and the Raphael rooms.

You cannot take any photographs in the Sistine Chapel. Elsewhere, you're free to photograph what you like— barring use of flash, tripod, or other special equipment, for which permission must be obtained.

With an average of 20,000 visitors per day, lines at the entrance to the Musei Vaticani can move slowly. It is always a good idea to reserve tickets in advance. It is sometimes possible to exit the museums from the Sistine Chapel into St. Peter's, saving further legwork.

Saint Peter, the Church's first pope. The original church stood for more than 1,000 years, undergoing a number of restorations and alterations, until, toward the middle of the 15th century, it was on the verge of collapse. In 1452, a reconstruction job began but was abandoned for lack of money. In 1503, Pope Julius II instructed the architect Bramante to raze all the existing buildings and build a new basilica, one that would surpass even Constantine's for grandeur. It wasn't until 1626 that the new basilica was completed and consecrated.

Though Bramante made little progress in rebuilding St. Peter's, he succeeded in outlining a basic plan. He also built the piers of the crossings—the massive pillars supporting the dome. After Bramante's death in 1514, Raphael, the Sangallos, and Peruzzi all proposed, at one time or another, variations on the original plan. In 1546, however, Pope Paul III turned to Michelangelo and forced the aging artist to complete the building. Michelangelo returned to Bramante's first idea of having a centralized Greek-cross plan—that is, with the "arms" of the church all the same length—and completed most of the exterior architecture except for the dome and the facade.

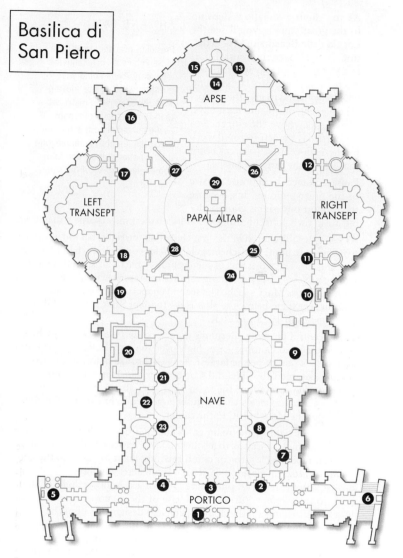

Basilica di San Pietro

As you climb the shallow steps up to the great church, you'll see the **Loggia delle Benedizioni** (Benediction Loggia) over the central portal. This is the balcony where newly elected popes are proclaimed, and where they stand to give their apostolic blessing on solemn feast days. The mosaic above the entrance to the portico is a much-restored work by the 14th-century painter Giotto that was in the original basilica.

Pause a moment to appraise the size of the great building. It's because the proportions of this giant building are in such perfect harmony that its vastness may escape you at first.

ART AND FAITH

Presiding over the great nave of St. Peter's is Michelangelo's legendary *Pietà*. Could you question whether this moving work, owes more to man's art than to man's faith? Perhaps, as we contemplate this masterpiece, we are able to understand a little better that art and faith sometimes partake of the same impulse.

As you enter the church in the first chapel on the right, behind a protective glass partition, is **Michelangelo's** *Pietà*, completed when the artist was only 24. The work was of such genius, some rivals spread rumors it was by someone else, prompting the artist to inscribe his name, unusual for him, across Mary's sash. The second chapel on the right is dedicated to Saint Sebastian; below the altar is the tomb of Saint John Paul II (who was pope from 1978 to 2005).

In the central crossing, Bernini's great bronze *baldacchino*—a huge, spiral-columned canopy—rises high over the papal altar. At 100,000 pounds, it's said to be the largest, heaviest bronze object in the world. Bernini designed the splendid **Cattedra di San Pietro** (Throne of St. Peter), in the apse above the main altar and, above, placed a window of thin alabaster sheets that diffuses a golden light around the dove, symbol of the Holy Spirit, in the center.

The farthest right of the main gates entering the basilica leads to the Cupola (dome), as well as to a souvenir shop and the Vatican Grottoes. You can take the elevator or climb the long flight of stairs to the roof (06/69883462; €7 elevator, €5 stairs). From here, you'll see a landscape of vast, sloping terraces, punctuated by domes. Another flight of stairs leads to the *tamburo* (drum)—the base of the dome—where there's a bust of Michelangelo, the dome's principal designer. Within the drum, another ramp and staircase give access to the gallery encircling the base of the dome. (You also have the option of taking an elevator to this point.) From here, you have a dove's-eye view of the interior of the church. If you're of stout heart and strong lungs, you can then take the stairs that wind around the elevator to reach the cramped space of the lantern balcony for a gorgeous panorama of Rome and the countryside on a clear day. There's also a nearly complete view of the palaces, courtyards, and gardens of the Vatican.

Under the Pope Pius V monument, the entrance to the sacristy also leads to the **Museo Storico-Artistico e Tesoro** (*Historical-Artistic Museum and Treasury*; 06/69881840; €5), a small collection of Vatican treasures. They range from the massive and beautiful bronze 15th-century tomb

CLOSE UP

Meet the Pope

Piazza di San Pietro is the scene of large papal audiences, as well as special commemorations, Masses, and beatification ceremonies. When he's in Rome, the pope makes an appearance every Sunday at noon at the window of the Vatican Palace. He addresses the crowd and blesses all present, a ceremony that lasts about 10 to 15 minutes. The pope also holds general audiences in the square on Wednesday morning at about 10:30 am; a ticket is usually necessary for a seat, but even with a ticket you will have to arrive early, as about 40,000 people arrive every week, sometimes many more for special occasions. The general audience lasts between an hour and an hour and a half. In the winter and inclement weather, the audience is held in a hall adjacent to the basilica (Aula Paolo Sesto), which houses far fewer people than the square. Audiences are suspended in July and August.

For admission to an audience, apply for free tickets by phone or fax, in advance, indicating your preferred date, preferred language, and your contact information during your stay in Rome. You can also apply for tickets at the Prefettura della Casa Pontifice, either by fax (☎ 06/69885863), or by going to the office Tuesday 3–7 pm or on the morning of the audience 7–10 am. You can reach the office through the Portone di Bronzo (Bronze Door) at the end of the right-hand colonnade. Or arrange your tickets for free for Wednesday general audience only (not for the papal Mass) through the Santa Susanna American Church (✉ *Via XX Settembre 15, near Termini station*; ☎ *06/69001821*); the best way is to fill out a booking form directly online at ⊕ *www.santasu-sanna.org/popeVatican/tickets.html.* You can pick up your tickets Tuesday 5–6:30 pm only.

of Pope Sixtus IV by Pollaiuolo, to a jeweled cross dating from the 6th century and a marble tabernacle by Donatello.

sThe entrance is tucked away to the right of the Basilica, by the entrance to the Cupola. The crypt is lined with marble-faced chapels and tombs and the confessional (directly beneath the high altar and on your left after you reach the bottom of the stairs), flanked by two angels and visible through glass, is the most sacred spot in the church, believed to be directly above the tomb of Saint Peter.

■ **TIP→** The Basilica is free to visit but a security check at the entrance can create very long lines. Arrive before 8:30 or after 5:30 to minimize the wait and avoid the crowds. ✉ *Piazza di San Pietro, Vatican* ☉ *Closed during Papal Audience (Wed. until 1 pm) and during other ceremonies in piazza* Ⓜ *Ottaviano.*

QUICK BITES

Fa-bio. This friendly shop, a stone's throw from the Musei Vaticani, special-izes in super-fresh, made-to-order sandwiches using organic ingredients. It also serves salads and great fresh juices and smoothies but has very limited seating. ✉ *Via Germanico 43, Vatican* ☎ *06/64525810* ⊕ *www. fa-bio.com* Ⓜ *Ottaviano.*

For St. Peter's, Michelangelo originally designed a dome much higher than the one ultimately completed by his follower Giacomo della Porta.

★

Cappella Sistina (*Sistine Chapel*). In 1508, the redoubtable Pope Julius II commissioned Michelangelo to fresco the more than 10,000 square feet of the Sistine Chapel's ceiling. (*Sistine,* by the way, is simply the adjective form of *Sixtus,* in reference to Pope Sixtus IV, who commissioned the chapel itself.) The task took four and a half years, and it's said that for many years afterward Michelangelo couldn't read anything without holding it over his head. The result, however, was arguably the greatest artwork of the Renaissance. A pair of binoculars helps greatly, as does finding a seat on the benches around the edge of the chapel.

Before the chapel was consecrated in 1483, its lower walls were decorated by famed artists including Botticelli, Ghirlandaio, Perugino, Signorelli, and Pinturicchio. They painted scenes from the life of Moses on one wall and episodes from the life of Christ on the other. Later, Pope Julius II, dissatisfied with the simple vault decoration (stars painted on the ceiling), decided to call in Michelangelo. At the time, Michelangelo was carving Julius II's resplendent tomb, a project that never neared completion. He had no desire to give the project up to paint a ceiling, considering the task unworthy of him. Julius was not, however, a man to be trifled with, and Michelangelo reluctantly began work.

More than 20 years later, Michelangelo was called on again, this time by Farnese Pope Paul III, to add to the chapel's decoration by painting the *Last Judgment* on the wall over the altar. The subject was well suited to the aging and embittered artist, who had been deeply moved by the horrendous Sack of Rome in 1527 and the confusions and disturbances of the Reformation. The painting stirred up controversy even before it was unveiled in 1541, shocking many Vatican officials, especially one Biagio

CLOSE UP

Tips on Touring the Vatican Museums

Remember that the Vatican's museum complex is humongous: only after walking through what seems like miles of galleries do you see the entrance to the Sistine Chapel (which cannot be entered from St. Peter's Basilica directly). Most people—especially those who rent an audio guide and must return it to the main desk—tour the complex, see the Sistine, then trudge back to the main museum entrance, itself a 15-minute walk from St. Peter's Square.

However, there is an "insider" exit directly from the Sistine Chapel to St. Peter's Basilica. Look for the "tour groups only" door on the right as you face the rear of the chapel and, when a group exits, go with the flow and follow them. This will deposit you on the porch of St. Peter's Basilica. While this served as a sly trick for years, guards and guides both have gotten stricter about the practice, meaning you might be the victim of

a stern guard or a head count that leaves you in the cold. Also note that if you run to the Sistine Chapel, using the "shortcut" exit into the basilica, you will have missed the rest of the Vatican Museum collection.

Plans are afoot to broaden the sidewalk leading to the museum, to install electronic information panels, and to build a streamlined roof to protect people in the line from sun or rain (until then, umbrellas are recommended).

Another possibility is to visit in the evening. This experiment began in 2009 and has been running intermittently ever since, with the Vatican opening on Friday evenings 7–11, May–October. While the major hits, like the Sistine Chapel, are usually open during these special evenings, many more off-the-beaten-path rooms and galleries are not. Reservations are required (and possible to secure online at ⊕ www.vatican.va).

da Cesena, who criticized its "indecent" nudes. Michelangelo retaliated by painting Biagio's face on Minos, judge of the underworld—the figure with donkey's ears in the lower right-hand corner of the work. Biagio pleaded with Pope Paul to have Michelangelo erase his portrait, but the pontiff replied that while he could intercede for those in purgatory, he had no power over hell. By way of signature on this, his late great fresco, Michelangelo painted his own face on the flayed-off human skin in St. Bartholomew's hand.

The best way to avoid long lines is to arrive at the museum entrance after 2:30, when lines will be very short or even nonexistent (reservations are always advisable)—except free Sundays, which are extremely busy and when admissions close at 12:30. Even better, schedule your visit during the Wednesday papal audience, held in the Piazza di San Petro or at Aula Paolo Sesto, at 10:30 am. ⊠ *Vatican Palace, enter through the Musei Vaticani, Vatican* ⊕ *mv.vatican.va* ⊒ *€16 (part of the Vatican Museums)* ⊙ *Closed Sun. except the last Sun. of every month* Ⓜ *Ottaviano.*

QUICK BITES

Castroni. There are the usual range of pastries and sandwiches at this old-school coffee shop; sit outside, or do as the Romans do and stand at the bar. The attached store sells all sorts of gourmet goodies (and, of course, fresh coffee)—ideal for souvenirs. ⊠ *Via Ottaviano 55, Vatican* ☎ *06/39723279* ⊕ *www.castroni.it* Ⓜ *Ottaviano.*

Fodor's Choice **Musei Vaticani** (*Vatican Museums*).
★ The Vatican palaces and museum spaces consist of an estimated 1,400 rooms, chapels, and galleries; one of the largest museums in the world for the smallest country in the world. Beyond the glories of the Sistine Chapel, the collection is so extraordinarily rich you'll only be able to skim the surface. But few will want to miss out on the great antique sculptures, Raphael Rooms, and the Sistine Chapel .

> ## LAW AND ORDER, 16TH-CENTURY STYLE
>
> The Raphael Room frescoes represent all the revolutionary characteristics of High Renaissance art: naturalism (Raphael's figures lack the awkwardness that pictures painted only a few years earlier conveyed); humanism (the idea that man is the most noble and admirable of God's creatures); and a profound interest in the ancient world (the result of the 15th-century rediscovery of archaeology and classical antiquity). The frescoes in this room virtually dared its occupants to aspire to the highest ideas of law and learning—an amazing feat for an artist not yet 30 years old.

The gems of the Vatican's ancient sculpture collection are in the **Pio-Clementino Museum.** Just off the hall in Room X, you can find the Apoxyomenos (Scraper), a beautiful 1st-century AD copy of the famous bronze statue of an athlete. There are other even more famous pieces in the **Octagonal Courtyard,** where Pope Julius II installed the pick of his private collection. On the left stands the celebrated Apollo Belvedere. In the far corner, on the same side of the courtyard, is the Laocoön group. Found on Rome's Esquiline Hill in 1506, this antique sculpture group influenced Renaissance artists perhaps more than any other.

In the **Hall of the Muses,** the Belvedere Torso occupies center stage: this is a fragment of a 1st-century BC statue, probably of Hercules, all rippling muscles and classical dignity, much admired by Michelangelo. The lovely Neoclassical room of the **Rotonda** has an ancient mosaic pavement and a huge porphyry basin from Nero's palace.

Rivaling the Sistine Chapel for artistic interest—and for the number of visitors—are the **Stanze di Raffaello** (Raphael Rooms). Pope Julius II moved into this suite in 1507, four years after his election. Reluctant to continue living in the Borgia apartments downstairs, with their memories of his ill-famed predecessor Alexander VI, he called in Raphael to decorate his new quarters. When people talk about the Italian High Renaissance—thought to be the very pinnacle of Western art—it's probably Raphael's frescoes they're thinking about.

The **Stanza della Segnatura,** the first to be frescoed, was painted almost entirely by Raphael himself (his assistants painted much of the other rooms). The theme of the room, which may broadly be said to be

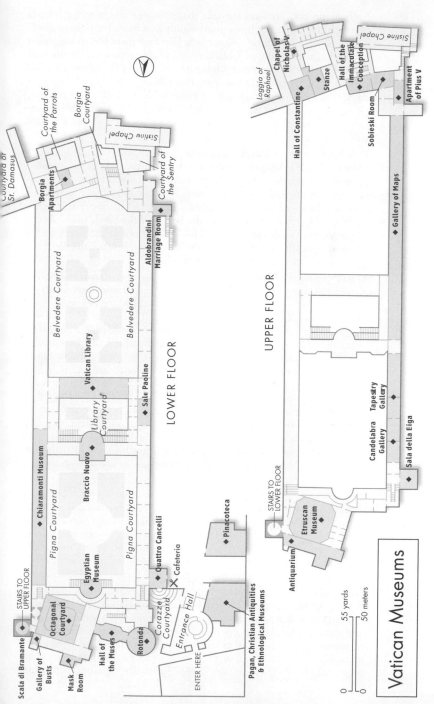

Vatican Museums

LOWER FLOOR

Courtyard of St. Damasus

Courtyard of the Parrots

Borgia Courtyard

Borgia Apartments

Sistine Chapel

Courtyard of the Sentry

Aldobrandini Marriage Room

Belvedere Courtyard

Belvedere Courtyard

Vatican Library

Sale Paoline

Library Courtyard

Braccio Nuovo

Chiaramonti Museum

Pigna Courtyard

Pigna Courtyard

Egyptian Museum

STAIRS TO UPPER FLOOR

Scala di Bramante

Gallery of Busts

Mask Room

Octagonal Courtyard

Hall of the Muses

Rotonda

Corazze Courtyard

Entrance Hall

Quattro Cancelli

Cafeteria

ENTER HERE

Pinacoteca

Pagan, Christian Antiquities & Ethnological Museums

UPPER FLOOR

Loggia of Raphael

Chapel of Nicholas V

Stanze

Hall of the Immaculate Conception

Sistine Chapel

Hall of Constantine

Sobieski Room

Apartment of Pius V

Gallery of Maps

STAIRS TO LOWER FLOOR

Antiquarium

Etruscan Museum

Candelabra Gallery

Tapestry Gallery

Sala della Biga

Sala della Eiga

0 — 55 yards
0 — 50 meters

4

"enlightenment," reflects the fact that this was meant to be Julius's private library. Instead, it was used mainly as a room for signing documents, hence *"segnatura"* (signature). Theology triumphs in the fresco known as the *Disputa,* or *Debate on the Holy Sacrament,* on the wall in front of you as you enter. Opposite, the *School of Athens* glorifies philosophy in its greatest exponents. Plato (likely a portrait of Leonardo da Vinci), in the center, debates a point with Aristotle. The pensive, gloomy figure on the stairs is thought to be modeled after Michelangelo, who was painting the Sistine ceiling at the same time Raphael was working here.

Downstairs are the **Borgia apartments,** where some of the Vatican's most fascinating historic figures are depicted on elaborately painted ceilings. Pinturicchio designed the frescoes at the end of the 15th century, though the paintings were greatly retouched in later centuries. It's generally believed that Cesare Borgia murdered his sister Lucrezia's husband, Alphonse of Aragon, in the Room of the Sibyl. In the Room of the Saints, Pinturicchio painted his self-portrait in the figure to the left of the possible portrait of the architect Antonio da Sangallo. (His profession is made clear by the fact that he holds a T-square.)

Equally celebrated are the works on view in the **Pinacoteca** (Picture Gallery). These often world-famous paintings, almost exclusively of religious subjects, are arranged in chronological order, beginning with works of the 12th and 13th centuries. Room II has a marvelous Giotto triptych, painted on both sides, which formerly stood on the high altar in the old St. Peter's. In Room III you'll see paintings of Madonna by the Florentine 15th-century painters Fra Angelico and Filippo Lippi. Room VIII contains some of Raphael's greatest creations, including the exceptional *Transfiguration,* the *Coronation of the Virgin,* and the *Foligno Madonna,* as well as the tapestries that Raphael designed to hang in the Sistine Chapel. The next room contains Leonardo's beautiful (though unfinished) *St. Jerome* and a Bellini *Pietà.* A highlight for many is Caravaggio's gigantic *Deposition,* in Room XII. In the courtyard outside the Pinacoteca you can admire a beautiful view of the dome of St. Peter's, as well as the reliefs from the base of the now-destroyed column of Antoninus Pius.

The best way to avoid long lines into the museums, which can be a three-hour wait in the high season, is to arrive between noon and 2, when lines will be very short or even nonexistent, except Sunday when admissions close at 12:30. Even better is to schedule your visit during the Wednesday Papal Mass, held in the piazza of St. Peter's or at Aula Paolo Sesto, usually 10:30 am. Also consider booking your ticket in advance online (*biglietteriamusei.vatican.va*); there is a €4 surcharge.

For those interested in guided visits to the Vatican Museums, tours start at €32, including entrance tickets, and can also be booked online. Other offerings include a regular two-hour guided tour of the Vatican gardens and the semi-regular Friday night openings, allowing visitors to the museums until 11 pm; call or check online to confirm. For more information, call 06/69884676 or go to *mv.vatican.va.* For information on tours, call 06/69883145 or 06/69884676; visually impaired visitors can arrange tactile tours by calling *06/69884947*. Wheelchairs are available (free) and can be booked in advance by emailing *accoglienza.musei@scv.va* or by request at the Special Permits desk in the entrance hall.

Ushers at the entrance of St. Peter's and sometimes the Vatican Museums will bar entry to people with bare knees or bare shoulders. ⊠ *Viale Vaticano, near intersection with Via Leone IV, Vatican* ⊕ *www.museivaticani.va/* ≊ *€20 with online reservations, €16 without. Free last Sun. of month* ⊙ *Closed Sun. (except last Sun. of month) and church holidays* Ⓜ *Cipro–Musei Vaticani or Ottaviano–San Pietro. Bus 64, 40.*

<table>
<tr><td>NEED A
BREAK</td><td>✕ **Hostaria Dino e Toni.** Many restaurants immediately near the Vatican are touristy rip-off joints. So, while not worth a special journey, this eatery stands in sharp relief: dine here on typical Roman fare, fresh from the nearby Trionfale market, and pizza. It's closed on Sunday. ⊠ *Via Leone IV 60, Prati* ☎ *06/39733284* Ⓜ *Ottaviano.*</td></tr>
</table>

Necropoli Vaticana (*Vatican Necropolis*). With advance notice you can take a 1¼-hour guided tour in English of the Vatican Necropolis, under the Basilica di San Pietro, which gives a rare glimpse of Early Christian Roman burial customs and a closer look at the tomb of St. Peter. Apply by fax or email at least two months in advance, specifying the number of people in the group (all must be age 15 or older), preferred language, preferred time, available dates, and your contact information in Rome. ⊠ *Piazza di San Pietro, Vatican* ☎ *06/69885318* ⊕ *www. vatican.va* ≊ *€13* ⊙ *Closed Sun.* Ⓜ *Ottaviano-San Pietro.*

WORTH NOTING

Giardini Vaticani (*Vatican Gardens*). Neatly trimmed lawns and flower beds extend over the hills behind St. Peter's Basilica, an area dotted with some interesting constructions and other, duller ones that serve as office buildings. The Vatican Gardens occupy almost 40 acres of land on the Vatican hill. They include a formal Italian garden, a flowering French garden, a romantic English landscape, and a small forest. There's also the little-used Vatican railroad station, which now houses a museum of coins and stamps made in the Vatican, and the Torre di San Giovanni (Tower of St. John), restored by Pope John XXIII as a retreat for work, and now used as a residence for distinguished guests.

To visit the gardens, join a two-hour guided walking tour or a 45-minute open-bus tour (no stops). ⊠ *Vatican* ☎ *06/69883145 for tour info,* ⊕ *mv.vatican.va* ≊ *€32 for 2-hr walking tour, €36 for 45-min open-bus tour (includes €16 admission to Musei Vaticani)* Ⓜ *Ottaviano.*

BORGO

Between the Vatican and the once-moated bulk of Castel Sant'Angelo—erstwhile mausoleum of Emperor Hadrian and now an imposing relic of medieval Rome—is the old Borgo neighborhood, whose workaday charm has largely succumbed to gentrification. Be wary of the tourist-trap lunch spots and souvenir shops right outside the Vatican walls.

Continued on page 112

DID YOU KNOW?

Designed to be Hadrian's tomb, the Castel Sant'Angelo was originally topped by a marble-sheathed tumulus and crowned by a gigantic bronze of the emperor in his chariot.

HEAVEN'S ABOVE:
THE SISTINE CEILING

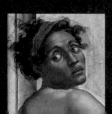

Forming lines that are probably longer than those
waiting to pass through the Pearly Gates, hordes of
visitors arrive at the Sistine Chapel daily to view what
may be the world's most sublime example of artistry:

Michelangelo: *The Creation of Adam,* Sistine Chapel, The Vatican, circa 1511.

Michelangelo's Sistine Ceiling. To paint this 12,000-square-foot barrel vault, it took four years, 343 frescoed figures, and a titanic battle of wits between the artist and Pope Julius II. While in its typical fashion, Hollywood focused on the element of agony, not ecstasy, involved in the saga of creation, a recently completed restoration of the ceiling has revolutionized our appreciation of the masterpiece of masterpieces.

By Martin Bennett

View of the Cappella Sistina

MICHELANGELO'S
MISSION IMPOSSIBLE

Designed to match the proportions of Solomon's Temple described in the Old Testament, the Sistine Chapel is named after Pope Sixtus VI, who commissioned it as a place of worship for himself and as the venue where new popes could be elected. Before Michelangelo, the barrel-vaulted ceiling was an expanse of azure fretted with golden stars. Then, in 1504, an ugly crack appeared. Bramante, the architect, managed do some patchwork using iron rods, but when signs of a fissure remained, the new Pope Julius II summoned Michelangelo to cover it with a fresco 135 feet long and 44 feet wide.

Taking in the entire span of the ceiling, the theme connecting the various participants in this painted universe could be said to be mankind's anguished waiting. The majestic panel depicting the Creation of Adam leads, through the stages of the Fall and the expulsion from Eden, to the tragedy of Noah found naked and mocked by his own sons; throughout all runs the underlying need for man's redemption. Witnessing all from the side and end walls, a chorus of ancient Prophets and Sibyls peer anxiously forward, awaiting the Redeemer who will come to save both the Jews and the Gentiles.

APOCALYPSE NOW

The sweetness and pathos of his Pietà, carved by Michelangelo only ten years earlier, have been left behind. The new work foretells an apocalypse, its congregation of doomed sinners facing the wrath of heaven through hanging, beheading, crucifixion, flood, and plague. Michelangelo, by nature a misanthrope, was already filled with visions of doom thanks to the fiery orations of Savonarola, whose thunderous preachments he had heard before leaving his hometown of Florence. Vasari, the 16th-century art historian, coined the word "terrabilità" to describe Michelangelo's tension-ridden style, a rare case of a single word being worth a thousand pictures.

Michelangelo wound up using a *Reader's Digest* condensed version of the stories from Genesis, with the dramatis personae overseen by a punitive and terrifying God. In real life, poor Michelangelo answered to a flesh-and-blood taskmaster who was almost as vengeful: Pope Julius II. Less vicar of Christ than latter-day Caesar, he was intent on uniting Italy under the power of the Vatican, and was eager to do so by any means, including riding into pitched battle. Yet this "warrior pope" considered his most formidable adversary to be Michelangelo. Applying a form of blackmail, Julius threatened to wage war on Michelangelo's Florence, to which the artist had fled after Julius canceled a commission for a grand papal tomb unless Michelangelo agreed to return to Rome and take up the task of painting the Sistine Chapel ceiling.

MICHELANGELO, SCULPTOR

A sculptor first and foremost, however, Michelangelo considered painting an inferior genre—"for rascals and sissies" as he put it. Second, there was the sheer scope of the task, leading Michelangelo to suspect he'd been set up by a rival, Bramante, chief architect of the new St. Peter's Basilica. As Michelangelo was also a master architect, he regarded this fresco commission as a Renaissance mission-impossible. Pope Julius's powerful will prevailed—and six years later the work of the Sistine Ceiling was complete. Irving Stone's famous novel *The Agony and the Ecstasy*—and the granitic 1965 film that followed—chart this epic battle between artist and pope.

THINGS ARE LOOKING UP

To enhance your viewing of the ceiling, bring along opera-glasses, binoculars, or just a mirror (to prevent your neck from becoming bent like Michelangelo's). Note that no photos are permitted. Insiders know the only time to see the chapel to yourself is during the papal blessings and public audiences held in St. Peter's Square. Failing that, get there during lunch hour. Admission and entry to the Sistine Chapel is only through the Musei Vaticani (Vatican Museums).

SCHEMATIC OF THE SISTINE CEILING

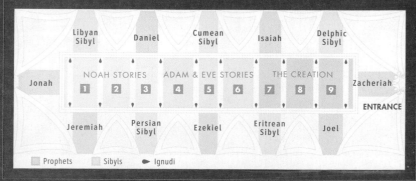

The ceiling's biblical symbols were ideated by three Vatican theologians, Cardinal Alidosi, Egidio da Viterbo, and Giovanni Rafanelli, along with Mi-

chelangelo. As for the ceiling's painted "framework," this *quadratura* alludes to Roman triumphal arches because Pope Julius II was fond of mounting "triumphal entries" into his conquered cities (in imitation of Christ's

procession into Jerusalem on Palm Sunday).

THE CENTER PANELS
Prophet turned art-critic or, perhaps doubling as ourselves, the ideal viewer, Jonah the prophet (painted at the altar end) gazes up at the

Creation, or Michelangelo's version of it.

1 The first of three scenes taken from the Book of Genesis: God separates Light from Darkness.

2 God creates the sun and a craterless pre-Galilean moon while the panel's other half offers an unprecedented rear view of the Almighty creating the vegetable world.

3 In the panel showing God separating the Waters from the Heavens, the Creator tumbles towards us as in a self-made whirlwind.

4 Pausing for breath, next admire probably Western Art's most famous image— God giving life to Adam.

5 The Creation of Eve from Adam's rib leads to the sixth panel.

6 In a sort of diptych divided by the trunk of the Tree of Knowledge of Good and Evil, Michelangelo retells the Temptation and the Fall.

7 Illustrating Man's fallen nature, the last three panels narrate, in un-chronological order, the Flood. In the first Noah offers a pre-Flood sacrifice of thanks.

8 Damaged by an explosion in 1794, next comes Michelan-

gelo's version of Flood itself.

9 Finally, above the monumental Jonah, you can just make out the small, wretched figure of Noah, lying drunk—in pose, the shrunken anti-type of the majestic Adam five panels down the wall.

THE CREATION OF ADAM

Michelangelo's Adam was partly inspired by the Creation scenes Michelangelo had studied in the sculpted doors of Jacopo della Quercia in Bologna and Lorenzo Ghiberti's Doors of Paradise in Florence. Yet in Michelangelo's version Adam's hand hangs limp, waiting God's touch to impart the spark of life. Facing his Creation, the Creator—looking a bit like the pagan god Jupiter—is for the first time ever depicted as horizontal, mirroring the Biblical "in his own likeness." Decades after its completion, a crack began to appear, amputating Adam's fingertips. Believe it or not, the most famous fingers in Western art are the handiwork, at least in part, of one Domenico Carnevale.

PIAZZA DI SAN PIETRO

✉ *West end of Via della Conciliazione, Vatican*
☎ *06/69881662* Ⓜ *Cipro or Ottaviano.*

TIPS

■ The Vatican post offices (known for fast handling of outgoing mail) can be found on both sides of St. Peter's Square and inside the Musei Vaticani complex. You can also buy Vatican stamps and coins at the shop annexed to the information office. Although postage rates are the same at the Vatican as elsewhere in Italy, the stamps are not interchangeable, so any material stamped with Vatican stamps must be placed into a blue or yellow Posta Vaticana mailbox.

■ Public restrooms are near the Information Office, under the colonnade on the side closest to Via di Porta Angelica, and at the entrance to the Basilica after the statue of Saint Paul.

Mostly enclosed within high walls that recall the papacy's stormy history, the Vatican opens the arms of Bernini's colonnade to embrace the world only at St. Peter's Square, scene of the pope's public appearances. One of Bernini's most spectacular masterpieces, the elliptical Piazza di San Pietro was completed in 1667 after only 11 years' work and holds about 100,000 people.

Surrounded by a pair of quadruple colonnades, it is topped with 140 statues of saints and martyrs. Look for the two disks set into the piazza's pavement to either side of the central obelisk. If you stand on either disk, a trick of perspective makes the colonnades look like a single row of columns.

Bernini had an even grander visual effect in mind when he designed the square. By opening up this immense, airy, and luminous space in a neighborhood of narrow, shadowy streets, he created a contrast that would surprise and impress anyone who emerged from the darkness into the light, in a characteristically Baroque metaphor.

At the piazza center, the 85-foot-high Egyptian obelisk was brought to Rome by Caligula in AD 37 and moved here in 1586 by Pope Sixtus V. The emblem at the top of the obelisk is the Chigi star, in honor of Pope Alexander VII, a member of the powerful Chigi family, who commissioned the piazza.

Alexander demanded that Bernini make the pope visible to as many people as possible from the Loggia delle Benedizioni (Benediction Loggia) and to provide a covered passageway for papal processions.

WORTH NOTING

FAMILY **Castel Sant'Angelo.** Situated between the Tiber and the Vatican, this medieval "castle" has long been one of Rome's most distinctive landmarks. Opera lovers know it well as the setting for the final scene of Puccini's *Tosca*; the tempestuous diva throws herself from the rampart on the upper terrace. In fact, the structure began life many centuries before as a mausoleum for the emperor Hadrian. Started in AD 135, it was completed by the emperor's successor, Antoninus Pius, about five years later. It initially consisted of a great square base topped by a marble-clad cylinder on which was planted a ring of cypress trees. Above them towered a gigantic statue of Hadrian. From the mid-6th century the building became a fortress, a place of refuge for popes during wars and sieges. Its name dates to AD 590, when Pope Gregory the Great, during a procession to plead for the end of a plague, saw an angel standing on the summit of the castle, sheathing his sword. Taking this as a sign that the plague was at an end, the pope built a small chapel at the top, placing a statue next to it to celebrate his vision—thus the name, Castel Sant'Angelo.

Enter the building through the original Roman door of Hadrian's tomb. You'll then enter a vaulted brick corridor that hints at grim punishments in dank cells. On the right, a spiral ramp leads up to the chamber in which Hadrian's ashes were kept. Where the ramp ends, the Borgia pope Alexander VI's staircase begins. Part of it consisted of a wooden drawbridge, which could isolate the upper part of the castle completely. The staircase ends at the Cortile dell'Angelo, a courtyard that has become the resting place of neatly piled stone cannonballs, as well as the marble angel that stood above the castle. (It was replaced by a bronze sculpture in 1753.) In the rooms off the Cortile dell'Angelo, look for the **Cappella di Papa Leone X** (Chapel of Pope Leo X), with a facade by Michelangelo.

In the courtyard named for Pope Alexander VI, a wellhead bears the Borgia coat of arms. The courtyard is surrounded by gloomy cells and huge storerooms that could hold great quantities of oil and grain in case of siege.

Take the stairs at the far end of the courtyard to the open terrace for a view of the Passetto, the fortified corridor connecting Castel Sant'Angelo with the Vatican. Pope Clement VII used the Passetto to make his way safely to the castle during the Sack of Rome in 1527. In the *appartamento papale* (papal apartment) the Sala Paolina (Pauline Room), the first room you enter, was decorated in the 16th century by Perino del Vaga and assistants with lavish frescoes of scenes from the Old Testament and the lives of Saint Paul and Alexander the Great. Look for the trompe-l'oeil door with a figure climbing the stairs. From another false door, a black-clad figure peers into the room. This is believed to be a portrait of an illegitimate son of the powerful Orsini family. ⊠ *Lungotevere Castello 50, Prati* ☎ *06/6819111 for central line, 06/6896003 for tickets* ⊕ *castelsantangelo.beniculturali.it* ⬛ *€10* Ⓜ *Lepanto.*

4

Ponte Sant'Angelo. Angels designed by Baroque master Bernini line the most beautiful of central Rome's 20-odd bridges. Bernini himself carved only two of the angels (those with the scroll and the crown of thorns), both of which were moved to the church of Sant'Andrea delle Fratte shortly afterward at the behest of the Bernini family. Though copies, the angels on the bridge today convey forcefully the grace and characteristic sense of movement—a key element of Baroque sculpture—of Bernini's best work. Originally built in AD 133–134, the Ponte Elio, as it was originally called, was a bridge over the Tiber to Hadrian's Mausoleum. Pope Gregory changed the bridge's name after he had a vision of an angel sheathing its sword to signal the ending of the plague of 590. In medieval times, continuing its sacral function, the bridge became an important element in funneling pilgrims toward St. Peter's. As such, in 1667 Pope Clement IX commissioned Bernini to design 10 angels bearing the symbols of the Passion, turning the bridge into a sort of Via Crucis. ⊠ *Between Lungotevere Castello and Lungotevere Altoviti, Borgo* Ⓜ *Ottaviano.*

PRATI

Outside the Vatican walls, but slightly upriver from the Borgo neighborhood, Prati is starting to come into its own as a foodie destination.

PIAZZA NAVONA, CAMPO DE' FIORI, AND THE JEWISH GHETTO

Getting Oriented

Piazza Navona,
Campo de' Fiori,
and the Jewish Ghetto

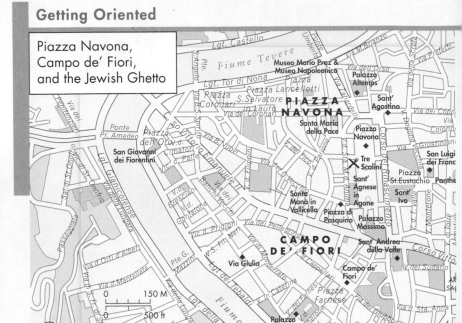

See Historic Heart Detail Map

GETTING HERE

The Piazza Navona and Campo de' Fiori are an easy walk from the Vatican or Trastevere, or a half-hour stroll from the Spanish Steps. From Termini or the Vatican, take Bus No. 40 Express or the No. 64 to Largo Torre Argentina; then walk 10 minutes to either piazza. Bus No. 116 winds from Via Veneto past the Spanish Steps to Campo de' Fiori.

From the Vatican or the Spanish Steps, it's a 30-minute walk to the Jewish Ghetto, or take the No. 40 Express or the No. 64 bus from Termini station to Largo Torre Argentina.

MAKING THE MOST OF YOUR TIME

Start at Campo de' Fiori, where the popular market takes place every morning Monday–Saturday. The cobblestone streets that stretch out from the square are still lined with artisanal workshops. Wind your way west through the Jewish Ghetto, the historic home of Rome's once-vibrant Jewish community (and a good place for lunch); don't miss the area around the Portico d'Ottavia, with some of the city's most atmospheric ruins. Heading north will take you across busy Corso Vittorio Emanuele toward the Pantheon. Duck into the piazza of Santa Maria Sopra Minerva, which contains Rome's most delightful Baroque conceit, the 17th-century elephant obelisk memorial designed by Bernini, and pop into the church, which has the only Gothic interior in Rome. Straight ahead is one of the wonders of the world, the ancient Pantheon, with that postcard icon, Piazza Navona, just a few blocks to the west. You could spend about five hours exploring, not counting breaks—but taking breaks is what this area is all about.

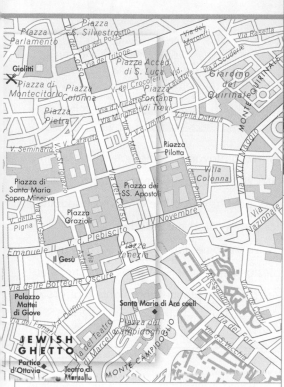

5

TOP REASONS TO GO

Piazza Navona: This is the city's most glorious piazza—the showcase for Rome's exuberant Baroque style. Savor Bernini's fantastic fountain, set off by the curves and steeples of Borromini's church of Sant'Agnese.

Caravaggio: Feel the power of 17th-century Rome's rebel artist in three of his finest paintings at the church of San Luigi dei Francesi.

The Pantheon: Gaze up to the heavens through the dome of Rome's best-preserved ancient temple—could this be the world's only architecturally perfect building?

Campo de' Fiori: Stroll through the morning market for a taste of the sweet life.

Via Giulia: Lined with regal palaces—still home to some of Rome's *princeliest* families—this is a Renaissance-era diorama you can walk through.

Portico d'Ottavia: This famed ancient Roman landmark casts a spell over Rome's time-honored Jewish Ghetto.

QUICK BITES

Giolitti. The Pantheon area is ice-cream heaven, with some of Rome's best gelaterias within a few steps of each other. But for many Romans, a scoop at Giolitti, which opened in 1900, is tradition. The scene at the counter often looks like the storming of the Bastille; remember to pay the cashier first, and hand the stub to the counter-person when you order your cone. Giolitti also has a good snack counter. ✉ *Via Uffizi del Vicario 40, Piazza Navona* ☎ *06/6991243* ⊕ *www.giolitti.it.*

Tre Scalini. The sidewalk tables of the caffè, along with its restaurant annex, offer a grandstand view of all the action of the Piazza Navona. This is the place that invented the *tartufo,* a luscious chocolate ice-cream specialty—and, it's worth noting, one found with far more frequency in the United States than Italy. ✉ *Piazza Navona 30, Piazza Navona* ☎ *06/6879148* ⊕ *www.ristorante-3scalini.com.*

Sightseeing
★★★★★
Nightlife
★★★★
Dining
★★★
Lodging
★★★★★
Shopping
★★★★

The area around Piazza Navona, Campo de' Fiori, and the Jewish Ghetto, also known as the Campo Marzio (Field of Mars) for its martial past, is one of the city's most beautiful, most atmospheric, and liveliest neighborhoods. More than almost anywhere else in Rome, this is an area worth getting lost in, with cobblestone side streets and artisanal shops just around the corner from the piazze and sights that crowd with tourists (and the establishments that cater to them).

PIAZZA NAVONA

Updated
by Agnes
Crawford

In terms of sheer sensual enjoyment—from a mouthwatering range of restaurants and caffè to the ornate Baroque settings—it's tough to top this area of Rome. Just a few blocks (and some 1,200 years) separate the two main showstoppers: Piazza Navona and the Pantheon. The first is the most beautiful Baroque piazza in the world, and it serves as the open-air salon for this quarter of Rome. As if this is not grandeur enough, across Corso di Rinascimento—and more than a millennium away—is the Pantheon, the grandest extant building still standing from ancient Rome, topped by the world's largest unreinforced concrete dome. Near the same massive hub, Bernini's delightful elephant obelisk proves that small can also be beautiful. And beautiful is the word to describe this entire area, one that is packed with Baroque wonders, charming stores, and very happy sightseers.

TOP ATTRACTIONS

Fodor's Choice
★

Palazzo Altemps. Containing some of the finest ancient Roman statues in the world, Palazzo Altemps is part of the Museo Nazionale Romano. The palace's sober exterior belies a magnificence that appears as soon as you walk into the majestic courtyard, studded with statues and covered in part by a retractable awning. The restored interior hints at the

Roman lifestyle of the 16th–18th centuries while showcasing the most illustrious pieces from the Museo Nazionale, including the collection of the Ludovisi noble family. In the frescoed salons you can see the Galata Suicida, a poignant work portraying a barbarian warrior who chooses death for himself and his wife, rather than humiliation by the enemy. Another highlight is the large Ludovisi sarcophagus, magnificently carved from marble. In a place of honor is the Ludovisi Throne, which shows a goddess emerging from the sea and being helped by her acolytes. For centuries this was heralded as one of the most sublime Greek sculptures, but, today, at least one authoritative art historian considers it a colossally overrated fake. Look for the framed explanations of the exhibits that detail (in English) how and exactly where Renaissance sculptors, Bernini among them, added missing pieces to the classical works. In the lavishly frescoed Loggia stand busts of the Caesars. In the wing once occupied by early-20th-century poet Gabriele d'Annunzio (who married into the Altemps family), three rooms host the museum's Egyptian collection. ⊠ *Piazza Sant'Apollinare 46, Piazza Navona* ☏ *06/39967700* ⊕ *www.coopculture.it* ▣ *€7, includes 3 other Museo Nazionale Romano sites (Crypta Balbi, Palazzo Massimo, Museo Diocleziano); €10 if any one of them has a special exhibit* ☉ *Closed Mon.* Ⓜ *Bus Nos. 70, 81, 87, 116T, 186, 492, and 628.*

Fodor's Choice
★

Pantheon. One of the wonders of the ancient world, this former Roman pagan temple is a marvel of architectural harmony and proportion, and the best-preserved ancient building in the city. It was entirely rebuilt by the emperor Hadrian around AD 120 on the site of an earlier Pantheon (from the Greek: *pan,* or all, and *theon,* or gods) erected in 27 BC by Augustus's right-hand man and son-in-law, Agrippa.

The most striking thing about the Pantheon is not its size, immense though it is, nor even the phenomenal technical difficulties posed by so massive a construction; rather, it's the remarkable unity of the building. The diameter described by the dome is exactly equal to its height. It's the use of such simple mathematical balance that gives classical architecture its characteristic sense of proportion and its nobility, and why some call it the world's only architecturally perfect building. The great opening at the apex of the dome, the *oculus,* is nearly 30 feet in diameter and was the temple's only source of light. It was intended to symbolize the "all-seeing eye of heaven."

To do the interior justice defied even Byron. He piles up adjectives, but none seems to fit: "Simple, erect, severe, austere, sublime." Although little is known for sure about the Pantheon's origins or purpose, it's worth noting that the five levels of trapezoidal coffers (sunken panels in the ceiling) represent the course of the five then-known planets and their concentric spheres. Ruling over them is the sun, represented symbolically and literally by the 30-foot-wide eye at the top. The heavenly symmetry is further paralleled by the coffers: 28 to each row, the number of lunar cycles. In the center of each would have shone a small bronze star. Down below the seven large niches were occupied not by saints, but, it's thought, by statues of Mars, Venus, the deified Caesar, and the other "astral deities," including the moon and sun, the "sol

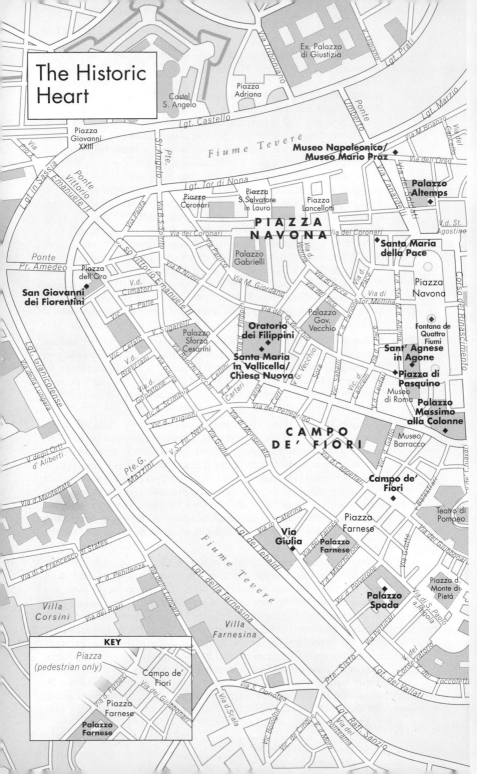

The Historic Heart

Ex. Palazzo di Giustizia

Piazza Adriana

Castel S. Angelo

Piazza Giovanni XXIII

V. Ulpiano

V. Umberto

Lgt. Prati

Lgt. Marzio

Via del Cancello

Via M. Brianzo

Via dell'Orso

Ponte Umberto

Museo Napoleonico/ Museo Mario Praz

Palazzo Altemps

Via Zanardelli

V.d. St. Agostino

Lgt. Castello

Fiume Tevere

Lgt. Tor di Nona

Piazza Coronari

Piazza S. Salvatore in Lauro

Piazza Lancellotti

PIAZZA NAVONA

Via dei Coronari

Via dei Coronari

Via d. Vettina

Santa Maria della Pace

Ponte Pr. Amedeo

Piazza dell'Oro

Palazzo Gabrielli

Via di Pace

Piazza Navona

V.d. Cimatori

V.d. Palle

Via M. Giordano

Via della Fico

Via di Tor Millina

Corso del Rinascimento

San Giovanni dei Fiorentini

V. Sugarelli

Vic. Celso

Via B. Nuovi

Palazzo Sforza Cesarini

Palazzo Gov. Vecchio

Fontana de Quattro Fiumi

Lgt. Gran Colonese

V.d. Bresciani

Via Giulia

Oratorio dei Filippini

Via d. Governo Vecchio

Vic. S. Salieri

Sant' Agnese in Agone

Via d. Cancell.

Vic. d. Cellini

Via d. Leutari

Santa Maria in Vallicella/ Chiesa Nuova

Cora

Piazza di Pasquino

Via d. Goglatore

Via Cartari

Vic. d. Scimmia

Via Largo

Museo di Roma

Palazzo Massimo alla Colonne

Vic. d. Prigioni

Via del Pellegrino

CAMPO DE' FIORI

Museo Barracco

Via d. Gallo

V.S. Fil. Neri

Via Giulia

Via Monserrato

Via d. Cappellari

Via del Teatro di Pompeo

Pte. G. Mazzini

Via de Giubbonari

Campo de' Fiori

Via di Banchi Vecchi

V. d. Mantellate

Lgt. della Lungara

Via di S. Francesco di Stato

V. d. Penitenza

Via di S. Caterina

Via d. Balestrari

Teatro di Pompeo

Fiume Tevere

Lgt. dei Tebaldi

Via Giulia

Piazza Farnese

Palazzo Farnese

Via d. Farnesi

Via del Mascherone

Via di Monserrato

Piazza d. Monte di Pietà

Via d. Polverone

Via d. Giubbonari

Villa Corsini

Via dei Riari

Palazzo Spada

Via d. S. Paolo a Regola

Villa Farnesina

Lgt. della Farnesina

Via Pettinari

V. del Conservatorio

Pte. Sisto

Lgt. dei Vallati

Lgt. Sanzio

Zoccolette

KEY
Piazza (pedestrian only)

Campo de' Fiori

Piazza Farnese

Palazzo Farnese

Via d. Scala

Vic. de Cinque

V. d. Moro

Via S. Donatea

Via d. Ponte Teama

Via Baulana

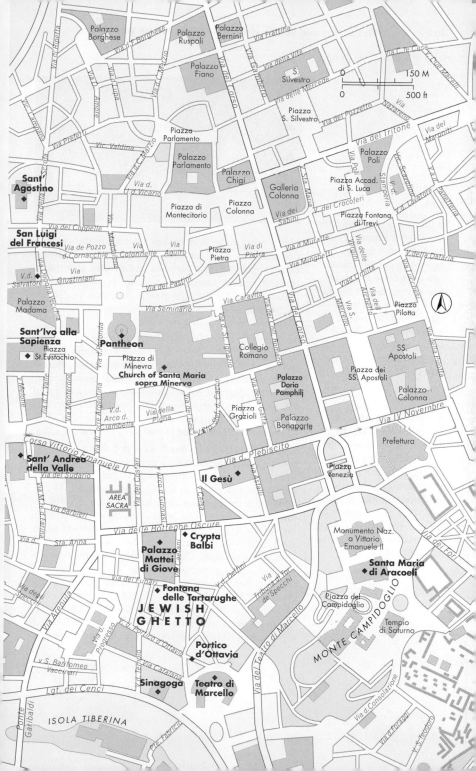

PIAZZA NAVONA

✉ *Piazza Navona.*

TIPS

■ On the eve of the Epiphany (the night of January 5), Piazza Navona's toy fair explodes in joyful conclusion, with much noise and rowdiness to encourage *la Befana*, an old woman who brings toys to good children and pieces of coal (represented by coal-looking candy) to the naughty. Meanwhile, the toy stores of Al Sogno (at No. 53) and Berté (at No. 3) enchant year-round.

■ If you want a caffè with one of the most beautiful, if pricey, views in Rome, grab a seat at Piazza Navona. Just be aware that all of the restaurants here are heavily geared toward tourists, so while it's a beautiful place for a coffee, you can find cheaper, more authentic, and far better meals elsewhere.

Here, everything that makes Rome unique is compressed into one beautiful Baroque piazza. Always camera-ready, Piazza Navona has Bernini sculptures, three gorgeous fountains, a magnificently Baroque church (Sant'Agnese in Agone), and, best of all, the excitement of so many people strolling, admiring the fountains, and enjoying the view.

The piazza has been an entertainment venue for Romans ever since being built over Domitian's circus (pieces of the arena are still visible near the adjacent Piazza Sant'Apollinare). Although undoubtedly more touristy today, the square still has the carefree air of the days when it was the scene of medieval jousts and 17th-century carnivals. Today, it's the site of a lively Christmas "Befana" fair.

The piazza still looks much as it did during the 17th century, after the Pamphilij pope Innocent X decided to make it over into a monument to his family to rival the Barberini's palace at the Quattro Fontane. At center stage is the Fontana dei Quattro Fiumi, created for Innocent by Bernini in 1651. Bernini's powerful figures of the four rivers represent the four corners of the world: the Nile; the Ganges; the Danube; and the Plata, with its hand raised. One story has it that the figure of the Nile—the figure closest to Sant'Agnese in Agone—hides its head because it can't bear to look upon the church's "inferior" facade designed by Francesco Borromini, Bernini's rival. In fact, the facade was built after the fountain, and the statue hides its head because it represents a river whose source was then unknown.

invictus." (Academics still argue, however, about which gods were most probably worshipped here.)

One of the reasons the Pantheon is so well preserved is the result of it being consecrated as a church in AD 608. (It's still a working and Mass-holding church today, and it's the church name, the Santa Maria degli Angeli e dei Martiri, that you'll see on official signs.) No building, church or not, though, escaped some degree of plundering through the turbulent centuries of Rome's history after the fall of the empire. In 655, for example, the gilded bronze covering the dome was stripped. Similarly, in the early 17th century, Pope Urban VIII removed the bronze beams of the portico. Most of its interior marble facing has also been stripped and replaced over the centuries. Nonetheless, the Pantheon suffered less than many other ancient structures. The temple's original bronze doors have remained intact, if restored and even melted down and recast at one point, for more than 1,800 years.

The Pantheon is also one of the city's important burial places. Its most famous tomb is that of Raphael (between the second and third chapels on the left as you enter).

Mass takes place on Sunday and mass on religious holidays at 10:30; it's open to the public, but you are expected to arrive before the beginning and stay until the end. General access usually resumes at about 11:30. ✉ *Piazza della Rotonda, Piazza Navona* ☎ *06/68300230* ⊕ *www.pantheonroma.com* ☞ *free; audio guide €5* Ⓜ *Closest bus hub: Argentina (Bus Nos. 40, 85, 53, 46, 64, 87, and 571; Tram No. 8).*

✘ **Tazza d'Oro.** On the east corner of the piazza in front of the Pantheon, the Tazza d'Oro coffee bar is the place for serious coffee drinkers—there are no tables, no frills. Indulge in their *granita di caffè con panna* (coffee ice with whipped cream). ✉ *Via degli Orfani 86, Piazza Navona* ☎ *06/678-9792* ⊕ *www.tazzadorocoffeeshop.com.*

Fodor's Choice **San Luigi dei Francesi.** A pilgrimage spot for art lovers, San Luigi's Con-
★ tarelli Chapel is adorned with three stunningly dramatic works by Cara-vaggio (1571–1610), the Baroque master of the heightened approach to light and dark. At the altar end of the left nave, they were commissioned for San Luigi, the official church of Rome's French colony (San Luigi is St. Louis, patron saint of France). The inevitable coin machine will light up his *Calling of St. Matthew, Saint Matthew and the Angel,* and *Martyrdom of Saint Matthew* (seen from left to right), and Caravag-gio's mastery of light takes it from there. When painted, they caused considerable consternation to the clergy of San Luigi, who thought the artist's dramatically realistic approach was scandalously disrespectful. A first version of the altarpiece was rejected; the priests were not par-ticularly happy with the other two, either. Time has fully vindicated Caravaggio's patron, Cardinal Francesco del Monte, who secured the commission for these works and stoutly defended them. ✉ *Piazza di San Luigi dei Francesi, Piazza Navona* ☎ *06/688271* ⊕ *www.saintlouis-rome.net* Ⓜ *Bus Nos. 40 and 87.*

Sant'Agnese in Agone. The quintessence of Baroque architecture, this church has a facade that is a wonderfully rich mélange of bell towers, concave spaces, and dovetailed stone and marble. It's the creation of Francesco Borromini (1599–1667), a contemporary and rival of Bernini. Next to his new Pamphilj family palace, Pope Innocent X had the adjacent chapel expanded into this full-fledged church. The work was first assigned to the architect Rainaldi. However, Donna Olimpia, the pope's famously domineering sister, became increasingly impatient with how the work was going and brought in Borromini, whose wonderful concave entrance has the magical effect of making the dome appear much larger than it actually is. The name of this church comes from the Greek *agones,* the source of the word *navona* and a reference to the agonistic competitions held here in Roman times. The saint associated with the church is Agnes, who was martyred here in the piazza's forerunner, the Stadium of Domitian. As she was stripped nude before the crowd, her hair miraculously grew to maintain her modesty before she was killed. The interior is a marvel of modular Baroque space and is ornamented by giant marble reliefs sculpted by Raggi and Ferrata. ⊠ *Via di Santa Maria dell'Anima, 30/A, Piazza Navona* 🕾 *06/68192134* ⊕ *www.santagneseinagone.org* ⊘ *Closed Mon.* Ⓜ *Bus Nos. 87, 40, and 64.*

Santa Maria della Pace. In 1656, Pietro da Cortona (1596–1669) was commissioned by Pope Alexander VII to enlarge the tiny Piazza della Pace in front of the 15th-century church of Santa Maria, to accommodate the carriages of its wealthy parishioners. His architectural solution was to design a new church facade complete with semicircular portico, demolish a few buildings here and there to create a more spacious approach to the church, add arches to give architectural unity to the piazza, and then complete it with a series of bijou-size palaces. The result was one of Rome's most delightful little architectural set pieces. Within are several great Renaissance treasures. Raphael's fresco above the first altar on your right depicts the *Four Sibyls*—almost exact replicas of Michelangelo's, if more relaxed. The fine decorations of the Cesi Chapel, second on the right, were designed in the mid-16th century by Sangallo. Opposite is Peruzzi's wonderful fresco of the *Madonna and Child*. Meanwhile, the octagon below the dome is something of an art gallery in itself, with works by Cavalliere Arpino, Orazio Gentileschi, and others as Cozzo's *Eternity* fills the lantern above. Behind the church is its cloister, designed by Bramante (architect of St. Peter's) as the very first expression of High Renaissance style in Rome. The cloister has an exhibition space and a lovely caffè on the upper level. ⊠ *Via Arco della Pace 5, Piazza Navona* 🕾 *06/6861156* ⊘ *Closed Thurs., Fri., Sun., and Tues.* Ⓜ *Bus Nos. 87, 40, and 64.*

Fodor's Choice **Santa Maria sopra Minerva.** The name of the church reveals that it was
★ built *sopra* (over) the ruins of a temple of Minerva, the ancient goddess of wisdom. Erected in 1280 by Dominicans along severe Italian Gothic lines, it has undergone a number of more or less happy restorations to the interior. Certainly, as the city's major Gothic church, it provides a refreshing contrast to Baroque flamboyance. Have a €1 coin handy to illuminate the **Cappella Carafa** in the right transept, where Filippino Lippi's (1457–1504) glowing frescoes are well worth the small investment, opening up the deepest azure expanse of sky where musical

angels hover around the Virgin. Under the main altar is the tomb of St. Catherine of Siena, one of Italy's patron saints. Left of the altar you'll find Michelangelo's *Risen Christ* and the tomb of the gentle artist Fra Angelico. Bernini's unusual and little-known monument to the Blessed Maria Raggi is on the fifth pier from the door on the left as you leave the church. In front of the church, the little obelisk-bearing elephant carved by Bernini is perhaps the city's most charming sculpture. An inscription on the base of **Bernini's Elephant Obelisk,** which was recently cleaned and restored, references the church's ancient patroness, reading something to the effect that it takes a strong mind to sustain solid wisdom. ⊠ *Piazza della Minerva, Piazza Navona* ☎ *06/6793926* ⊕ *www.santamariasopraminerva.it.*

Sant'Ivo alla Sapienza. The main facade of this eccentric Baroque church, probably Borromini's best, is on the stately courtyard of an austere building that once housed Rome's university. Sant'Ivo has what must surely be one of the most delightful "domes" in all of Rome—a dizzying spiral said to have been inspired by a bee's stinger. The apian symbol is a reminder that Borromini built the church on commission from the Barberini pope Urban VIII (a swarm of bees figure on the Barberini family crest). The interior, open only for three hours on Sunday, is worth a look, especially if you share Borromini's taste for complex mathematical architectural idiosyncrasies. "I didn't take up architecture solely to be a copyist," he once said. Sant'Ivo is certainly the proof. ⊠ *Corso del Rinascimento 40, Piazza Navona* ☎ *06/6864987* ⊕ *www.060608. it* ⊙ *Closed July and Aug. and Mon.–Sat.* Ⓜ *Bus Nos. 130, 116, 186, 492, 30, 70, 81, and 87.*

WORTH NOTING

Museo Mario Praz. On the top floor of the Palazzo Primoli—the same building (separate entrance) that houses the Museo Napoleonico—is one of Rome's most unusual museums. As if preserved in amber, the apartment in which the famous Italian essayist Mario Praz lived survives intact, decorated with a lifetime's accumulation of delightful Baroque and Neoclassical art and antiques, arranged and rearranged to create symmetries that take the visitor by surprise like the best trompe-l'oeil. As author of *The Romantic Sensibility* and *A History of Interior Decoration,* Praz was fabled for his taste for the arcane and the bizarre; here his reputation for the same lives on. You are obliged to follow a custodian through the museum; the visit takes about 50 minutes. ⊠ *Via Zanardelli 1, Piazza Navona* ☎ *06/6861089* ⊕ *www.060608.it* ⊙ *Closed Sun.–Wed.* Ⓜ *Bus Nos. 492, 70, 628, 81, and 116.*

Museo Napoleonico. Housed in an opulent collection of velvet-and-crystal salons that hauntingly capture the fragile charm of early-19th-century Rome, this small museum in the Palazzo Primoli contains a specialized and rich collection of Napoléon memorabilia, including a bust by Canova of the general's sister, Pauline Borghese (as well as a plaster cast of her left bust). You may well ask why this outpost of Napoléon is in Rome, but in 1798 the French emperor sent his troops to Rome, kidnapping Pope Pius VII and proclaiming his young son the King of

Rome—though it all ultimately came to naught. Upstairs is the Museo Mario Praz. ⊠ *Palazzo Primoli, Piazza di Ponte Umberto I, Piazza Navona* ☎ *06/68806286* ⊕ *www.museonapoleonico.it* ⊙ *Closed Mon.* Ⓜ *Bus Nos. 70, 30, 81, 628, and 492.*

Oratorio dei Filippini. Housed in a Baroque masterwork by Borromini, this former religious residence named for Saint Philip Neri, founder in 1551 of the Congregation of the Oratorians, now contains Rome's Archivio Storico. Like the Jesuits, the Oratorians—or Filippini, as they were commonly known—were one of the new religious orders established in the mid-16th century as part of the Counter-Reformation. Neri, a man of rare charm and wit, insisted that the members of the order—most of them young noblemen whom he had recruited personally—not only renounce their worldly goods, but also work as common laborers in the building of Neri's great church of Santa Maria in Vallicella. The Oratory itself, once headquarters of the order, was built by Borromini between 1637 and 1662. Its gently curving facade is typical of Borromini's insistence on introducing movement into everything he designed. The inspiration here is that of arms extended in welcome to the poor. The building houses the Vallicelliana Library found by Philip Neri, and the courtyard is usually accessible during the library's opening hours. ⊠ *Piazza della Chiesa Nuova (Corso Vittorio Emanuele), Piazza Navona* ☎ *06/6892537* ⊕ *www.060608.it* ⊙ *Closed Sun.*

Palazzo Massimo alle Colonne. Following the shape of Emperor Domitian's Odeon arena, a curving, columned portico identifies this otherwise inconspicuous palace on a traffic-swept bend of Corso Vittorio Emanuele. In the 1530s, Renaissance architect Baldassare Peruzzi built this new palace for the Massimo family, after their previous dwelling had been destroyed during the Sack of Rome. (High in the papal aristocracy, they claimed an ancestor who had been responsible for the defeat of Hannibal.) If you visit on March 16, you'll be able to go upstairs to visit the family chapel in commemoration of a miracle performed here in 1583 by St. Philip Neri, who is said to have recalled a young member of the family, one Paolo Massimo, from the dead (expect a line). Any other day of the year, though, you'll only be able to view the building from the outside. The palazzo's name comes from the columns from Domitian's Odeon, of which one still stands in the square at the back of the palazzo. ⊠ *Corso Vittorio Emanuele II 141, Piazza Navona.*

Piazza di Pasquino. This tiny piazza takes its name from the figure in the corner, the remnant of an old Roman statue depicting Menelaus. The statue underwent a name change in the 16th century when Pasquino, a cobbler or barber (and part-time satirist), started writing comments around the base. The habit caught on; soon everyone was doing it. The most loquacious of Rome's "talking statues," its lack of arms or face is more than made up for with commentary of any topic of the day. ⊠ *Piazza di Pasquino, Piazza Navona.*

Sant'Agostino. Caravaggio's celebrated *Madonna of the Pilgrims*—which scandalized all of Rome for depicting a kneeling pilgrim all too realistically for the era's tastes, with dirt on the soles of his feet, and the Madonna standing in a less-than-majestic pose in a dilapidated doorway—is in the first chapel on the left. At the third column down the nave, admire Raphael's blue-robed *Isaiah*, said to be inspired by Michelangelo's prophets on the Sistine ceiling (Raphael, with the help of Bramante, had taken the odd peek at the master's original against strict orders of secrecy). Directly below is Sansovino's Leonardo-influenced sculpture, *St. Anne and the Madonna with Child*. As you leave, in a niche just inside the door, is the sculpted *Madonna and Child*, known to the Romans as the "Madonna del Parto" (of Childbirth) and piled high with ex-votos. The artist is Jacopo Tatti, also sometimes confusingly known as Sansovino after his master. ⊠ *Piazza Sant'Agostino, Piazza Navona* ☎ 06/68801962.

Santa Maria in Vallicella/Chiesa Nuova. This church, sometimes known as Chiesa Nuova (New Church), was built toward the end of the 16th century at the urging of Philip Neri and, like Il Gesù, is a product of the fervor of the Counter-Reformation. It has a sturdy Baroque interior, all white and gold, with ceiling frescoes by Pietro da Cortona depicting a miracle reputed to have occurred during the church's construction: the Virgin and strong-armed angels hold up the broken roof to prevent it from crashing down upon the congregation below. The Church is most famous for its three magnificent altarpieces by Rubens. ⊠ *Piazza della Chiesa Nuova, Corso Vittorio Emanuele II, Piazza Navona* ☎ 06/6875289 ⊕ *www.vallicella.org.*

CAMPO DE' FIORI

In the mornings, Campo de' Fiori, an evocative piazza ringed by medieval palazzi, is one of the city's most popular markets. The market, like the square, is no longer a mainly local haunt—some stalls now hawk souvenirs and T-shirts, and tour groups are as common as bag-toting nonnas—it remains one of the most beloved, and bustling, institutions in the centro storico. In the evening until past midnight, outdoor bars and restaurants transform this humble square into a hot spot.

TOP ATTRACTIONS

Campo de' Fiori. A bustling marketplace in the morning (Monday–Saturday 8–2) and a trendy meeting place the rest of the day and night, this piazza has plenty of earthy charm. Just after lunchtime all the fruit and vegetable vendors disappear, and this so-called *piazza trasformista* takes on another identity, becoming a circus of bars particularly favored by study-abroads, tourists, and young expats. Brooding over the piazza is a hooded statue of the philosopher Giordano Bruno, who was burned at the stake here in 1600 for heresy, one of many victims of the Roman Inquisition. ⊠ *Intersection of Via dei Baullari, Via Giubbonari, Via del Pellegrino, and Piazza della Cancelleria, Campo de' Fiori.*

Fodor'sChoice
★

Il Gesù. The mother church of the Jesuits in Rome is the prototype of all Counter-Reformation churches. Considered the first fully Baroque church, it has a spectacular interior that tells a great deal about an era of religious triumph and turmoil. Its architecture influenced ecclesiastical buildings in Rome for more than a century (the overall design was

Continued on page 133

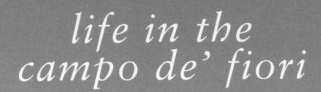

life in the
campo de' fiori

A small square with two personalities as
different as day and night, the Campo
de' Fiori is Rome's mecca for people
with a picky purpose—whether it is
picking out food or picking out that
night's amorous adventure.

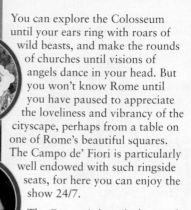

You can explore the Colosseum until your ears ring with roars of wild beasts, and make the rounds of churches until visions of angels dance in your head. But you won't know Rome until you have paused to appreciate the loveliness and vibrancy of the cityscape, perhaps from a table on one of Rome's beautiful squares. The Campo de' Fiori is particularly well endowed with such ringside seats, for here you can enjoy the show 24/7.

The Campo is heavily foot trafficked at any given hour, whether for its sunlit market stalls or its moon-shadowed cobblestones. If you only have 24 hours in Rome (and especially if the past 20 have been dedicated to sightseeing), take a breather here and inhale a truly Roman social scene, no matter what time of day or night.

In the daytime, the piazza is a buzzing produce market where ancient vendors shout out the day's specialties and caffè-goers gossip behind newspapers while enjoying the morning's cappuccino. In the late afternoon, the Campo de' Fiori transforms into the ultimate hangout with overflowing bars, caffès, and restaurants filled with locals and tourists all vying for the perfect seat to check out passersby.

Campo life is decidedly without pause. The only moment of repose happens in the very wee hours of the morning when the remaining stragglers start the stumble home and just before the produce-filled mini-trucks begin their magnificent march in to the square. At any given hour, you will always find something going on in Campo, the "living room" of today's Rome.

By Erica Firpo

5

IN FOCUS LIFE IN THE CAMPO DE' FIORI

24 HOURS IN THE CAMPO DE' FIORI

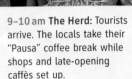

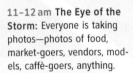

5–6 am The Flight of the Bumble-Bees: *Ape* ("bee" in Italian) trucks file into the Campo to unload the day's goods. These mini-trucks are very cute, no? *Ao! Claudia che sta a fa?!* ("Hey, Claudia how ya doin'"), Daniele yells across to Claudia as market guys and gals joke around. Good lessons in Roman slang.

7–8 am The Calm before the Storm: The only time the Campo seems a bit sluggish, as stands have just opened, shoppers have yet to arrive, and everyone is just waking up. Market locals gather before heading off to work and school.

9–10 am The Herd: Tourists arrive. The locals take their "Pausa" coffee break while shops and late-opening caffès set up.

11–12 am The Eye of the Storm: Everyone is taking photos—photos of food, market-goers, vendors, models, caffè-goers, anything.

1–2 pm Pranzo: Lunchtime in the Campo. Everyone is looking for an outdoor table. Meanwhile, the vendors start to pack up.

3–4 pm The Denoument: The Campo is officially shutting down, marked by the notable odor of Campo refuse and the loud din of the cleaning trucks. This is perhaps the absolute worst time to be in Campo. When the trucks depart, they leave the square to parents and toddlers.

5–6 pm Gelato Time: Shoppers and strollers replace replace market-goers. The first of Campo's many musicians begin warming up for the evening's concert. Favorites always include: "Guantanamera," "My Way," and "Volare."

7–8 pm Happy Hours:
The pre-aperitivi people enjoy the cocktail before the cocktails. Always good for the punctual. By 6 aperitivi have been served. Are you "in" or "out"? Outside means picking any of the umbrella *tavoli* that line the piazza. If you prefer to be on the sly, try an indoor *enoteca*. Late-comers arrive for a last sip of wine before deciding where to dine.

9–10 pm Dining Hour:
Dining in Rome is an all-evening experience. It's common custom to argue for a half-hour about the perfect restaurant.

11 pm–12 am After-dinner Drinks: Everyone moves back to the Campo for a drink (or many). Drunkenness can include catcalls, stiletto falls, volleyed soccer balls, and the cops (polizia or carabinieri, take your pick).

1–2 am Time to Go Home:
Bars begin to shut down, with lingering kisses and hugs ("Dude, I love you!"). Clean-up crews come back. The din returns, this time as trucks clean up broken bottles and plastic cups.

3–4 am Some stragglers are still hanging around. For the first time Campo de' Fiori is silent, to the delight of the residents around it. They have to hurry…because the Ape (see 5 am) are pressing to get back in.

Piazza Campo de' Fiori

Via del Baullari

To Via del Giubbonari

5

IN FOCUS LIFE IN THE CAMPO DE' FIORI

THE COGNOSCENTI'S CAMPO

WHAT TO KNOW

No longer a simple flower market, from Monday through Saturday mornings the Campo de' Fiori is Rome's most famous produce market. This is where you'll find standard Italian favorites (like Pacchino tomatoes, peppers, and eggplant), as well as seasonal delicacies such as *puntarelle* (a variety of chicory) and Roman artichokes. There are also meat, regional cheese, and homegrown honey vendors. The *bancarelle* (tchotchke stands) sell T-shirts, purses, bangles, and cookware; sometimes they're good for souvenir shopping.

This is one of the best places for people-watching in Rome so hang out for a while. The many bars and caffès may look different but all have very similar menus and similar food. Mornings mean coffee and pastries; in the evening there is wine, beer, and mixed drinks. Most also have Wi-Fi.

A word of advice: leave the high heels at home—the uneven cobblestones can be treacherous.

It's worth noting that the Campo de' Fiori and the adjacent Piazza Farnese have two of the best newspaper kiosks for international publications; so if you want something to read while you sip your coffee, stop by.

by Vignola, the facade by della Porta) and was exported by the Jesuits throughout the rest of Europe. Though consecrated as early as 1584, the interior of the church wasn't decorated for another 100 years. It was originally intended that the interior be left plain to the point of austerity—but, when it was finally embellished, the mood had changed and no expense was spared. Its interior drips with gold and lapis lazuli, gold and precious marbles, gold and more gold, all covered by a fantastically painted ceiling by Baciccia. Unfortunately, the church is also one of Rome's most crepuscular, so its visual magnificence is considerably dulled by lack of light.

The architectural significance of Il Gesù extends far beyond the splendid interior. As the first of the great Counter-Reformation churches, it was put up after the Council of Trent (1545–63) had signaled the determination of the Roman Catholic Church to fight back against the Reformed Protestant heretics of northern Europe. The church decided to do so through the use of overwhelming pomp and majesty, in an effort to woo believers. As a harbinger of ecclesiastical spectacle, Il Gesù spawned imitations throughout Italy and the other Catholic countries of Europe as well as the Americas.

The most striking element is the ceiling, which is covered with frescoes that swirl down from on high to merge with painted stucco figures at the base, the illusion of space in the two-dimensional painting becoming the reality of three dimensions in the sculpted figures. Baciccia, their painter, achieved extraordinary effects in these frescoes, especially in the *Triumph of the Holy Name of Jesus,* over the nave. Here, the figures representing evil cast out of heaven and seem to be hurtling down onto the observer. To appreciate in detail, the spectacle is best viewed through a specially tilted mirror in the nave.

The founder of the Jesuit order himself is buried in the Chapel of St. Ignatius, in the left-hand transept. This is surely the most sumptuous Baroque altar in Rome; as is typical, the enormous globe of lapis lazuli that crowns it is really only a shell of lapis over a stucco base—after all, Baroque decoration prides itself on achieving stunning effects and illusions. The heavy, bronze altar rail by architect Carlo Fontana is in keeping with the surrounding opulence. ⊠ *Piazza del Ges, off Via del Plebiscito, Campo de' Fiori* ☎ *06/697001* ⊕ *www.chiesadelgesu.org.*

Fodor's Choice **Palazzo Farnese.** The most beautiful Renaissance palace in Rome, the
★ Palazzo Farnese is fabled for the Galleria Carracci, whose ceiling is to the Baroque age what the Sistine ceiling is to the Renaissance. The Farnese family rose to great power and wealth during the Renaissance, in part because of the favor Pope Alexander VI showed to the beautiful Giulia Farnese. The massive palace was begun when, with Alexander's aid, Giulia's brother became cardinal; it was further enlarged on his election as Pope Paul III in 1534. The uppermost frieze decorations and main window overlooking the piazza are the work of Michelangelo, who also designed part of the courtyard, as well as the graceful arch over Via Giulia at the back. The facade on Piazza Farnese has geometrical brick configurations that have long been thought to hold some occult meaning. When looking up at the palace, try to catch a glimpse

of the splendid frescoed ceilings, including the **Galleria Carracci** vault painted by Annibale Carracci between 1597 and 1604. The Carracci gallery depicts the loves of the gods, a supremely pagan theme that the artist painted in a swirling style that announced the birth of the Baroque. Other opulent salons are among the largest in Rome, including the Salon of Hercules, which has an overpowering replica of the ancient *Farnese Hercules,* front and center. The French Embassy, which occupies the palace, offers tours (in English) on Wednesdays; book at least eight days in advance through the website, and bring photo ID. ✉ *French Embassy, Servizio Culturale, Piazza Farnese 67, Campo de' Fiori* ☎ *06/686011* ⊕ *www.inventerrome.com* ▨ *€9.*

Palazzo Spada. In this neighborhood of huge, austere palaces, Palazzo Spada strikes an almost frivolous note, with its upper stories covered with stuccos and statues and its pretty ornament-encrusted courtyard. While the palazzo houses an impressive collection of old-master paintings, it's most famous for its trompe-l'oeil garden gallery, a delightful example of the sort of architectural games rich Romans of the 17th century found irresistible. Even if you don't go into the gallery, step into the courtyard and look through the glass window of the library to the colonnaded corridor in the adjacent courtyard. See—or seem to see—an 8-meter-long gallery quadrupled in depth, a sort of optical telescope taking the Renaissance's art of perspective to another level, as it stretches out for a great distance with a large statue at the end. In fact the distance is an illusion: the corridor grows progressively narrower and the columns progressively smaller as they near the statue, which is just two feet tall. The Baroque period is known for special effects, and this is rightly one of the most famous. It was long thought that Borromini was responsible for this ruse; it's now known that it was designed by an Augustinian priest, Giovanni Maria da Bitonto. Upstairs is a seignorial picture gallery with the paintings shown as they would have been, piled on top of each other clear to the ceiling. Outstanding works include Brueghel's *Landscape with Windmills,* Titian's *Musician,* and Andrea del Sarto's *Visitation.* Look for the fact-sheets that have descriptive notes about the objects in each room. ✉ *Piazza Capo di Ferro 13, Campo de' Fiori* ☎ *06/6861158* ⊕ *www.galleriaborghese. it* ▨ *€5* ⊗ *Closed Tues.*

Sant'Andrea della Valle. Topped by the highest dome in Rome after St. Peter's (designed by Maderno), this huge and imposing 17th-century church is remarkably balanced in design. Fortunately, its facade, which had turned a sooty gray from pollution, has been cleaned to a near-sparkling white. Use one of the handy mirrors to examine the early-17th-century frescoes by Domenichino in the choir vault and those by Lanfranco in the dome. One of the earliest ceilings done in full Baroque style, its upward vortex was influenced by Correggio's dome in Parma, of which Lanfranco was also a citizen. (Bring a few coins to light the paintings, which can be very dim.) The three massive paintings of Saint Andrew's martyrdom are by Maria Preti (1650–51). Richly marbled and decorated chapels flank the nave, and in such a space, Puccini set the first act of *Tosca.* ✉ *Piazza Vidoni 6, Corso Vittorio Emanuele II, Campo de' Fiori* ☎ *06/6861339.*

Fodor'sChoice
★ **Via Giulia.** Still a Renaissance-era diorama and one of Rome's most exclusive addresses, Via Giulia was the first street in Rome since ancient times to be laid out in a straight line. Named for Pope Julius II (of Sistine Chapel fame), who commissioned it in the early 1500s as part of a scheme to open up a grandiose approach to St. Peter's Basilica (using funds from the taxation of prostitutes), it became flanked with elegant churches and palaces. Though the pope's plans to change the face of the city were only partially completed, Via Giulia became an important thoroughfare in Renaissance Rome. Today, after more than four centuries, it remains the "salon of Rome," address of choice for Roman aristocrats, although controversy has arisen about a recent change—the decision to add a large parking lot along one side of the street—that meant steamrolling through ancient and medieval ruins underneath. A stroll will reveal elegant palaces and churches (one, **San Eligio,** on the little side street Via di Sant'Eligio, was designed by Raphael himself). The area around Via Giulia is wonderful to wander through and get the feel of daily life as carried on in a centuries-old setting. Among the buildings that merit your attention are **Palazzo Sacchetti** (Via Giulia 66), with an imposing stone portal (inside are some of Rome's grandest state rooms, still, after 300 years, the private quarters of the Marchesi Sacchetti), and the forbidding brick building that housed the **Carceri Nuove** (New Prison; Via Giulia 52), Rome's prison for more than two centuries and now the offices of Direzione Nazionale Antimafia. Near the bridge that arches over the southern end of Via Giulia is the church of **Santa Maria dell'Orazione e Morte** (Holy Mary of Prayer and Death), with stone skulls on its door. These are a symbol of a confraternity that was charged with burying the bodies of the unidentified dead found in the city streets. Home since 1927 to the Hungarian Academy, the **Palazzo Falconieri** (Via Giulia 1; 06/6889671) was designed by Borromini—note the architect's rooftop belvedere adorned with statues of the family "falcons," best viewed from around the block along the Tiber embankment. (The Borromini-designed salons and loggia are sporadically open as part of a guided tour; call the Academy for information.) Remnant of a master plan by Michelangelo, the arch over the street was meant to link massive Palazzo Farnese, on the east side of Via Giulia, with the building across the street and a bridge to the Villa Farnesina, directly across the river. Finally, on the right and rather green with age, dribbles that star of many a postcard, the Fontana del Mascherone. ⊠ *Via Giulia, between Piazza dell'Oro and Piazza San Vincenzo Palloti, Campo de' Fiori.*

5

WORTH NOTING

San Giovanni dei Fiorentini. Imbued with the supreme grace of the Florentine Renaissance, this often-overlooked church dedicated to Florence's patron saint, John the Baptist, stands in what was the heart of the Florentine colony in Rome's *centro storico.* Many of these Florentines were goldsmiths, bankers, and money changers who contributed to the building of the church. Talented goldsmith and sculptor Benvenuto Cellini of Florence, known for his vindictive nature as much as for his genius, lived nearby. While the church was designed by Sansovino,

Raphael (yes, he was also an architect) was among those who competed for this commission. Today, the church interior makes you feel you have wandered inside a perfect Renaissance space, one so harmonious it seems to be a 3-D Raphael painting. Borromini executed a splendid altar for the Falconieri family chapel in the choir. He's buried under the dome, despite the fact that those who committed suicide normally were refused a Christian burial. ⊠ *Via Acciaioli 2, Piazza dell'Oro, Campo de' Fiori* ☎ *06/68892059* ⊕ *www.sangiovannideifiorentini.net.*

JEWISH GHETTO

Although today most of Rome's Jews live outside the Ghetto, the area remains the spiritual and cultural home of Jewish Rome, and that heritage permeates its small commercial area of Judaica shops, kosher bakeries, and restaurants. The Jewish Ghetto was established by papal decree in the 16th century. It was by definition a closed community, where Roman Jews lived under lock and key until Italian unification in 1870. In 1943–44, the already small Jewish population there was decimated by deportations.

The turn-of-the-20th-century synagogue, with its museum dedicated to the history of Jewish Rome, is a must for understanding the Ghetto. Tight, teeming alleys lead from there up to Giacomo della Porta's unmistakable Fontana delle Tartarughe; nearby is the picture-perfect Palazzo Mattei. Via Portico d'Ottavia is a walk through the olden days. Most businesses in the Ghetto observe the Jewish Sabbath, so it's a ghost town on Saturday. At its east end, the street leads down to a path past the 1st-century Teatro di Marcello. The Tiber River separates the Ghetto and Trastevere, with the lovely Isola Tiberina (Tiber Island) in the middle. Cross the river via the Ponte Fabricio, the oldest bridge in Rome.

TOP ATTRACTIONS

Fodor'sChoice
★ **Crypta Balbi.** The fourth component of the magnificent collections of the Museo Nazionale Romano (and visitable on the same ticket), this museum is unusual in how many periods of Roman history it represents. The crypt is part of the Balbus Theater complex (13 BC) and other parts of the complex are from the medieval period, up through the 20th century. The written explanations accompanying the well-lit exhibits are excellent, and this museum is a popular field trip for teachers and school groups. ⊠ *Via delle Botteghe Oscure 31, Jewish Ghetto* ☎ *06/39967700* ⊕ *www.coopculture.it* ⊠ *€7, includes 3 other Museo Nazionale Romano sites (Palazzo Altemps, Palazzo Massimo, Museo Diocleziano); €10 if any one of them has a special exhibit.* Ⓜ *Bus Nos. 64 and 40, Tram No. 8.*

Fodor'sChoice
★ **Fontana delle Tartarughe.** Designed by Giacomo della Porta in 1581 and sculpted by Taddeo Landini, this 16th-century fountain, set in venerable Piazza Mattei, is one of Rome's most charming. The focus of the fountain is four bronze boys, each grasping a dolphin spouting water into a marble shell. Bronze turtles held in the boys' hands drink from

the upper basin. The turtles are thought to have been added in the 17th century by Bernini. ⊠ *Piazza Mattei, Jewish Ghetto.*

Fodor's Choice
★

Palazzo Mattei di Giove. Graceful and opulent, the arcaded, multistory courtyard of this palazzo is a masterpiece of turn-of-the-17th-century style. Designed by Carlo Maderno, it is a veritable panoply of sculpted busts, heroic statues, sculpted reliefs, and Paleo-Christian epigrams, all collected by Marchese Asdrubale Mattei. Inside are various scholarly institutes, including the Centro Studi Americani (Center for American Studies, centrostudiamericani.org), which also contains a library of American books. Salons in the palace (not usually open to visitors) are decorated with frescoes by Cortona, Lanfranco, and Domenichino. ⊠ *Via Michelangelo Caetani 32, other entrance in Via dei Funari, Jewish Ghetto* ☎ 06/68801613 *Centro Studi Americani.*

Fodor's Choice
★

Portico d'Ottavia. Looming over the Jewish Ghetto, this huge portico enclosure, with a few surviving columns, is one of the area's most picturesque set pieces, with the time-stained church of Sant'Angelo in Pescheria (seemingly under perpetual restoration) built right into its ruins. Named by Augustus in honor of his sister Octavia, it was originally 390 feet wide and 433 feet long, encompassed two temples, a meeting hall, and a library, and served as a kind of grandiose entrance foyer for the adjacent Teatro di Marcello. The ruins of the portico became Rome's *pescheria* (fish market) during the Middle Ages. A stone plaque on a pillar (a copy; the original is in the Musei Capitolini) states in Latin that the head of any fish surpassing the length of the plaque was to be cut off "up to the first fin" and given to the city fathers, or else the vendor was to pay a fine of 10 gold florins. The heads were used to make fish soup and were considered a great delicacy. ⊠ *Via Tribuna di Campitelli 6, Jewish Ghetto.*

NEED A BREAK

✕ **Franco e Cristina.** The kosher pizza at this fast food joint is served by the slice and is some of the crispiest in town. There are a few tables outside. ⊠ *Via Portico d'Ottavia 5, Jewish Ghetto* ☎ 06/687–9262.

Santa Maria di Aracoeli. Sitting atop its 124 steps, Santa Maria di Aracoeli perches on the north slope of the Capitoline Hill. The church rests on the site of the temple of Juno Moneta (Admonishing Juno), which also housed the Roman mint (hence the origin of the word "money"). According to legend, it was here that the Sibyl, a prophetess, predicted to Augustus the coming of a Redeemer. He in turn responded by erecting an altar, the Ara Coeli (Altar of Heaven). This was eventually replaced by a Benedictine monastery, and then a church, which was passed in 1250 to the Franciscans, who restored and enlarged it in Romanesque-Gothic style. Today, the Aracoeli is best known for the **Santo Bambino,** a much-revered olivewood figure of the Christ Child (today a copy of the 15th-century original that was stolen in 1994). At Christmas, everyone pays homage to the "Bambinello" as children recite poems from a miniature pulpit. In true Roman style, the church interior is a historical hodgepodge: classical columns and large marble fragments from pagan buildings, as well as a 13th-century Cosmatesque pavement. The richly gilded Renaissance ceiling commemorates the naval victory at Lepanto in 1571 over the Turks. The first chapel on the right is noteworthy for Pinturicchio's frescoes of San Bernardino of Siena (1486). ⊠ *Via del Teatro di Marcello, at top of steep stairway, Piazza Venezia* ☎ *06/69763838* Ⓜ *Colosseo; Bus Nos. 44, 160, 170, 175, and 186.*

Sinagoga. This synagogue has been the city's largest Jewish temple, and a Roman landmark with its aluminium dome, since its 1904 construction. The building also houses the Jewish Museum, with its precious ritual objects and other exhibits, which document the uninterrupted presence of a Jewish community in the city for nearly 22 centuries. Until the 16th century, Jews were esteemed citizens of Rome. Among them were bankers and physicians to the popes, who had themselves given permission for the construction of synagogues. But in 1555, during the Counter-Reformation, Pope Paul IV decreed the building of the walls of the Ghetto, confining the Jews to this small area and imposing a series of restrictions, some of which continued to be enforced until 1870. For security reasons, guided visits are mandatory, and tours in English start every hour at about 10 minutes past the hour; entrance to the synagogue is through the museum located in Via Catalana (*Largo 16 Ottobre 1943*). ⊠ *Lungotevere Cenci 15, Jewish Ghetto* ☎ *06/68400661* ⊕ *www.museoebraico.roma.it* 🖃 *€11* ☉ *Closed Sat.* Ⓜ *Bus Nos. 46, 64, and 87; Tram No. 8.*

Teatro di Marcello. Begun by Julius Caesar and completed by the emperor Augustus in 13 BC, this theater could house around 14,000 spectators. Like other Roman monuments, it was transformed into a fortress during the Middle Ages. During the Renaissance, it was converted into a residence by the Savelli, one of the city's noble families. Today the archaeological park around the theater is used as a summer venue for open-air classical music concerts. ⊠ *Via del Teatro di Marcello, Jewish Ghetto* ☎ *06/87131590 for concert info* ⊕ *www.tempietto.it for concert info.*

PIAZZA DI SPAGNA

Getting Oriented

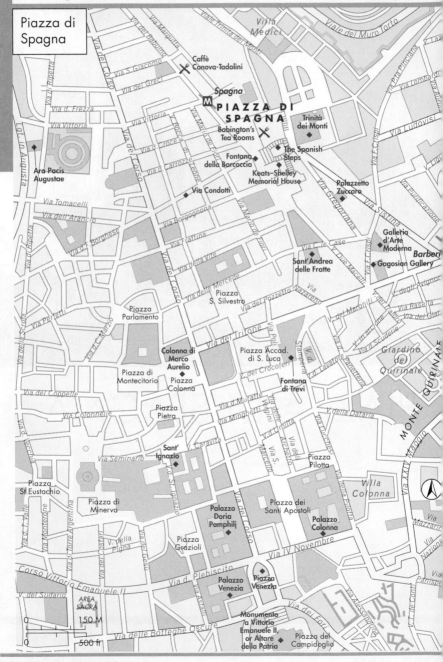

Piazza di Spagna

Caffè Conova-Tadolini

Spagna

PIAZZA DI SPAGNA

Trinità dei Monti

Babington's Tea Rooms

The Spanish Steps

Fontana della Barcaccia

Keats–Shelley Memorial House

Ara Pacis Augustae

Palazzetto Zuccaro

Via Condotti

Galleria d'Arte Moderna

Barberi

Sant'Andrea delle Fratte

Gagosian Gallery

Piazza S. Silvestro

Piazza Parlamento

Colonna di Marco Aurelio

Piazza Accad. di S. Luca

Piazza di Montecitorio

Piazza Colonna

Fontana di Trevi

Piazza Pietra

Giardino del Quirinale

MONTE QUIRINALE

Sant' Ignazio

Piazza Pilotta

Piazza St. Eustachio

Villa Colonna

Piazza di Minerva

Palazzo Doria Pamphilj

Piazza dei Santi Apostoli

Palazzo Colonna

Piazza Grazioli

Palazzo Venezia

Piazza Venezia

AREA SACRA

Monumento a Vittorio Emanuele II, or Altare della Patria

Piazza del Campidoglio

Villa Medici

0 ___ 150 M
0 ___ 500 ft

TOP REASONS TO GO

Trevi Fountain: In the pantheon of waterworks, this is Elvis—overblown, flashy, and reliably thronged by legions of fans.

The Spanish Steps: Sprawl seductively on the world's most celebrated stairway—everyone's doing it.

The Ceiling of San Ignazio: Stand beneath the stupendous ceiling of San Ignazio—Rome's most splendiferous Baroque church—and, courtesy of painter-priest Fra Andrea Pozzo, prepare to be transported heavenward.

Fabulous Palazzos: Visit the Palazzo Doria Pamphilj and the Palazzo Colonna for an intimate look at the homes of Rome's 17th-century grandees.

Luxe Shopping on Via Condotti: You can get from Bulgari to Gucci to Valentino to Ferragamo with no effort at all.

MAKING THE MOST OF YOUR TIME

This neighborhood is chock-full of postcard-worthy sights, including the Spanish Steps, the Trevi Fountain, and the Victor Emanuel monument (Il Vittoriano), which means a rewarding walk but plenty of tourists. Consider starting early or taking an evening stroll, when many of the area's must-sees (including the Trevi Fountain) are lighted. Shoppers flock to Via del Corso, though in recent years the street has been given over mostly to multinational chains. Poke through backstreets instead; Rome's swankiest boutiques and designers are on Via del Babuino and the surrounding streets.

GETTING HERE

The Piazza di Spagna is a short walk from Piazza del Popolo, the Pantheon, and the Trevi Fountain. One of Rome's handiest subway stations, Spagna, is tucked just left of the steps. Buses No. 117 (from the Colosseum) and No. 119 (from Piazza del Popolo) hum through the area; the latter tootles up Via del Babuino, famed for its shopping.

6

Sightseeing
★★★★★

Nightlife
★

Dining
★★★★★

Lodging
★★★★★

Shopping
★★★★★

In spirit, and in fact, this area of Rome is grandiose. The overblown Vittoriano monument, the labyrinthine treasure-chest palaces of Rome's surviving aristocracy—even the diamond-draped denizens of Via Condotti—all embody the exuberant ego of a city at the center of its own universe. Here's where you'll see ladies in fur as you walk through a thousand snapshots while climbing the famous Spanish Steps.

Updated
by Agnes
Crawford

At the top of everyone's sightseeing list is that great Baroque confection, the Trevi Fountain. Since pickpockets favor this tourist-heavy spot, be particularly aware as you withdraw that wallet. Once you've chucked your change in the fountain, follow the crowds and get ready to take some serious time to explore this neighborhood.

If Rome has a Main Street, it's Via del Corso, which is often jammed with swarms of Roman teenagers, in from the city's outlying districts for a ritual stroll that resembles a strutting migration of lemmings in blue jeans. Along this thoroughfare it's easy to forget that the gray and stolid atmosphere comes partially from the enormous palaces lining both sides of the street. Many were built over the past 300 years by princely families who wanted to secure front-row seats for the frantic antics of Carnevale. But once you make it past their entrances, you'll discover some of Rome's grandest 17th- and 18th-century treasures, including Baroque ballrooms, glittering churches, and great Old Master paintings.

Via del Corso begins at noisy, chaotic Piazza Venezia, the imperial-size hub of all this ostentation, presided over by Il Vittoriano, also known as the Altare della Patria (Altar of the Nation)—or, less piously, "the typewriter," "the wedding cake," or "the Eighth Hill of Rome." Sitting grandly off the avenue are the Palazzo Doria Pamphilj and the Palazzo Colonna, two of the city's great art collections housed in magnificent family palaces.

Extending just east of Via del Corso, but miles away in style, Piazza di Spagna and its surrounding streets are where the elite meet. The piazza's main draw remains the 18th-century Spanish Steps, which connect the ritzy shops at the bottom of the hill with the ritzy hotels (and one lovely church) at the top. The reward for climbing the *scalinata* is a dizzying view of central Rome. Because the steps face west, the views are especially good around sunset.

TOP ATTRACTIONS

Fodor's Choice
★

Ara Pacis Augustae (*Altar of Augustan Peace*). This vibrant monument of the Imperial age is housed in one of Rome's newest architectural landmarks: a gleaming, rectangular glass-and-travertine structure designed by American architect Richard Meier. Overlooking the Tiber on one side and the ruins of the marble-clad **Mausoleo di Augusto** (Mausoleum of Augustus) on the other, the result is a serene, luminous oasis right in the center of Rome. The altar itself dates back to 13 BC; it was commissioned to celebrate the Pax Romana, the era of peace ushered in by Augustus's military victories. Like all ancient Roman monuments of this kind, you have to imagine its spectacular and moving relief sculptures painted in vibrant colors, now long gone. The reliefs on the short sides portray myths associated with Rome's founding and glory; the long sides display a procession of the imperial family. It's fun to try to play who's who—although half of his body is missing, Augustus is identifiable as the first full figure at the procession's head on the south-side frieze—but academics still argue over exact identifications of other figures. The small museum has a model and useful information about the Ara Pacis's original location and the surrounding Augustan monuments. ⊠ *Lungotevere in Augusta, Piazza di Spagna* ☎ *06/0608* ⊕ *www.arapacis.it* ⊠ *€13* Ⓜ *Flaminio.*

Keats-Shelley Memorial House. Sent to Rome in a last-ditch attempt to treat his consumptive condition, English Romantic poet John Keats lived—and died—in this house at the foot of the Spanish Steps. At that point, this was the heart of the colorful bohemian quarter of Rome that was especially favored by the English. Keats had become celebrated through such poems as "Ode to a Nightingale" and "Endymion," but his trip to Rome was fruitless. He took his last breath here on February 23, 1821, at only 25, forevermore the epitome of the doomed poet. In this "Casina di Keats," you can visit his rooms, though all his furnishings were burned after his death, as a sanitary measure by the local authorities. You'll also find a rather quaint collection of memorabilia of English literary figures of the period—Lord Byron, Percy Bysshe Shelley, Joseph Severn, and Leigh Hunt, as well as Keats—and an exhaustive library of works on the Romantics. ⊠ *Piazza di Spagna 26, Piazza di Spagna* ☎ *06/6784235* ⊕ *www.keats-shelley-house.org* ⊠ *€5* ⊗ *Closed Sun.* Ⓜ *Spagna.*

Monumento a Vittorio Emanuele II, or Altare della Patria (*Victor Emmanuel Monument, or Altar of the Nation*). The huge white mass of the "Vittoriano" is an inescapable landmark—Romans say you can only avoid looking at it if you're actually standing on it. Some have likened it to

Rome's Fountains

Anyone who's thrown a coin backward over their shoulder into the Fontana di Trevi to ensure a return to Rome appreciates the magic of the city's fountains. From the magnificence of the Fontana dei Quattro Fiumi in Piazza Navona to the graceful caprice of the Fontana delle Tartarughe in the Jewish Ghetto, the water-spouting sculptures seem as essential to their piazzas as the cobblestones and ocher buildings that surround them.

Rome's original fountains date back to ancient times, when they were part of the city's remarkable aqueduct system. But from AD 537 to 1562, the waterworks were in disrepair, and the city's fountains lay dry and crumbling. Romans were left to draw their water from the Tiber and from wells. During the Renaissance, the popes brought running water back to the city as a means of currying political favor. To mark the restoration of the Virgin Aqueduct, architect Giacomo della Porta designed 18 unassuming, functional fountains. Each consisted of a large basin with two or three levels of smaller basins in the center, which were built and placed throughout the city at points along the water line.

Although nearly all of della Porta's fountains remain, their spare Renaissance design is virtually unrecognizable. With the Baroque era, most

were elaborately redecorated with dolphins, obelisks, and sea monsters. Of this next generation of Baroque fountaineers, the most famous is Gian Lorenzo Bernini. Bernini's writhing, muscular creatures of myth adorn most of Rome's most visible fountains, including the Fontana di Trevi (perhaps named for the three streets, or "*tre vie*," that converge at its piazza); the Fontana del Nettuno, with its tritons, in Piazza Barberini; and, in Piazza Navona, the Fontana dei Quattro Fiumi, whose hulking figures represented the four great rivers of the known world: the Nile, the Ganges, the Danube, and the Plata.

The most common type of fountain in Rome, however, is a kind rarely noted by visitors: the small, inconspicuous drinking fountains that burble away from side-street walls, old stone niches, and fire hydrant–like installations on street corners. You can drink this water, and many of these *fontanelle* even have pipes fitted with a little hole from which water shoots up when you hold your hand under the main spout.

To combine the glorious Roman fountain with a drink of water, head to Piazza di Spagna, where the Barcaccia fountain is outfitted with spouts from which you can wet your whistle.

a huge wedding cake; others, to an immense typewriter. Though not held in the highest esteem by present-day citizens, it was the source of great civic pride at the time of its construction at the turn of the 20th century. To create this elaborate marble monster and the vast piazza on which it stands, architects blithely destroyed many ancient and medieval buildings and altered the slope of the Campidoglio (Capitoline Hill), which abuts it. Built to honor the unification of Italy and the nation's first king, Victor Emmanuel II, it also shelters the eternal flame at the tomb of Italy's Unknown Soldier killed during World War I. The flame is guarded day and night by sentinels, while inside the building there is the (rather dry) Institute of the History of the Risorgimento. You can't avoid the Monumento, so enjoy neo-imperial grandiosity at its most bombastic.

The views from the top are some of Rome's most panoramic. The only way up is by elevator (located to the right as you face the monument); stop at the museum entrances (to the left and right of the structure) to get a pamphlet identifying the sculpture groups on the monument itself and the landmarks you will be able to see once at the top. Opposite the monument, note the enclosed olive-green wooden veranda fronting the palace on the corner of Via del Plebiscito and Via del Corso. For the many years that she lived in Rome, Napoléon's mother had a fine view of the local goings-on from this spot. The monument also houses the Caffetteria Italia, which has great views and follows the same hours as the elevator. ✉ *Entrances on Piazza Venezia, Piazza del Campidoglio, and Via di San Pietro in Carcere, Piazza di Spagna* ☎ *06/0608* ⊕ *www.060608.it* ✍ *Free, elevator €7* Ⓜ *Colosseo.*

Fodor's Choice ★ **Palazzo Colonna.** Rome's grandest family built themselves Rome's grandest private palazzo, a fusion of 17th- and 18th-century buildings on a spot they have occupied for a millennium. It's so immense that it faces Piazza dei Santi Apostoli on one side and the Quirinal Hill on the other (a little bridge over Via della Pilotta links the palace with the gardens on the hill). While still home to some Colonna patricians, the palace also holds the family picture gallery, which is open to the public on Saturday mornings. The gallery is itself a setting of aristocratic grandeur; you might recognize the **Sala Grande** as the site where Audrey Hepburn meets the press in *Roman Holiday.* At one end looms the ancient red marble column (*colonna* in Italian), which is the family's emblem; above the vast room is the spectacular ceiling fresco of the Battle of Lepanto painted by Giovanni Coli and Filippo Gherardi in 1675—the center scene almost puts the computer-generated special effects of Hollywood to shame. Adding redundant luster to the opulently stuccoed and frescoed salons are works by Poussin, Tintoretto, and Veronese, and a number of portraits of illustrious members of the family such as Vittoria Colonna, Michelangelo's muse and longtime friend, and Marcantonio Colonna, who led the papal forces in the great naval victory at Lepanto in 1577. Lost in the array of madonnas, saints, goddesses, popes, and cardinals is Annibale Carracci's lonely *Beaneater,* spoon at the ready and front teeth missing. (As W. H. Auden put it, "Grub first, art later.") At noon, there's a guided tour in English, included in your entrance fee. The gallery also boasts a caffè with a pleasant terrace when weather permits. ✉ *Via della Pilotta 17, Piazza di Spagna* ☎ *06/6784350* ⊕ *www.galleriacolonna.it* ✍ *€12* ⊙ *Closed Sun.–Fri.* Ⓜ *Barberini.*

Fodor's Choice ★ **Palazzo Doria Pamphilj.** Along with the Palazzo Colonna and the Galleria Borghese, this spectacular family palace provides the best glimpse of aristocratic Rome. Here, the main attractions are the legendary old master paintings, including treasures by Velázquez and Caravaggio; the splendor of the main galleries; and a unique suite of private family apartments. The beauty of the graceful facade, designed by Gabriele Valvassori in 1730, may escape you unless you take time to cross to the opposite side of the street for a good view. While the foundations of the immense complex of buildings probably date from classical times, the current building dates to the 15th century. It passed through several hands before becoming the property of the Pamphilj family, who married into the famous seafaring Doria family of Genoa in the 18th century. The family still lives in part of the palace.

The gallery contains 550 paintings, including three by Caravaggio—a young *St. John the Baptist, Mary Magdalene,* and the breathtaking *Rest on the Flight to Egypt.* Off the eye-popping **Galleria degli Specchi** (Gallery of Mirrors)—a smaller version of the one at Versailles—are the famous Velázquez *Pope Innocent X,* considered by some historians to be the greatest portrait ever painted, and the Bernini bust of the same Pamphilj pope. Elsewhere you'll find a Titian, a double portrait by Raphael, and some noted 17th-century landscapes by Claude Lorrain and Gaspard Dughet. The delightful audio guide is included in the ticket price. Narrated by the current heir, Prince Jonathan Doria Pamphilj, it provides an intimate family history well worth listening to. ⊠ *Via del Corso 305, Piazza di Spagna* ☎ *06/6797323* ⊕ *www.doriapamphilj.it* ⌨ *€12* Ⓜ *Barberini.*

Palazzetto Zuccaro. This amusing *palazzo* was designed in 1591 by noted painter Federico Zuccaro to form a monster's face. Typical of the outré Mannerist style of the period, the eyes are the house's windows and the entrance portal is through the monster's mouth. Zuccaro (1540–1609)—whose frescoes adorn many Roman churches, including Trinità dei Monti just up the block—sank all of his money into his new home, dying in debt before his curious memorial, as it turned out to be, was completed. Today, it is home to the German state-run Bibliotheca Hertziana, a prestigious fine-arts library. Access is reserved for scholars, but the pristine facade can be admired for free. Leading up to the quaint Piazza della Trinità del Monti, the nearby Via Gregoriana is quite charming and has long been one of Rome's most elegant addresses, home to such residents as 19th-century French painter Ingres and Valentino's first couture salon. ⊠ *Via Gregoriana 30, Piazza di Spagna* ☎ *06/69993242 for Bibliotheca Hertziana* Ⓜ *Spagna.*

Sant'Andrea delle Fratte. Copies may have replaced Bernini's original angels on the Ponte Sant'Angelo, but two of the originals can be found here, to either side of the choir. The door in the right aisle leads into one of Rome's hidden gardens, where orange trees bloom in the cloister. Borromini's fantastic contributions—the dome and a curious bell tower with its droop-winged angels looking out over the city—are best seen from Via di Capo le Case, across Via dei Due Macelli. ⊠ *Via di Sant'Andrea delle Fratte 1, at Via della Mercede, Piazza di Spagna* ☎ *06/6793191* ⊕ *www.santandreadellefratte.it* Ⓜ *Spagna.*

Fodor'sChoice ★ **Sant'Ignazio.** Rome's second Jesuit church, this 17th-century landmark harbors some of the most city's magnificent trompe-l'oeil. To get the full effect of the marvelous illusionistic ceiling by priest-artist Andrea Pozzo, stand on the small disk set into the floor of the nave. The heavenly vision above you, seemingly extending upward almost indefinitely, represents the *Allegory of the Missionary Work of the Jesuits* and is part of Pozzo's cycle of works in this church exalting the early history of the Jesuit

Order, whose founder was the reformer Ignatius of Loyola. The saint soars heavenward, supported by a cast of thousands; not far behind is Saint Francis Xavier, apostle of the Indies, leading a crowd of Eastern converts; a bare-breasted, spear-wielding America in American Indian headdress rides a jaguar; Europe with crown and scepter sits serene on a heftily rumped horse; while a splendid Africa with gold tiara perches on a lucky crocodile. The artist repeated this illusionist technique, so popular in the late 17th century, in the false dome, which is actually a flat canvas—a trompe l'oeil trick used when the budget drained dry. The overall effect of the frescoes is dazzling (be sure to have coins handy for the machine that switches on the lights) and was fully intended to rival that produced by Baciccia in the nearby mother church of Il Gesù. Scattered around the nave are several awe-inspiring altars; their soaring columns, gold-on-gold decoration, and gilded statues make these the last word in splendor. The church is often host to concerts of sacred music performed by choirs from all over the world. Look for posters at the church doors or see www.chiesasantignazio.it for more information. ⊠ *Piazza Sant'Ignazio, Piazza Navona* ☎ *06/6794406* ⊕ *www. chiesasantignazio.it.*

FAMILY
Fodor's Choice
★

The Spanish Steps. The iconic Spanish Steps (often called *la scalinata*—"the staircase"—by Italians) and the Piazza di Spagna from which they ascend both get their names from the Spanish Embassy to the Vatican on the piazza—even though the staircase was built with French funds by an Italian in 1723. In honor of a diplomatic visit by the King of Spain, the hillside was transformed by architect Francesco de Sanctis with a spectacular piece of urban planning to link the church of Trinità dei Monti at the top with the Via Condotti below. In an allusion to the church, the staircase is divided by three landings (beautifully banked by azaleas mid-April–mid-May). For centuries, the scalinata and its neighborhood have welcomed tourists, artists, and writers in search of inspiration—among them Stendhal, Honoré de Balzac, William Makepeace Thackeray, and Byron. Bookending the bottom of the steps are two monuments to the 18th century, when the area was known as the "English Ghetto": to the right, the Keats-Shelley House, and to the left, Babington's Tea Rooms—both beautifully redolent of the era of the Grand Tour. For weary sightseers, there is an elevator at Vicolo del Bottino 8, next to the Metro entrance. (Those with mobility problems should be aware that there is still a small flight of stairs after, however, and that the elevator is sporadically closed for repair.) At the bottom of the steps, Bernini's splendid "Barcaccia" (sinking ship) fountain dates to the early 17th century and is fed by the ancient Aqua Vergine aqueduct; the spouts at either end still provide drinking water. Watch your step—it gets slippery. ⊠ *Piazza di Spagna* Ⓜ *Spagna.*

WORTH NOTING

Colonna di Marco Aurelio. Inspired by Trajan's Column, this 2nd-century-AD column is composed of 27 blocks of marble covered in reliefs recording Marcus Aurelius's victory over the Germanic tribes. A bronze statue of St. Paul, which replaced the effigy of Marcus Aurelius in the

TREVI FOUNTAIN

✉ *Piazza di Trevi, Piazza di Spagna* Ⓜ *Barberini.*

6

TIPS

■ Everyone knows the famous legend that if you throw a coin into the Trevi Fountain you will ensure a return trip to the Eternal City, but not everyone knows how to do it the right way. You must toss a coin with your right hand over your left shoulder, with your back to the fountain. One coin means you'll return to Rome; two, you'll return *and* fall in love; three, you'll return, find love, and marry.

■ The fountain grosses some €600,000 a year, and aside from incidences of opportunists fishing coins from the water, all of the money goes to the Italian Red Cross. Roll up on a Monday morning when the collection is made and you'll find it empty.

■ Even though you might like to reenact Anita Ekberg and Marcello Mastroianni's famous Trevi dip in *La Dolce Vita*, be forewarned that police guard the fountain 24 hours a day to keep out movie buffs and lovebirds alike. (Transgressors risk a fine of up to €500.)

■ Around the corner, the Gelateria San Crispino (*Via della Panetteria 42; 06/6793924*) is the best gelato in the immediate area.

Alive with rushing waters commanded by an imperious Oceanus, the Fontana di Trevi (Trevi Fountain) earned full-fledged iconic status in 1954 when it starred in 20th Century Fox's *Three Coins in the Fountain*. As the first color film in Cinemascope to be filmed on location, it caused practically half of America to pack their bags for the Eternal City.

From the very start, though, the Trevi has been all about theatrical effects. An aquatic marvel in a city filled with them, the fountain's unique drama is largely due to the site: its vast basin is squeezed into the tight confluence of three little streets (the "tre vie," which may give the fountain its name), with cascades emerging as if from the wall of Palazzo Poli. The conceit of a fountain emerging full-force from a palace was first envisioned by Bernini and Pietro da Cortona for Pope Urban VIII's plan to rebuild the fountain, which had earlier marked the end-point of the ancient Acqua Vergine aqueduct, created in 18 BC by Agrippa. Three popes later, under Pope Clement XIII, Nicolo Salvi finally broke ground with his winning design.

Salvi had his cake and ate it, too, for while he dazzles the eye with Baroque pyrotechnics—the sculpted seashells, the roaring sea beasts, the diva-like mermaids—he has slyly incorporated them in a stately triumphal arch (Clement was then restoring Rome's Arch of Constantine). Unfortunately, Salvi did not live to see his masterpiece completed in 1762: working in the culverts of the aqueduct 11 years earlier, he caught a cold and died.

16th century, stands at the top. The column is the centerpiece of Piazza Colonna. ✉ *Piazza Colonna, Piazza di Spagna.*

Fontana della Barcaccia (*Leaky Boat Fountain*). At the foot of the Spanish Steps, this curious, half-sunken boat in Piazza di Spagna is powered by Rome's only surviving ancient aqueduct, the Acqua Vergine. The fountain's design, a ship sinking into the piazza, is a clever solution to low water pressure and was created by fountain genius Gian Lorenzo Bernini, together with his father Pietro. The project was commissioned by Barberini Pope Urban VIII as part of his restoration, which had built up considerably during the 17th century, of the ancient aqueduct in an effort to bring more water to the area,. The bees and suns on the boat are symbols of the Barberini family. Some insist that the Berninis intended the fountain to be a reminder that this part of town was often flooded by the Tiber; others claim that it represents the Ship of the Church; and still others think that it marks the presumed site of the emperor Domitian's water stadium in which sea battles were reenacted in the glory days of the Roman Empire. ✉ *Piazza di Spagna, Piazza di Spagna* Ⓜ *Spagna.*

Gagosian Gallery. One of the most prestigious contemporary galleries in the world opened its Rome branch in 2007 in a former bank. Temporary exhibitions have included mega-stars such as Cy Twombly, Damien Hirst, and Jeff Koons. ✉ *Via Francesco Crispi 16, Piazza di Spagna* ☎ *06/42086498* ⊕ *www.gagosian.com* Ⓜ *Spagna.*

Fodor'sChoice
★
Galleria d'Arte Moderna. The city of Rome's modern art gallery is housed in the 18th-century Convent of the Discalced Carmelites, the perfect spot for the Roman 19th- and 20th-century paintings, drawings, prints, and sculptures. With more than 3,000 pieces by artists including Giorgio de Chirico, Gino Severini, Scipione, Antonio Donghi, and Giacomo Manzù, the permanent collection is too large to be displayed at once, so exhibits rotate. Regardless of what the particular exhibit is, stop by to soak in another side of the city—one where, in the near-empty halls, tranquillity and contemplation reign. ✉ *Via Francesco Crispi 24, Piazza di Spagna* ☎ *06/0608,* ⊕ *www.galleriaartemodernaroma.it* ☞ *€7.50* ☾ *Closed Mon.* Ⓜ *Spagna.*

Palazzo Venezia. Centerpiece of the eponymous piazza, this palace was originally built for Venetian cardinal Pietro Barbo, who became Pope Paul II. It was also the backdrop used by Mussolini to harangue crowds with dreams of empire from the balcony over the main portal. Lights were left on through the night during his reign to suggest that the Fascist leader worked without pause. The palace shows a mixture of Early Renaissance grace and heavy Late Medieval lines; rooms include frescoes by Giorgio Vasari and an Algardi sculpture of Pope Innocent X. The loggia has a pleasant view over the tranquil garden courtyard, a million miles away from the chaos of Piazza Venezia on the other side of the building. The ticket price includes an audio guide. ✉ *Via del Plebiscito 118, Piazza di Spagna* ☎ *06/69994388* ⊕ *www.museopalazzovenezia.beniculturali.it* ☞ *€5* ☾ *Closed Mon.*

Piazza Venezia. The geographic heart of the city, this is the spot from which all distances from Rome are calculated and the main center of city traffic. Piazza Venezia stands at what was the beginning of Via Flaminia, the ancient Roman road leading northeast across Italy to Fano on the Adriatic Sea. The Via Flaminia was, and remains, a vital artery. Its initial tract, from Piazza Venezia to Piazza del Popolo, is now known as Via del Corso, after the horse races (*corse*) that were run here during the wild Roman carnival celebrations of the 17th and 18th centuries. It also happens to be one of Rome's busiest shopping streets. The massive female bust near the church of San Marco in the corner of the piazza, a fragment of a statue of Isis, is known to the Romans as Madama Lucrezia. This was one of the "talking statues" on which anonymous poets hung verses pungent with political satire, a practice that has not entirely disappeared. ⊠ *Piazza Venezia, Piazza di Spagna.*

Trinità dei Monti. Standing high above the Spanish Steps, this 16th-century church has a rare double-tower facade, suggestive of late–French Gothic style; in fact, the French crown paid for the church's construction. Today, it is beautiful primarily for its dramatic location and magnificent views. ⊠ *Piazza della Trinità dei Monti, Piazza di Spagna* ☎ *06/6794179* ⊘ *Closed Mon.* Ⓜ *Spagna.*

6

REPUBBLICA AND QUIRINALE

Getting Oriented

Repubblica and Quirinale

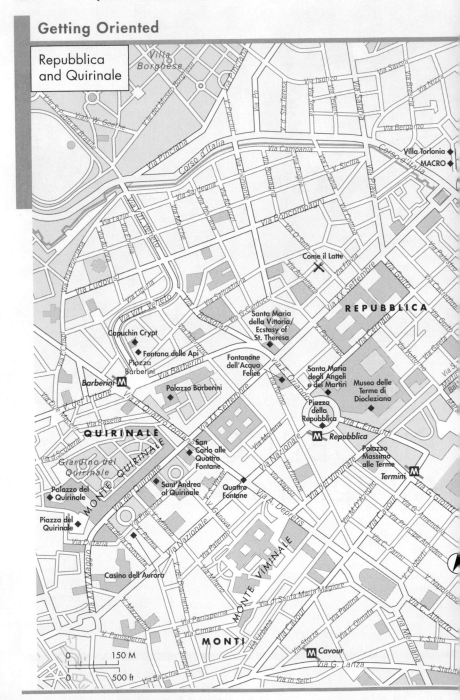

Villa Borghese

Viale W. Goethe

Viale del Museo Borghese

Corso d'Italia

Via Campania

Via Isonzo

Via Savoia

Via Brescia

Via Nizza

Via Bergamo

Via Sicilia

Villa Torlonia ◆
MACRO ◆

Via Pinciana

Via Sardegna

Via Lazio

Via Boncompagni

Come il Latte ✕

Via Flavia

Via XX Settembre

REPUBBLICA

Via Ludovisi

Santa Maria
della Vittoria/
Ecstasy of
St. Theresa

Via Vitt. Veneto

Capuchin Crypt ◆

◆ Fontana delle Api
Piazza
Barberini

Fontanone
dell'Acqua
Felice

Santa Maria
degli Angeli
e dei Martiri

Museo delle
Terme di
Diocleziano

Barberini Ⓜ

Via Barberini

◆ Palazzo Barberini

Piazza
della
Repubblica

Via del Tritone

Via Quattro Fontane

QUIRINALE

Via Nazionale

Ⓜ **Repubblica**

Via Rasella

San
Carlo alle
Quattro
Fontane

Palazzo
Massimo
alle Terme

Giardino del
Quirinale

Quattro
Fontane

Termini Ⓜ

Palazzo del ◆
Quirinale

Sant'Andrea
al Quirinale

MONTE QUIRINALE

Piazza del
Quirinale

Via Nazionale

Via Depretis

Casino dell'Aurora

MONTE VIMINALE

Via di Santa Maria Maggiore

MONTI

Via Panisperna

Via Cavour

Ⓜ **Cavour**

Via G. Lanza

Via in Selci

MAKING THE MOST OF YOUR TIME

While slightly off Rome's bustling tourist path, this central (and well-connected) area has a number of intriguing sights, from the stunning sweep of Piazza della Repubblica and the excellent ancient art collection of the Palazzo Massimo alle Terme to the bones of the Capuchin Crypt and Bernini's breathtaking sculpture, the *Ecstasy of St. Theresa*. It's possible to walk the whole area, but walking from one attraction to the other can be a bit of a slog; this part of town is so well-connected by bus and metro that it's sometimes easier to take public transport instead. When choosing a time of day to visit, remember that many churches (like Santa Maria della Vittoria, home of the Bernini sculpture) close at midday, reopening around 4 or 5.

GETTING HERE

Located between Termini station and the Spanish Steps, this area is about a 15-minute walk from either. Bus No. 40 will get you from Termini to the Quirinale in two stops; from the Vatican take Bus No. 64. The very busy and convenient Repubblica Metro stop is on the piazza of the same name.

QUICK BITES

Come il Latte. Located just a five-minute walk from Piazza della Repubblica, Come il Latte has a serious following for its super-creamy, all-natural gelato. The pistachio may be the best in town, though you can't go wrong with any of the flavors, some particularly creative (like rice and cinnamon). Top off your scoop with homemade *panna* (whipped cream) in a variety of flavors and either dark or white chocolate from the shop's chocolate fountain. ⊠ *Via Silvio Spaventa 24/26, Repubblica* ☎ *06/42903882* ⊕ *www.comeillatte.it* ▭ *No credit cards* Ⓜ *Castro Pretorio.*

TOP REASONS TO GO

Bernini's Ecstasy of St. Teresa: Admire (or just blush at) the worldly realism of Teresa's allegedly spiritual rapture. Star of the Cappella Cornaro, Bernini's piece represents an audacious fusion of architecture, painting, and sculpture.

Palazzo Barberini: Take in five centuries of art at one of Rome's greatest family palaces, where you can gape at Rome's biggest ballroom and Raphael's *La Fornarina*.

Palazzo Massimo alle Terme: Admire the spectacular Hellenistic *Boxer*, get your emperors straight in the portrait gallery, and marvel at breathtaking 2,000-year-old frescoes on the top floor.

Capuchin Crypt: Contemplate eternity in the creepy-yet-creative crypt under **Santa Maria della Concezione**, "decorated" with the skeletons of 4,000 monks, replete with fluted arches made of collarbones and arabesques of shoulder blades.

Piazza del Quirinale: Crowning the Quirinale—the loftiest of Rome's seven hills—is the Piazza del Quirinale, with spectacular views over the city, its horizon marked by "Il Cupolino," the dome of St. Peter's. Framing the vista are enormous ancient statues of Castor and Pollux, the Dioscuri (Horse-Tamers), which give the Quirinale its nickname "Monte Cavallo" (Horse Hill).

7

Sightseeing
★★★★
Nightlife
★★
Dining
★★★★
Lodging
★★★★★
Shopping
★★★

Just west of the modern Termini station, this area offers an extraordinary Roman blend of old and new. Think of it as the place where work gets done today: the stretch from Piazza della Repubblica to Piazza Barberini swarms with professionals going in and out of office buildings, as the Quirinale, home to the president of Italy, buzzes with political activity. More than just a workaday area, though, you will also find plenty of attractions for travelers, from the bizarre Capuchin Crypt to ancient artworks and great Bernini sculptures.

REPUBBLICA

Updated by Agnes Crawford

As a gateway, Piazza della Repubblica was laid out to serve as a monumental foyer between the Termini rail station and the rest of the city. Climbing the stairs out of the Metro here feels like stepping into a tornado. The clanging of sirens and car horns, the squeal of brakes, and the roar of mopeds, not to mention the smell of the fast-food joints, may make you want to duck back underground and get out at another stop. But to do so would be to miss out on a district with an array of fascinating attractions, like the one right before you: the piazza's main landmark, the vast ruins of the Terme di Diocleziano (Baths of Diocletian). They were subsequently transformed into a Renaissance monastery and then, by Michelangelo's design, to the church of Santa Maria degli Angeli. The streets here may not be conducive to wandering, but the ancient treasures at Palazzo Massimo delle Terme, Bernini's spectacular Capella Cornaro, and, farther afield, the modern Museo d'Arte Contemporanea (MACRO) will always be vying for your attention.

TOP ATTRACTIONS

Museo delle Terme di Diocleziano (*Baths of Diocletian*). Though part of this ancient bath complex (the largest in the Roman world) is now the church of Santa Maria degli Angeli, and other parts were transformed into a Carthusian monastery or razed to make room for later urban development, a visit gives you an idea of the scale and grandeur of this ancient bathing establishment. Upon entering the church you see the major structures of the baths, partly covered by 16th- and 17th-century overlay, some of which is by Michelangelo. The calm monastery cloister is filled with the Museo Nazionale Romano's collection of inscriptions; other rooms have pieces associated especially with remote Roman antiquity (think: huts), as well as archaeological finds from Rome's Republican and Imperial periods, including a rare painted relief of the god Mithras. ⊠ *Viale Enrico de Nicola 79, Repubblica* ☎ *06/39967700* ⊠ *€7, includes Crypta Balbi, Palazzo Massimo, Palazzo Altemps (valid for 3 days)* ⊗ *Closed Mon.* Ⓜ *Repubblica.*

Fodor's Choice
★ **Palazzo Massimo alle Terme.** Come here to get a real feel for ancient Roman art—the collection rivals even the Vatican's. The Museo Nazionale Romano, with a collection ranging from striking classical Roman paintings to marble bric-a-brac, has four locations: Palazzo Altemps, Crypta Balbi, the Museo delle Terme di Diocleziano, and this, the Palazzo Massimo alle Terme. This vast structure holds the great ancient treasures of the archaeological collection and also the coin collection. Highlights include the Dying Niobid, the famous bronze Boxer, and the Discobolus Lancellotti. Pride of place goes, however, to the great ancient frescoes on view on the top floor, stunningly set up to "re-create" the look of the homes they once decorated. These include stuccoes and wall paintings found in the area of the Villa della Farnesina (in Trastevere) and the legendary frescoes from Empress Livia's villa at Prima Porta, delightful depictions of a garden in bloom and an orchard alive with birds. Their colors are remarkably well preserved. These delicate decorations covered the walls of cool, sunken rooms in Livia's summer house outside the city. ⊠ *Largo Villa Peretti 1, Repubblica* ☎ *06/39967700* ⊕ *www.coopculture.it* ⊠ *€7, includes Crypta Balbi, Palazzo Massimo, Palazzo Altemps (valid for 3 days)* ⊗ *Closed Mon.* Ⓜ *Repubblica.*

Piazza della Repubblica. Often the first view that spells "Rome" to weary travelers walking from Termini station, this round piazza was laid out in the late 1800s and follows the line of the caldarium of the vast ancient Terme di Diocleziano. At its center, the exuberant **Fontana delle Naiadi** (Fountain of the Naiads) teems with voluptuous bronze ladies happily wrestling with marine monsters. The nudes weren't there when the pope unveiled the fountain in 1870—sparing him any embarrassment—but when the figures were added in 1901, they caused a scandal. It's said that the sculptor, Mario Rutelli, modeled them on the ample figures of two musical-comedy stars of the day. The colonnades now house the luxe Hotel Exedra, and a branch of foodie superstore Eataly recently opened in a former McDonald's, gradually helping Piazza della Repubblica to return to its original status as a smart section of town. ⊠ *Repubblica* Ⓜ *Repubblica.*

7

FodorśChoice **Santa Maria della Vittoria.** Like the church of Santa Susanna across Piazza
★ San Bernardo, this church was designed by Carlo Maderno, but this
one is best known for Bernini's sumptuous Baroque decoration of the
Cappella Cornaro (Cornaro Chapel, the last on the left as you face the
altar), which houses his interpretation of divine love, the *Ecstasy of St.
Teresa*. Your eye is drawn effortlessly from the frescoes on the ceiling
down to the marble figures of the angel and the swooning saint to the
earthly figures of the Cornaro family (some living, some dead at the
time), who observe the scene from the opera boxes on either side, to
the two inlays of marble skeletons in the pavement, representing the
hope and despair of souls in purgatory.

As evinced in other works of the period, the theatricality of the chapel
is the result of Bernini's masterly fusion of sculpture, light, architecture,
painting, and relief; it's a multimedia extravaganza, and one of the key
examples of the Roman High Baroque. Bernini's audacious conceit was
to model the chapel as a theater. The members of the Cornaro family
meditate on the communal vision of the great moment of divine love
before them: the swooning saint's robes appear to be on fire, quivering
with life, and the white marble group seems suspended in the heavens
as golden rays illuminate the scene. An angel assists at the mystical
moment of Teresa's vision as the saint abandons herself to the joys of
heavenly love. Bernini represented this mystical experience in what, to
modern eyes, may seem very earthly terms. Or, as the visiting French
dignitary President de Brosses put it in the 18th century, "If this is divine
love, I know all about it." No matter what your reaction, you'll have to
admit it's great theater. ⊠ *Via XX Settembre 17, Largo Santa Susanna,
Repubblica* ☎ *06/42740571* ⊕ *www.chiesasantamariavittoriaroma.it*
Ⓜ *Repubblica.*

FAMILY **Villa Torlonia.** Built for aristocrats-come-lately, the Torlonia family—
the Italian Rockefellers of the 19th century—this villa became Mussolini's residence and now serves as a public park. Long neglected,
the park's vegetation and buildings have recently been refurbished.
The **Casina Nobile,** the main palace designed by the great architect
Giuseppe Valadier is a grand, Neoclassical edifice, replete with a gigantic ballroom, frescoed salons, and soaring temple-like facade. While
denuded of nearly all their furnishings and art treasures, some salons
have important remnants of decor, including the reliefs once fashioned
by the father of Italian Neoclassical sculpture, Antonio Canova. In
the park, a complete contrast is offered by the **Casina delle Civette**
(Little House of Owls), a hyper-charming example of the Liberty (Art
Nouveau) style of the early 1900s: the gabled, fairy tale–like cottage-
palace now displays majolica and stained-glass decorations, including
windows with owl motifs—a stunning, oft-overlooked find for lovers of
19th-century decorative arts. Temporary exhibits are held in the small
and elegant **Il Casino dei Principi** (The House of Princes), designed
in part by Valadier. ⊠ *Villa Torlonia, Via Nomentana 70, Repubblica*
☎ *06/0608* ⊕ *www.museivillatorlonia.it* 🎫 *€6 Casina delle Civette with
exhibit, €7.50 Casino Nobile with exhibit; €9.50, includes both Casina
delle Civette and Casino Nobile, with exhibit* ☉ *Closed Mon.* Ⓜ *Repubblica; Bus Nos. 36 and 84.*

WORTH NOTING

Casino dell'Aurora. Set just off the Piazza del Quirinale is the Palazzo Pallavicini-Rospigliosi, and within its grounds you'll find the *Casino dell'Aurora*, originally built for Cardinal Scipione Borghese. The *casino* (a summer pavilion) has a fabulous ceiling fresco of Aurora (the personification of the Dawn) painted by Baroque artist Guido Reni—a painting once thought to be the last word in 17th-century style. The casino is only open to the public on the first day of every month except January. ⊠ *Via XXIV Maggio 43, Quirinale* ☏ *06/83467000* ⊕ *www. casinoaurorapallavicini.it* ▱ *Free* Ⓜ *Repubblica.*

Fontanone dell'Acqua Felice (*Fountain of Sixtus* V). When Pope Sixtus V (Felice Peretti) completed the restoration of the Acqua Felice toward the end of the 16th century, Domenico Fontana was commissioned to design this commemorative fountain. As the story goes, a sculptor named Prospero da Brescia had the unhappy task of executing the central figure, which was to represent Moses (Sixtus fancied himself a kind of "Moses," having provided water to his thirsting population). The comparison with Michelangelo's magnificent *Moses* in the church of San Pietro in Vincoli was inevitable, and the largely disparaging criticism of Prospero's work is said to have driven him to his grave. A full cleaning, however, has left the fountain—whose Moses in recent years had looked as if he were dipped in soot—sparkling white, revealing a great deal of its charm. ⊠ *Piazza San Bernardo, Repubblica* Ⓜ *Repubblica.*

MACRO. Formerly known as Rome's Modern and Contemporary Art Gallery, and before that formerly known as the Peroni beer factory, this redesigned industrial space has brought new life to the gallery and museum scene of a city formerly known for its "then," not its "now." The collection here covers Italian contemporary artists from the 1960s through today. Its sister museum, MACRO Testaccio (*Piazza O. Giustiniani*) is housed in a renovated slaughterhouse in the Testaccio neighborhood, a sort of Roman "Left Bank," and features temporary exhibits and installations by current artists. The goal of both spaces is to bring current art to the public in innovative spaces, and, not incidentally, to give support and recognition to Rome's contemporary art scene, which labors in the shadow of the city's artistic heritage. After a few days—or millennia—of dusty marble, it's a breath of fresh air. ■ TIP➔ Check the website for occasional late-night openings and events. ⊠ *Via Nizza 138, at Via Cagliari, Repubblica* ☏ *06/671070400* ⊕ *www.museomacro.org* ▱ *€13.50 MACRO; €14.50, includes MACRO and MACRO Testaccio (single-entry, valid for 7 days)* ⊙ *Closed Mon.* Ⓜ *Repubblica; Bus Nos. 719 and 38.*

Santa Maria degli Angeli e dei Martiri. The curving brick facade on the northeast side of Piazza della Repubblica is one small remnant of the colossal Terme di Diocleziano, the largest and most impressive of the baths of ancient Rome. A gift to the city from Emperor Diocletian, the complex was completed in AD 306. In 1561 Michelangelo was commissioned to convert the vast *frigidarium,* the central hall of the baths, into a church. His work was later altered by Vanvitelli in the 18th century, but the huge transept, which formed the nave in Michelangelo's plan,

Continued on page 168

BERNINI & BORROMINI

*By Martin
Wilmot Bennett*

ANGELS & DEMONS

Designed by Bernini, the ten angels of the Ponte Sant'Angelo bridge star along with other Berninis in Dan Brown's *Angels & Demons*, the Rome-based prequel to *The Da Vinci Code*.

THE TRAGIC RIVALRY OF BERNINI AND BORROMINI

Consider the famous feuding duos of Lennon vs. McCartney, Mozart vs. Salieri, Michelangelo vs. Raphael. None of them match the rivalry of Gian Lorenzo Bernini vs. Francesco Borromini. In a pitched battle of anything-you-can-do-I-can-do-better, these two great geniuses of the Baroque style transformed 17th-century Rome into a city of spectacle, the "theater of the entire world." While it was Bernini who triumphed and Borromini who wound up taking his own life, the real winner was Rome itself—a banquet for the eyes cooked up by these two Baroque masters.

Borromini's dome in San Carlo alle Quattro Fontane

United in genius, the two could not have been more different in fortune and character. Born within a year of each other at the turn of the 1600s, they spent decades laying out majestic squares, building precedent-shattering churches, all the while outdoing each other in Baroque bravado.

AN ARTISTIC THROWDOWN

Compared and contrasted, the pair form the ultimate odd couple: Bernini, perhaps the greatest master showman of all time, exulted in Technicolor-hued theatricality; Borromini, the purist and reclusive genius, pursued the pure light of geometry, although with an artisan's hankering after detail. Bernini grew into the famed lover and solid family man; Borromini seems not to have had any love life at all. Bernini became a smooth mingler with society's great and worthy ranks; Borromini remained the quirky outsider. Bernini triumphed as the all-rounder, he of the so-called *"bel composto,"* as in the Cornaro Chapel where his talents as sculptor/architect/dramatist come stunningly together. Borromini was an architect, pure and simple. Throughout their lives, they had tried to turn the tables—psychologically as well as architecturally—on each other, a struggle that ended with Borromini's tragic suicide.

OPERATION AMAZEMENT

Both, however, fervently believed in the Baroque style and its mission to amaze, as well as edify. Thanks to the Counter-Reformation, the Catholic church discovered, and exploited, the effects on its congregants of such overtly Baroque tricks-of-the-trade as *chiaroscuro* (light-and-dark) and *trompe l'oeil* (fool-the-eye) techniques. Using emotion and motion, Bernini and Borromini learned how to give stone wing. In Bernini's famed *Pluto and Persephone*, the solid stone seems transmuted into living flesh—sculpted effects previously thought possible only in paint. Together transforming the city into a "giant theater," the rivals thus became the principal dramaturges and stage managers of Baroque Rome.

(preceding page) Bernini's *Pluto and Persephone*, (left) Bernini's *Angel* on the Ponte St. Angelo

BERNINI (1598—1680): THE POPE'S FAVORITE

Born: December 7, 1598, in Naples, southern Italy.

Greatest Works: St. Peter's Square, *Ecstasy of St. Theresa*, Piazza Navona's *Fountain of Four Rivers, Apollo and Daphne*, Sant'Andrea al Quirinale.

Personality Profile: Extrovert and fully aware of his genius or, to quote his own mother, "He acts as if he were master of the world."

Scandal: Just imagine the headlines: "Brother Attacked with Crowbar/Costanza Slashed with Razor by Jealous Genius." Bernini went ballistic on learning his wife, Costanza Nonarelli, was having an affair with his brother Luigi. Protected by Pope Urban VIII, Bernini was let off with a fine of 3,000 scudi.

Career Low: Largely on Borromini's expert insistence, the two crack-ridden bell-towers Bernini designed for St. Peter's were subsequently pulled down.

"La Bella Morte": Death in Bernini becomes star performer. His tomb for Urban VIII has a skeleton writing the pope's name in a marble registry of death, while his tomb for Alexander VII has a golden skeleton riffling marble drapery (this pope kept a Bernini-designed coffin in his bedroom).

> *"An ignorant Goth who has corrupted architecture...."*
>
> Bernini on Borromini

Considered the "father of the Baroque," Bernini enjoyed almost too many career highs to count, starting from a drawing done as a youth, for which Pope Paul V awarded him a handful of gold ducats, to his being dubbed with the honorarium of "cavaliere" at age 23 (Borromini only received the same honor when he was past fifty). Born "under a happy star," as he himself put it, Bernini had patrons lining up, starting with church potentate and eventual pope, Maffeo Barberini, and Pope Paul's nephew, cardinal and art-dealer, Scipio Borghese, who claimed a bevy of Bernini's sculptures for his new Roman palace.

Bernini was a genius of self-promotion.

Cupola, Sant'Andrea al Quirinale

Trick No. 1: In an early bust of Cardinal Borghese, there was an unsightly crack across the forehead; as cardinal turns away in disappointment, Bernini whips out a perfect copy, no more crack. Trick No. 2: On inaugurating Piazza Navona's River Fountain, Innocent X is distressed upon realizing that the water isn't running; Bernini explains technical hitch; pope steps away; abracadabra, Bernini switches water on. Bravo, Bernini!?

Bernini's *David*

BORROMINI (1599—1667): THE ICONOCLAST

Born: September 27, 1599 in Bissone near Lake Lugano in Italy's far north, but with the name Castelli, the name-change coming later, partly to honor San Carlo Borromeo, whose San Carlo church will be Borromini's first major commission.

Greatest Works: San Carlo alle Quattro Fontane, Sant' Ivo della Sapienza, Sant'Agnese in Piazza Navona, Palazzo Falconieri.

Personality Profile: If Bernini is the "instant hit," Borromini is the "struggling genius," the introspective loner, and the complex, often misunderstood perfectionist.

Scandal: A young man, caught filching marble, was beaten and left for dead in San Giovanni in Lanterno, evidently on Borromini's orders. He avoids murder charges thanks to Pope Innocent's intervention.

Scale: Arguably his greatest work, San Carlo could be fitted into one of the four giant crossing-piers of the dome in St Peter's (in one of which towers Bernini's statue of St. Longinus).

"La Brutta Morte": His messy suicide was anything but "bella," as his brave note written in the hours it took him to expire after he fell on his sword attests.

> *"What I mind is not that the money goes to Bernini but that he should enjoy the honor of my labors."*
>
> Borromini on Bernini

Usually dressed in Spanish black, Borromini evidently had few attachments beyond his art. He not only had great artistic vision but an astounding command of geometry, an impeccable hankering after detail, and an artisan's willingness to get his hands dirty. The main influences on him range from Hiram, the builder of Solomon's temple in Jerusalem (who also died by falling on his sword) to Milan's Gothic cathedral, whose influence has been traced to S. Ivo's spiraled dome. On Urban VIII's death, Borromini's star began to ascend. The new pope, Innocent X, makes him papal architect, responsible for restructuring the S. Giovanni basilica and turning the S. Agnese church into a papal chapel. Bernini,

however, is again waiting in the wings, readying himself for a startling come back.

While he had a long run of patrons, Borromini was often overshadowed by Bernini's showmanship. He is done out of designing the *Four Rivers* fountain after Bernini submits a silver model of his own design to the new pope. After Innocent's death, commissions become scarce and depression followed. His suicide note is famously calm: "I've been wounded like this since half past eight this morning and I will tell you how it happened...." Once forgotten and derided, Francesco Borromini is now considered "the architect's architect."

Church of Sant' Agnese

BERNINI & BORROMINI TOP 20 MASTERPIECES

Bernini

1. Apollo and Daphne, Galleria Borghese

2. The Baldacchino, Basilica di San Pietro

3. Ecstasy of Saint Theresa, Santa Maria della Vittoria

4. David, Galleria Borghese

5. Pluto and Persephone, Galleria Borghese

6. Tomb of Pope Urban VIII, Basilica di San Pietro

7. Fountain of the Four Rivers, Piazza Navona

8. Two Angels, Ponte Sant'Angelo

9. Elephant and Obelisk, Piazza Sta Maria sopra Minerva

10. Ludovica Albertoni, San Francesco a Ripa

11. Fontana della Barcaccia, Piazza di Spagna

12. Fontana del Tritone, Piazza Barberini

Borromini

13. San Carlo alla Quattro Fontane, Quirinale

14. Sant' Agnese, Piazza Navona

15. Sant' Ivo alla Sapienza, Piazza Navona

16. Oratory of Saint Phillip Neri, Piazza Chiesa Nuova

17. Palazzo Spada, Piazza Capo di Ferro

18. Palazzo Barberini, Via Barberini

19. Sant'Andrea delle Fratte, Via dell Mercede

20. Palazzo Falconieri, Via Giulia

BERNINI VS. BORROMINI: A MINI-WALK

In Rome, you may become lost looking for the work of one rival, then suddenly find yourself gazing at the work of the other. As though an eerily twinned path was destined for the two giants, several of their greatest works are just a few blocks from each other.

A short street away (Via Orlando) from mammoth Piazza Repubblica stands **Santa Maria della Vittoria**, famed for Bernini's **Cornaro Chapel.** Out of favor with new anti-Barberini Pope Innocent X, Bernini was rescued by a commission from Cardinal Cornaro to build a chapel for his family. Here, as if in a "theater," sculpted figures of family members look down from two marble balconies on the so-called "transverberation" of Carmelite Saint Theresa of Avila being pierced by the arrow of the Angel of Divine Love, eyes shut in agony, mouth open in rapture. Spiritual ecstasy has become shockingly real—to quote the famed comment by President de Brosses, "If this is divine love, I know what it is."

Leave the church and head down Via Barberini to Piazza Barberini where perch three of the largest bees you'll ever see. The **Fountain of the Bees** is Bernini's tribute to his arch-patron from the Barberini family, Pope Urban VIII. The bees were family emblems. Another Bernini masterstroke is the **Triton Fountain** in the center of Piazza Barberini. Turn left up Via delle Quattro Fontane. On your left is spectacular **Palazzo Barberini,** where Bernini and Borromini worked together in an

uneasy partnership. The wonderful winding staircase off to the right is the work of Borromini, while the other more conventionally angled staircase on the left is by Bernini, who also has a self-portrait hanging in the art gallery upstairs.

Borromini's prospects soon took a turn for the better thanks to the Barefoot Spanish Trinitarians, who commissioned him to design **San Carlo alla Quatto Fontane**, set at the crossroads up the road. One of the

marvels of architecture, its dome—not much bigger than a down-turned bathtub is packed immaculately throughout with hexagons, octagons, and crosses. Like jigsaw pieces they diminish upwards until the tiny roof seems anything but: to a space that in another architect might turned out claustrophobic Borromini is able to bring a touch of infinity. In the adjoining cloister, revel in Borromini's rearrangement of columns, which transform what would be a conventional rectangle into an energetic octagon. Don't

forget to stop and admire the church's *movementé* facade.

On the same Via del Quirinale stands a famous Bernini landmark, the Jesuits' **Sant' Andrea al Quirinale.** With steps flowing out into the street, it could be viewed as Bernini's response to his rival's nearby masterpiece.

Ironically, the commission for the Jesuit church was originally earmarked for Borromini (but transferred when Pope Alexander VII took over). Note how the hexagons in Bernini's dome diminish upwards to create an illusion of space—in Borrominiesque fashion.

has remained. The eight enormous monolithic columns of red granite that support the great beams are the original columns of the tepidarium, 45 feet high and more than 5 feet in diameter. The great hall is 92 feet high. ⊠ *Via Cernaia 9, Repubblica* ☎ *06/4880812* ⊕ *www.santamariadegliangeliroma.it* Ⓜ *Repubblica.*

QUIRINALE

Rome's highest hill, the Quirinale, has housed ancient Roman senators, 17th and 18th century popes, and, with the end of papal rule, Italy's kings. West from Via Nazionale, the hill is set with various jewels of the Baroque era, including masterpieces by Bernini and Borromini. Nearby stands Palazzo Barberini, a grand and gorgeous 16th-century palace holding five centuries of masterworks.

Crowning the Piazza del Quirinale is the enormous Palazzo del Quirinale, built in the 16th century as a summer residence for the popes; it became the presidential palace in 1946. Today, you can tour its reception rooms, which are as splendid as you might imagine. The changing of the guard outside on the piazza (Sundays at 4 pm, 6 pm in summer months), is an old-fashioned exercise in pomp and circumstance.

While Bernini's work feels omnipresent in much of the city center, the vast range of his work is particularly notable here and in Repubblica. The artist as architect considered the church of Sant'Andrea al Quirinale one of his best; Bernini the urban designer and water worker wrought the muscle-bound sea gods who wrestle in the fountain at the center of Piazza Barberini; and Bernini the master sculptor gives religious passion corporeal treatment in what is perhaps his greatest work, the *Ecstasy of St. Teresa*, in the church of Santa Maria della Vittoria, in Repubblica.

TOP ATTRACTIONS

Capuchin Crypt. Not for the easily spooked, the crypt under the church of Santa Maria della Concezione holds the bones of some 4,000 dead Capuchin monks. Arranged in odd decorative designs around the shriveled and decayed skeletons of their kinsmen, a macabre reminder of the impermanence of earthly life, the crypt is strangely touching and beautiful. As one sign proclaims: "What you are, we once were. What we are, you someday will be." After a recent renovation, the crypt was reopened to the public with a new museum devoted to teaching visitors about the Capuchin order; the crypt is now located at the end of the museum circuit. Upstairs in the church, the first chapel on the right contains Guido Reni's mid-17th-century *St. Michael Trampling the Devil*. The painting caused great scandal after an astute contemporary observer remarked that the face of the devil bore a surprising resemblance to the Pamphilj Pope Innocent X, archenemy of Reni's Barberini patrons. Compare the devil with the bust of the pope that you saw in the Palazzo Doria Pamphilj and judge for yourself. ⊠ *Via Veneto 27, Quirinale* ☎ *06/88803695* ⊕ *www.cappuccinieviaveneto.it* ⊡ *€8, includes museum* Ⓜ *Barberini.*

PALAZZO BARBERINI/GALLERIA NAZIONALE

✉ *Via Barberini 18, Quiri-*
nale ☎ *06/32810* ⊕ *www.*
galleriaborghese.it ✉ *€7;*
€9, includes Palazzo Corsini
☉ *Closed Mon.* Ⓜ *Barberini;*
Bus Nos. 52, 56, 60, 95, 116,
175, and 492.

TIPS

■ Part of the family of
museums that make up the
Galleria Nazionale d'Arte
(others include the Palazzo
Corsini, Galleria Borghese,
Palazzo Spada, Palazzo
Venezia), the Palazzo Barberini
has gone into marketing in
a big way—visit the shop for
some distinctive gifts for Aunt
Ethel back home, includ-
ing tote bags bearing the
beloved visage of Raphael's
La Fornarina, bookmarks with
Caravaggio's Judith slicing off
Holofernes's head, and coffee
mugs bearing the famous
Barberini heraldic bees.

D'ARTE ANTICA

One of Rome's most splendid 17th-century palaces, the
Palazzo Barberini is a landmark of the Roman Baroque
style. Pope Urban VIII had acquired the property and
given it to a nephew, who was determined to build an
edifice worthy of his generous uncle and the ever-more-
powerful Barberini clan. The result was, architecturally, a precedent-shattering affair: a "villa suburbana"
set on what was then the edge of the city. The grand
facade was designed by Carlo Maderno (aided by his
nephew, Francesco Borromini), but when Maderno
died, Borromini was passed over in favor of his great
rival, Gianlorenzo Bernini.

Ascend Bernini's staircase to the Galleria Nazionale
d'Arte Antica. The splendid collection includes Raphael's *La Fornarina,* a luminous portrait of the artist's
lover (a resident of Trastevere, she was reputedly a
baker's daughter): study the bracelet on her upper arm
bearing the artist's name. Also noteworthy are Guido
Reni's portrait of the doomed *Beatrice Cenci* (beheaded
in Rome for patricide in 1599)—Hawthorne called it
"the saddest picture ever painted" in his Rome-based
novel, *The Marble Faun*—and Caravaggio's dramatic
Judith and Holofernes.

The showstopper here is the palace's Gran Salone, a
vast ballroom with a ceiling painted in 1630 by the
third (and too-often-neglected) master of the Roman
Baroque, Pietro da Cortona. It depicts the *Glorification
of Urban VIII's Reign* and has the spectacular conceit
of glorifying Urban VIII as the agent of Divine Provi-
dence, escorted by a "bomber squadron" (to quote art
historian Sir Michael Levey) of huge Barberini bees, the
heraldic symbol of the family.

7

Palazzo del Quirinale. Pope Gregory XIII started building this spectacular palace, now the official residence of Italy's president, in 1574. He planned to use it as a summer home. But less than 20 years later, Pope Clement VIII decided to make the palace—safely elevated above the malarial miasmas shrouding the low-lying location of the Vatican— the permanent residence of the papacy until 1870, undergoing various enlargements and alterations over time. When Italian troops under Garibaldi stormed Rome in 1870, making it the capital of the newly united Italy, the popes moved back to the Vatican, and the Palazzo del Quirinale became the official residence of the kings of Italy. After the Italian people voted out the monarchy in 1946, the palazzo passed to the presidency of the Italian Republic. The palace is now open to visitors, but you need to prebook a guided tour. Outside the gates, you can see the changing of the military guard at 4 pm on Sunday (at 6 pm July and August), and occasionally you can glimpse the impressive presidential guard. ⊠ *Piazza del Quirinale, Quirinale* ☏ *06/46991* ⊕ *www. quirinale.it* ✉ *By tour only: Itinerary No. 1 free (€1.50 booking fee), Itinerary No. 2 €10* ☙ *Closed Mon. and Thurs.* Ⓜ *Barberini.*

Piazza del Quirinale. This strategic location atop the Quirinale has long been of great importance. It served as home of the Sabines in the 7th century BC—at that time, deadly enemies of the Romans, who lived on the Campidoglio and Palatino (all of 1 km [½ mile] away). Today, it's the foreground for the presidential residence, Palazzo del Quirinale, and home to the **Palazzo della Consulta,** where Italy's Constitutional Court sits. The open side of the piazza has an impressive vista over the rooftops and domes of central Rome and St. Peter's. The **Fontana di Montecavallo,** or Fontana dei Dioscuri, comprises a huge Roman statuary group and an obelisk from the tomb of the emperor Augustus. The group of the Dioscuri trying to tame two massive marble steeds was found in the Baths of Constantine, which occupied part of the summit of the Quirinale. Unlike just about every other ancient statue in Rome, this group survived the Dark Ages intact and accordingly became one of the city's great sights, especially during the Middle Ages. Next to the figures, the ancient obelisk from the Mausoleo di Augusto (Tomb of Augustus) was put here by Pope Pius VI at the end of the 18th century. ⊠ *Quirinale* Ⓜ *Barberini.*

Quattro Fontane (*Four Fountains*). The intersection takes its name from its four Baroque fountains, which represent the Tiber (on the San Carlo corner), the Arno, Juno, and Diana. Despite the nearby traffic and the tightness of the sidewalk, it's worthwhile taking in the views from this point in all four directions: to the southwest, as far as the obelisk in Piazza del Quirinale; to the northeast, along Via XX Settembre to the Porta Pia; to the northwest, across Piazza Barberini to the obelisk of Trinità dei Monti; and to the southeast, as far as the obelisk and apse of Santa Maria Maggiore. The prospect is a highlight of Pope Sixtus V's campaign of urban beautification and an example of Baroque influence on city planning. ⊠ *Intersection of Via Quattro Fontane, Via XX Settembre, and Via del Quirinale, Quirinale* Ⓜ *Barberini.*

Fodor's Choice   **San Carlo alle Quattro Fontane.** Sometimes known as San Carlino because
★   of its tiny size, this is one of Borromini's masterpieces. In a space no
larger than the base of one of the piers of St. Peter's Basilica, he created
a church that is an intricate exercise in geometric perfection, with a coffered dome that seems to float above the curves of the walls. Borromini's
work is often bizarre, definitely intellectual, and intensely concerned
with pure form. In San Carlo, he invented an original treatment of
space that creates an effect of rippling movement, especially evident
in the double-S curves of the facade. Characteristically, the interior
decoration is subdued, in white stucco with no more than a few touches
of gilding, so as not to distract from the form. Don't miss the cloister:
a tiny, understated Baroque jewel, with a graceful portico and loggia
above, echoing the lines of the church. ⊠ *Via del Quirinale 23, Quiri-*
nale ☎ *06/4883109* ⊕ *www.sancarlino.eu* Ⓜ *Barberini.*

Fodor's Choice   **Sant'Andrea al Quirinale.** Designed by Bernini, this small church is one of
★   the triumphs of the Roman Baroque period. His son wrote that Bernini
considered it his best work and that he used to come here occasionally,
just to sit and contemplate. Bernini's simple oval plan, a classic form
in Baroque architecture, is given drama and movement by the church's
decoration, which carries the story of St. Andrew's martyrdom and
ascension into heaven, starting with the painting over the high altar,
up past the figure of the saint above, to the angels at the base of the
lantern and the dove of the Holy Spirit that awaits on high. ⊠ *Via del*
Quirinale 29, Quirinale ☎ *06/4740807* ⊕ *www.santandrea.gesuiti.it*
⊙ *Closed Mon.* Ⓜ *Barberini.*

WORTH NOTING

Fontana delle Api (*Fountain of the Bees*) Decorated with the famous
heraldic bees of the Barberini family, the upper shell and the inscription are from a fountain that Bernini designed for Pope Urban VIII;
the rest was lost when the fountain was moved to make way for a new
street. The inscription was the cause of a considerable scandal when
the fountain was first built in 1644. It said that the fountain had been
erected in the 22nd year of the pontiff's reign, although in fact the 21st
anniversary of Urban's election to the papacy was still some weeks
away. The last numeral was hurriedly erased, but to no avail—Urban
died eight days before the beginning of his 22nd year as pope. The
superstitious Romans, who had immediately recognized the inscription
as a foolhardy tempting of fate, were vindicated. ⊠ *Via Veneto at Piazza*
Barberini, Quirinale Ⓜ *Barberini.*

VILLA BORGHESE, PIAZZA DEL POPOLO, AND FLAMINIO

Getting Oriented

Villa Borghese,
Piazza del Popolo,
and Flaminio

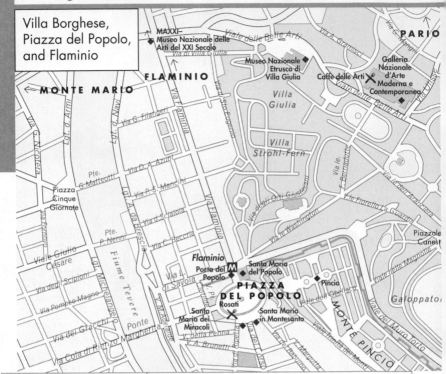

GETTING HERE

The Metro stop for Piazza del Popolo is Flaminio on Line A. The Villa Giulia, the Galleria Nazionale d'Arte Moderna e Contemporanea, and the Bioparco in Villa Borghese are accessible from Via Flaminia, 1 km (½ mile) from Piazza del Popolo. Tram No. 19 and Bus No. 3 stop at each.

Bus No. 119 connects Piazza del Popolo to Piazza Venezia. From the Colosseum, take No. 117 to Piazza del Popolo. Bus No. 116, starting near the Galleria Borghese, is the only bus that goes through the park.

TOP REASONS TO GO

Piazza del Popolo: At the end of three of the centro storico's most important streets—Via del Babuino, Via del Corso, and Via di Ripetta—the "People's Square" provides a front-row seat for some of Rome's best people-watching.

Villa Borghese: Drink in the fresh air in central Rome's largest park—stretches of green and plenty of leafy pathways encourage wandering, biking, or just chilling out.

The Pincio: Stroll through formal gardens in the footsteps of aristocrats out of a 19th-century fashion plate.

Santa Maria del Popolo: Marvel at the incredible realism of Caravaggio's gritty paintings in the Cerasi Chapel, then savor Raphael's Chigi Chapel.

Galleria Borghese: Appreciate the extravagant interior decor in one of Rome's most opulent—and pleasant—museums.

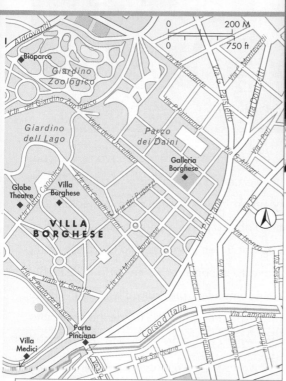

QUICK BITES

Caffè delle Arti. Attached to the Galleria d'Arte Moderna, inside the Villa Borghese, this elegant caffè with a pretty terrace is a favorite all-day rendezvous both for Romans from nearby upscale Parioli and for visitors to the Villa Borghese park and museums. ✉ *Via Gramsci 73, Villa Borghese* ☎ *06/32651236* ⊕ *www.caffe-delleartiroma.it.*

Rosati. A fixture of the Piazza del Popolo since 1922, this classic Roman caffè attracts locals and visitors for cappucino and aperitivo. It's a prime people-watching spot, especially if you sit outside. ✉ *Piazza del Popolo 5, Piazza del Popolo* ☎ *06/3225859* ⊕ *www.barro-sati.com* Ⓜ *Flaminio.*

MAKING THE MOST OF YOUR TIME

Explore this area on a clear day: the Villa Borghese park is at its best (and most bustling with strolling Italian families) on beautiful days, while the view from the top of the Pincio provides a stunning panorama over Rome's pastel rooftops. The Galleria Borghese, one of several museums within the Villa Borghese, is a Roman gem and a must-see for art lovers; just remember to book your tickets in advance (you can do so online), as walk-ins are rarely accommodated. After your "walk in the park," head down to Piazza del Popolo, one of Rome's loveliest piazzas, and duck into Santa Maria del Popolo for its gorgeous paintings by Baroque master Caravaggio—keeping in mind that, like many of Rome's churches, it closes in the middle of the day.

Sightseeing
★★★★
Nightlife
★
Dining
★★
Lodging
★★
Shopping
★

While it may not feel like it amid the dense warren of cobblestone streets in the *centro storico* (historic center), Rome is actually a very green city. All around the immediate city center are a number of vast public parks, the most central of which is the city's giant green lung: the Villa Borghese park, where residents love to escape for some serious R&R. But don't think you can completely prevent gallery gout—three of Rome's most important museums are inside the park, and Piazza del Popolo, which has more than one art-crammed church, is close by.

VILLA BORGHESE

Updated by Agnes Crawford

Central Rome's largest open space is filled with playful fountains, sculptured gardens, and picturesque forests of shady pine trees. But that's not the park's only purpose, for on the perimeter lie three of Rome's most important museums: the Galleria Borghese, for the very best of ancient, Renaissance, and Baroque art; the Villa Giulia, for the world's ultimate collection of Etruscan remains; and the Galleria Nazionale d'Arte Moderna, with its collection of 19th and 20th century art (Italian and other). For theatergoers, there are summer performances of Shakespeare (in Italian) in a replica of London's Globe Theatre. All in all, there's enough here to satisfy the most avid culture vulture. For a look at some real vultures and an excellent day out with the children, head for the new Bioparco, Rome's zoo.

TOP ATTRACTIONS

Fodor's Choice
★

Galleria Borghese. It's a real toss-up as to which is more magnificent: the museum built for Cardinal Scipione Borghese in 1612, or the art that lies within it. The luxury-loving cardinal had the museum custom-built as a showcase for his fabulous collection of both antiquities and more "modern" works, including those he commissioned from the masters Caravaggio and Bernini. Today, it's a monument to Roman interior decoration at its most extravagant.

Like the gardens, the "Museo" and its collections have undergone many changes since the 17th century. Much of the building was redecorated in the late 18th century, when the villa received many of its eye-popping ceiling frescoes (although some original decorations also survive). The biggest change to the collection, however, came thanks to Camillo Borghese. After marrying Napoléon's sister Pauline, he sold 154 statues, 170 bas-reliefs, 160 busts, 30 columns, and a number of vases—all ancient pieces—to his new brother-in-law. Today, those sculptures, including the so-called Borghese Gladiator and Borghese Hermaphrodite, are in the Louvre in Paris. At the end of the 19th century, a later member of the family, Francesco Borghese, attempted damage control with his fellow Romans (outraged that many of their art treasures had been shipped off to Paris) with some new acquisitions; he also transferred to the casino the remaining works of art then housed in Palazzo Borghese. In 1902 the building, its contents, and the estate were sold to the Italian government.

One of the most famous works in the collection is Canova's Neoclassical sculpture *Pauline Borghese as Venus Victrix*. Scandalously, Pauline reclines on a Roman sofa, bare-bosomed, her hips swathed in classical drapery—the very model of haughty detachment and sly come-hither allure. You can imagine what the 19th-century gossips were saying!

The next three rooms hold three key early Baroque sculptures: Bernini's *David, Apollo and Daphne,* and *Rape of Persephone.* All were done when the artist was in his 20s, and all illustrate Bernini's extraordinary skill. They also demonstrate the Baroque desire to invest sculpture with a lifelike quality, to imbue inert marble with a sense of real flesh. Whereas Renaissance sculptors wanted to capture the idealized beauty of the human form that they had admired in ancient Greek and Roman works, later sculptors like Bernini wanted movement and drama as well, capturing not an essence but an instant, infused with theatricality and emotion. The *Apollo and Daphne* shows the moment when, to aid her escape from the pursuing Apollo, Daphne is turned into a laurel tree. Leaves and twigs sprout from her fingertips as she stretches agonizingly away from Apollo. In *Pluto and Persephone,* Pluto has just plucked Persephone (or Proserpina) from her flower-picking, or perhaps he's returning to Hades with his prize. (Don't miss the realistic way his grip causes dimples in Proserpina's flesh.) This is the stuff that makes the Baroque exciting—and moving. Other Berninis on view in the collection include a large, unfinished figure called *Verità,* or *Truth.* Bernini began work on this brooding figure after the death of his principal patron, Pope Urban VIII. It was meant to form part of a work titled *Truth Revealed by Time.* The next pope, Innocent X, had little love for the ebullient Urban, and, as was the way in Rome, this meant that Bernini would be excluded from the new pope's favors. However, Bernini's towering genius was such that the new pope came around with his patronage with almost indecent haste.

8

Room 8 contains six paintings by Caravaggio, the hotheaded genius who died at age 37. All of his paintings, even the charming *Boy with a Basket of Fruit*, seethe with an undercurrent of darkness. The disquieting *Sick Bacchus* is a self-portrait of the artist who, like the god, had a fondness for wine. *David and Goliath*, painted in the last year of Caravaggio's life—while he was on the run, murder charges hanging over his head—includes his self-portrait in the head of Goliath.

Upstairs, the Pinacoteca (Picture Gallery) boasts paintings by Raphael (including his moving *Deposition*), Pinturicchio, Perugino, Bellini, and Rubens. Probably the gallery's most famous painting is Titian's allegorical *Sacred and Profane Love*, a mysterious and yet-unsolved image with two female figures, one nude, one clothed.

■TIP➔ **Admission to the Galleria is by reservation only.** Visitors are admitted in two-hour shifts 9–5. Prime-time slots can sell out days in advance, so reserve directly through the Borghese's website. ⊠ *Piazza Scipione Borghese 5, off Via Pinciana, Villa Borghese* ☏ *06/32810 for reservations, 06/8413979 for info* ⊕ *www.galleriaborghese.it* ⌑ *€15, includes €2 reservation fee; audio guide €5* ⊙ *Closed Mon.* Ⓜ *Bus No. 910 from Piazza della Repubblica; Tram No. 19 or Bus No. 3 from Policlinico.*

Fodor'sChoice **Museo Nazionale Etrusco di Villa Giulia.** The world's most outstanding
★ collection of Etruscan art and artifacts is housed in Villa Giulia, built around 1551 for Pope Julius III (hence its name). Among the team called in to plan and construct the villa were Michelangelo and fellow Florentine Vasari. Most of the actual work, however, was done by Vignola and Ammannati. The villa's *nymphaeum*—or sunken sculpture garden—is a superb example of a refined late-Renaissance setting for princely pleasures. No one knows precisely where the Etruscans originated. Many scholars maintain they came from Asia Minor, appearing in Italy about 2000 BC, and creating a civilization that was a dazzling prelude to the ancient Romans. Unfortunately, the exhibitions here are rather dry—hundreds of glass vitrines stuffed with objects. Even so, you'll find a few great artistic treasures. Among the most striking pieces are the terra-cotta statues, such as the *Apollo of Veio* and the serenely beautiful *Sarcophagus of the Wedded Couple*. Dating to 530–500 BC, this couple (or Sposi) look at the viewer with almond eyes and archaic smiles, suggesting an openness and joie de vivre rare in Roman art. Also look for the cinematic frieze from a later temple (480 BC) in Pyrgi, resembling a sort of Etruscan Elgin marbles in terra-cotta. Note the fabulous Etruscan jewelry, which makes Bulgari look like your village blacksmith. ⊠ *Piazzale Villa Giulia 9, Villa Borghese* ☏ *06/3226571* ⊕ *villagiulia.beniculturali.it* ⌑ *€8* ⊙ *Closed Mon.* Ⓜ *Tram No. 19, Bus No. 3.*

FAMILY **Pincio.** Redolent of the bygone era of Henry James and Edith Wharton,
Fodor'sChoice the Pincian gardens have long been a classic setting for a walk. Grand
★ Tourists—and even a pope or two—would head here to see and be seen among the beau monde of Rome. Today, the Pincian terrace remains a favorite spot for locals taking a springtime Sunday stroll. The rather formal, early-19th-century style contrasts with the far more elaborate

terraced gardens of Lucullus, the Roman gourmand who held legendary banquets here. Today, off-white marble busts of Italian Risorgimento heroes and artists line the pathways. Along with similar busts on the Gianicolo (Janiculum Hill), their noses have been targets of vandalism.

A stretch of ancient walls separates the Pincio from the southwest corner of Villa Borghese. From the balustraded terrace, you can look down at Piazza del Popolo and beyond, surveying much of Rome. Southeast of the Pincian terrace is the **Casina Valadier** (*06/69922090; www.casinavaladier.it*), a magnificently decorated Neoclassical building, which houses an upscale restaurant and cafeteria with glorious views. ✉ *Piazzale Napoleone I and viale dell'Obelisco, Villa Borghese* Ⓜ *Flaminio (Piazza del Popolo).*

FAMILY **Villa Borghese.** Rome's Central Park, the Villa Borghese was originally laid out as a pleasure garden in the early 17th century by Cardinal Scipione Borghese, a worldly and cultivated cleric and nephew of Pope Paul V. The word "villa" was used to mean suburban estate, of the type developed by the ancient Romans and adopted by Renaissance nobles. Today's gardens bear little resemblance to the originals. Not only do they cover a much smaller area—by 1630, the perimeter wall was almost 5 km (3 miles) long—but they also have been almost entirely remodeled. This occurred at the end of the 18th century, when a Scottish painter, Jacob More, was employed to transform them into the style of the "cunningly natural" park so popular in 18th-century England. Until then, the park was probably the finest example of an Italian-style garden in the entire country.

In addition to the gloriously restored Galleria Borghese, the highlights of the park are Piazza di Siena, a graceful amphitheater, and the botanical garden on Via Canonica, where there is a pretty little lake, a Neoclassical faux-Temple of Aesculapius (a favorite photo-op), the newly designed Biopark zoo, Rome's own replica of London's Globe Theatre, and the Villa Giulia museum.

The recently opened Carlo Bilotti Museum is particularly visitable for Giorgio de Chirico fans, although there is more modern art in the nearby Galleria Nazionale d'Arte Moderna e Contemporanea. The park is dotted with bike, in-line skating, and electric scooter–rental concessions and has a children's movie theater (showing films for adults in the evening). It also has a cinema center, Casa del Cinema, where film buffs can screen films or sit at the sleek, cherry-red, indoor-outdoor caffè (you can find a schedule of events at www.casadelcinema.it). ✉ *Main entrances at Porta Pinciana, the Pincio, Piazzale Flaminio (Piazza del Popolo), Viale delle Belle Arti, and Via Mercadante, Villa Borghese* Ⓜ *Flaminio (Piazza del Popolo).*

Villa Medici (*The French Academy of Rome*). Purchased by Napoléon to create an academy where artists could study Italian art and put it toward the (French) national good, the villa originally belonged to Cardinal Ferdinando I de' Medici, who also laid out the immaculate Renaissance garden to set off his sculpture collection. Garden tours in English are offered, allowing you to walk in the footsteps of Velázquez, Fragonard, and Ingres, who all worked here (at what is now officially

Principessa Pauline Borghese, Napoleon's sister, scandalized all Europe by posing as a half-naked Venus for Canova; the statue is on view at the Galleria Borghese.

called the French Academy in Rome). The guided tour is the only way you can see the gardens and the incredibly picturesque garden facade, which is studded with Mannerist and Rococo sculpted reliefs and overlooks a loggia with a beautiful fountain devoted to Mercury. There is also a pleasant cafeteria (daily 8 am–7 pm) at the loggia level, by the Galleria del Cardinale Ferdinando de' Medici. ⊠ *Viale Trinità dei Monti 1, Villa Borghese* ☎ *06/67611* ⊕ *www.villamedici.it* 🎟 *€12, includes garden tour and exhibit* ☉ *Closed Mon* Ⓜ *Spagna.*

WORTH NOTING

FAMILY **Bioparco.** Especially good for a day out with the children, this zoo has been remodeled along eco-friendly lines: there is now more space for the animals, most of which were brought from other zoos or born from animals already in captivity (rather than those snatched from the wild). There aren't any rhinos, koalas, pandas, or polar bears, but there are big cats, elephants, chimpanzees, and local brown bears from Abruzzo among others. Other features include the Reptilarium, the Bioparco train (€1.50), a picnic area next to the flamingos, and a farm. ⊠ *Piazzale del Giardino Zoologico 1, Villa Borghese* ☎ *06/3608211* ⊕ *www. bioparco.it* 🎟 *€16* Ⓜ *Tram No. 19 or Bus Nos. 3, 88, 95, 490, 495.*

Galleria Nazionale d'Arte Moderna e Contemporanea (*National Gallery of Modern Art*). This massive white Beaux Arts building, built for the 1911 World Exposition in Rome, contains one of Italy's leading collections of 19th- and 20th-century works. It's primarily dedicated to the history of Italian Modernism, examining the movement's development over the last two centuries, but crowd-pleasers Degas, Monet, Courbet, Van Gogh, and Cézanne put in appearances, along with an out-standing Dadaist collection. You can mix coffee and culture at the Art Nouveau Caffè delle Arti in the columned alcove of the museum. ✉ *Via delle Belle Arti 131, Villa Borghese* ☎ *06/32298221,* ⊕ *www.lagallerianazionale.com* 🎫 *€10* ☉ *Closed Mon.* Ⓜ *Tram No. 19 or 3, Bus Nos. 88, 95, 490, 495.*

Globe Theatre. Directed by pro-lific Roman actor Gigi Proietti, this theater replicates the London original inaugurated in 1576. Rome's homage to Shakespeare is built entirely of wood, and seats 1,250 with standing room for 420 groundlings (following Elizabethan custom). Performances run July–September and are usually works

by Shakespeare translated into Italian. Set in the Villa Borghese park, it is roughly midway between the Bioparco and the Museo Carlo Bilotti. ■**TIP→** Check the website for admission, as prices vary. ✉ *Largo Aqua Felix on Viale Pietro Canonica, Villa Borghese* ☎ *06/0608* ⊕ *www.globetheatreroma.com* Ⓜ *Flaminio.*

Porta Pinciana (*Pincian Gate*). Framed by two squat, circular towers, this gate was constructed at the beginning of the 5th century during a renovation of the 3rd century Aurelian Walls. Here you can see just how well the walls have been preserved and imagine hordes of Visigoths trying to break through them. Sturdy as they look, these walls couldn't always keep out the barbarians: Rome was sacked three times during the 5th century alone. ✉ *Piazzale Brasile, corner of Via Veneto and Corso d'Italia, Villa Borghese.*

PIAZZA DEL POPOLO

The formal garden terraces of the Pincio, on the southwestern side of Villa Borghese, give way to a stone staircase down to Piazza del Popolo, a mercifully traffic-free piazza that is one of Rome's best people-watch-ing spots. Very round, very explicitly defined, and very picturesque, the Piazza del Popolo (the People's Square) is one of Rome's biggest. Papal architect Giuseppe Valadier (1762–1839) laid out this square with twin churches at one end and the Porta del Popolo, Rome's northern city gate, at the other. Part of an earlier urban plan, the three streets to the south radiate straight as spokes to other parts of the city, form-ing the famed *tridente* that gives this neighborhood its nickname. The center is marked with an obelisk taken from Egypt, one so old it makes the Pantheon look like the Sears Tower; it was carved for Ramses II in the 13th century BC. Today, the obelisk is guarded by four water-gushing lions and steps that mark the end of many a sunset passeggiata (stroll). The most fascinating pieces of art—including masterpieces by Raphael and Caravaggio—are hidden within the northeast corner's often-overlooked church of Santa Maria del Popolo, snuggled against the 400-year-old Porta del Popolo.

If you're looking to rest your feet, there are caffè and restaurant tables aplenty.

TOP ATTRACTIONS

NEED A BREAK

✕ **Buccone.** This old-school wine shop serves food at lunchtime and wine by the glass all day long in atmospheric surroundings. ✉ *Via di Ripetta 19, Piazza del Popolo* ☏ *06/3612154* ⊕ *www.enotecabuccone.com* Ⓜ *Spagna.*

Fodor's Choice ★

Santa Maria del Popolo. Standing inconspicuously in a corner of the vast Piazza del Popolo, this church often goes unnoticed, but the treasures inside make it a must for art lovers, as they include an entire chapel designed by Raphael and one adorned with two striking Caravaggio masterpieces. Bramante enlarged the apse of the church, which was rebuilt in the 15th century on the site of a much older place of worship. Inside, in the first chapel on the right, you'll see some frescoes by Pinturicchio from the mid-15th century; the adjacent **Cybo Chapel** is a 17th-century exercise in decorative marble. Raphael's famous **Chigi Chapel**, the second on the left, was built around 1513 and commissioned by the banker Agostino Chigi (who also had the artist decorate his home across the Tiber, the Villa Farnesina). Raphael provided the cartoons for the vault mosaic—showing God the Father in benediction—and the designs for the statues of Jonah and Elijah. More than a century later, Bernini added the oval medallions on the tombs and the statues of Daniel and Habakkuk, when, in the mid-17th century another Chigi, Pope Alexander VII, commissioned him to restore and decorate the building.

The organ case by Bernini in the right transept bears the Della Rovere family oak tree, part of the Chigi family's coat of arms. Behind the main altar the **choir,** with vault frescoes by Pinturicchio, contains the handsome tombs of Ascanio Sforza and Girolamo della Rovere—both designed by Andrea Sansovino—and 16th-century stained glass, a rarity in central Italy. To visit the choir ask at the information booth; tours are free.

The best is for last: the **Cerasi Chapel,** to the left of the high altar, holds two Caravaggios: the *Crucifixion of St. Peter* and *Conversion of St. Paul.* Exuding drama and realism, both are key early Baroque works that show how "modern" 17th-century art can appear. Compare their style with the much more restrained and classically "pure" *Assumption of the Virgin* by Caravaggio's contemporary and rival, Annibale Carracci, which hangs over the altar of the chapel. ✉ *Piazza del Popolo 12, near Porta Pinciana, Piazza del Popolo* ☏ *06/3610836* ⊕ *www.santamariadelpopolo.it* Ⓜ *Flaminio.*

WORTH NOTING

Porta del Popolo (*City Gate*). The medieval gate in the Aurelian walls was replaced by the current one between 1562 and 1565, by Nanni di Bacco Bigio. Bernini further embellished it in 1655 for the much-heralded arrival of Queen Christina of Sweden, who had abdicated her throne to become a Roman Catholic. ✉ *Piazza del Popolo and Piazzale Flaminio, Piazza del Popolo* Ⓜ *Flaminio.*

Santa Maria dei Miracoli. A twin to Santa Maria in Montesanto, this church was built in the 1670s by Carlo Fontana as an elegant frame for the entrance to Via del Corso from Piazza del Popolo. ✉ *Via del Corso 528, Piazza del Popolo* ☎ *06/3610250* ☉ *Closed Sat.* Ⓜ *Flaminio.*

Santa Maria in Montesanto. Located on the eastern side of the Piazza del Popolo, Santa Maria dei Miracoli's "twin church" was built in the 1670s by Carlo Fontana and supervised by his brilliant teacher, Bernini (whose other pupils are responsible for the saints topping the facade). ✉ *Via del Babuino 197, Piazza del Popolo* ☎ *06/3610594* ⊕ *www. chiesadegliartisti.it* ☉ *Closed Sat.* Ⓜ *Flaminio.*

FLAMINIO

The Flaminio neighborhood, in northern Rome near the Tiber, was the focus of urban renewal plans for many years. Renzo Piano's Auditorium Parco della Musica put the area on the map in 2002, and the MAXXI museum, several years later, solidified the area as a destination.

MAXXI—Museo Nazionale delle Arti del XXI Secolo (*National Museum of 21st-Century Arts*). It took 10 years and cost some €150 million, but for art lovers, Italy's first national museum devoted to contemporary art and architecture was worth it. The building alone impresses, as it should: the design, by the late Anglo-Iraqi star-architect Zaha Hadid, triumphed over 272 other contest entries. The building plays with lots of natural light, curving and angular lines, and big open spaces, all meant to question the division between "within" and "without" (think glass ceilings and steel staircases that twist through the air).

The MAXXI hosts temporary exhibitions of art, architecture, film, and more. The permanent collection, exhibited on a rotating basis, boasts more than 350 works from artists including Andy Warhol, Francesco Clemente, and Gerhard Richter. ✉ *Via Guido Reni 4, Flaminio* ☎ *06/32810* ⊕ *www.fondazionemaxxi.it* 🎫 *€10* ☉ *Closed Mon.* Ⓜ *Flaminio, then Tram No. 2 to Apollodoro; Bus Nos. 53, 217, 280, 910.*

MONTE MARIO

In the northwest part of Rome, perched on the city's highest hill, the neighborhood of Monte Mario has fabulous views. Although not the easiest to get to by public transportation, there are a few noteworthy hotels and restaurants here.

PARIOLI

The elegant residential neighborhood of Parioli, north of the Villa Borghese, is home to some of the city's poshest hotels and restaurants. However, it's not especially convenient if you're planning to do any sightseeing.

TRASTEVERE

Getting Oriented

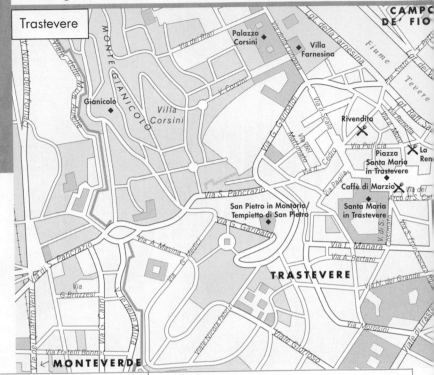

Trastevere

CAMPO
DE' FIO

MONTE GIANICOLO

Palazzo Corsini

Villa Farnesina

Gianicolo

Villa Corsini

Rivendita

Piazza Santa Maria in Trastevere

La Ren

Via S. Pancrazio

Caffè di Marzio

San Pietro in Montorio/ Tempietto di San Pietro

Santa Maria in Trastevere

Via G. Garibaldi

Via A. Masina

TRASTEVERE

Via
G. Bruzzesi

MONTEVERDE

Via Fratelli Bonnet

GETTING HERE

From the Vatican or Spanish Steps, expect a 20- to 30-minute walk to reach Trastevere. From Termini station, take Bus No. 40 Express or No. 64 to Largo Torre Argentina, where you can switch to Tram No. 8 to get to Trastevere.

If you don't feel like climbing the steep Gianicolo, take Bus No. 115 from Largo dei Fiorentini, then enjoy the stately walk down to the northern reaches of Trastevere or explore the leafy residential area of Monteverde Vecchio on the other side of the hill. Monteverde is a five-minute tram ride from Trastevere.

TOP REASONS TO GO

Santa Maria in Trastevere: Tear yourself away from the piazza scene outside to take in the gilded glory of one of the city's oldest and most beautiful churches, fabled for its medieval mosaics.

Isola Tiberina: Cross the river on the Ponte Fabricio—the city's oldest bridge—for a stroll on the paved shores of the adorable Isola Tiberina (and don't forget to detour for the lemon ices at La Grattachecca).

Nightlife: Trastevere has become one of Rome's hottest nighttime-scene arenas, with hipsterious clubs at nearly every turn.

Get a Feel for the Middle Ages: With cobblestone alleyways and medieval houses, the area around Trastevere's Piazza in Piscinula offers a magical dip into Rome's Middle Ages.

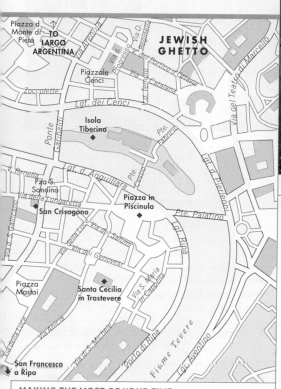

Piazza d.
Monte di **TO**
Pietá **LARGO
ARGENTINA**

Via d. Arenula

Via d. Progresso

Via D.

Via Reginella

**JEWISH
GHETTO**

Via del Portico d'Ottavia

Via S. Maria in Monticelli

Piazzale
Cenci

V.d. Tempio

Via Catalana

Via del Teatro di Marcello

Zoccalette

Lgt. dei Cenci

Isola
Tiberina

Pte.
Fabricia

Ponte Garibaldi

Lgt. d. Anguillara

Pte.
D.

Lgt. dei Pierleoni

V. Renella

Pza S.
Sonnino

Via della Lungaretta

San Crisogono

Via d. S. Gallicano

Via D. Salumi

Via de' Genovesi

Stella del Salumi

Piazza in
Piscinula

Pte. Palatino

Via in Piscinula

Via Titta Scarpetta

Via dei Genovesi

Via S. Maria

in Cappella

Via della Luce

Piazza
Mastai

Via della Luce

**Santa Cecilia
in Trastevere**

Via di S. Michele

Via di Genovesi

Via Anicia

Via Madonna dell'Orto

Via Lungaretta

Via della Luce

Porto di Ripa

Lgt. di Ripa

Fiume Tevere

Lgt. Aventino

**San Francesco
a Ripa**

MAKING THE MOST OF YOUR TIME

It's easy to get to Trastevere from Piazza Venezia: just take Tram No. 8 to the first stop on the other side of the river. You'll probably want to head right to the Piazza di Santa Maria in Trastevere, the heart of this lively area. Heading to the opposite side of Viale di Trastevere, though, is a treat many tourists miss. The cobblestone streets around Piazza in Piscinula and Via della Luce—locals peering down from balconies and the smell of fresh-baked bread floating from bakeries—are much more reminiscent of how Trastevere used to be than the touristic area to the north. Either way, remember that many of Trastevere's lovely small churches close, like others in Rome, in the afternoons. In the evenings, the neighborhood heats up with locals and visitors alike, drinking, eating, and going for *passeggiate* (strolls)—a not-to-be-missed atmosphere, especially for those with energy to burn.

QUICK BITES

Caffè di Marzio. Over a coffee or a cocktail, sit and gaze upon Santa Maria in Trastevere's glistening golden facade at Caffè di Marzio. The outdoor seating is lovely but the interior is warm and welcoming, too. ✉ *Piazza di Santa Maria in Trastevere 15, Trastevere* ☎ *06/5816095.*

La Renella (*Forno La Renella*). This no-frills pizzeria *al taglio* (by the slice) and bakery is hidden just off Piazza Trilussa. As in many traditional bakeries, pizza and cookies are sold by weight, so get yours sliced to the size you want. ✉ *Via del Moro 15, Trastevere* ☎ *06/5817265* ▭ *No credit cards.*

Rivendita. The full name is "Rivendita: Libri Cioccolata e Vino," and that's exactly what you'll find in this charming hole-in-the-wall: books, chocolate, and wine. Options like Barolo, fruity cocktails, or coffee served in cups of pure chocolate are enticing. ✉ *Vicolo del Cinque 11/a, Trastevere* ☎ *06/58301868* ▭ *No credit cards.*

9

Sightseeing
★★★★★
Nightlife
★★★★
Dining
★★★★
Lodging
★★★
Shopping
★★★

Updated
by Agnes
Crawford

Trastevere (literally, "across the Tiber") can feel a world apart from the rest of Rome and despite galloping gentrification, the bohemian neighborhood remains about the most tightly knit community in Rome.

Perfectly picturesque piazzas, tiny winding medieval alleyways, and time-burnished Romanesque houses all cast a frozen-in-time spell, while grand art awaits at Santa Maria in Trastevere, San Francesco a Ripa, and the Villa Farnesina. The neighborhood's greatest attraction, however, is simply its atmosphere—traditional shops set along crooked streets, peaceful during the day and alive with throngs of restaurant- and partygoers at night. From here, a steep hike upstairs and along the road to the Gianicolo, Rome's highest hill, earns you a panoramic view of the city.

The inhabitants of Trastevere don't even call themselves Romans but Trasteverini, claiming that they, not the citizens east of the river, are the true remaining Romans. A visit here still feels a bit like entering a different time and place, as the district remains an enchanting confusion of past and present.

TOP ATTRACTIONS

FAMILY **Gianicolo** (*Janiculum Hill*). The Gianicolo is famous for its panoramic views of the city, a noontime cannon shot, and statues of Giuseppe and Anita Garibaldi (the guiding spirit behind the unification of Italy in the 19th century, and his long-suffering wife). The view, with the foothills of the Appennini in the background, is especially breathtaking at dusk. It's also a great view for dome-spotting, from the Pantheon to the myriad of city churches. It all looks very peaceful and pastel from up here. ⊠ *Via Garibaldi and Passeggiata del Gianicolo, Trastevere.*

FAMILY **Piazza Santa Maria in Trastevere.** At the very heart of the Trastevere *rione* (district) lies this beautiful piazza, with its elegant raised fountain and sidewalk caffè. The centerpiece is the 12th-century church of Santa Maria in Trastevere, first consecrated in the 4th century. Across countless generations, this piazza has seen the comings and goings of tourists and travelers, intellectuals and artists, who lounge on the steps of the

ISOLA TIBERINA

✉ *Isola Tiberina can be accessed by Ponte Fabricio or the Ponte Cestio, Trastevere.*

TIPS

■ Sometimes called the world's most beautiful movie theater, the open-air Cinema d'Isola di Tiberina operates from mid-June to early September as part of Rome's big summer festival, Estate Romana (*www.estateromana. comune.roma.it*). The 450-seat Arena unfolds its silver screen against the backdrop of the ancient Ponte Fabricio, while the 50-seat CineLab is set against Ponte Garibaldi facing Trastevere. Screenings usually start at 9:30 pm; admission is €6 for the Arena, €6 CineLab. Call *06/58333113* or go to *isoladelcinema.com* for more information.

■ Line up at the kiosk of "La Grattachecca del 1915" (near the Ponte Cestio) for the most yum-ptious frozen ices in Rome.

It's easy to overlook this tiny island in the Tiber. Don't. In terms of history and sheer loveliness, the charming Isola Tiberina—shaped like a boat about to set sail—gets high marks.

Cross onto the island via Ponte Fabricio, constructed in 62 BC, Rome's oldest remaining bridge; on the north side of the island crumbles the romantic ruin of the Ponte Rotto (Broken Bridge), which dates back to 179 BC. Descend the steps to the lovely river embankment to see the island's claim to fame: a Roman relief of the intertwined-snakes symbol of Aesculapius, the great god of healing. In 291 BC, a temple to Aesculapius was erected on the island. A ship had been sent to Epidaurus in Greece, heart of the cult of Aesculapius, to obtain a statue of the god.

As the ship sailed back up the Tiber, a great serpent was seen escaping from it and swimming to the island—a sign that a temple to Aesculapius should be built here.

In Imperial times, Romans sheathed the entire island with marble to make it look like Aesculapius's ship, replete with a towering obelisk as a mast. Amazingly, a fragment of the ancient sculpted ship's prow still exists. You can marvel at it on the downstream end of the embankment.

Today, medicine still reigns here. The island is home to the hospital of Fatebenefratelli (literally, "Do good, brothers"). Nearby is San Bartolomeo, built at the end of the 10th century by the Holy Roman Emperor Otto III and restored in the 18th century.

9

fountain or eat lunch at an outdoor table at Sabatini's. At night, it's the center of Trastevere's action, with street festivals, musicians, and gamboling dogs vying for attention from the throngs of people taking the evening air. ⊠ *Via della Lungaretta, Via della Paglia, and Via San Cosimato, Trastevere.*

San Pietro in Montorio. Built by order of Ferdinand and Isabella of Spain in 1481 near the spot where medieval tradition believed St. Peter was crucified (the crucifixion site at the Vatican is much more probable), this church is a handsome and dignified edifice. It contains a number of well-known works, including, in the first chapel on the right, the *Flagellation* painted by the Venetian Sebastiano del Piombo from a design by Michelangelo, and *St. Francis in Ecstasy,* in the next-to-last chapel on the left, in which Bernini made one of his earliest experiments with concealed lighting effects.

The most famous work here, though, is the circular **Tempietto** (Little Temple) in the monastery cloister next door. This small sober building (it holds only 10 people and is a church in its own right) marks the spot where Peter was thought to have been crucified. Designed by Bramante (the first architect of the "new" St. Peter's Basilica) in 1502, it represents one of the earliest and most successful attempts to create an entirely classical building. The Tempietto is reachable via the Royal Spanish Academy next door. ⊠ *Piazza di San Pietro in Montorio 2 (Via Garibaldi), Trastevere* ☎ *06/5813940 for San Pietro in Montorio, 06/5812806 for Tempietto (Accademia di Spagna)* ⊕ *www.sanpietro-inmontorio.it* ⊙ *Tempietto closed Sun. and Mon.*

Fodor's Choice ★ **Santa Cecilia in Trastevere.** This basilica commemorates the aristocratic St. Cecilia, patron saint of musicians. One of ancient Rome's most celebrated Early Christian martyrs, she was most likely put to a supernaturally long death by the Emperor Diocletian just before the year AD 300. After an abortive attempt to suffocate her in the baths of her own house (a favorite means of quietly disposing of aristocrats in Roman days), she was brought before the executioner. But not even three blows of the executioner's sword could dispatch the young girl. She lingered for several days, converting others to the Christian cause, before finally dying. In 1595, her body was exhumed—it was said to look as fresh as if she still breathed—and the heart-wrenching sculpture by eyewitness Stefano Maderno that lies below the main altar was, the sculptor insisted, exactly how she looked. Time your visit to enter the cloistered convent to see what remains of Pietro Cavallini's *Last Judgment,* dating to 1293. It's the only major fresco in existence known to have been painted by Cavallini, a contemporary of Giotto. To visit the frescoes, ring the bell of the convent to the left of the church entrance. ⊠ *Piazza di Santa Cecilia in Trastevere 22, Trastevere* ☎ *06/5899289* ☐ *Frescoes €2.50, underground €2.50.*

Fodor's Choice ★ **Santa Maria in Trastevere.** Originally built during the 4th century and rebuilt in the 12th century, this is one of Rome's oldest and grandest churches. It is also the earliest foundation of any Roman church to be dedicated to the Virgin Mary. With a nave framed by a processional of two rows of gigantic columns (22 in total) taken from the ancient

Baths of Caracalla, and an apse studded with gilded mosaics, the interior conjures the splendor of ancient Rome better than any other in the city. Overhead is Domenichino's gilded ceiling (1617). The 18th-century portico draws attention to the facade's 800-year-old mosaics, which represent the parable of the Wise and Foolish Virgins. They enhance the whole piazza, especially at night, when the church front and bell tower are illuminated. The church's most important mosaics, Pietro Cavallini's six panels of the *Life of the Virgin,* cover the semicircular apse. Note the building labeled "Taberna Meritoria" just under the figure of the Virgin in the Nativity scene, with a stream of oil flowing from it. It recalls the legend that a fountain of oil appeared on this spot, prophesying the birth of Christ. Off the piazza's northern side is a street called Via delle Fonte dell'Olio in honor of this miracle. ⊠ *Piazza Santa Maria in Trastevere, Trastevere* ☎ *06/5814802.*

Fodors Choice **Villa Farnesina.** Money was no object to the extravagant Agostino Chigi,
★ a banker from Siena who financed many papal projects. His munificence is evident in this elegant villa, built for him about 1511. He was especially proud of the decorative frescoes in the airy loggias, now glassed in to protect them. When Raphael could steal a little time from his work on the Vatican Stanze, he came over to execute some of the frescoes himself, notably a luminous *Triumph of Galatea.* In his villa, Agostino entertained the popes and princes of 16th-century Rome. He delighted in impressing his guests at alfresco suppers held in riverside pavilions by having his servants clear the table by casting the precious silver and gold dinnerware into the Tiber. His extravagance was not quite so boundless as he wished to make it appear, however: nets were unfurled a foot or two beneath the water's surface to catch the valuable ware.

In the magnificent Loggia of Psyche on the ground floor, Giulio Romano and others worked from Raphael's designs. Raphael's lovely *Galatea* is in the adjacent room. On the floor above you can see the trompe-l'oeil effects in the aptly named Hall of Perspectives by Peruzzi. Agostino Chigi's bedroom, next door, was frescoed by Il Sodoma with scenes from the life of Alexander the Great, notably the *Wedding of Alexander and Roxanne,* which is considered to be the artist's best work. The palace also houses the **Gabinetto Nazionale delle Stampe,** a treasure trove of old prints and drawings. When the Tiber embankments were built in 1879, the remains of a classical villa were discovered under the Farnesina gardens, and their decorations are now in the Museo Nazionale Romano's collections in Palazzo Massimo alle Terme. ⊠ *Via della Lungara 230, Trastevere* ☎ *06/68027268 for info, 06/68027397 tour reservations* ⊕ *www.villafarnesina.it* ☎ *€6.*

WORTH NOTING

Palazzo Corsini. A brooding example of Baroque style, the palace (once home to Queen Christina of Sweden) is across the road from the Villa Farnesina and houses part of the 16th- and 17th-century sections of the collection of the Galleria Nazionale d'Arte Antica. Among the star paintings in this manageably sized collection are Rubens's *St. Sebastian*and Caravaggio's *St. John the Baptist.* Stop in if only to climb the

17th-century stone staircase, itself a drama of architectural shadows and sculptural voids. Behind, but separate from, the palazzo is the University of Rome's **Orto Botanico**, home to 3,500 species of plants, with various greenhouses around a stairway/fountain with 11 jets. ✉ *Via della Lungara 10, Trastevere* ☎ *06/68802323 for Galleria Corsini, 06/32810 for Galleria Corsini tickets, 06/49912436 for Orto Botanico* ⊕ *galleriacorsini.beniculturali.it* 🎫 *€5* ⊙ *Closed Tues.*

Piazza in Piscinula. One of Trastevere's most historic and time-burnished squares, this piazza takes its name from ancient Roman baths on the site (*piscina* means "pool"). It's said that the tiny church of **San Benedetto** on the piazza was built on the home of Roman nobles in which St. Benedict lived in the 5th century. Opposite is the medieval **Casa dei Mattei** (House of the Mattei), where the rich and powerful Mattei family lived until the 16th century, when, after a series of murders on the premises, colorful legend has it that they were forced to move out of the district, crossing the river to build their magnificent palace close to the Jewish Ghetto. ✉ *Via della Lungaretta, Piazza della Gensola, Via in Piscinula, and Via Lungarina, Trastevere.*

San Crisogono. This pretty church, which dates back to the 4th or 5th century, might be Rome's first parish church. The soaring medieval bell tower can best be seen from the little piazza flanking the church or from the other side of Viale di Trastevere. Inside, ring the bell of the room to the left of the apse to gain access to the underground area, where you can explore the ruins of the ancient basilica, discovered in 1907 beneath the "new" 12th-century structure. The eerie space is dotted with gems like 8th-century frescoes, ancient marble sarcophagi, and even a 6th-century marble altar. ✉ *Piazza Sonnino 44, Trastevere* ☎ *06/5818225* 🎫 *€3 for underground area.*

San Francesco a Ripa. In a quiet part of Trastevere, south of Viale di Trastevere, this church's dedication refers to the fact that St. Francis of Assisi stayed nearby during a visit to Rome. The medieval church was rebuilt in the 17th century and houses one of Bernini's last works, a statue of the *Blessed Ludovica Albertoni*. This is perhaps Bernini's most hallucinatory sculpture, a dramatically lighted figure ecstatic at the prospect of entering heaven as she expires on her deathbed. The cell in which Saint Francis is said to have stayed (Il Santuario di San Francesco) is often visitable. Fans of Giorgio de Chirico can ask to visit his tomb in a chapel that contains three paintings by the 20th-century metaphysical painter. ✉ *Piazza San Francesco d'Assisi 88, Trastevere* ☎ *06/5819020* ⊕ *www.sanfrancescoaripa.com.*

MONTEVERDE

Southwest of Trastevere, adjacent to Villa Pamphili park, Monteverde is a residential area that's been getting more and more foot traffic from travelers in recent years. It has some destination-worthy dining spots.

AVENTINO AND TESTACCIO

Getting Oriented

Aventino and
Testaccio

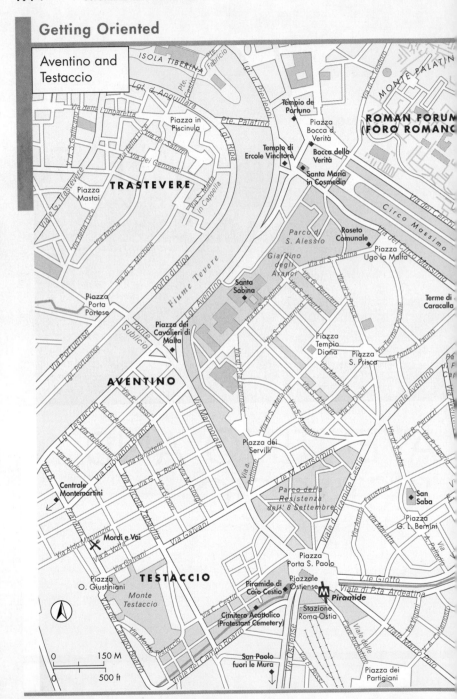

ISOLA TIBERINA
Pte. Fabricio
Pte. Cestio
Lgt. d'Anguillara
Via della Lungaretta
Piazza in Piscinula
Pte. Palatino
Lgt. Ripa
Lgt. de' Pierleoni
Tempio de Portuno
Piazza Bocca d. Verità
Via della Lungaretta
Via delle Salara
Via dei Genovesi
Tempio di Ercole Vincitore
Bocca della Verità
Santa Maria in Cosmedin
ROMAN FORUM (FORO ROMANO
MONTE PALATIN

TRASTEVERE
Piazza Mastai
Via S. Maria in Cappella
Via di Ponte Rotto
Circo Massimo
Via dei Cerchi

Via Anicia
Via S. Michele
Via di S. Sabina
Parco di S. Alessio
Giardino degli Aranci
Roseto Comunale
Piazza Ugo la Malta
Via dei Circo Massimo
Via di S. Sabina

Fiume Tevere
Porto di Ripa
Lgt. Aventino
Santa Sabina
Via di S. Sabina
Via S. Alberto
Via S. Domenica
Terme di Caracalla
Via delle Terme Deciane

Piazza Porta Portese
Via Portuense
Lgt. Portuense
Ponte Sublicio
Piazza dei Cavalieri di Malta
Via di S. Melania
Piazza Tempio Diana
Piazza S. Prisca
Via Aventino

AVENTINO
Via G. Bezzi
Via A. Pollaio
Piazza dei Servilli

Via Testaccio
Via G. Branca
Via Robatino
Via Florio
Via Giovanni Branca
Via G. B. Bodoni
Via Mastro Giorgio
Via di S. Saba
Parco della Resistenza dell' 8 Settembre
Viale M. Gelsomini
San Saba
Piazza G. L. Bernini

Centrale Montemartini
Mordi e Vai
Via Galvani
Via A. Volta
Via Galvani
Piazza O. Giustiniani
TESTACCIO
Monte Testaccio
Piazza Porta S. Paolo
Piazza Porta S. Paolo
Piramide di Caio Cestio
Piazzale Ostiense
Viale Giotto
M **Piramide**
Stazione Roma-Ostia
Viale di Pta. Ardeatina

Cimitero Acattolico (Protestant Cemetery)
Via Ostiense
San Paolo fuori le Mura
Piazza dei Partigiani

0 — 150 M
0 — 500 ft

TOP REASONS TO GO

Santa Maria in Cosmedin: Test your truthfulness (or someone else's) at the mouth of the Bocca della Verità.

Cimitero Acattolico "Protestant Cemetery": Swoon over Keats's body and Shelley's heart in this romantic graveyard.

Piazza Cavalieri di Malta: Peek through the keyhole of the Priorato di Malta for a privileged view—one of Rome's most surprising delights.

Tempting Testaccio: Like New York City's Meatpacking District, this neighborhood is a combination of factories and nightclubs.

Roseto Comunale: Overlooking the Circo Massimo, this rose garden offers a fitting and fragrant vestibule to Rome's most poetic hill.

Baths of Caracalla: South of the lovely Villa Celimontana park are the imposing ruins of the Terme di Caracalla, once the second-largest bathing complex of the Roman world.

QUICK BITES

Mordi e Vai. Sergio Esposito's stand at what will forever be called the "New" Testaccio Market (it moved in 2012) sells the best sandwiches in town. Meatballs, tongue, tripe, and other Roman classics make it worth the journey, and there are usually vegetarian options, too. There are a couple of counters but no formal seating. It's open during market hours (Monday–Saturday 8–2:30). ✉ *Testaccio Market Box 15, Via Beniamino Franklin, Testaccio* ☎ *06/69920945* ⊕ *www. mordievai.it* ⊟ *No credit cards.*

MAKING THE MOST OF YOUR TIME

Travelers with limited time often see just one sight here: the Bocca della Verità, or "Mouth of Truth." There are other gems, though, especially on a nice day. The Giardino degli Aranci (Garden of the Orange Trees) has spectacular views over Rome and the Tiber. Next to the giardino is Santa Sabina, one of Rome's finest ancient churches, and the Piazza dei Cavalieri di Malta, whose keyhole has a special surprise.

Visit Testaccio in the evening, when locals take their *passeggiata* (stroll) and restaurants fill with diners. Admire the Piramide di Caio Cestio and duck into the Cimitero Acattolico, or "Protestant Cemetery," one of the most atmospheric spots in Rome. You can stay out till the wee hours here, as it's a popular area for dance clubs and music.

GETTING HERE

It's a a spectacular 20-minute walk through ancient ruins like the Circo Massimo to reach the Aventine hill from either the Roman Forum or the Campidoglio. There's a Metro stop by the same name at the foot of Aventino, too. If you're coming from the Colosseum or Trastevere, take Bus No. 3; from the Spanish Steps, take Bus No. 160; from Termini, Bus No. 175. For Testaccio, use the Piramide (Ostiense) Metro stop.

10

Sightseeing
★★
Nightlife
★★★
Dining
★★
Lodging
★★★
Shopping
★

While Romans consider these neighborhoods central, they are just far enough off the beaten path to be little known to tourists—and to have retained their unique character, from the well-heeled, flower-draped residential quarter of Aventino to the traditional-yet-trendy riverside neighborhood of Testaccio. For travelers who have a little extra time (or who simply want to see a Rome beyond the Trevi Fountain and Spanish Steps), making a visit to these areas allows a glimpse of what the Eternal City really means to its residents.

AVENTINO

Updated
by Agnes
Crawford

One of the seven hills on which the city was founded, the Aventine Hill enjoys a serenity hard to find elsewhere in Rome. Trills of birdsong win out over the din of traffic—appropriate, since the hill's name derives from the Latin *avis*, or bird. Indeed, legend says that the sighting of eagles was used by Romulus and Remus to determine the prime spot for the city's foundation. In the end, though, Romulus's site on the Palatine Hill won, and Remus's Aventino was abandoned. It would remain for centuries thereafter the hill of the plebei, who looked across the valley to the grandeur of Palatine Hill.

Things have long since changed, however, and today this is a rarefied district, in which some houses still have their own bell towers, and private gardens are called "parks" without exaggeration. Like the emperors of old on Palatino, the fortunate residents here look out over the Circus Maximus and the Tiber, winding its way far below. Today's travelers still enjoy great views, famously including that from the peculiar keyhole at the gates to the headquarters of the Cavalieri di Malta (Knights of Malta), which may be the most peered-through in the world.

TOP ATTRACTIONS

FodorśChoice **Centrale Montemartini.** After visiting Rome's many old palazzi, the Cen-
★ trale Montemartini feels like a breath of fresh air. Rome's first electricity
plant, reopened as a permanent museum in 2005, houses the overflow
of ancient art from the Musei Capitolini collection. With Roman sculptures and mosaics set against industrial machinery and pipes, nowhere
else in Rome is the contrast between ancient and modern more apparent
or enjoyable. A pleasure, too, is the sheer space of the building—but
even better than soaring ceilings and high walls is the fact that you're
likely to be one of the only visitors here, making it the perfect stop
for those feeling claustrophobic from Rome's crowds. Unusually, the
collection is organized by the area in which the ancient pieces were
found. Highlights include the 4th-century-AD mosaic of a hunting
scene, complete with horseman driving his sword into a boar, and the
two portrait heads, so well preserved that they still, incredibly, retain
flakes of the gold that once gilded them. ⊠ *Via Ostiense 106, Aventino*
🕾 *06/0608* ⊕ *www.centralemontemartini.org* ✏*€7.50* ☺ *Closed Mon.*
Ⓜ *Garbatella. Bus Nos. 23, 271, 769, and 770.*

FodorśChoice **Piazza dei Cavalieri di Malta.** Peek through the keyhole of the **Priorato di**
★ **Malta,** the walled compound of the Knights of Malta, and you'll get a
surprising eyeful: a picture-perfect view of the dome of St. Peter's Basilica, far across the city. Giovanni Battista Piranesi, 18th-century Rome's
foremost engraver, is more famous for rendering architecture than for
realizing it, yet the square is his work along with the priory (1765)
within. Stone insignia of the Knights notwithstanding, the square's most
famed feature is that initially nondescript keyhole in the dark green
door of No. 3. Bend slightly and surprise your eyes with a view that is
worth walking miles for. As for the Order of the Knights of Malta, it
is the world's oldest and most exclusive order of chivalry, founded in
the Holy Land during the Crusades. Though nominally ministering to
the sick in those early days—a role that has since become the order's
raison d'être—the knights amassed huge tracts of land in the Middle
East. From 1530 they were based on the Mediterranean island of Malta,
but in 1798 Napoléon expelled them and, in 1834, they established
themselves in Rome. Tours are sometimes available if you would like
to go inside; call for information. ⊠ *Via Santa Sabina and Via Porta
Lavernale, Aventino* 🕾 *06/577 9193 for tour reservations* Ⓜ *Circo Massimo; Bus Nos. 60, 81, 118, 175, 271, and 715; Tram No. 3.*

Roseto Comunale. As suggested by the paths shaped like a menorah, what
is now the city rose garden was once a Jewish cemetery: one tombstone
is still visible on the side of the garden across from Valle Murcia, the
name for the swamp that once separated this area from the Palatine.
The garden is laid out to reflect the history of roses from antiquity to the
present day. If you happen to be in town when the roses are in bloom,
stop by: it's closed the rest of the year. ⊠ *Viale di Valle Murcia, Aventino*
🕾 *06/5746810* ☺ *Closed July–late Apr.* Ⓜ *Circo Massimo. Bus Nos. 60,
81, 118, 160, 271, 628, and 715; Tram No. 3.*

10

FAMILY

Fodor's Choice

★

Santa Maria in Cosmedin. Although this is one of Rome's oldest churches, with a haunting, almost exotic interior, it plays second fiddle to the renowned artifact installed in the church portico. The **Bocca della Verità** (Mouth of Truth) is in reality nothing more than an ancient drain cover, unearthed during the Middle Ages. Legend has it, however, that the teeth will clamp down on a liar's hand, and to tell a lie with your hand in the fearsome mouth is to risk losing it. Hordes of tourists line up to take the test every day (kids especially get a kick out of it), although entering the church itself requires no wait. Few churches, inside or out, are as picturesque as this one. The church was built in the 6th century for the city's burgeoning Greek population. Heavily restored at the end of the 19th century, it has the typical basilica form and stands across from the **Piazza della Bocca della Verità**, originally the location of the Forum Boarium, ancient Rome's cattle market, and later the site of public executions. ⊠ *Piazza Santa Maria in Cosmedin, Aventino* ☎ *06/6787759* Ⓜ *Circo Massimo. Bus Nos. 3, 60, 75, 81, 118, 160, 175, 271, and 628.*

Santa Sabina. This early Christian basilica demonstrates the severe but lovely simplicity common to churches of its era. Although some of the side chapels were added in the 16th and 17th centuries, the essential form is as Rome's Christians knew it in the 5th century. Once bright with mosaics, today the church has only one: that above the entrance door (its gold letters announce how the church was founded by Peter of Illyria, "rich for the poor," under Pope Celestine I). Meanwhile, the mosaics in the apse have been at least partially reproduced in Taddeo Zuccari's Renaissance fresco of Christ and his apostles. The beautifully carved, 5th-century cedar doors to the left of the outside entrance are the oldest of their kind in existence. ⊠ *Piazza Pietro d'Illiria 1, Via di Santa Sabina, Aventino* ☎ *06/579401* Ⓜ *Circo Massimo; Bus Nos. 60, 75, 81, 118, 160, 175, and 715; Tram No. 3.*

Tempio di Portuno. A picture-perfect, if dollhouse-size, Roman temple, this rectangular edifice from the 2nd century BC is built in the Greek style. Positioned by the old river port and long known as the Temple of Fortuna Virilis ("Manly Fortune"), it was appropriately dedicated to Portunus, the protector of ports. It owes its fine state of preservation to the fact that it was consecrated as a church. ⊠ *Piazza Bocca della Verità, Aventino* Ⓜ *Circo Massimo; Bus Nos. 60, 75, 81, 118, 160, 175, and 271; Tram No. 3.*

Tempio di Ercole Vincitore. Long called the Temple of Vesta because of its similarity in shape to the building of that name in the Roman Forum, it's now recognized as the Temple of Hercules Victor. All but one of the 20 Corinthian columns of this evocative ruin remain intact. Like its next-door neighbor, the Tempio di Portuno, it was built in the 2nd century BC. The little park around the temples have benches to rest weary feet. ⊠ *Piazza Bocca della Verità, Aventino* Ⓜ *Circo Massimo; Bus Nos. 60, 75, 81, 118, 160, 175, and 271; Tram No. 3.*

FAMILY

Terme di Caracalla (*Baths of Caracalla*). The Terme di Caracalla are some of Rome's most massive—yet least visited—ruins. They're also a peek into how Romans turned "bathing" into one of the most lavish leisure activities imaginable.

Begun in AD 206 by the emperor Septimius Severus and completed by his son, Caracalla, the 28-acre complex could accommodate 1,600 bathers at a time. Along with an Olympic-size swimming pool and baths, the complex also had two gymnasiums for weightlifting, boxing, and wrestling; a library with both Latin and Greek texts; and gardens. All the services depended on slaves, who checked clients' robes, rubbed them down, and saw to all of their needs. Under the magnificent marble pavement of the stately halls, other slaves toiled in a warren of tiny rooms and passages, stoking the fires that heated the water.

Taking a bath was a long and complex process—which makes more sense if you see it, first and foremost, as a social activity. You began in the sudatoria, a series of small rooms resembling saunas, where you sat and sweated. From these you moved to the *caldarium*, a large, circular room that was humid rather than simply hot. This was where the actual business of washing went on. You used a strigil, or scraper, to get the dirt off; if you were rich, your slave did this for you. Next stop: the warm(-ish) *tepidarium*, which helped you start cooling down. Finally, you splashed around in the *frigidarium*, a swimming pool filled with cold water.

Today, the complex is a shell of its former self. Some black-and-white mosaic fragments remain, but you'll need your imagination to see the interior as it would have been, filled with opulent mosaics, frescoes, and sculptures. But for getting a sense of the sheer size of ancient Rome's ambitions, few places are better. The walls still tower, the spaces still dwarf, and—if you try—you almost can hear the laughs of long-gone bathers, splashing in the pools. If you're here in summer, don't miss the chance to catch an open-air opera or ballet in the baths, put on by the **Teatro dell'Opera di Roma**. ⊠ *Via delle Terme di Caracalla 52, Aventino* ☎ *06/39967700* ⊕ *www.coopculture.it* ⊠ *€6 (includes Villa dei Quintili and Mausoleo di Cecilia Metella)* Ⓜ *Circo Massimo.*

WORTH NOTING

San Saba. A former monastery, founded by monks of the order of San Saba after they fled Jerusalem following the Arab invasion, this is a major monument of Romanesque Rome. Inside, an almost rustic interior harbors a famed Cosmatesque mosaic pavement and a hodgepodge of ancient marble pieces. ⊠ *Piazza Gian Lorenzo Bernini 20, Via San Saba, Aventino* ☎ *06/64580140* ⊕ *www.sansaba.it* Ⓜ *Circo Massimo.*

TESTACCIO

Testaccio is perhaps the world's only neighborhood built on broken pots: the eponymous hill grew from discarded amphorae used to store oil, wine, and other goods loaded from the nearby Ripa, when Rome had a port and the Tiber was once a mighty river to an empire. Quiet during the day but buzzing on Saturday—with the very loud music from rows of discos and clubs, it's sometimes hailed as Rome's new "Left

Bank" neighborhood. The area is also a must for those seeking authentic and comparatively cheap Roman cuisine.

TOP ATTRACTIONS

Fodor's Choice
★

Cimitero Acattolico (*Non-Catholic or Protestant Cemetery*). Piled up against the ancient Aurelian Walls, this famed cemetery was intended for the interment of non-Catholics. This is where you'll find the tomb of John Keats, who tragically died in Rome after succumbing to consumption at age 25 in 1821. The stone is famously inscribed, "Here lies one whose name was writ in water" (the poet requested that no name or dates should appear). Nearby is the place where Shelley's heart was buried, as well as the tombs of Goethe's son, founder of the Italian Communist Party and vehement anti-Fascist Antonio Gramsci, and America's famed beat poet Gregory Corso. The cemetery is about a 20-minute walk south from the Arco di Constantino along Via San Gregorio and Viale Aventino, but the easiest way to get here is to catch the Metro Linea B from Termini station to the Piramide stop just around the corner from the entrance to the cemetery. ⊠ *Via Caio Cestio 6, Testaccio* ☎ *06/5741900* ⊕ *www.cemeteryrome.it* ⊠ *€3 suggested donation* ☞ *If door is closed, ring bell for cemetery custodian* Ⓜ *Piramide; Buses Nos. 23, 30, 60, 75, 95, 118, and 715; Tram No. 3.*

FAMILY
Piramide di Caio Cestio. This monumental tomb was designed in 12 BC for the immensely wealthy praetor Gaius Cestius in the form of a 120-foot-tall pyramid; according to an inscription, it was completed in a little less than a year. Though little else is known about him, he clearly had a taste for grandeur and liked to show off his travels to far parts of the nascent empire. The pyramid was recently restored in a project funded by a €1 million donation from Japanese fashion tycoon Yuzo Yagi. ⊠ *Piazzale Ostiense, Testaccio* ⊕ *www.060608.it* Ⓜ *Piramide; Bus Nos. 3, 30, 60, 75, 95, 118, 130, 175, and 719.*

San Paolo fuori le Mura (*St. Paul's Outside the Walls*). A couple of Metro stops farther down Via Ostiense from Testaccio, in a rather dreary location near the river, St. Paul's is one of Rome's most historic and important churches. Its size, second only to St. Peter's Basilica, allows ample space for the 272 roundels depicting every pope from St. Peter to the current Pope Francis (found below the ceiling, with spaces left blank for pontiffs to come). Built in the 4th century AD by Constantine over the site where St. Paul had been buried, the church was later enlarged, but in July 1823, a fire burned it almost to the ground. Although the rebuilt St. Paul's has a sort of monumental grandeur, it's only in the cloisters (€4) that you get a real sense of the magnificence of the original building. In the middle of the nave is the famous baldacchino created by sculptor Arnolfo di Cambio. ⊠ *Piazzale San Paolo, Via Ostiense 190, Testaccio* ☎ *06/69880800* ⊕ *www.basilicasanpaolo.org* ⊠ *Cloister €4* Ⓜ *Basilica San Paolo.*

MONTI, ESQUILINO, CELIO, AND THE VIA APPIA ANTICA

Getting Oriented

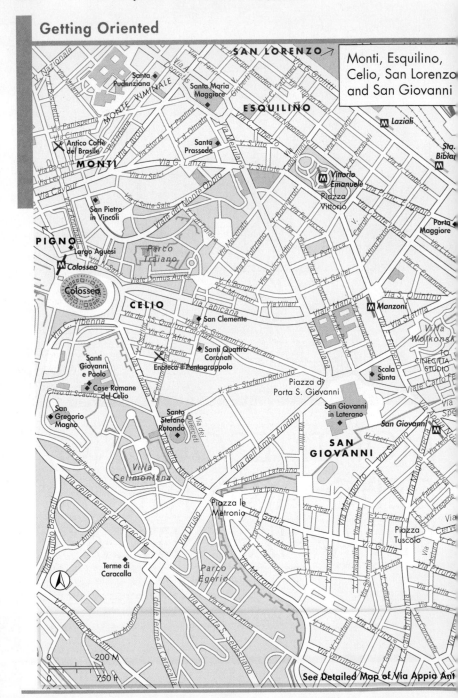

Monti, Esquilino,
Celio, San Lorenzo
and San Giovanni

TOP REASONS TO GO

San Pietro in Vincoli: Hike uphill past Lucrezia Borgia's palace to visit Michelangelo's magisterial *Moses*.

San Clemente: Hurtle back through three eras—the Middle Ages, early Christianity, and ancient Rome—by descending four excavated levels of this venerated church.

Magnificent Mosaics: In a neighborhood once home to the first Christians, Santa Pudenziana gleams with a stunning early 5th-century mosaic of Christ while Santa Prassede shimmers with Byzantine beauty nearby.

Catacomb Country: Be careful exploring the underground graves of the earliest Christians—one wrong turn and it may be days before you surface.

QUICK BITE

Antico Caffè del Brasile. This caffè in the heart of Monti has been a local favorite since 1908. Even Pope John Paul II was a fan: as a student, he regularly got coffee here. Try the caffè's own coffee blends, chocolates, and pastries. ⌧ *Via dei Serpenti 23, Monti* ☎ *06/4882319* Ⓜ *Cavour.*

Enoteca Il Pentagrappolo. With its exposed-brick arches, soft lighting and close proximity to the Colosseum, this attractive wine bar has an ample spread of cheeses and salamis, and more than 250 wines. ⌧ *Via Celimontana 21/B, Celio* ☎ *06/7096301* ⊕ *www.ilpentagrappolo.com.*

GETTING HERE

The Esquilino hill can be reached via the Vittorio Emanuele subway station, one stop from Termini station. The Monti area (running down one side of the Esquilino to the Roman Forum) can be reached by the Cavour stop on Line B. Bus No. 117 runs from Piazza del Popolo and the Corso to both Celio and Monti districts on the Esquilino. Bus No. 3 from Trastevere and Bus No. 75 from Termini reach Celio, about a five-minute walk from the Colosseo stop.

MAKING THE MOST OF YOUR TIME

Some of central Rome's least touristy and best-loved neighborhoods, these areas also have a great deal to explore—especially in the way of ancient sights. If you have limited time, combine your exploration here with your discovery of the ancient Forum and Colosseum, which are nearby. From those sights, it's a short walk to the multilayered Basilica of San Clemente and the Santi Quattro Coronati, a gem of medieval church architecture. Head back to the Colosseum area and then toward the Esquilino hill via the steps in the Colosseo Metro station to reach the Largo Agnesi overlook, which offers a great view of the Colosseum, and the Palatine Hill beyond.

On the north side of the Colosseum, in the quarter known as Monti, you'll find San Pietro in Vincoli, home to Michelangelo's *Moses*. As you head farther northeast, don't miss gigantic Santa Maria Maggiore; nearby are wonderful mosaics in San Prassede and Santa Pudenziana.

Make sure to give yourself at least a couple of hours to explore the neighborhood of Monti itself, with its artisanal shops, fine trattorias, and high-end boutiques—the best of old and new Rome, all in one tiny, proud *rione* (district).

Sightseeing
★★★★
Nightlife
★★
Dining
★★★
Lodging
★★★★
Shopping
★★

Several neighborhoods come together here, just north of the Roman Forum and the Colosseum. They range from the bustling, multicultural Esquilino neighborhood to the super-trendy (yet still traditional), ancient rione of Monti. Most travelers will find themselves passing through at least part of the area, either when they come into the Termini train station or when they pay a visit to Michelangelo's *Moses* at the Church of San Pietro in Vincoli. Head farther south for the evocative Via Appia Antica, dotted with ruins and ancient catacombs.

MONTI

Updated by Agnes Crawford

As the hill starts to slope downward from Termini station, right around Santa Maria Maggiore, the streets become cobblestone, the palazzos prettier, and the boutiques higher-end. This is the area known as Monti, the oldest rione in Rome. Gladiators, prostitutes, and even Caesar made their homes in this area that stretches from Santa Maria Maggiore down to the Forum. Today, Monti is one of the best-loved neighborhoods in Rome, known for its appealing mix of medieval streets, old-school trattorias, and hip boutiques.

TOP ATTRACTIONS

Fodor'sChoice ★ **San Pietro in Vincoli.** Michelangelo's *Moses,* carved in the early 16th century for the never-completed tomb of Pope Julius II, has put this church on the map. The tomb was to include dozens of statues and stand nearly 40 feet tall when installed in St. Peter's Basilica. But only three statues—*Moses* and the two that flank it here, *Leah* and *Rachel*—had been completed when Julius died. Julius's successor as pope, from the rival Medici family, had other plans for Michelangelo, and the tomb was abandoned unfinished. The fierce power of this remarkable sculpture dominates its setting. People say that you can see the sculptor's profile in the lock of Moses's beard right under his lip, and that the pope's profile can also be seen. As for the rest of the church, St. Peter takes second billing to Moses. The reputed sets of chains (*vincoli*) that bound St. Peter during his imprisonment by the Romans in both Jerusalem and Rome are in a bronze and crystal urn under the main altar. Other treasures include a 7th-century mosaic of St. Sebastian, in front of the second altar to the left of the main altar, and, by the door, the tomb of the Pollaiuolo brothers, two lesser 15th-century Florentine artists. ⊠ *Piazza di San Pietro in Vincoli, Monti* ☎ *06/97844952* Ⓜ *Cavour.*

Fodor'sChoice **Santa Maria Maggiore.** Despite it's florid 18th-century facade, Santa
★ Maria Maggiore is one of the oldest churches in Rome, built around 440 by Pope Sixtus III. One of the four great pilgrimage churches of Rome, it's also the city center's best example of an Early Christian basilica—one of the immense, hall-like structures derived from ancient Roman civic buildings and divided into thirds by two great rows of columns marching up the nave. The other three major basilicas in Rome (San Giovanni in Laterano, Basilica di San Pietro, and St. Paul's Outside the Walls) have been largely rebuilt. Paradoxically, the major reason why this church is such a striking example of Early Christian design is that the same man who built the undulating exteriors circa 1740, Ferdinando Fuga, also conscientiously restored the interior, throwing out later additions and, crucially, replacing a number of the great columns.

Precious 5th-century mosaics high on the nave walls and on the triumphal arch in front of the main altar bear splendid testimony to the basilica's venerable age. Those along the nave show 36 scenes from the Old Testament (unfortunately, tough to see clearly without binoculars), and those on the arch illustrate the Annunciation and the Youth of Christ. The resplendent carved-wood ceiling dates to the early 16th century; it's supposed to have been gilded with the first gold brought from the New World. The inlaid marble pavement (called Cosmatesque, after the family of master artisans who developed the technique) in the central nave is even older, dating to the 12th century.

The **Cappella Sistina** (Sistine Chapel), in the right-hand transept, was created by architect Domenico Fontana for Pope Sixtus V in 1585. Elaborately decorated with precious marbles "liberated" from the monuments of ancient Rome, the chapel includes a lower-level museum in which some 13th-century sculptures by Arnolfo da Cambio are all that's left of what was the once richly endowed chapel of the *presepio* (Christmas crèche), looted during the Sack of Rome in 1527.

Directly opposite, on the church's other side, stands the **Cappella Paolina** (Pauline Chapel), a rich Baroque setting for the tombs of the Borghese popes Paul V—who commissioned the chapel in 1611 with the declared intention of outdoing Sixtus's chapel across the nave—and Clement VIII. The **Cappella Sforza** (Sforza Chapel) next door was designed by Michelangelo and completed by Della Porta. Just right of the altar, next to his father, lies Gian Lorenzo Bernini; his monument is an engraved slab, as humble as the tombs of his patrons are grand.

Above the loggia, the outside mosaic of Christ raising his hand in blessing is one of Rome's most beautiful sights, especially when lighted at night. The loggia mosaics can be seen close-up by following a 30-minute guided tour (€5). Tours run roughly every hour, though have no fixed timetable. For information or to join either tour, go through the souvenir shop inside the church on the right and down the stairs to the right to the museum entrance. ⊠ *Piazza di Santa Maria Maggiore, Monti* ☎ *06/69886802* 🖃 *Museum tour €4, loggia mosaics tour €5* Ⓜ *Termini.*

Fodor'sChoice
★
Santa Prassede. This small, inconspicuous 9th-century church is known above all for the exquisite **Cappella di San Zenone,** just to the left of the entrance. It gleams with vivid mosaics that reflect their Byzantine inspiration. Though much less classical and naturalistic than the earlier mosaics of Santa Pudenziana, they are no less splendid, and the composition of four angels hovering on the sky-blue vault is one of the masterstrokes of Byzantine art. Note the square halo over the head of Theodora, mother of St. Paschal I, the pope who built this church. It indicates that she was still alive when she was depicted by the artist. The chapel also contains one curious relic: a miniature pillar, supposedly part of the column at which Christ was flogged during the Passion. It was brought to Rome in the 13th century. Over the main altar, the magnificent mosaics on the arch and apse are also in rigid Byzantine style. In them, Pope Paschal I wears the square halo of the living and holds a model of his church. ⊠ *Via di Santa Prassede 9/a, Monti* ☎ *06/4882456* Ⓜ *Cavour.*

Fodor'sChoice
★
Santa Pudenziana. Apart from Ravenna, Rome has some of the most opulent mosaics in Italy, and this church has one of the most striking examples. Commissioned during the papacy of Innocent I, its early 5th-century apse mosaic represents Christ Teaching the Apostles and sits above a Baroque altarpiece surrounded by a bevy of florid 18th-century paintings. The mosaic is remarkable for its iconography; at the center sits Christ Enthroned, shown as an emperor or as a philosopher holding court, surrounded by his apostles. Each apostle faces the spectator, literally rubbing shoulders with his companion (unlike later hieratic styles in which each figure is isolated), and bears an individualized expression. Above these figures and a landscape symbolizing Heavenly Jerusalem float the signs of the four evangelists in a blue sky flecked with the orange of sunset, made from thousands of *tesserae* (mosaic tiles).

To either side of Christ, Sts. Praxedes and Pudentiana hold wreaths over the heads of Sts. Peter and Paul. These two women were actually daughters of the Roman senator Pudens (probably the one mentioned in 2 Timothy 4:21), whose family befriended both apostles. During the persecutions of Nero, both sisters collected the blood of many martyrs before suffering their fate. Pudentiana transformed her house into a church, but her namesake church was constructed over a 2nd-century bathhouse. Beyond the sheer beauty of the mosaic work, the size, rich detail, and number of figures make this both the last gasp of ancient Roman art and one of the first monuments of early Christianity. ⊠ *Via Urbana 160, Monti* ☎ *06/4814622* Ⓜ *Termini.*

ESQUILINO

Rome's most sprawling hill—the Esquilino—lies at the very edge of most tourist maps. Even imperial Rome could not have matched this minicosmopolis for sheer internationalism. Right around Termini, sons of the soil—the so-called "romani romani"—mingle with Chinese, Sri Lankans, Sikhs, and a hundred nationalities in between. One highlight is the Nuovo Mercato Esquilino, a covered market hall where goods from the four corners of the earth are bought and sold in a multitude of languages. This is also where you can find some of the city's best ethnic restaurants and cheapest B&Bs—just not the cobblestone atmosphere that most think of when they think of Rome.

WORTH NOTING

Porta Maggiore (*Main Gate*). The massive 1st-century-AD arch was built as part of the original Aqua Claudia and then incorporated into the walls hurriedly erected in the late 3rd century as Rome's fortunes began to decline; the great arch of the aqueduct subsequently became a *porta* (city gate). It gives an idea of the grand scale of ancient Roman public works. On the Piazzale Labicano side, to the east, is the curious **Baker's Tomb,** erected in the 1st century BC by a prosperous baker (predating both the aqueduct and the city walls); it's shaped like an oven to signal the deceased's trade. The site is now in the middle of a public transport node, and is close to Rome's first tram depot (going back to 1889). ⊠ *Piazza di Porta Maggiore, Esquilino* Ⓜ *Tram No. 3, 5, 14, or 19.*

PIGNETO

A hip neighborhood, famed for its street art and full of young people, Pigneto comes to life at night and is a good spot for cool restaurants and caffè. A short ride from Termini station (Bus No. 105, Tram No. 19 or 14), the majority of bars and restaurants are clustered around the section of Via del Pigneto between Via l'Aquila and Circonvallazione Casilina, and around the junction of Via Braccio da Montone and Via Fanfulla da Lodi.

CELIO

On the border of Monti, from the Colosseum west toward Piazza San Giovanni, the Celio neighborhood is a tranquil, lovely residential area replete with medieval churches and ruins. Sights not to miss here include the Basilica of San Clemente, the church of Santi Quattro Coronati, and the church of Santo Stefano Rotondo.

TOP ATTRACTIONS

Fodor'sChoice ★ **Case Romane del Celio.** Formerly accessible only through the church of Santi Giovanni e Paolo, this important ancient Roman excavation was opened in 2002 as a museum in its own right. An underground honeycomb of rooms, the site comprises the lower levels of a so-called *insula*, or apartment block, the heights of which were a wonder to ancient Roman contemporaries. Through the door on the left of the Clivo di Scauro lane a portico leads to the Room of the Genie, where painted figures grace the walls virtually untouched over two millennia. Farther on is the Confessio altar of Saint John and Saint Paul, officials at Constantine's court who were executed under Julian the Apostate. Still lower is the Antiquarium, where state-of-the-art lighting showcases amphorae, pots, and ancient Roman bricks, with stamps so fresh they might have been imprinted yesterday. ⊠ *Clivio di Scauro, Celio* ☎ *06/70454544* ⊕ *www.caseromane.it* ⌑ *€6* ☉ *Closed Tues. and Wed.* Ⓜ *Colosseo; Bus Nos. 60, 75, 81, 117, 118, 175; Tram No. 3.*

Fodor'sChoice   **San Clemente.** One of the most impressive archaeological sites in Rome,
★   San Clemente is a historical triple-decker. A 12th-century church was built on top of a 4th-century church, which had been built over a 2nd-century pagan temple to the god Mithras and 1st-century Roman apartments. The layers were uncovered in 1857, when a curious prior, Friar Joseph Mullooly, started excavations beneath the present basilica. Today, you can descend to explore all three.

The **upper church** (at street level) is a gem in its own right. In the apse, a glittering 12th-century mosaic shows Jesus on a cross that turns into a living tree. Green acanthus leaves swirl and teem with small scenes of everyday life. Early Christian symbols, including doves, vines, and fish, decorate the 4th-century marble choir screens. In the left nave, the Castiglioni chapel holds frescoes painted around 1400 by the Florentine artist Masolino da Panicale (1383–1440), a key figure in the introduction of realism and one-point perspective into Renaissance painting. Note the large Crucifixion and scenes from the lives of Saints Catherine, Ambrose, and Christopher, plus the Annunciation (over the entrance).

To the right of the sacristy (and bookshop), descend the stairs to the **4th-century church**, used until 1084, when it was damaged beyond repair during a siege of the area by the Norman prince Robert Guiscard. Still intact are some vibrant 11th-century frescoes depicting stories from the life of St. Clement. Don't miss the last fresco on the left, in what used to be the central nave. It includes a particularly colorful quote—including "Go on, you sons of harlots, pull!"—that's not only unusual for a religious painting, but one of the earliest examples of written vernacular Italian.

Descend an additional set of stairs to the **mithraeum,** a shrine dedicated to the god Mithras. His cult spread from Persia and gained a foothold in Rome during the 2nd and 3rd centuries AD. Mithras was believed to have been born in a cave and was thus worshipped in cavernous, underground chambers, where initiates into the all-male cult would share a meal while reclining on stone couches, some visible here along with the altar block. Most such pagan shrines in Rome were destroyed by Christians, who often built churches over their remains, as happened here. ⊠ *Via San Giovanni in Laterano 108, Celio* ☎ *06/7740021* ⊕ *www. basilicasanclemente.com* ⌑ *Archaeological area €10* Ⓜ *Colosseo.*

Fodor'sChoice   **Santi Giovanni e Paolo.** Perched up the incline of the Clivio di Scauro—
★   a magical time-machine of a street, where the dial seems to be stuck

somewhere in the 13th century—Santi Giovanni e Paolo is an image that would tempt most landscape painters. Marked by one of Rome's finest Romanesque bell towers, it looms over a picturesque piazza. Underneath, however, are other treasures, whose excavations can be seen in the **Case Romane del Celio** museum. A basilica erected on the spot was, like San Clemente, destroyed in 1084 by attacking Normans. Its half-buried columns, near the current church entrance, are visible through misty glass. The current church's origins date to the start of the 12th century, but most of the interior dates to the 17th century and later. The lovely, incongruous chandeliers are a hand-me-down from New York's Waldorf-Astoria hotel, a gift arranged by the late Cardinal Francis Spellman of New York, whose titular church this was. Spellman also initiated the excavations here in 1949. ⊠ *Piazza di Santi Giovanni e Paolo 13, Celio* ☎ *06/772711* Ⓜ *Colosseo.*

Fodor's Choice
★
Santi Quattro Coronati. Situated on one of those evocative cul-de-sacs in Rome where history seems to be holding its breath, this church is strongly imbued with the sanctity of the Romanesque era. Marvelously redolent of the Middle Ages, this is one of the most unusual and unexpected corners in Rome, a quiet citadel that has resisted the tides of time and traffic. The church, which dates back to the 4th century, honors the Four Crowned Saints: the four brothers Severus, Severianus, Carpophorus, and Victorinus, all Roman officials who were whipped to death for their faith by Emperor Diocletian (284–305). After its 9th century reconstruction, the church was twice as large as it is now; the abbey was partially destroyed during the Normans' sack of Rome in 1084 but reconstructed about 30 years later. This explains the inordinate size of the apse in relation to the small nave. Don't miss the **cloister**, with its well-tended gardens and 12th-century fountain. The entrance is the door in the left nave; ring the bell if it's not open.

There's another medieval gem hidden away off the courtyard at the church entrance: the **Chapel of San Silvestro.** (Enter the door marked "Monache Agostiniane" and ring the bell at the left for the nun; give her the appropriate donation through a grate, and she will press a button to open the chapel door.) The chapel has remained, for the most part, as it was when consecrated in 1246. Some of the best-preserved medieval frescoes in Rome decorate the walls, telling the story of the Christian emperor Constantine's recovery from leprosy thanks to Pope Sylvester I. Note, too, the delightful *Last Judgment* fresco above the door, in which the angel on the left neatly rolls up sky and stars like a backdrop, signaling the end of the world. ⊠ *Via Santi Quattro Coronati 20, Celio* ☎ *06/70475427* ⌸ *Chapel of San Silvestro €2* Ⓜ *Colosseo.*

Santo Stefano Rotondo. This 5th-century church is thought to have been inspired by the design of the Church of the Holy Sepulchre in Jerusalem. Its unusual round plan and timbered ceiling set it apart from most other Roman churches. So do the frescoes, which lovingly depict 34 of the goriest martyrdoms in Catholicism—a catalogue, above the names of different emperors, of every type of violent death conceivable. (You've been warned: these are not for the fainthearted.) ⊠ *Via Santo Stefano Rotondo 7, Celio* ☎ *06/421199* ⊘ *Closed Mon.* Ⓜ *Colosseo.*

WORTH NOTING

San Gregorio Magno. Set amid the greenery of the Celian Hill, this church wears its Baroque facade proudly. Dedicated to St. Gregory the Great (who served as pope 590–604), it was built about 750 by Pope Gregory II to commemorate his predecessor and namesake. The church of San Gregorio itself has the appearance of a typical Baroque structure, the result of remodeling in the 17th and 18th centuries. But you can still see what's said to be the stone slab on which the pious St. Gregory the Great slept; it's in the far right-hand chapel. Outside are three chapels. The right chapel is dedicated to Gregory's mother, Saint Sylvia, and contains a Guido Reni fresco of the *Concert of Angels.* The chapel in the center, dedicated to Saint Andrew, contains two monumental frescoes showing scenes from the saint's life. They were painted at the beginning of the 17th century by Domenichino (*The Flagellation of St. Andrew*) and Guido Reni (*The Execution of St. Andrew*). It's a striking juxtaposition of the sturdy, if sometimes stiff, classicism of Domenichino with the more flamboyant and heroic Baroque manner of Guido Reni. ⊠ *Piazza di San Gregorio, Celio* ☎ *06/7008227* ⊕ *www.camaldolesiromani.com* Ⓜ *Colosseo.*

SAN GIOVANNI

The crown jewel of San Giovanni, just west of Celio, is the Basilica of San Giovanni in Laterano, Rome's cathedral. Today, it is largely a residential neighborhood with 19th- and 20th-century apartment buildings and modern shops. Reach San Giovanni by walking south along Via Merulana from the Colosseum.

TOP ATTRACTIONS

Fodor'sChoice   **San Giovanni in Laterano.** The cathedral of Rome is San Giovanni in Lat-
★   erano, not St. Peter's. The church was built here by Emperor Constantine 10 years before he built the church dedicated to Peter, and because of its primacy it is the ecclesiastical seat of the Bishop of Rome—also known as the Pope. Constantine obtained the land from the wealthy Laterani family and donated it to the Church. But thanks to vandals, earthquakes, and fires, today's building owes most of its form to 16th- and 17th-century restorations, including an interior designed by Baroque genius Borromini. Before you go inside, look up: at the top of the towering facade, built for Pope Clement X in 1736, 15 colossal statues (the 12 apostles plus Christ, John the Baptist, and the Virgin Mary) stand watch over the suburbs spreading from Porta San Giovanni.

Despite the church's Baroque design, some earlier fragments do remain. Under the portico on the left stands an ancient statue of Constantine, while the central portal's ancient bronze doors were brought here from the Forum's Curia. Inside, the fragment of a fresco on the first pillar is attributed to the 14th-century Florentine painter Giotto; it depicts Pope Boniface VIII proclaiming the first Holy Year in 1300. The altar's rich Gothic tabernacle—holding what the faithful believe are the heads of Sts. Peter and Paul—dates to 1367. Head to the last chapel at the end of the left aisle to check out the **cloister.** Encrusted with 12th-century Cosmatesque mosaics by father-and-son team the Vassallettos, it's a break from the Baroque ... and from the big tour groups that tend to fill the church's interior. Around the corner, meanwhile, stands one of the oldest Christian structures in Rome. Emperor Constantine built the standalone octagonal **Baptistery** in AD 315. Despite several restorations, a 17th-century interior redecoration, and even a Mafia-related car bombing in 1993, the Baptistery remains much as it would have been in ancient times. ⊠ *Piazza di Porta San Giovanni, San Giovanni* 🕾 *06/69886433* 🖾 *Cloister €3, museum €4* Ⓜ *San Giovanni.*

WORTH NOTING

Scala Santa. According to tradition, the Scala Santa was the staircase from Pilate's palace in Jerusalem—and, therefore, the one trod by Christ himself. St. Helena, Emperor Constantine's mother, brought the 28 marble steps to Rome in 326. As they have for centuries, pilgrims still come to climb the steps on their knees. At the top, they can get a glimpse of the **Sancta Sanctorum** (Holy of Holies), the richly decorated private papal chapel containing an image of Christ "not made by human hands." You can sneak a peek, too, by taking one of the (nonsanctified) staircases on either side. The splendid Sancta Sanctorum—the Pope's private chapel long before the Sistine Chapel—is itself visitable, and well worth the price of admission. ⊠ *Piazza di San Giovanni in Laterano, San Giovanni* 🕾 *06/69886433* 🖾 *Scala Santa free, Sancta Sanctorum €3.50* ⊘ *Sancta Sanctorum closed Sun.* Ⓜ *San Giovanni.*

SAN LORENZO

This traditionally working-class neighborhood north of Termini station is close to the University. The area is inundated with students and faculty, which makes for quite a lively scene in the evening.

VIA APPIA ANTICA

Far south of the Celio lies catacomb country—the haunts of the fabled underground graves of Rome's earliest Christians, arrayed to either side of the Queen of Roads, the Via Appia Antica (Appian Way). Strewn with classical ruins and dotted with grazing sheep, the road stirs images of chariots and legionnaires returning from imperial conquests. It was completed in 312 BC by Appius Claudius, who laid it out to connect Rome with settlements in the south, in the direction of Naples. Though time and vandals have taken their toll on the ancient relics along the road, the catacombs remain to cast their spirit-warm spell. Although Jews and pagans also used the catacombs, the Christians expanded the idea of underground burials to a massive scale. Persecution of Christians under pagan emperors made martyrs of many, whose bones, once interred underground, became objects of veneration. Today, the dark, gloomy catacombs contrast strongly with the Appia Antica's fresh air, verdant meadows, and evocative classical ruins.

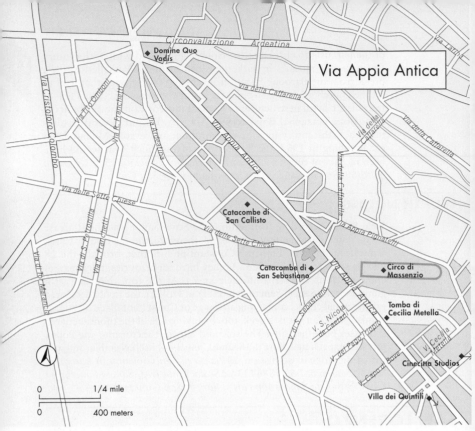

The initial stretch of the Via Appia Antica is not pedestrian-friendly—there is fast, heavy traffic and no sidewalk all the way from Porta San Sebastiano to the Catacombe di San Callisto. To reach the catacombs, take Bus No. 218 from San Giovanni in Laterano. Alternatively, take Metro Line A to Colli Albani and then Bus No. 660 to the Tomba di Cecilia Metella. A more expensive option is the big, green Archeobus from Piazza Venezia (Friday–Sunday, early June–early November only). With an open-top deck, these buses allow you to hop on and off as you please (€20 for 24 hours). Another attractive alternative is to rent a bike—for example, at the Appia Antica Caffè near the Cecilia Metella bus stop.

TOP ATTRACTIONS

Catacombe di San Callisto (*Catacombs of St. Calixtus*). Burial place of several 3rd-century popes, this is Rome's oldest and best-preserved underground cemetery. One of the (English-speaking) friars who act as custodians of the catacomb will guide you through its crypts and galleries, some adorned with early Christian frescoes. Watch out for wrong turns: this catacomb is five stories deep! ■ **TIP→ The large parking garage makes a visit easy—both for you and for large groups—and it can get busy.** ✉ *Via Appia Antica 110/126, Via Appia Antica*

Walk in the footsteps of St. Peter along the Via Appia Antica, stretches of which seem barely altered from the days of the Caesars.

☎ 06/5310151 ⊕ www.catacombe.roma.it ▭ €8 ⊙ Closed Wed. and mid-Jan.–Feb. Ⓜ Bus Nos. 118, 218.

Fodor'sChoice **Catacombe di San Sebastiano** (*Catacombs of St. Sebastian*). The 4th-cen-
★ tury church was named after the saint who was buried in the catacomb, which burrows underground on four different levels. This was the only early Christian cemetery to remain accessible during the Middle Ages, and it was from here that the term "catacomb" is derived—it's in a spot where the road dips into a hollow, known to the Romans as *catacumba* (Greek for "near the hollow"). The Romans used the name to refer to the cemetery that had existed here since the 2nd century BC, and it came to be applied to all the underground cemeteries discovered in Rome in later centuries. As well as Christian burial areas, some very well preserved pagan mausolea were found here in the early 20th century making this one of the more varied catacomb complexes in the area. ⊠ *Via Appia Antica 136, Via Appia Antica* ☎ 06/7850350 ⊕ *www. catacombe.org* ▭ *€8* ⊙ *Closed Sun.* Ⓜ *Bus Nos. 118, 218, 660.*

Domine Quo Vadis (*Church of Quo Vadis*). This church was built on the spot where tradition says Christ appeared to St. Peter as the apostle was fleeing Rome and persuaded him to return and face martyrdom. A paving stone in the church bears an imprint said to have been made by the feet of Christ. ⊠ *Via Appia Antica at Via Ardeatina, Via Appia Antica* ☎ 06/5120441.

Tomba di Cecilia Metella. For centuries, sightseers have flocked to this famous landmark, one of the most complete surviving tombs of ancient Rome. One of the many round mausoleums that once lined the Appian

Way, this tomb is a smaller version of the Mausoleum of Augustus, but impressive nonetheless. It was the burial place of a Roman noblewoman—wife of the son of Crassus, who was one of Julius Caesar's rivals and known as the richest man in the Roman Empire (infamously entering the English language as "crass"). The original decoration includes a frieze of bulls' skulls near the top. The travertine stone walls were made higher and the medieval-style crenellations were added when the tomb was transformed into a fortress by the Caetani family in the 14th century. An adjacent chamber houses a small museum of the area's geological phases. Entrance to this museum also includes the Terme di Caracalla (Baths of Caracalla) and the Villa dei Quintili, but you can also get a super view without going in. ⊠ *Via Appia Antica 162, Via Appia Antica* ☎ *06/39967700* ⊕ *www.archeoroma.beniculturali.it* 🎫 *€6, includes Terme di Caracalla and Villa dei Quintili (valid for 7 days)* ⊘ *Closed Mon.*

WORTH NOTING

OFF THE BEATEN PATH

Cinecittà Studios. Film buffs may want to make the trip out to Cinecittà Studios—stomping ground of Fellini, Audrey Hepburn, and Elizabeth Taylor and birthplace of such classics as *Roman Holiday,* *Cleopatra,* and *La Dolce Vita.* You can take a guided tour of the sets and see the exhibition *Cinecittà Shows Off,* with memorabilia like Elizabeth Taylor's *Cleopatra* gown and the dolphin-shape statue that marked the chariot laps in *Ben-Hur.* Cinecittà is located about 25 minutes southeast of the city center on Metro Line A. ⊠ *Via Tuscolana 1055, Rome* ☎ *06/722931* ⊕ *www.cinecittastudios.it* 🎫 *€10 exhibition, €20 exhibition and tour* Ⓜ *Cinecittà.*

Villa dei Quintili. Even in ruins, this once splendid villa gives a real sense of ancient Rome's opulence, and the small on-site museum includes archaeological finds that add to the vision. Even today, two millennia later, it remains clear why Emperor Commodus—the villain in the 2000 film epic *Gladiator*—coveted this sumptuous property. To get the villa from its owners, the Quintili, he accused the family of plotting against him and had them executed, before moving in himself. He may have used the exedra for training for his fights with ostriches back in the Colosseum. Note that the villa is best included in a separate itinerary from the catacombs, being 5 km (3 miles) away. It is accessible from both the modern Appia Nuova and from the Appia Antica, the ancient road ((by bicycle or on foot only). ⊠ *Via Appia Nuova 1092, Via Appia Antica* ☎ *06/39967700* ⊕ *www.archeoroma.beniculturali.it* 🎫 *€6 (includes entrance to Terme di Caracalla and Tomba di Cecilia Metella, ticket valid for 7 days.)* ⊘ *Closed Mon.* Ⓜ *Colli Albani, then Bus No. 664.*

WHERE TO EAT

EAT LIKE A LOCAL

In Rome, tradition is the dominant feature of the cuisine, with a focus on freshness and simplicity, so when Romans continue ordering the standbys, it's easy to understand why. That said, Rome is the capital of Italy, and the influx of residents from other regions of the country has yielded many variations on the staples.

Artichokes

There are two well-known preparations of *carciofo*, or artichoke in Rome. *Carciofi alla romana* are stuffed with wild mint, garlic, and pecorino, then braised in olive oil, white wine, and water. *Carciofi alla giudia* (Jewish-style) are whole artichokes, deep-fried twice, so that they open like a flower, the outer leaves crisp and golden brown, while the heart remains tender. When artichokes are in season—late winter through the spring—they're served everywhere.

Gelato

For many travelers, their first taste of gelato is revelatory. Its consistency is often said to be a cross between regular American ice cream and soft-serve. The best versions of gelato are extremely flavorful, and almost always made fresh daily. When choosing a *gelateria,* watch for signs that say *gelato artigianale* (artisan- or homemade): otherwise, keep an eye out for the real deal by avoiding gelato that looks too bright or fluffy.

Pizza

There are two kinds of Roman pizza: *al taglio* (by the slice) and *tonda* (round

12

pizza). The former has a thicker, focaccia-like crust and is cut into squares; these are sold by weight and generally available all day. The typical Roman pizza tonda has a very thin crust and is served almost charred—it's cooked in wood-burning ovens that reach extremely high temperatures. Because they're so hot, the ovens are usually fired up only in the evening, which is why Roman pizzerie tend to open for dinner only.

Cacio e pepe

The name means "cheese and pepper" and it's a simple pasta dish from the *cucina povera*, or rustic cooking, tradition. It's a favorite Roman primo, usually made with *tonnarelli* (fresh egg pasta a bit thicker than spaghetti), which is coated with a pecorino-cheese sauce and lots of freshly ground black pepper. Some restaurants serve the dish in an edible bowl of paper-thin baked cheese, for added delicious effect.

Fritti

The classic Roman starter in a trattoria and especially at the pizzeria, is *fritti*: an assortment of fried treats, usually crumbed or in batter. Often, before ordering a pizza, locals will order their fritti—a *filetti di baccala* (salt cod in batter), *fiori di zucca* (zucchini flowers, usually stuffed with anchovy and mozzarella), *suppli* (rice balls stuffed with mozzarella and other ingredients), or *olive ascolane* (stuffed olives). Fritti can

also be found at many pizza al taglio joints or at *tavola caldas* (caffè). They make a great quick snack.

Bucatini all'amatriciana

It might look like spaghetti with red sauce, but there's much more to *bucatini all'amatriciana*. It's a spicy, rich, and complex dish that owes its flavor to *guanciale*, or cured pork jowl, as well as tomatoes and crushed red pepper flakes. It's often served over bucatini, a hollow, spaghetti-like pasta, and topped with grated pecorino Romano.

La Gricia

This dish is often referred to as a "white amatriciana," because it's precisely that: pasta (usually spaghetti or rigatoni) served with pecorino cheese and guanciale—thus amatriciana without the tomato sauce. It's a lighter alternative to *carbonara* in that it doesn't contain egg, and its origins date back further than the amatriciana.

Coda alla vaccinara

Rome's largest slaughterhouse in the 1800s was in the Testaccio neighborhood and that's where you'll find dishes like *coda alla vaccinara*, or "oxtail in the style of the cattle butcher." This dish is made from ox or veal tails stewed with tomatoes, carrots, celery, and wine, and it's usually seasoned with cinnamon. It's simmered for hours and then finished with raisins and pine nuts or bittersweet chocolate.

Updated
by Maria
Pasquale

In Rome, the Eternal(ly culinarily conservative) City, simple yet traditional cuisine reigns supreme. Most chefs prefer to follow the mantra of freshness over fuss, and simplicity of flavor and preparation over complex cooking techniques.

Rome has been known since antiquity for its grand feasts and banquets, and dining out has alway been a favorite Roman pastime. Until recently, the city's *buongustaii* (gourmands) would have been the first to tell you that Rome is distinguished more by its enthusiasm for eating out than for a multitude of world-class restaurants—but this is changing. There is an ever-growing promotion of slow-food practices, a focus on sustainably and locally sourced produce. The economic crisis has forced the food industry in Rome to adopt innovative ways to maintain a clientele who are increasingly looking to dine out but want to spend less. The result has been the rise of "street food" restaurants, selling everything from inexpensive and novel takes on the classic *supplì* (Roman fried-rice balls) to sandwich shops that use a variety of organic ingredients.

Generally speaking, Romans like Roman food, and that's what you'll find in many of the city's trattorias and wine bars. For the most part, today's chefs cling to the traditional and excel at what has taken hundreds, sometimes thousands, of years to perfect. This is why the basic trattoria menu is more or less the same wherever you go. And it's why even the top Roman chefs feature their versions of simple trattoria classics like carbonara, and why those who attempt to offer it in a "deconstructed" or slightly varied way will often come under criticism. To a great extent, Rome is still a town where the Italian equivalent of "What are you in the mood for?" still gets the answer, "Pizza or pasta."

Nevertheless, Rome is the capital of Italy, and because people move here from every corner of the Italian peninsula, there are more variations on the Italian theme in Rome than you'd find elsewhere in Italy: Sicilian, Tuscan, Pugliese, Bolognese, Marchegiano, Sardinian, and northern Italian regional cuisines are all represented. And reflecting the increasingly cosmopolitan nature of the city, you'll find a growing number of good-quality international foods here as well—particularly Japanese, Indian, and Ethiopian.

Oddly enough, though, for a nation that prides itself on *la bella figura* ("looking good"), most Romans don't fuss about music, personal space, lighting, or decor. After all, who needs flashy interior design when so much of Roman life takes place outdoors, when dining alfresco in Rome can take place in the middle of a glorious ancient site or a centuries-old piazza?

12

PLANNING

RESTAURANT TYPES

Until relatively recently, there was a distinct hierarchy delineated by the names of Rome's eating places. A **ristorante** was typically elegant and expensive, and a **trattoria** served more traditional, home-style fare in a relaxed atmosphere. An **osteria** was even more casual, essentially a wine bar and gathering spot that also served food, although the latest species of wine bars generally goes under the moniker of **enoteca**. All these terms still exist but their distinction has blurred considerably. Now, an osteria in the center of town may be pricier than a ristorante across the street.

Although Rome may not boast the grand **caffè** of Paris or Vienna, it does have hundreds of small places on pleasant side streets and piazze. The coffee is routinely of high quality. Locals usually stop in for a quickie at the bar, where prices are much lower than for the same drink taken at the table. If you place your order at the counter, ask if you can sit down: some places charge more for table service. Often you'll pay a cashier first, then give your *scontrino* (receipt) to the person at the counter who fills your order.

HOW TO ORDER: FROM PRIMO TO DOLCE

In a Roman sit-down restaurant, whether a ristorante, trattoria, or osteria, you're expected to order at least two courses. It could be a *primo* (first course, usually pasta or an appetizer) followed by a *secondo* (second course, really a "main course" in English parlance, usually meat or fish); an *antipasto* (starter) followed by a primo or secondo; or a secondo and a *dolce* (dessert). Many people consider a full meal to consist of a primo, a secondo, and a dolce.

If you're not too hungry, try a pizzeria, where it's common to order just one dish. The handiest places for an afternoon snack are bars, caffè, and pizzerie. For a quick lunch or dinner, head to a *tavola calda*, kind of like a cafeteria where you can order from what's available at the counter and sit and eat at a table.

MEAL TIMES AND CLOSURES

Breakfast (*la colazione*) is usually served 7 am–10:30 am, lunch (*il pranzo*) 12:30 pm–2:30 pm, dinner (*la cena*) 7:30 pm–11 pm. Peak times are around 1:30 pm for lunch and 9 pm for dinner.

Enoteche are sometimes open in the morning and late afternoon for snacks. Most pizzerie open at 8 pm and close around midnight or 1 am. Most bars and caffè are open 7 am–8 or 9 pm.

Almost all restaurants close one day a week (in most cases Sunday or Monday) and for at least two weeks in August. The city is zoned, however, so that there are always some restaurants in each zone that remain open.

Local regulations are in the process of changing in Rome to give proprietors greater leeway in setting their hours. This is meant to allow establishments to stay open later and make more money in a down economy, and to offer patrons longer hours and more time to eat, drink, and be merry. It has yet to be seen whether Italians will find the law "flexible" and use it as an excuse to close early when they feel like it. *Tutto è possibile*: anything's possible in Rome.

PRICES, TIPPING, AND TAXES

All prices include tax and service (*servizio*) unless indicated otherwise on the menu. It's customary to leave a small tip in cash (anywhere from a euro to 10% of the bill) in appreciation of good service. Most restaurants have a "cover" charge, usually listed on the menu as *pane e coperto*. It should be modest (€1–€2.50 per person) except at the most expensive restaurants. Some instead charge for bread, which should be brought to you (and paid for) only if you order it. When in doubt, ask before ordering.

Note that the price of fish dishes is often given by weight (before cooking); the price on the menu will be for 100 grams (*l'etto*), not for the whole fish. An average fish portion is about 300 grams.

	$	$$	$$$	$$$$
WHAT IT COSTS IN EUROS				
AT DINNER	under €14	€14–€24	€25–€34	over €34

Restaurant prices are the average cost of a main course at dinner or, if dinner is not served, at lunch.

WITH KIDS

In ristoranti and trattorie you may find a high chair or a cushion for a child to sit on, but there's rarely a children's menu. Order a *mezza porzione* (half portion) of any dish, or ask the waiter for a *porzione da bambino* (child's portion).

WHAT TO WEAR

We mention dress only when men are required to wear a jacket, or a jacket and tie. Italian men rarely wear shorts in a ristorante or enoteca and infrequently wear sneakers or running shoes or baseball caps—no matter how humble the establishment. The same "rules" apply to ladies' casual shorts, running shoes, and flip-flops. Shorts are acceptable in pizzerie and caffès.

RESTAURANT REVIEWS

Listed alphabetically within neighborhoods. Use the coordinate (⌖ 1:B2) at the end of each listing to locate a property on the dining and lodging atlas at the end of this chapter.

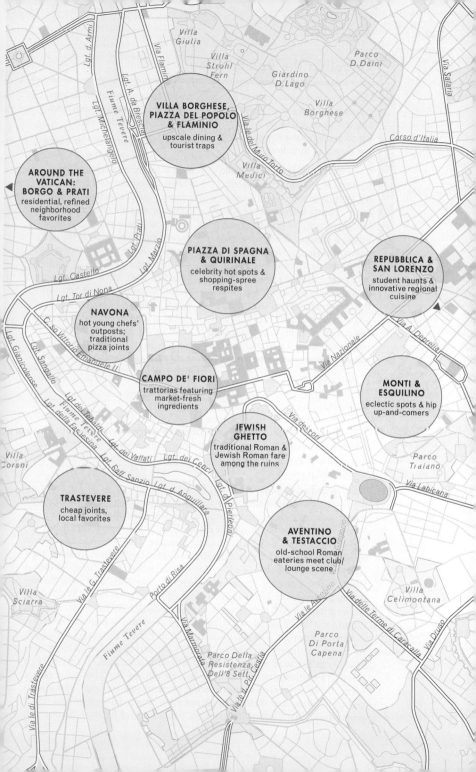

VILLA BORGHESE, PIAZZA DEL POPOLO & FLAMINIO
upscale dining & tourist traps

AROUND THE VATICAN: BORGO & PRATI
residential, refined neighborhood favorites

PIAZZA DI SPAGNA & QUIRINALE
celebrity hot spots & shopping-spree respites

REPUBBLICA & SAN LORENZO
student haunts & innovative regional cuisine

NAVONA
hot young chefs' outposts; traditional pizza joints

CAMPO DE' FIORI
trattorias featuring market-fresh ingredients

MONTI & ESQUILINO
eclectic spots & hip up-and-comers

JEWISH GHETTO
traditional Roman & Jewish Roman fare among the ruins

TRASTEVERE
cheap joints, local favorites

AVENTINO & TESTACCIO
old-school Roman eateries meet club/lounge scene

CLOSE UP

Refueling the Roman Way

Staggering under the weight of a succession of three-course meals, you may ask yourself, how do the Romans eat so much, twice a day, every day? The answer is: they don't.

If you want to do as the Romans do, try lunch at a *tavola calda* (literally, hot table), a cross between a caffè and a cafeteria where you'll find fresh food in manageable portions. There's usually a selection of freshly prepared pastas, cooked vegetables such as *bietola all'agro* (cooked beet greens with lemon), roasted potatoes, and grilled or roasted meat or fish. Go to the counter to order an assortment and quantity that suits your appetite, and pay by the plate, usually about €5 plus drinks. Tavole calde aren't hard to find, particularly in the city center, as they're often marked with "tavola calda" or "self-service" signs.

Other ubiquitous options for a light lunch or between-meal snack include pizza al taglio, bars, and enoteche. At bars throughout Italy, coffee is the primary beverage served (drinking establishments are commonly known as pubs or American bars); at a bar you can curb your appetite with a *panino* (a simple sandwich) or *tramezzino* (triangular sandwich on crustless, untoasted white bread, usually heavy on the mayonnaise). Wine bars vary widely in the sophistication and variety of food available, but you can count on cheese and cured meats, at the very least.

AROUND THE VATICAN

BORGO

Many tourists think the area around the Vatican is rip-off central when it comes to drinking and dining. Although there are an overwhelming number of tourist "trap-torias," the Borgo area, just outside the Vatican walls, is home to some genuinely good restaurants off the usual tourist radar.

$$$
ROMAN
Fodor's Choice
★

✕ **La Veranda dell'Hotel Columbus.** Deciding where to sit at La Veranda isn't easy, because both the shady courtyard (torchlit at night), and the frescoed dining room are among Rome's most spectacular settings. While La Veranda is known for classic Roman cuisine, some dishes are served with refreshing twists on the familiar. The seasonal menu may include an eggplant *caponata* with *burrata* (fresh cheese made from mozzarella and cream) and *bottarga* (salted fish roe) from Sardinia; Piedmontese oxtail soup; a risotto with Barolo wine and blue cheese; or quail carpaccio with mustard seeds. $ *Average main: €25* ⌂ *Hotel Columbus, Borgo Santo Spirito 73, Borgo* ☎ *06/6872973* ⊕ *www.laveranda.net* ⊘ *Closed Mon. No lunch* ⌐ *Reservations essential* ✛ *1:D3.*

$$
MODERN ITALIAN

✕ **Taverna Angelica.** The Borgo area near St. Peter's Basilica hasn't been known for culinary excellence, but this is starting to change, and Taverna Angelica was one of the first refined restaurants in this part of town. The dining room is small, which allows the chef to create a menu that's inventive without being pretentious: perhaps pasta with pistachio pesto and shrimp, or turbot with crushed almonds and white wine sauce. Spaghetti with crunchy pancetta and leeks is wonderful, as is the warm seafood soup. Fresh sliced tuna in a pistachio crust with orange sauce is light and delicious. Desserts here go beyond the staples of tiramisù and panna cotta. $ *Average main: €22* ⊠ *Piazza A. Capponi 6, Borgo* ☎ *06/6874514* ⊕ *www.tavernaangelica.it* ⊙ *Closed 2 wks in Aug. No lunch Mon.–Sat.* ⬧ *Reservations essential* Ⓜ *Ottaviano* ✛ *1:D2.*

PRATI

Near the Vatican, but slightly farther up the river than Borgo, Prati has become a hotbed of niche foodic spots.

$ ✗**Al Settimo Gelo.** The unusual flavors of gelato scooped up here include
ITALIAN cardamom, chestnut, and ginger, but the classics also get rave reviews. If you can't decide on one, mix and match. Ask for a taste of the *passito* flavor, if it's available: it's inspired by the popular sweet Italian dessert wine. There's a second location in Via Aurelia. $ *Average main: €5* ⊠ *Via Vodice 21/a, Prati* ☎ *06/3725567* ⊕ *www.alsettimogelo. it* ⊙ *Closed Mon., and 1 wk in Aug.* Ⓜ *Leganto* ✛ *1:A1.*

$$ ✗**Cesare.** An old standby in Prati, Cesare is a willing slave to tradition.
TUSCAN Classic fish dishes like marinated fresh anchovies and sardines, and an excellent mixed seafood salad, quell seafood cravings. Homemade pasta with meat sauce is the primo to order, and *saltimbocca* (thinly sliced veal with prosciutto and sage) or the thick Florentine steak are the ultimate meat lover's dishes. The €40 *menu toscano* is a great, multicourse value. The general menu's tendency toward hearty, stick-to-your-ribs comfort food makes this a popular spot in the autumn and winter. Look for dishes featuring truffles and game. $ *Average main: €20* ⊠ *Via Crescenzio 13, Prati* ☎ *06/6861227* ⊕ *www.ristorantecesare.com* ⊙ *Closed Easter wk and 3 wks in Aug.* Ⓜ *Lepanto* ✛ *1:E2.*

$$ ✗**Del Frate.** This impressive wine bar, adjacent to one of Rome's noted
MODERN ITALIAN wineshops, matches sleek, modern decor with creative cuisine and three
Fodor's Choice dozen wines available by the glass. The house specialty is marinated
★ meat and fish, but you can also get cheeses, smoked meats, and composed salads. Try a risotto or the braised oxtail–stuffed tortelli in a celery sauce for primo, and monkfish alla cacciatora with bitter Roman *puntarelle* (a type of chicory) for secondo. For dessert, the molten chocolate cake with banana cream is outstanding. $ *Average main: €19* ⊠ *Via degli Scipioni 118, Prati* ☎ *06/3236437* ⊕ *www.enotecadelfrate. it* ⊙ *Closed Sun., and Aug.* Ⓜ *Ottaviano* ✛ *1:C1.*

$$$ ✗**Il Simposio di Costantini.** At the most upscale wine bar in town, you
MODERN ITALIAN come for the wine but return for the food. Everything here is appropriately *raffinato* (refined): marinated and smoked fish, salads, and top-quality *salumi* (salted meat) and other cured meats and pâtés. There are plenty of dishes with classic Roman leanings, including artichokes prepared three ways. Main courses favor meat, with options that might include roast lamb, a fillet with foie gras, or game in season—all of which complement the vast offerings of top-notch red wines. There is a choice of roughly 80 cheeses to savor with your dessert wine. $ *Average main: €30* ⊠ *Piazza Cavour 16, Prati* ☎ *06/3203575* ⊕ *www. pierocostantini.it* ⊙ *Closed 2 wks in Aug.* ⬧ *Reservations essential* Ⓜ *Lepanto* ✛ *1:E2.*

$$
MODERN ITALIAN
Fodor's Choice
★

✕ **Il Sorpasso.** The focus at this happening spot, open from early morning till late in the evening, is on using excellently sourced products to make simple but wonderful food. Start your meal with a meat and cheese board—there are Italian selections, of course, as well as *jamón ibérico* (Spanish-style cured ham)—then move on to appetizers that put a twist on the familiar, like eggplant parmigiana with pesto. Innovative primi might include *strozzapretti* (a short pasta) served with eggplant, pistachio, and chili breadcrumbs, with hearty secondi that include prime cuts of steak. In the morning and afternoon, this is the perfect place to stop in for freshly baked sweet treats, while evenings are popular for aperitivo, when people spill out into the street, cocktail in hand. ⑤ *Average main: €15* ✉ *Via Properzio 31, Prati* ☎ *06/89024554* ⊕ *www. passaguai.it* ☾ *Closed Sun., and Aug.* Ⓜ *Ottaviano* ✛ *1:D2.*

$$
MODERN ITALIAN

✕ **La Zanzara.** This bright and modern restaurant functions as a bar, caffè, and restaurant all in one, with plenty of indoor and outdoor seating. The menu runs the international gamut, with salads, pasta, steak, and seafood—standouts include the tuna tartare and the beef burger. This is a busy spot from morning till night, but especially in the late afternoon and early evening, when attentive waitstaff serve cocktails and light bites, and the bustle extends well into dinner. ⑤ *Average main: €16* ✉ *Via Crecenzio 84, Prati* ☎ *06/68392227* ⊕ *www.lazanzararoma. com* Ⓜ *Ottaviano* ✛ *1:C2.*

$$
PIZZA

✕ **L'Isola della Pizza.** Right near the Vatican Metro stop, the "Island of Pizza" is also known for its copious antipasti. Ask for the house appetizers, and a waiter will swoop down numerous plates of salad, seafood, bruschetta, prosciutto, and crispy pizza bianca to choose from. Though it's easy to fill up on starters—you can order just one, or a selection for a fixed price—the pizza is dependably good, and meat lovers appreciate the steak. ⑤ *Average main: €14* ✉ *Via degli Scipioni 45, Prati* ☎ *06/39733483* ⊕ *www.isoladellapizza.com* ☾ *Closed Wed., Aug., and Christmas wk* Ⓜ *Ottaviano* ✛ *1:C2.*

$$
MODERN ITALIAN

✕ **Romeo: Chef and Baker.** The sprawling space here—it used to be an Alfa Romeo workshop; hence, the name—is an über-modern, multifaceted affair. In front is a casual bakery and deli counter, serving pizzas; gourmet sandwiches like pita stuffed with chicken, walnuts, celery, and pomegranate; and freshly baked breads, cakes, muffins, and tarts. In back, a more upscale menu is available, with pasta dishes like the classic carbonara, and secondi like lamb, or calamari stuffed with ricotta, sea urchin, ginger, and orange. This is the second restaurant from Michelin-starred chef Cristina Bowerman; the other is Glass Hostaria, in Trastevere. ⑤ *Average main: €20* ✉ *Via Silla 26A, Prati* ☎ *06/32110120* ⊕ *www.romeo.roma.it* Ⓜ *Ottaviano* ✛ *1:C1.*

$$
MODERN ITALIAN
Fodor's Choice
★

✕ **Settembrini.** The modern, intimate dining room here hints at what to expect from the kitchen and staff: elegant and restrained cooking, friendly yet unobtrusive service, and an interesting and well-curated wine list. The menu puts creative twists on classic Italian ingredients—think risotto with sea urchins, basil, and licorice, or cod with burrata, watermelon, and cardamom. This is a gem in a reasonably quiet neighborhood. ⑤ *Average main: €20* ✉ *Via Luigi Settembrini 27, Prati*

☎ 06/3232617 ⊕ *www.viasettembrini.com* ☉ *Closed Sun., and 2 wks in Aug. No lunch Sat.* ⚔ *Reservations essential* Ⓜ *Lepanto* ✛ *1:C1.*

PIAZZA NAVONA, CAMPO DE' FIORI, AND THE JEWISH GHETTO

12

PIAZZA NAVONA

The narrow, cobblestone *vicoli* (alleys) around Piazza Navona are home to a vast range of dining options. You'll find everything from casual pizzerie, where hurried waiters scribble your bill on a paper tablecloth, to several of the city's most revered gourmet temples, featuring star chefs and inventive cuisine, with decidedly higher bills placed on the finest high-threadcount damask tablecloths. The area around the Pantheon is full of classic, old-school trattorias and midrange to upscale restaurants, including many in gorgeous piazze that could double as opera sets. You'll feel the grandeur of Rome here, sometimes with prices to match.

$$
ROMAN

✗ **Armando al Pantheon.** In the shadow of the Pantheon, this trattoria, open since 1961, delights the tourists who tend to come for lunch. There's an air of authenticity here, and you'll see Roman antiques-shop owners who've been regulars here for decades. This is the place to try Roman artichokes or *vignarola* (a fava bean, asparagus, pea, and guanciale stew) in the spring, or the wild boar bruschetta in winter. Pastas are wonderful and filling, and secondi deliver all the Roman staples: oxtail, baby lamb chops, tripe, meatballs, and other hearty fare. Ⓢ *Average main: €15* ⊠ *Salita dei Crescenzi 31, Piazza Navona* ☎ 06/68803034 ⊕ *www.armandoalpantheon.it* ☉ *Closed Sun., and Dec.–Jan. 6. No dinner Sat.* ✛ *4:E2.*

$
ITALIAN
FAMILY

✗ **Bar del Fico.** Everyone in Rome knows Bar del Fico, located right behind Piazza Navona, so if you're looking to hang out with the locals, this is the place to come. Just about every evening of the year, it's packed with people sipping cocktails in the square. Inside, diners sit on mismatched chairs, at eclectic tables, and order local specialties like their excellent rendition of cacio e pepe. For dessert, order the profiteroles. An Italian-style brunch is served on Sunday, in the style of lunch at Nonna's (grandma's), complete with pasta *al forno* (baked) and crumbed schnitzel—though you can also order pancakes and American-style coffee. Ⓢ *Average main: €12* ⊠ *Piazza de Fico 26, Piazza Navona* ☎ 06/68891373 ⊕ *www.bardelfico.com* ✛ *4:C2.*

$
NORTHERN
ITALIAN

✗ **Birreria Peroni.** With its long wooden tables, hard-back booths, and free-flowing beer, this casual restaurant in a 16th-century palazzo might seem more like a Munich beer hall than a popular Roman hangout (around since 1906). But remember that in the far northern reaches of Italy, locals speak as much German as they do Italian, and that's where Birreria Peroni draws its inspiration. Goulash and a number of sausage specialties provide a respite from pasta and tomato sauce. And the added bonus is that this is one of the few places in the historic center of Rome where you can fill up on protein for very few euros. Ⓢ *Average main: €10* ⊠ *Via di San Marcello 19, Piazza Navona* ☎ 06/6795310 ⊕ *www.anticabirreriaperoni.it* ☉ *Closed Sun.* ⚔ *Reservations not accepted* ✛ *4:H3.*

$ ✗ **Caffè Sant'Eustachio.** Traditionally frequented by Rome's literati, this
CAFÉ cafe is considered by many to make Rome's best coffee. Servers are
hidden behind a huge espresso machine, where they vigorously mix
the sugar and coffee to protect their "secret method" for the perfectly
prepared cup. (If you want your caffè without sugar here, ask for it
amaro.) Note that as in most caffè in Rome, it costs more if you want
to sit and sip your coffee—but there is nice outdoor seating when the
weather is pleasant, so it's often worth it. **$** *Average main: €2* ⊠ *Piazza
Sant'Eustachio 82, Piazza Navona* ☎ *06/68802048* ⊕ *www.santeusta-
chioilcaffe.it* ✛ *4:E3.*

$ ✗ **Cremeria Monteforte.** Immediately beside the Pantheon is this gelat-
ITALIAN eria, which is well known for its flavors, like mango, pistachio, and
chocolate chip. The chocolate *sorbetto*—an icier version of gelato, made
without the dairy—is also excellent, and even better with a dollop of
whipped cream on top. The shop is small but the service is fast and
friendly. **$** *Average main: €3* ⊠ *Via della Rotonda 22, Piazza Navona*
☎ *06/6867720* ☾ *Closed Mon., and mid-Dec.–mid-Jan.* ✛ *4:E2.*

$$ ✗ **Cul de Sac.** This popular wine bar near Piazza Navona is among the
WINE BAR city's oldest and offers a book-length selection of wines from Italy,
Fodor's Choice France, the Americas, and elsewhere. The food is eclectic, ranging from
★ a huge assortment of Italian meats and cheeses (try the delicious *lonza*,
cured pork loin, or *speck*, a northern Italian smoked prosciutto), and
various Mediterranean dishes, including delicious baba ghanoush, a
tasty Greek salad, and a spectacular wild boar pâté. Outdoor tables get
crowded fast, so arrive early, or come late—they usually serve food until
just past midnight, though they're closed in the late afternoon (about
4–5:30). **$** *Average main: €14* ⊠ *Piazza Pasquino 73, Piazza Navona*
☎ *06/68801094* ⊕ *www.enotecaculdesacroma.it* ⌲ *Reservations not
accepted* ✛ *4:D3.*

$ ✗ **Da Francesco.** For good, hearty, Roman cuisine in an area filled with
ROMAN mediocre touristy restaurants, head to this authentic trattoria that's
FAMILY been on the scene since the late 1950s. Food-wise, stick to the classics:
start off with a mixed salumi plate, then hit the primi—the gricia and
the amatriciana are usually the standouts. Desserts are made fresh daily
and the tiramisù is always a winner. As at most trattorie in Rome, the
house wine is pretty good, but here you can also choose from a decent
list of wines local and otherwise. In the warmer months, tables spill
out on the popular Piazza del Fico, making this an especially wonderful
spot in the evening. **$** *Average main: €13* ⊠ *Piazza del Fico 29, Piazza
Navona* ☎ *06/6864009* ⊕ *www.dafrancesco.it* ✛ *4:C2.*

$ ✗ **Enoteca Corsi.** Very convenient to the centro storico for lunch or an
ITALIAN afternoon break, this small, hole-in-the-wall spot looks undeniably old-
Fodor's Choice school—renovations were done a few years back, but you wouldn't
★ know it—and that's all part of the charm. The prices and decor are *come
una volta* (like once upon a time) when the shop sold, as the sign says,
wine and oil. You can still get wine here by the liter, or choose from a
good variety of fairly priced bottles. It's packed at lunch, when a few
specials—classic pastas, a delicious octopus salad, and some secondi
like roast veal with peas—are offered. A longtime lunch-only spot, it's
now also open on Thursday and Friday evenings. The restaurant also

An *alimentari* is a specialty food shop. Visit one to stock up on lunch or picnic fixings; some will give you samples to taste.

runs cooking classes in and around Rome. $ *Average main: €12* ⊠ *Via del Gesù 88, Piazza Navona* ☎ *06/6790821* ⊕ *www.enotecacorsi.com* ☉ *Closed Sun., and 3 wks in Aug. No dinner Mon.–Wed. and Sat.* ✛ *4:F3.*

$ ✕ **Etabli.** On a narrow *vicolo* (alley) off lovely cobblestone Piazza del

MEDITERRANEAN Fico, this multifunctional restaurant and lounge space is decorated

Fodor's Choice according to what could be called a modern Italian farmhouse-chic

★ aesthetic, with vaulted wood-beam ceilings, wrought-iron touches, plush leather sofas, and chandeliers. The food is Mediterranean, with touches of Asia in the raw-fish appetizers. Pastas are more traditionally Italian, and secondi range from land to sea. It gets busy *dopo cena* (after dinner), when it becomes a popular spot for sipping and posing. If you want a more low-key experience, come for breakfast or lunch, which are served daily. $ *Average main: €12* ⊠ *Vicolo delle Vacche 9/a, Piazza Navona* ☎ *06/97616694* ⊕ *www.etabli.it* ✛ *4:C2.*

$ ✕ **Fiocco di Neve.** The gelato is certainly excellent—the chocolate chip

CAFÉ and After Eight (mint chocolate chip) flavors are delicious—but this

FAMILY small spot is also known for its *granita di caffè* (coffee ice slush). Look for intriguing seasonal gelato flavors like pear-cinnamon. $ *Average main: €4* ⊠ *Via del Pantheon 51, Piazza Navona* ☎ *06/6786025* ✛ *4:F2.*

$ ✕ **Gelateria del Teatro.** Not far from Piazza Navona, this is one of the

ITALIAN top gelaterie in the city. They make their creamy, artisan-style gelato

FAMILY from scratch every day, using top-quality products like pistachios from Bronte (Sicily) and hazelnuts from Piedmont. Classic flavors like caffè, strawberry, lemon, and chocolate are available, but this is a good place to get adventurous and try interesting combinations like cherry and ricotta, raspberry and sage, lemon cheesecake, and even beer-flavored gelato. $ *Average main: €5* ✉ *Via dei Coronari 65/6, Piazza Navona* ☎ *06/45474880* ☎ *No credit cards* ✚ *4:C2*.

$$$$
MODERN ITALIAN
Fodor's Choice
★

✕ **Il Convivio.** In a tiny, nondescript alley north of Piazza Navona, the three Troiani brothers—Angelo in the kitchen, and brothers Giuseppe and Massimo presiding over the dining room and wine cellar—have quietly been redefining the experience of Italian *alta cucina* (haute cuisine) for many years. Antipasti include "speck" of amberjack fish, herbs, pears, pomegranate, nuts, and raspberry oil, while pastas include spelt spaghetti with shrimp, mint, cocoa beans, and chili pepper. The renowned secondi might include options like Ischian-style rabbit or a "cannoli" of sole, artichokes, and saffron. Service is attentive without being overbearing, and the wine list is exceptional. $ *Average main: €40* ✉ *Vicolo dei Soldati 31, Piazza Navona* ☎ *06/6869432* ⊕ *www. ilconviviotroiani.it* ☉ *Closed Sun., and 1 wk in Aug. No lunch* ⌖ *Reservations essential* ✚ *4:D1*.

$$$$
MODERN ITALIAN
Fodor's Choice
★

✕ **Il Pagliaccio.** Some of the most innovative interpretations of Roman fine dining can be found in this starkly chic restaurant on a back street between upscale Via Giulia and the popular Campo de' Fiori. Chef Anthony Genovese was born in France to Calabrese parents, and spent time cooking in Japan and Thailand, so it's no surprise that the food he turns out makes use of nontraditional spices, ingredients, and preparations—all of which have gained him a loyal following and prized Michelin stars. The prices are exorbitant, but the food is exemplary. Dishes include items like pasta bundles filled with onion, tapioca, and red currant in a saffron broth, or duck with black salsify, caramelized pear, and chocolate sauce. You can choose one of the elaborate tasting menus or order à la carte. $ *Average main: €48* ✉ *129 Via dei Banchi Vecchi, Piazza Navona* ☎ *06/68809595* ⊕ *www.ristoranteilpagliaccio. com* ☉ *Closed Sun. and Mon., and Aug. No lunch Tues.* ⌖ *Reservations essential* ✚ *4:B3*.

$$
ITALIAN
FAMILY

✕ **La Campana.** Thought to be the oldest restaurant in Rome (a document dates it back to 1518), La Campana remains a favorite of both locals and visitors. It's well liked for its honest Roman cuisine and its old-school, slightly upmarket feel—think white tablecloths and unflappable waiters in black tie who have been there since the beginning of time. This is the place to have one of the best *coda alla vaccinara* (oxtail stew) in Rome, along with other specialties like saltimbocca and pasta *all'amatriciana* (a classic Roman tomato sauce with bacon-like pork cheek). $ *Average main: €18* ✉ *Vicolo della Campana 18, Piazza Navona* ☎ *06/6875273* ⊕ *www.ristorantelacampana.com* ☎ *No credit cards* ☉ *Closed Mon.* Ⓜ *Spagna* ✚ *4:E1*.

$$
ITALIAN

✕ **La Ciambella.** The sprawling space is styled after American restaurants, with a lively bar in front, but the structure itself is all Roman, with brick archways, high ceilings, and a skylight in one of the dining rooms that allows guests to gaze at the fantastic Roman sky. The emphasis here is on high-quality ingredients and classic Italian culinary traditions, evident in the incomparable Pugliese burrata, thin-crust pizzas, flavorful pastas (both classic and seasonal specialties), and grilled meats on offer. $ *Average main: €17* ✉ *Via dell'Arco della Ciambella 20, Piazza*

Navona ☏ *06/6832930* ⊕ *www.laciambellaroma.com* ⊗ *Closed Sun. No lunch in Aug.* ✛ *4:E3.*

$ ✕ **La Fraschetta di Castel Sant'Angelo.** A *fraschetta* is the name given to one of the casual, boisterous countryside spots just outside of Rome, where the menu focuses on porchetta, the Italian version of roast pork. This is a city-styled version of the same, and the atmosphere is typical, with waiters yelling across the room and frequently breaking into song. Order porchetta (of course) and a cheese and charcuterie board, and follow with pasta carbonara or amatriciana. The tiramisù here, served in a jar, is worth saving room for. Don't bother asking for a wine list—the only choice is the daily house wine, served in a tumbler, as it would be at a true fraschetta. ⑤ *Average main: €12* ⊠ *Via del Banco di Santo Spirito 20, Piazza Navona* ☏ *06/68307661* ⊕ *www.fraschettadicastelsantangelo.it* ⊗ *Closed Sun. No lunch in Aug.* ✛ *4:B2.*

ROMAN

$ ✕ **La Montecarlo.** The crusts on the pizza at this casual, perennially popular spot just off the Piazza Navona are super-thin and charred around the edges a little—the sign of a good wood-burning oven. This is one of a few pizzerie open for both lunch and dinner, and it's busy day and night. Service is friendly and when the weather is nice, there are tables outside, making this one of the most pleasant places for a meal in the neighborhood. ⑤ *Average main: €12* ⊠ *Vicolo Savelli 13, Piazza Navona* ☏ *06/6861877* ⊕ *www.lamontecarlo.it* ⊗ *Closed Mon., and 3 wks in Aug.* ✛ *4:C3.*

PIZZA
FAMILY

$$$$ ✕ **La Rosetta.** Chef-owner Massimo Riccioli may have taken the nets and fishing gear off the walls of the trattoria he inherited from his parents, but this is still widely known as *the* place to go in Rome for first-rate seafood. Make sure to start with any of the marinated seafood appetizers, like carpaccio of fresh, translucent fish drizzled with olive oil and perhaps fresh herbs. Pastas tend to mix varieties of shellfish, usually with a touch of oil, white wine, and lemon, and classic secondi like *zuppa di pesce* (fish soup) deserve top billing. The experience here includes friendly staff and undeniably high-quality fish, but be prepared for simple preparations and high prices. ⑤ *Average main: €50* ⊠ *Via della Rosetta 9, Piazza Navona* ☏ *06/6861002* ⊕ *www.larosetta.com* ⊗ *Closed 2 wks in Aug.* ⌲ *Reservations essential* 🏛 *Jacket required* ✛ *4:E2.*

SEAFOOD

$$ ✕ **Osteria dell'Ingegno.** This casual, trendy place is a great spot to enjoy a glass of wine or a gourmet meal in an ancient piazza in the city center, but the modern interior—vibrant with colorful paintings by local artists—brings you back to the present day. The simple but innovative menu includes dishes like *panzanella* (Tuscan bread salad), beef *tagliata* (sliced grilled steak) with a red-wine reduction, and a perfectly cooked duck breast with seasonal fruit sauce. Outdoor tables (April–October) make you feel as if you're on an opera stage set, since your perch looks out over the Tempio d'Adriano (AD 145). If ever there was a place to linger outdoors over limoncello, this is it. ⑤ *Average main: €19* ⊠ *Piazza di Pietra 45, Piazza Navona* ☏ *06/6780662* ⊕ *www.osteriadellingegno.com* ⊗ *Closed 1 wk in Aug.* ✛ *4:F2.*

MODERN ITALIAN
Fodor's Choice
★

12

CAMPO DE' FIORI

Campo de' Fiori is home to one of Rome's largest open-air produce markets, and is historically the secular crossroads of the city: even in ancient Rome, pilgrims gathered here to eat, drink, and be merry. Today's shoppers at the market include local chefs who head here to concoct menus based on what looks good.

$ ✕ **Alberto Pica.** Beloved owner Alberto Pica sadly died in 2015, but his
CAFÉ name lives on in the gelato shop he ran in Trastevere. Gelato production
FAMILY is artisanal, and the selection of seasonal *sorbetti* and *cremolate* (the latter is similar to sorbetto but made with the fruit pulp, rather than just fruit juice). An interesting gelato flavor to try here is the *riso a cannella*, like a cinnamon rice pudding. The treats are sweet but the owners can be grumpy, so remember: in, out, and nobody gets hurt. $ *Average main: €4* ✉ *Via della Seggiola 12, Campo de' Fiori* ☎ *06/6868405* ⊙ *Closed Sun., and 2 wks in Aug. No lunch in summer* ✛ *4:D5.*

$ ✕ **Carapina.** There are plenty of ordinary gelaterie around the Campo
ITALIAN de' Fiori but it's worth searching out Carapina. Of course the highest-
FAMILY quality ingredients go into the gelato here and the flavors are wonderfully unique, from extra-virgin olive oil flavor to gelato *al vin santo* (flavored with the Tuscan wine famous for biscotti dipping) to *crema del artusi* (egg-based, vanilla custard). More mainstream options like nougat and strawberry are standouts, too, and Christmastime means panettone-flavor gelato (that's traditional Italian Christmas cake)— winter may be the best time to eat gelato, since it doesn't melt so fast. $ *Average main: €5* ✉ *Via dei Chiavari 37, Campo de' Fiori* ☎ *06/06 6893843* ⊕ *www.carapina.it/wp* ⊙ *Closed 1 wk in Aug.* ✛ *4:D4.*

$$ ✕ **Ditirambo.** Don't let the country-kitchen ambience fool you: at this
ITALIAN little spot off Campo de' Fiori, the constantly changing selection of offbeat takes on Italian classics makes this a step beyond the ordinary. Antipasti can be delicious and unexpected, like Gorgonzola-pear soufflé drizzled with aged balsamic vinegar, or a mille-feuille of mozzarella, sundried tomatoes, and fresh mint. But people really love this place for rustic dishes like roast lamb, suckling pig, and hearty pasta with guinea fowl and porcini mushrooms. Vegetarians love the cheesy potato gratin with truffle shavings. Desserts, though homemade, can be skipped in favor of a *digestivo*. $ *Average main: €16* ✉ *Piazza della Cancelleria 74, Campo de' Fiori* ☎ *06/6871626* ⊕ *www.ristoranteditirambo.it* ⊙ *Closed Aug. No lunch Mon.* ✛ *4:D4.*

$$ ✕ **Emma.** Opened by Rome's renowned family of bakers, the Rosciolis,
ROMAN this large, sleek, modern pizzeria is smack in the middle of the city,
FAMILY with the freshest produce right outside the door. Start your meal with
Fodor's Choice the artichoke salad if it's in season and an order of golden-fried sup-
★ plì, then choose among the excellent pastas and thin-crust pizzas. The pancetta and chicory pizza is simple but outstanding—you really can't go wrong here. The wine list features many local Lazio options. If you have room, the warm apple cake with vanilla bean gelato, is deliciously decadent. You can walk it off tomorrow. $ *Average main: €15* ✉ *Via Monte della Farina 28-29, Campo de' Fiori* ☎ *06/64760475* ⊕ *www. emmapizzeria.com* ✛ *4:E4.*

12

$ × **Filetti di Baccalà.** The window says "Filetti di Baccalà," but the official
ITALIAN name of this small restaurant that specializes in one thing—deliciously
battered and deep-fried fillets of salt cod—is Dar Filettaro a Santa Barbara. There are a few basic starters on the menu, like *bruschette al
pomodoro* (garlic-rubbed toast topped with fresh tomatoes and olive
oil), and sautéed zucchini and, in the winter, the cod is served alongside
puntarelle (chicory stems tossed with a delicious anchovy-garlic-lemon
vinaigrette). The location, down the street from Campo de' Fiori in a
little piazza in front of the beautiful Santa Barbara church, practically
begs you to eat at one of the outdoor tables. Be prepared for the service
to be as Roman as the food: that is, brusque. ⑤ *Average main: €12
⊠ Largo dei Librari 88, Campo de' Fiori* ☎ *06/6864018* ▭ *No credit
cards* ⊘ *Closed Sun., and Aug. No lunch* ✥ *4:D4.*

$$$$ × **Il Sanlorenzo.** This gorgeous space with its chandeliers and soaring
SEAFOOD original brickwork ceilings, houses one of the best seafood restaurants
Fodor's Choice in the Eternal City. The eight-course tasting menu is extremely tempt-
★ ing—it might include the likes of cuttlefish-ink tagliatelle with mint,
artichokes, and roe, or shrimp from the island of Ponza with rosemary,
bitter herbs, and porcini mushrooms—and, for Rome, a relative bargain at €85. There are also plenty of à la carte items: a *crudo* (raw fish)
appetizer, for instance, might include a perfectly seasoned fish tartare
trio, sweet scampi, and a wispy carpaccio of red shrimp. The restaurant's version of spaghetti with sea urchin is exquisite and delicate;
follow up with a main course of freshly caught seasonal fish prepared
to order. ⑤ *Average main: €36* ⊠ *Via dei Chiavari 4/5, Campo de' Fiori*
☎ *06/6865097* ⊕ *www.ilsanlorenzo.it* ⊘ *Closed 2 wks in Aug. No lunch
Sat.–Mon.* ⌕ *Reservations essential* ✥ *4:D4.*

$$ × **L'Angolo Divino.** There's something about this cozy wine bar that
WINE BAR feels as if it's in a small university town instead of a bustling metropo-
lis. Serene blue-green walls lined with wooden shelves of wines from
around the Italian peninsula add to the warm atmosphere. There are
always a few fresh pastas to choose from, and you can order smoked
fish, cured meats, cheeses, and salads to make a nice lunch or light din-
ner. The kitchen stays open until the wee hours on weekends. ⑤ *Aver-
age main: €15* ⊠ *Via dei Balestrari 12, Campo de' Fiori* ☎ *06/6864413*
⊕ *www.angolodivino.it* ⊘ *Closed 2 wks in Aug.* ✥ *4:D5.*

$$ × **Open Baladin.** The craft beer movement has taken hold in Italy and
BURGER this gorgeous, sprawling space down the road from Campo de' Fiori
is headed up by the Baladin beer company. Staff members take their
jobs—and brews—seriously, and they're helpful with recommendations
from the more than 40 options on tap and the more than 100 bottles
to choose from. The food is mostly burgers and sandwiches, in many,
many incarnations, and the hand-cut potato chips come in interesting
flavors like cacio e pepe or paprika. ⑤ *Average main: €14* ⊠ *Via Degli
Specchi 5–6, Campo de' Fiori* ☎ *06/6838989* ⊕ *www.baladin.it* ✥ *4:E5.*

$$ × **Osteria La Quercia.** Looking for a pleasant escape from the chaos of
ROMAN the Campo de' Fiori? The menu at this casual trattoria is simple and
traditional, but the setting in the pretty piazza with tables under the
gorgeous, looming oak tree is undoubtedly the real highlight. ⑤ *Average*

main: €15 ✉ *Piazza della Quercia 23, Campo de' Fiori* ☎ *06/68300932* ⊕ *www.osterialaquercia.com* ✛ *4:C4.*

$$
SOUTHERN ITALIAN ✗ **Pesci Fritti.** This cute jewel box of a restaurant on the amphitheater-shape street behind Campo de' Fiori serves the namesake fried fish and much more. Step inside, and the whitewashed walls with touches of pale sea blue will make you feel like you've escaped to the Mediterranean. Much of the cuisine echoes this theme, with heavy incorporation of seaside favorites like octopus, *spigola* (sea bass), and *bottarga* (salted, cured fish roe). The pasta with clams is a highlight, as is the fish prepared many different ways. The few missteps happen when the cooks try to get too creative, so stick to the southern classics and enjoy this virtual seaside escape. Ⓢ *Average main: €18* ✉ *Via della Grottapinta 8, Campo de' Fiori* ☎ *06/68806170* ⊘ *Closed Mon., and Aug. No lunch* ✛ *4:D4.*

$$$
ITALIAN ✗ **Pierluigi.** This popular seafood restaurant is a fun spot on balmy summer evenings with tables out on the pretty piazza de'Ricci. As at many Italian fish ristoranti, any antipasto featuring crudi is always a smart choice: delicious tartare, carpaccio, shrimp, clams, and oysters are all in abundance. So are pastas and risotto with seafood, and secondi like roasted turbot with potatoes, cherry tomatoes, and black olives. Make sure to end your meal with a refreshing *sgroppino* (lemon sorbet, vodka, and prosecco). If you're ordering fresh fish, double-check the cost after it's been weighed so you don't get overcharged. Ⓢ *Average main: €28* ✉ *Piazza de Ricci 144, Campo de' Fiori* ☎ *06/6861302* ⊕ *www.pierluigi.it* ⊘ *Closed Mon.* ⌂ *Reservations essential* ✛ *4:B4.*

$$
WINE BAR
Fodor's Choice
★
✗ **Roscioli.** The shop in front of this wine bar will beckon you in with top-quality comestibles like hand-sliced cured ham from Italy and Spain, more than 300 cheeses, and a dizzying array of wines—but venture further inside to where you can sit and order artisanal cheeses and smoked meats, as well as an extensive selection of unusual dishes and interesting takes on classics. Try the burrata with Norwegian herring caviar, pasta with sardines, or Sicilian linguini with red prawns and cumin. The menu ranges from meat, seafood (including a nice selection of crudi), to vegetarian-friendly items. You can also reserve a table in the cozy wine cellar downstairs for an even more intimate experience. After your meal, head around the corner to their bakery for rightfully famous breads and sweets. Ⓢ *Average main: €22* ✉ *Via dei Giubbonari 21/22, Campo de' Fiori* ☎ *06/6875287* ⊕ *www.salumeriaroscioli.com/restaurant* ⊘ *Closed Sun., and 1 wk in Aug.* ⌂ *Reservations essential* ✛ *4:D4.*

$$
ITALIAN ✗ **Trattoria Moderna.** The space is as advertised: modern, and in neutral shades, with an oversize chalkboard displaying daily specials, such as a delicious chickpea and baccalà soup. The food leans generally toward the traditional but with a twist, like a pasta all'amatriciana with kosher beef instead of the requisite pork guanciale. Main courses are also creative but can be hit-or-miss. The friendly staff and reasonable prices are pluses, as is the outdoor seating—a few tables surrounded by greenery, off a lovely cobblestone street. Ⓢ *Average main: €16* ✉ *Vicolo dei Chiodaroli 16, Campo de' Fiori* ☎ *06/68803423* ⊕ *www.trattoriamodernaroma.com* ✛ *4:E4.*

JEWISH GHETTO

Across Via Arenula from the Campo de' Fiori, the Ghetto is home to Europe's oldest Jewish population, who have lived in Rome uninterrupted for more than 2,000 years. There are excellent restaurants not just along its main drag, Via del Portico d'Ottavia, but also hidden in the narrow back streets that wind between the river, Via Arenula, and Piazza Venezia.

> ### INSTEAD OF PORK...
>
> Variations on cured pork, such as guanciale, prosciutto, and pancetta, are signature flavorings for Roman dishes. When Jewish culinary culture started intermingling with Roman, it was discovered that Jewish cooks used *alici* (anchovies) to flavor dishes the way Romans used cured pork. For excellent-quality anchovies, check out the Jewish *alimentari* (food shops) in the Ghetto.

12

$$$
ROMAN

✗**Al Pompiere.** The nondescript entrance on a narrow side street leads upstairs to the main dining room of this neighborhood favorite, where those in the know enjoy dining on classic Roman fare under arched ceilings. Fried zucchini flowers, battered salt cod, and gnocchi are all consistently excellent, and the menu has some nice, historic touches, like a beef-and-citron stew from an ancient Roman recipe of Apicius. If the porchetta is on the menu, order it. Back in 2004, there was a terrible fire in a shop below the restaurant, but the kitchen was soon back in business, though the irony here is as thick as the chef's tomato sauce: Al Pompiere means "the fireman." ⑤ *Average main: €25* ⊠ *Via Santa Maria dei Calderari 38, Jewish Ghetto* ☎ *06/6868377* ⊕ *www.alpompiereroma.com* ☉ *Closed Sun., and Aug.* ✦ *4:E5.*

$$
ISRAELI
Fodor's Choice
★

✗**Ba' Ghetto.** This hot spot on the main promenade in the Jewish Ghetto has been going strong for years, with pleasant indoor and outdoor seating. The kitchen is kosher (many places featuring Roman Jewish fare are not) and serves meat dishes (so no dairy); the menu features an assortment of Roman Jewish delights, as well as Mediterranean and Middle Eastern Jewish fare. Enjoy starters like phyllo "cigars" stuffed with ground meat and spices, or the mixed appetizer platter with hummus. Forego pasta for couscous (the one with spicy fish is delicious) or baccalà with raisins and pine nuts. Down the street is **Ba'Ghetto Milky** (*Via del Portico d'Ottavia 2/a*), the kosher dairy version of the original. ⑤ *Average main: €22* ⊠ *Via del Portico d'Ottavia 57, Jewish Ghetto* ☎ *06/68892868* ⊕ *www.kosherinrome.com* ☉ *No dinner Fri.; no lunch Sat.* ✦ *4:F5.*

$$
ROMAN

✗**Bellacarne.** *Bellacarne* means "beautiful meat," and that's the focus of the menu here, though the double entendre is that it's also what a Jewish Italian grandmother might say while pinching her grandchild's cheek. The kosher kitchen makes its own pastrami—a pretty good version of what one might find in Jewish delis in NYC, but the difference is that here the meat is served on its own, thinly sliced, at room temperature, and on a platter with mustard—much like how cured meats are served in Italy. It's culturally on-point, though it might leave you longing for two slices of rye bread to make a sandwich—and the setting is definitely more fine-dining than deli. The fried artichokes are excellent, as is the shawarma with hummus, and the chopped Israeli salad. ⑤ *Average*

234 < **Where to Eat**

main: €17 ⊠ *Via Portico d'Ottavia 51, Jewish Ghetto* ☎ *06/6833104* ⊕ *www.bellacarne.it* ⊘ *Closed Jewish holidays. No dinner Fri.; no lunch Sat.* ⊹ *4:F5.*

$
ROMAN
✕ **Nonna Betta.** Right on the main street of the Jewish Ghetto, Nonna Betta is an institution in the neighborhood. All the Roman Jewish classics are on the menu here, and the carciofi alla giudia are outstanding, as are most of the fried starters. A perfect meal might also include the kosher carbonara, which substitutes dried beef for the guanciale, or the semolina gnocchi baked in a terra-cotta ramekin. The restaurant gets extremely busy, so don't expect service to be all that attentive, but the food more than makes up for it. ⑤ *Average main: €12* ⊠ *Via del Portico d'Ottavia 16, Jewish Ghetto* ☎ *06/68806263* ⊕ *www.nonnabetta. it* ⊘ *Closed Tues.* ⊹ *4:F5.*

$
CAFÉ
✕ **Pasticceria Boccioni.** *Forno* means "oven" in Italian, but it's also the word for a bakery that specializes in bread and simple baked goods, like biscotti and pine-nut tarts. A *pasticceria,* on the other hand, specializes in more complicated Italian sweets, like fruit tarts, *montebianco* (a chestnut-cream creation resembling an alpine mountain), and *millefoglie* (puff pastry layered with pastry cream). Straddling the line between a forno and a pasticceria, Pasticceria Boccioni—commonly known as Forno del Ghetto (aka "the Burnt Bakery," for the dark brown crust most everything here seems to have)—is famed for its Roman Jewish specialties. Try the delicious ricotta cheesecake, filled with cherries or chocolate, baked in an almond crust. Come early on Friday, as they sell out before closing for the Sabbath. ⑤ *Average main: €4* ⊠ *Via del Portico d'Ottavia 1, Jewish Ghetto* ☎ *06/6878637* ⊘ *Closed Sat.* ⊹ *4:F5.*

$$
ROMAN
✕ **Piperno.** *The* place to go for Rome's extraordinary carciofi alla giudia, Piperno has been in business since 1860. The location, up a tiny hill in a piazza tucked away behind the palazzi of the Jewish Ghetto, lends the restaurant a rarefied air. In addition to the artichokes, try the exquisite prosciutto and buffalo mozzarella plate, the *fiori di zucca ripieni e fritti* (fried stuffed zucchini flowers), and filetti di baccalà to start. The display of fresh, local fish is enticing enough to lure diners to try offerings from sea instead of land. Service is in the old-school style of dignified formality. This is a very popular destination for Sunday lunch. ⑤ *Average main: €20* ⊠ *Monte dei Cenci 9, Jewish Ghetto* ☎ *06/68806629* ⊕ *www.ristorantepiperno.it* ⊘ *Closed Mon., and Aug. No dinner Sun.* ⚇ *Reservations essential* ⊹ *4:E5.*

$$$
ROMAN
✕ **Sora Lella.** The draw here—in addition to the wonderful food—is the fact that this is the only restaurant on Isola Tiberina, the wondrously picturesque island set in the middle of the Tiber river between the Jewish Ghetto and Trastevere, that's open year-round. The dining rooms, spread over two floors, are elegant, and service is discreet. As for the food, try the delicious prosciutto and mozzarella to start, and move on to classics like pasta all'amatriciana, meatballs in tomato sauce, or Roman baby lamb chops. The stuffed calamari in white wine sauce is worthy of *facendo una scarpetta*—taking a piece of bread to sop up the savory sauce. ⑤ *Average main: €26* ⊠ *Via di Ponte Quattro Capi 16, Jewish Ghetto* ☎ *06/6861601* ⊕ *www.soralella.com* ⊘ *Closed Tues.,*

and 1 wk in Aug. No lunch Sun. in July and Aug. ⋐ *Reservations essential* ✛ *3:D1.*

$$ ✕ **Vecchia Roma.** Though the frescoed dining rooms are lovely, the choice

SEAFOOD place to dine is outside on the piazza, under the big white umbrellas, in the shadow of Santa Maria in Campitelli. For appetizers, the seafood selection may include an assortment of fresh anchovies in vinegary goodness, seafood salad, or baby shrimp. Chef Raffaella generally doles out large portions, so share one of her wonderful pasta dishes or skip straight to the secondo. Seafood is the specialty, and simple southern Italian preparations, such as grilled calamari with Sicilian tomatoes, are excellent no-fail choices. Homemade fruit desserts provide a light(ish) finish to the meal. ⑤ *Average main: €22* ⊠ *Piazza Campitelli 18, Jewish Ghetto* ☎ *06/6864604* ⊕ *www.ristorantevecchiaroma.com* ⊗ *Closed Wed., and 1 wk in Aug.* ⋐ *Reservations essential* ✛ *4:F5.*

PIAZZA DI SPAGNA

During the day, the area around the Spanish Steps is a hotbed of tourists, shoppers, and office workers. It gets significantly quieter at night and, as a result, it's easy to fall into tourist traps and overpriced hotel dining. Stick to recommended restaurants.

$ ✕ **Antico Caffè Greco.** Pricey Antico Caffè Greco is a national landmark;

CAFÉ its red-velvet chairs, marble tables, and Neoclassical sculpted busts have hosted the likes of Byron, Shelley, Keats, Goethe, and Casanova, and the antique artwork lining the walls lends the place the air of a gorgeously romantic, bygone era. Add to this the fact that it's in the middle of the shopping madness on the upscale Via dei Condotti, and you won't be surprised that the place is often filled with tourists. But there are some locals who love to breathe the air of history—more than 250 years of it—within these dark-wood walls. Take a coffee at the counter for a much less expensive experience. ⑤ *Average main: €12* ⊠ *Via dei Condotti 86, Piazza di Spagna* ☎ *06/6791700* ⊕ *www.anticocaffegreco.eu* Ⓜ *Spagna* ⬥ *1:H2.*

$$$ ✕ **Caffè Romano dell'Hotel d'Inghilterra.** With *orario continuato,* or non-

ECLECTIC stop operating hours (10 am till late at night), this sleek spot in the Hotel d'Inghilterra caters to jet-setters and hotel guests. The global menu can mean international misfires, so it's best to select from among the authentic northern Italian meat and southern Italian seafood dishes such as boar with polenta, seafood soup, or classic pastas. Tables are close together, but perhaps you won't mind eavesdropping on your supermodel neighbor. ⑤ *Average main: €28* ⊠ *Hotel d'Inghilterra, Via Borgognna 4M, Piazza di Spagna* ☎ *06/69981500* ⊕ *www.royaldemeure.com* Ⓜ *Spagna* ✛ *1:H2.*

$ ✕ **Gelateria Venchi.** Established in 1878, Venchi is one of Italy's premier

ITALIAN chocolate and confectionary makers, and you'll see the brand all over the country. At this brick-and-mortar shop, you can buy chocolate as well as artisanal gelato, made fresh daily. The nougat and caramel flavors are fabulous, and of course there are several different chocolate variations to choose from. ⑤ *Average main: €5* ⊠ *Via della Croce 25/26, Piazza di Spagna* ☎ *06/69797790* Ⓜ *Spagna* ✛ *1:H2.*

$　✕**GiNa.** "Homey minimalism" isn't a contradiction at this multilevel
CAFÉ　whitewashed caffè with a modern edge. The menu offers various bruschette, mixed salads, and sandwiches, making this a great spot for a
light lunch or aperitivo at a reasonable price (considering the high-end
neighborhood); and the sweets are top-notch, whether you're in the
mood for gelato, pastries, fruit with yogurt, or even American pie and
cheesecake. A mug of their decadent hot chocolate is the perfect way to
warm up a cold Roman afternoon, while summers mean fully stocked
gourmet picnic baskets to take to Villa Borghese Gardens. ⑤ *Average
main: €10* ✉ *Via San Sebastianello 7A, Piazza di Spagna* ☎ *06/6780251*
⊕ *www.ginaroma.com* ⊘ *No dinner* Ⓜ *Spagna* ✛ *1:H2.*

$　✕**Il Gelato di San Crispino.** Many people say this is the best gelato in
CAFÉITALIAN　Rome, and though it's hard to pick just one, this is definitely the place
to go if you want a delicious iced treat in the shadow of the Pantheon.
You might even recognize the shop from a cameo in the movie *Eat,
Pray, Love.* Creative flavors like black fig, chocolate rum, armagnac,
and ginger-cinnamon are all fresh and make use of top-notch ingredi-
ents. There are additional locations behind the Pantheon (*Piazza della
Maddalena 3*) and San Giovanni (*Via Acaia 56*). ⑤ *Average main: €4*
✉ *Via della Panetteria 42, Piazza di Spagna* ☎ *06/6793924* ⊕ *www.
ilgelatodisancrispino.it* Ⓜ *Barberini* ✛ *4:H2.*

$　✕**Il Leoncino.** The no-reservation policy and long lines of locals out
PIZZA　the door attest to the popularity of this fluorescent-lighted pizzeria in
Fodor's Choice　the otherwise big-ticket neighborhood around Piazza di Spagna, but if
★　you arrive early (between 7 and 8), you probably won't have to wait.
The atmosphere is noisy and cheerful, and the service is dished out by
a Fellinian cast of characters that falls just on the right side of chaotic.
The Tridente area might not have much in the way of budget dinner
options, but a pizza at Il Leoncino is a good start. ⑤ *Average main:
€12* ✉ *Via del Leoncino 28, Piazza di Spagna* ☎ *06/6876306* ⊘ *Closed
Wed., and August.* Ⓜ *Spagna* ✛ *1:G3.*

$$$　✕**Imàgo.** Excellence is at the forefront of everything at Imàgo, the
MODERN ITALIAN　Michelin-starred restaurant inside the legendary Hotel Hassler, and it's
all a memorable ode to the international travels of executive chef Fran-
cesco Apreda. You can order à la carte, but this is the place to splurge on
a tasting menu. Each carefully and meticulously created dish will leave
you in awe: from the Mumbai spiced penne all'arrabiata with fresh
yogurt, to Roman risotto cacio e pepe, to New York–inspired cheese-
cake with local berries and sour-apple sorbet. The waitstaff bring spice
jars to the table at the beginning of each course, which is believed to
heighten the sensory journey. Take your coffee up to the rooftop terrace
for a magical, bird's-eye view of the city. ⑤ *Average main: €30* ✉ *Hotel
Hassler, Piazza Trinità dei Monti 6, Piazza di Spagna* ☎ *06/69934726*
⊕ *www.hotelhasslerroma.com/en/restaurants-bars/imago* ⊘ *No lunch*
⚱ *Reservations essential* Ⓜ *Spagna* ✛ *2:A2.*

$$$　✕**Moma.** Across the street from Hotel Aleph, a favorite of the design
MODERN ITALIAN　*trendoisie*, modern Moma attracts the same clientele. The kitchen turns
out hits along with a few misses as it experiments with nouvelle cuisine;
but seared scallops, plump and sweet, are a real find, and the rigatoni
all'amatriciana is extremely tasty. Secondi like lamb with spices and

12

yogurt and a Jerusalem artichoke salad are flavorful twists on classics. There are several basic desserts, but the molten chocolate cake served with pear sorbetto and chocolate sauce usually wins any contests. ⑤ *Average main: €25* ✉ *Via San Basilio 42/43, Piazza di Spagna* ☎ *06/42011798* ⊕ *www.ristorantemoma.it* ⊙ *Closed Sun.* ⚐ *Reservations essential* Ⓜ *Barberini* ✚ *2:C2.*

$$$ ✕ **Nino.** A favorite among international journalists and the rich and
ITALIAN   famous for decades, Nino is Rome's best-loved dressed-up trattoria.
Fodor's Choice The interior is country rustic alla toscana, and the menu accordingly
★   sticks to the classics, featuring Roman and Tuscan staples. Start with a selection of antipasti or the warm crostini spread with pâté. Move on to pappardelle *al lepre* (a rich hare sauce) or hearty Tuscan ribollita, and go for the gold with a piece of juicy grilled beef. If you're not Italian or a regular or a celebrity, the chance of brusque service multiplies—insist on good service and you'll win the waiters' respect. ⑤ *Average main: €28* ✉ *Via Borgognona 11, Piazza di Spagna* ☎ *06/6786752,* ⊕ *www. ristorantenino.it* ⊙ *Closed Sun., and Aug.* ⚐ *Reservations essential* Ⓜ *Spagna* ✚ *1:H2.*

$$ ✕ **Palatium Enoteca Regionale.** This wine bar and restaurant is just a short
MODERN ITALIAN walk from the Spanish Steps on one of the nearby fashion-forward
Fodor's Choice streets, but it's unique for the fact that it's owned and operated by the
★   Regione Lazio (the state government within which Rome sits), and the mantra is local Laziale produce: everything from the cheeses to the wines to bottled water is local. The menu changes seasonally, but if the ricotta and tomato flan or the gnocchi with clams and asparagus are on offer, they're must-orders. Come for a drink, and share a plate or two if you don't want a full meal. ⑤ *Average main: €16* ✉ *Via Frattina 94, Piazza di Spagna* ☎ *06/69202132* ⊕ *www.enotecapalatium.com* ⊙ *Closed Sun., and Aug.* Ⓜ *Barberini* ✚ *1:H3.*

REPUBBLICA AND QUIRINALE

REPUBBLICA

The areas around Piazza della Repubblica and Termini station aren't known as gastronomic hot spots, but there are some classic Roman wine bars.

$$ ✕ **Il Cuore di Napoli.** Once you've been in Rome long enough to familiar-
NEAPOLITAN ize yourself with Roman cuisine and, especially, Roman-style pizza, it's time to try something for comparison. At Il Cuore di Napoli the pizza is perfect Neapolitan style—that is, thin but with a thick crust—and the classic margherita is a must. Paccheri pasta with fresh tomato and the sea bass are also winners. For dessert, the *torta caprese,* a chocolate and almond torte that originates from the island of Capri, is a must. ⑤ *Average main: €14* ✉ *Via Cernaia 31, Repubblica* ☎ *06/44340252* ⊕ *www.ilcuoredinapoli.info* ⊙ *No lunch Sun.* Ⓜ *Castro Pretorio or Repubblica* ✚ *2:D2.*

$
PIZZA
FAMILY
Fodor'sChoice
★

✕ **Pinsere.** In Rome, you'll usually find either pizza tonda or pizza al taglio, but there's also pizza *pinsa*: it's an oval-shape pie, and a little thicker than the classic Roman pizza. Pinsere is mostly a take-out shop, with people eating on the street for their lunch break, so it's the perfect quick meal. The pizzas are sold individually, and there is a large selection of meat and vegetarian toppings. The big winners are the tomato and buffalo mozzarella and the mortadella and pistachio versions. $ *Average main: €8* ✉ *Via Flavia 98, Repubblica* ☎ *06/42020924* ⊕ *www.pinsereroma.com* ⊘ *Closed weekends, and Aug. No dinner* Ⓜ *Castro Pretorio* ✛ *2:D2.*

$$$
MODERN ITALIAN

✕ **Pipero al Rex.** In the lobby of Hotel Rex, not far from Termini station, this Michelin-starred restaurant is a winning collaboration between well-known Roman restaurateur Alessandro Pipero and chef Luciano Monosilio. You can order à la carte, but the tasting menus—served at lunch and dinner—are the way to go so that you can experience items like algae crisps with miso cream; rigatoni with brocoletti, pork sausage, and pecorino foam; with perhaps a slice of sangria-soaked watermelon to cleanse your palate. They also make one of the best carbonaras in the city. A meal here is all class, in an intimate setting. $ *Average main: €30* ✉ *Via Torino 149, Repubblica* ☎ *06/4815702* ⊕ *www.hotelrex.net/restaurant.htm* ⩘ *Reservations essential* Ⓜ *Termini* ✛ *2:D4.*

$$
WINE BAR

✕ **Trimani Il Winebar.** Operating nonstop 11 am–midnight, this wine bar serves hot food at lunch and dinner. The interior is minimalist in style, but the second floor provides a subdued, candlelit space to sip wine. There's always a choice of soup and pasta, as well as second courses and *torte salate* (savory tarts). Around the corner is a wine shop, one of the oldest in Rome, by the same name. They also offer wine tastings and classes (in Italian). $ *Average main: €15* ✉ *Via Cernaia 37/b, Repubblica* ☎ *06/4469630* ⊕ *www.trimani.com* ⊘ *Closed Sun., and Aug.* Ⓜ *Castro Pretorio* ✛ *2:E2.*

QUIRINALE

This area has lots of government offices, hotels, and museums, and the tourist traps and expense-account stalwarts that go with them. There are some reasonable standouts though.

$$
MODERN ITALIAN

✕ **Baccano.** There are plenty of options for good food at reasonable prices around the Trevi Fountain, but this large French brasserie is a good bet, open for breakfast and dinner and everything in between. The extensive menu has something for everyone, from salads to pasta to main courses—the tuna tartare is a standout and if you're looking for oysters, this is the place. For lunch, the burger is solid, but they also serve sandwich staples, like a classic club. There are platters of cured meats and cheeses to accompany your aperitivo in the evening. Service is friendly and attentive. $ *Average main: €16* ✉ *Via delle Muratte 23, Quirinale* ☎ *06/69941166* ⊕ *www.baccanoroma.com* Ⓜ *Barberini* ✛ *4:G2.*

$$$
MODERN ITALIAN

✕ **Giuda Ballerino.** The name is a catchphrase from the Italian comic strip "Dylan Dog," and the restaurant picks up the theme in decor as well—but this is not a gimmicky dining destination. Indeed, chef Andrea Fusco has a Michelin star to his name, and the food he serves is inventive and delicious. The menu might feature scallops in a squid-ink tempura crust

12

or a twist on the classic Roman cacio e pepe, served with mussel powder and mint. Add to that some of the most stunning views in all of Rome: the restaurant is on the roof of the old-world Hotel Bernini Bristol in Piazza Barberini, at the end of the famed Via Veneto. The city stretches out below, from the piazza to the dome of St. Peter's Basilica. ⑤ *Average main: €30* ✉ *Piazza Barberini 23, Quirinale* ☎ *06/42010469* ⊕ *www. giudaballerino.com* ⌔ *Reservations essential* Ⓜ *Barberini* ✦ *2:B3.*

$$$ ✗ **Tullio.** Just off Piazza Barberini, this upscale trattoria serves Tuscan
TUSCAN classics like white beans and high-quality meat dishes, including the famed *bistecca alla fiorentina* (Tuscan porterhouse), as well as other cuts of beef, lamb, and veal. The homemade pappardelle *al cinghiale* (wide, flat noodles in a wild boar sauce) is excellent. There are also a few key Roman dishes on the menu, as well as brocoletti sautéed to perfection with garlic and olive oil. The wine list favors robust Tuscan reds and thick wallets. The decor is basic wood paneling and white linens, with the requisite older—and often grumpy—waiters. ⑤ *Average main: €32* ✉ *Via San Nicola da Tolentino 26, Quirinale* ☎ *06/4745560* ⊕ *www.tullioristorante.it* ⊘ *Closed Sun., and Aug.* ⌔ *Reservations essential* Ⓜ *Barberini* ✦ *2:C2.*

VILLA BORGHESE, PIAZZA DEL POPOLO, FLAMINIO, AND MONTE MARIO

VILLA BORGHESE

One of Rome's two large parks borders the famed-but-faded Via Veneto, the former haunt of the Hollywood-on-the-Tiber scene. The upscale neighborhood is home to historic dining destinations as well as the café culture that formed the backdrop for those living *la dolce vita.*

$$$ ✗ **Al Ceppo.** The well-heeled, the business-minded, and those of refined
ITALIAN palates frequent this outpost of tranquility. The owners hail from Le Marche, the region northeast of Rome that encompasses inland mountains and the Adriatic coastline, and these ladies dote on their customers as you'd wish a sophisticated Italian *mamma* would. There's always a selection of dishes from their native region, such as olive ascolane, fresh pasta dishes, succulent roast lamb, and a delicious *marchigiano*-style rabbit. Other temptations include a beautiful display of seafood and a wide selection of meats ready to be grilled in the fireplace in the front room. There's also an excellent and well-priced wine list. ⑤ *Average main: €32* ✉ *Via Panama 2, Villa Borghese* ☎ *06/8419696* ⊕ *www. ristorantealceppo.it* ⊘ *Closed 3 wks in Aug.* ⌔ *Reservations essential* ✦ *2:C1.*

$$$ ✗ **Duke's International Bar and Restaurant.** It dubs itself an American West
AMERICAN Coast–style restaurant, and the decor is very Malibu beach house, with a gorgeous patio out back. But the menu takes a few liberties: the California rolls contain tuna and carrot, and there are mint leaves in the Caesar salad. It's a nice change from eating Italian, though, and everything is high quality. Up front, the bar opens out onto the street and attracts the neighborhood beautiful people. ⑤ *Average main: €26* ✉ *Viale Parioli 200, Villa Borghese* ☎ *06/80662455* ⊕ *www.dukes.it* ⊘ *Closed Sun. and Mon. No lunch* ⌔ *Reservations essential* ✦ *2:C1.*

$$$$ ✕ **Metamorfosi.** Chef Roy Caceres heads up this chic but understated
FUSION Michelin-starred restaurant. There are several tasting menus to choose
from (as well as à la carte), but it's worth the splurge to partake of the
surprising and satisfying wonders that come out of the kitchen: from
spaghetti with mussel powder, to scallop and razor-clam ceviche, to
prime wagyu beef with hazelnuts, to red shrimp carpaccio with oyster
emulsion. The presentation is dramatic and the wine list is, unsurpris-
ingly, outstanding. ⑤ *Average main: €35* ✉ *Via Giovanni Antonelli
30-32, Parioli* ☎ *06/68076839* ⊕ *www.metamorfosiroma.it* ⊘ *Closed
Sun. No lunch Sat.* ⚏ *Reservations essential* ✛ *2:C1.*

PIAZZA DEL POPOLO

This high-traffic shopping and tourist zone has both casual pizzerie and
upscale eateries, as well as classic caffè where you can have a restorative
espresso and a light bite.

$$$$ ✕ **Dal Bolognese.** The darling of the media, film, and fashion commu-
EMILIAN nities, this classic restaurant off Piazza del Popolo is a perennial hot
spot, and a convenient lunch break mid–shopping spree. Their offerings adhere to the hearty tradition of Bologna, so start with a plate of
sweet prosciutto di Parma, then move on to the traditional egg pastas of
Emilia-Romagna. Secondi include the famous *bollito misto,* a steaming
tray of an assortment of boiled meats (some recognizable, some inde-
cipherable) served with its classic accompaniment: a tangy, herby *salsa
verde* (green sauce). Linger for dessert and take in the passing parade of
destination diners as they air kiss their way around the room. ⑤ *Average main: €35* ✉ *Piazza del Popolo 1, Piazza del Popolo* ☎ *06/3222799*
⊕ *www.dalbolognese.it* ⊘ *Closed 3 wks in Aug.* ⚏ *Reservations essential* Ⓜ *Flaminio* ✛ *1:G1.*

$$ ✕ **Il Brillo Parlante.** The location near Piazza del Popolo makes Il Brillo
WINE BAR especially convenient for lunch or dinner after shopping in the Via del
Corso area. You can eat at the cozy bar, outside on the patio, or down-
stairs in one of several wood-paneled rooms. There are 20 wines by the
glass to choose from, and the menu is more extensive than the typical
wine bar, with cured meats, crostini, pastas, grilled meats, and pizzas.
⑤ *Average main: €16* ✉ *Via della Fontanella 15, Piazza del Popolo*
☎ *06/3243334* ⊕ *www.ilbrilloparlante.com* Ⓜ *Flaminio* ✛ *1:G1.*

$$ ✕ **Il Margutta.** Parallel to posh Via del Babuino, Via Margutta was once
VEGETARIAN a street of artists' studios, and home to Fellini. This chic restaurant,
with changing displays of modern art, sits on the far end of this gal-
lery-lined street. The added element of interest here is that this is a
vegetarian kitchen, which turns out tasty meat-free versions of classic
Mediterranean dishes, as well as more daring tofu concoctions. Lunch
is essentially a pasta-and-salad bar to which you help yourself, while
dinner offers à la carte and prix-fixe options. ⑤ *Average main: €14*
✉ *Via Margutta 118, Piazza del Popolo* ☎ *06/32650577* ⊕ *www.ilm-
arguttavegetariano.it* Ⓜ *Flaminio* ✛ *1:G1.*

FLAMINIO

Long a residential area, Flaminio is starting to come into its own, with
several new and interesting bars and restaurants opening.

12

$$$ ✕ **Acquolina.** Angelo Troiani, one of the brothers who run the excel-
SEAFOOD lent restaurant Il Convivio, near the Piazza Navona, moved outside
the city center to open this high-quality seafood restaurant with chef
Giulio Terrinoni. The kitchen turns out delicious and understated dishes
reflecting, for the most part, the time-honored Italian tradition of let-
ting great seafood speak for itself. The crudo is ultrafresh, and pastas
like the seafood carbonara and the cacio e pepe with skate and zuc-
chini flowers are upscale aquatic riffs on Roman classics. Main dishes
range from fish stew to *gran fritto misto* (deep-fried seafood platter).
Desserts are surprisingly sophisticated. Service is helpful and thorough,
but beware of the sometimes-slow kitchen. $ *Average main: €28* ⊠ *Via
Antonio Serra 60, Flaminio* ☎ *06/3337192* ⊕ *www.acquolinahostaria.
it* ⊘ *Closed Sun., and 10 days in Aug. No lunch* ✥ *1:F1.*

$$ ✕ **Tree Bar.** One of the influx of new dining spots in the area, Tree
CAFÉ Bar is, as the name suggests, set amid lush greenery and decorated in
wooden treehouse style. Functioning as a bar, restaurant, and enoteca
all at once, it's open for lunch and dinner as well as for appertivi and
late-night drinks. The marinated anchovies are an excellent snack; for
larger plates, you can expect pizzas, salads, and pastas—look for hearty
specialties like *pasta e ceci* (pasta with chickpeas) in winter. $ *Aver-
age main: €14* ⊠ *Via Flaminia 226, Flaminio* ☎ *06/32652754* ⊕ *www.
treebar.it* ⊘ *Closed Mon., and 2 wks in Aug.* ✥ *1:F1.*

MONTE MARIO

This neighborhood is home to some of Rome's fanciest restaurants.

$$$$ ✕ **La Pergola.** Dinner here is a truly spectacular and romantic event,
MODERN ITALIAN with incomparable views across the city matched by the spectacular
Fodor's Choice three–Michelin star dining experience. The difficulty comes in choos-
★ ing from among Chef Heinz Beck's alta cucina specialties. Expect such
temptations as John Dory fillet with white truffles, pumpkin purée, and
mushrooms, or deep-fried zucchini flowers with caviar in a shellfish-
and-saffron consommé. Everything from the bread to the wine to the
service is top-notch, and the dessert course is always an extravagant,
multicourse event. $ *Average main: €65* ⊠ *Waldorf Astoria Rome Cav-
alieri, Via Alberto Cadlolo 101, Monte Mario* ☎ *06/35092152* ⊕ *www.
romecavalieri.com/lapergola.php* ⊘ *Closed Sun. and Mon., 3 wks in
Aug., and most of Jan. No lunch* ⌲ *Reservations essential* 🎩 *Jacket
and tie* ✥ *1:A1.*

TRASTEVERE AND MONTEVERDE

TRASTEVERE

Trastevere has always been known for its Left Bank bohemian appeal.
A hip expat enclave with working-class Roman roots, the neighborhood
is lined with an abundance of trattorias and wine bars. The Gianicolo
area, at the top of the hill, is more subdued, with breathtaking views.

$ ✕ **Ai Marmi** (*Panattoni*). The official name of this popular pizzeria is Pan-
PIZZA attoni, but everyone calls it "Ai Marmi" or "L'Obitorio" (the morgue)
FAMILY for its marble-slab tables. Contrary to what that might imply, this place
is actually about as lively as it gets—indeed, it's packed pretty much

every night, with diners munching on crisp pizzas that come out of the wood-burning ovens at top speed. The fried starters, like a nice baccalà, are light and tasty. The restaurant stays open well past midnight, convenient for a late meal after the theater or a movie nearby. $ *Average main: €12* ⊠ *Viale Trastevere 53–57, Trastevere* ☎ *06/5800919* ☉ *Closed Wed., and 3 wks in mid-Aug. No lunch* ⌂ *Reservations not accepted* ✚ *3:C2.*

$$$ ✕ **Antico Arco.** Founded by three friends with a passion for wine and

MODERN ITALIAN fine food, Antico Arco attracts foodies from Rome and beyond with

Fodor's Choice its refined culinary inventiveness. The location on top of the Janiculum

★ Hill makes for a charming setting, and inside, the dining rooms are plush, modern spaces, with whitewashed brick walls, dark floors, and black velvet chairs. The seasonal menu offers delights such as amberjack tartare with lime, ginger, and a salad of chicory stems; classic pasta alla carbonara enriched with black truffle; and duck with artichokes and foie gras. The molten chocolate cake has made a name for itself among chocoholics the city over. $ *Average main: €28* ⊠ *Piazzale Aurelio 7, Trastevere* ☎ *06/5815274* ⊕ *www.anticoarco.it* ⌂ *Reservations essential* ✚ *3:A1.*

$ ✕ **Baylon Cafe.** With eclectic vintage decor, colorful mismatched tables

CAFÉ and chairs, free Wi-Fi, and waiters with hipster beards, this low-key neighborhood hot spot lures lots of expats and American travelers. The caffè menu features American-style sandwiches and salads, and weekend brunch is popular for the French toast, pancakes, and eggs Benedict. In the evenings, order an aperitivo and you can accompany it with a variety of small plates brought to you at minimal cost. $ *Average main: €13* ⊠ *Via San Francesco a Ripa 151, Trastevere* ☎ *06/5814275* ✚ *3:B2.*

$ ✕ **Biscottificio Innocenti.** People from all over Rome come to this family-

BAKERY run bakery that's been turning out sweet and savory biscuits since 1920.

FAMILY Try the *brutti ma buoni* ("ugly but good") almond cookies or anything with chocolate or jam. Stefania runs the place with her daughters, Michela and Manuela, and says her fondest memories of the bakery are from when she was a child, watching her father operate the 1950s oven, still in use today. $ *Average main: €5* ⊠ *Via della Luce 21, Trastevere* ☎ *06/5803926* ☉ *Closed Sun. in early July and Sept.; Closed mid-July–Aug.* ▭ *No credit cards* ✚ *3:C2.*

$$ ✕ **Da Enzo al 29.** In the quieter part of Trastevere, the family-run Da

ROMAN Enzo is everything you would imagine a classic Roman trattoria to be.

Fodor's Choice There are just a few tables, but locals line up to eat here—a testament

★ to the quality of the food. The classics are truly exceptional, from the carbonara to the cacio e pepe. Start with *carciofi all giudia* (Jewish artichokes), mozzarella- and anchovy-stuffed zucchini flowers, and fresh burrata that arrives daily from Andria in Puglia. The *coda alla vaccinara* (oxtail stew) is the absolute standout of the secondi, made the old way with a hint of cocoa. Finish with the marscarpone mousse served with wild strawberries. Because it's so small, there's almost invariably a wait, but it's worth it. $ *Average main: €14* ⊠ *Via dei Vascellari 29, Trastevere* ⊕ *www.daenzoal29.com* ☉ *Closd Sun., and 2 wks in Aug.* ✚ *3:C2.*

$$ ✕ **Da Ivo.** This always-busy pizzeria opens early and closes late, and

PIZZA in between it's packed with locals, some tourists, and sports fans who know they can watch the Roma soccer team play on big, flat-screen TVs in good company. The selection of pizzas is large, with larger dishes available as well. The coveted streetside tables are a great spot from which to view Trastevere's people parade. ⑤ *Average main: €14* ⊠ *Via di San Francesco a Ripa 158, Trastevere* ☎ *06/5817082* ⊙ *Closed Tues., and 2 wks in Jan.* ✛ *3:B2.*

$$
ROMAN
✕ **Da Lucia.** There's no shortage of old-school trattorias in Trastevere, but Da Lucia has a strong following among them. Both locals and expats enjoy the brusque but "authentic" service and the hearty Roman fare, like classic *bombolotti* all'amatriciana (short, fat tubular pasta) and spaghetti cacio e pepe; and meat dishes like beef *involtini* with peas and Roman-style tripe. Snag a table outside in warm weather for the true Roman experience of dining on the cobblestones. ⑤ *Average main: €14* ⊠ *Vicolo del Mattonato 2b, Trastevere* ☎ *06/5803601* ⊙ *Closed Mon., and Aug.* ✛ *3:A1.*

$
PIZZA
✕ **Dar Poeta.** Romans drive across town for great pizza from this neighborhood institution on a small street in Trastevere. It doesn't accept reservations, so arrive early or late, or expect to wait in line. They offer both thin-crust pizza and a thick-crust (*alta*) Neapolitan-style pizza with any of the given toppings. For dessert, there's a calzone with Nutella and ricotta cheese for those with a sweet tooth, so save some room. Service from the owners and friendly waitstaff is smile-inducing. ⑤ *Average main: €12* ⊠ *Vicolo del Bologna 45, Trastevere* ☎ *06/5880516* ⊕ *www. darpoeta.com* ⊙ *No lunch* ✛ *4:B6.*

$$$$
MODERN ITALIAN
Fodor's Choice
★
✕ **Glass Hostaria.** After 14 years in Austin, Texas, chef Cristina Bowerman returned to Rome to reconnect with her Italian roots, and her cooking is as innovative as the building she works in (the latter has received numerous recognitions for its design). The menu changes frequently, featuring dishes like a standout steak tartare, risotto with aged parmesan or truffle; tagliatelle with eggplant, prunes, and smoked ricotta; scallops with brussels sprouts, lentils, and radishes in dashi broth; and desserts like passion fruit frozen custard with lychees, cornbread, and popcorn granita. Looking for wine to accompany your meal? There are more than 600 labels for oenophiles. ⑤ *Average main: €35* ⊠ *Vicolo del Cinque 58, Trastevere* ☎ *06/58335903* ⊕ *www.glass-restaurant.it* ⊙ *Closed Mon., and 2 wks in July. No lunch* ⌫ *Reservations essential* ✛ *4:C6.*

$
ROMAN
✕ **I Supplì.** Trastevere's best supplì have been served at this hole-in-the-wall takeout spot since 1979. At lunchtime, the line spills out on to the street with locals who've come for the namesake treats, as well as fried baccalà fillets and stuffed zucchini flowers. The thin-crust pizza al taglio is baked the old-fashioned way—in low-rise rectangular pans—and the marinara version is a must, but you might have to order the pizza with zucchini and *straciatella* (kind of like a burrata cheese) if it's available. A few daily pasta specials are available too, and there are always gnocchi on Thursday (the traditional day for it in Rome). ⑤ *Average main: €5* ⊠ *Via San Francesco a Ripa 137, Trastevere* ☎ *06/5897110* ⊙ *Closed Sun., and 2 wks in Aug.* ▭ *No credit cards* ✛ *3:B2.*

$$
INDIAN
✕ **Jaipur.** Named after the Pink City in India, this restaurant serves the highest-quality curries in a large space just off the main Viale di

Trastevere. It's a festive and fun destination if you're craving something quite different from Italian food. The portions are small but made for sharing, so you can order an assortment. There are tables outside when the weather is good. $ *Average main: €16* ⊠ *Via di San Francesco a Ripa 56, Trastevere* ☎ *06/5803992* ⊕ *www.ristorantejaipur.it* ☉ *No lunch Mon.* ✛ *3:C2.*

$

WINE BAR

✕**Ombre Rosse.** Set on lovely Piazza Sant'Egidio in the heart of Trastevere, this open-day-and-night spot is a great place to pass the time. You can have a morning cappuccino and read one of their international newspapers; have a light lunch (soups and salads are fresh and delicious) while taking in some sun or working on your laptop (free Wi-Fi); enjoy an aperitivo and nibbles at an outdoor table; or finish off an evening with friends at the bar. Ombre Rosse bustles with regulars and expats who know the value of a well-made cocktail and an ever-lively atmosphere. $ *Average main: €12* ⊠ *Piazza Sant'Egidio 12, Trastevere* ☎ *06/5884155* ⊕ *www.ombrerossecaffe.it* ☉ *No lunch Sun.* ⚞ *Reservations not accepted* ✛ *3:B1.*

$$

ROMAN

FAMILY

✕**Osteria der Belli.** One might overlook Osteria der Belli because of its proximity to the central square of Trastevere, Piazza Santa Maria in Trastevere—and that would be a crying shame. Leo, the owner, is Sardinian and has been running this place daily for over 35 years. While Roman dishes are on the menu, it excels at seafood and Sardinian cuisine. Try the sea bass carpaccio to start, the ravioli or fettuccine *alla sarda* (in a creamy mushroom sauce) to follow. All of the homemade pasta is supplied by Leo's sister, who runs the pasta house around the corner. Ask what fresh fish has just arrived and how it's recommended to be cooked. Between the friendly service and quality food, this one's a real find in an otherwise-touristy part of Trastevere. $ *Average main: €18* ⊠ *Piazza di Sant'Apollonia 11, Trastevere* ☎ *06/5803782* ☉ *Closed Mon., and Feb.* ✛ *3:B1.*

$

MODERN ITALIAN

Fodor's Choice

★

✕**Pianostrada Laboratorio di Cucina.** This gourmet sandwich shop and caffè has an open kitchen, where you can watch the talented women owners cook up a storm of inventive delights—this is a "kitchen *lab*," after all. The baccalà patty, with tomato confit, zucchini flowers, and homemade mayonnaise on a homemade squid-ink bun, is one of the signature dishes, and the unusual combination is a delicious indication of how interesting the food can get. More mainstream options include freshly baked focaccia topped with whatever is fresh and in season, local-style fish 'n' chips, porchetta sandwiches, and roasted eggplant, along with a daily main course and a pasta. The restaurant is tiny, so plan for an early meal to avoid missing out on a table. $ *Average main: €12* ⊠ *Vicolo del Cedro 26, Trastevere* ☎ *06/689572296* ⊕ *www.pianostrada.com* ☉ *Closed Mon., and 3 wks in Aug.* ✛ *3:A1.*

$$

ITALIAN

✕**Spirito di Vino.** At this restaurant on the less traveled side of Viale Trastevere, diners get to enjoy an evening of historical interest alongside an excellent meal. The building was constructed on the site of an 11th-century synagogue, and the spot is rich with history—several ancient sculptures, now in the Vatican and Capitoline museums, were unearthed in the basement in the 19th century. The food ranges from the inventive (marinated duck salad with grapes, walnuts, and pomegranate

12

seeds) to the traditional (spaghetti cacio e pepe) to the historical (an ancient Roman recipe for braised pork shoulder with apples and leeks). The proud owner is happy to explain every dish on the menu, and offers a post-dinner tour of the wine cellar—and the famed basement. $ *Average main: €18* ⊠ *Via dei Genovesi 31, Trastevere* ☎ *06/5896689* ⊕ *www.spiritodivino.com* ⊙ *Closed Sun., and Aug.* ✦ *3:C2*.

$$
JAPANESE

✕ **Take Sushi.** An increasingly familiar sight on the streets of Rome are all-you-can-eat Japanese restaurants, popular for their inexpensive prices—but Take Sushi couldn't be further from this concept. It's all about top-quality, authentic food and decor here. The pan-fried *gyoza*-dumplings are a good way to start, followed by an order of a variety of sashimi and classic hand rolls (the menu features predominantly familiar options like spicy tuna and California rolls). The algae salad is good, too. And of course there is imported Japanese beer and sake. $ *Average main: €20* ⊠ *Viale di Trastevere 4, Trastevere* ☎ *06/65810075* ⊕ *www.takesushi.it* ⊙ *Closed Mon.* ✦ *3:C1*.

MONTEVERDE

$$
ROMAN
FAMILY

✕ **Cesare al Caseletto.** This beloved neighborhood trattoria does many things well, from the fried starters to the pastas to the meaty secondi, so it's no surprise that it's won the hearts—and stomachs—of Romans all over town. Favorite dishes include any of the fried starters, *polpette di bollito* (broiled meatballs), or *melanzane* (eggplant), as well as the hearty gnocchi with *sugo alla coda alla vaccinara* (oxtail sauce). The wine list is extensive, but the friendly waitstaff are happy to offer advice. There's also a pleasant outdoor seating area when weather allows. $ *Average main: €15* ⊠ *Via del Casaletto 45* ☎ *06/536015* ✦ *3:A6*.

$$
PIZZA
FAMILY

✕ **La Gatta Mangiona.** The pizza at this neighborhood spot is Roman-style—with a thin crust, charred on the edges. All the standard toppings are represented, from margherita to buffalo mozzarella and prosciutto, but try one of the new-fangled combinations like ricotta and pancetta and edible wild flowers. The supplì here are outstanding, and the perfect start to a meal. There are close to 100 varieties of craft beers to choose from, and the desserts are all homemade. $ *Average main: €15* ⊠ *Via Federico Ozanam 30-32* ☎ *06/65346702* ⊕ *www.lagattamangiona.com* ⊙ *No lunch* ✦ *3:A6*.

$$
MODERN ITALIAN
FAMILY

✕ **L'Osteria di Monteverde.** Romans are starting to recognize Monteverde as a foodie hub, and this trattoria is one of the neighborhood's outstanding spots. The food ranges from the classics to carefully thought-out modern dishes, but whatever you order, the quality of the produce shines. Try the tuna tartare with sesame, poppy seeds, and homemade guacamole; the tortellini filled with shrimp and served with a tomato, 'nduja (Calabrian spicy pork paste), and burrata sauce; or go with the simple but delicious carbonara. Desserts like cinnamon and pear cheesecake or tiramisù pair well with the selection of local dessert wines, like moscato from Terracina, a coastal town not far from Rome. $ *Average main: €18* ⊠ *Via Pietro Cartoni 163-165* ☎ *06/53273887* ⊕ *www.losteriadimonteverde.it* ⊙ *Closed 3 wks in Aug. No lunch Mon.* ✦ *3:A6*.

TESTACCIO

This working-class neighborhood is where the old slaughterhouses once stood and where the butchers invented the (in)famous meat and offal dishes you can still find in authentic old-school restaurants. Relatively low rents have meant an influx of young people which has made this one of the up-and-coming areas of the city.

$$ ✕ **Checchino dal 1887.** Literally carved out of a hill of ancient shards
ROMAN   of amphorae, Checchino is an example of a classic, upscale, family-run Roman restaurant, with one of the best wine cellars in the region. Though the slaughterhouses of Testaccio are long gone, an echo of their existence carries on in the restaurant's classic dishes—mostly offal and other cuts like *trippa* (tripe), *pajata* (intestines), and *coratella* (sweetbreads and beef heart) are all still on the menu for Roman purists. For the less adventurous, house specialties include braised milk-fed lamb with seasonal vegetables. ⑤ *Average main: €23* ✉ *Via di Monte Testaccio 30, Testaccio* ☎ *06/5746318* ⊕ *www.checchino-dal-1887. com* ⊘ *Closed Mon., Aug., and 1 wk at Christmas. No dinner Sun.* ⚐ *Reservations essential* Ⓜ *Piramide* ✛ *3:C5.*

$$ ✕ **Flavio al Velavevodetto.** It's everything you're looking for in a true
ROMAN   Roman eating experience: authentic, in a historic setting, and filled
Fodor's Choice   with Italians eating good food at good prices. In this very "romani di
★   Roma" working-class neighborhood, surrounded by discos and bars sharing Monte Testaccio, you can enjoy a meal of classic Roman pasta dishes (carbonara, amatriciana, etc .) and delicious fettucine with baby calamari and cherry tomatoes with some very good antipasti (try the mixed vegetable plate); and great meat mains like *polpette di bollito* (broiled meatballs) and flame-grilled lamb. The menu is simple and seasonal, and served either in the cozy, cavelike indoor dining rooms or outside under the umbrellas. For dessert order the tiramisù with a Nutella chocolate center. ⑤ *Average main: €16* ✉ *Via di Monte Testaccio 97, Testaccio* ☎ *06/5744194* ⊕ *www.ristorantevelavevodetto.it* ⚐ *Reservations essential* Ⓜ *Piramide* ✛ *3:C5.*

$$ ✕ **La Torricella.** This family-run institution has been serving seafood in the
SEAFOOD   working-class Testaccio neighborhood for over 40 years, and fresh fish
FAMILY   arrives here from all over the country (but mainly Puglia) every morning and sometimes twice daily. The tuna and mixed-seafood carpaccio are standard but excellent starters, and from there, look for house specialties like paccheri with *totani* (baby calamari) and the wondrously simple spaghetti with lobster. There are non-seafood Roman classics on the menu, too, like cacio e pepe and pajata, but this is the place to order seafood. ⑤ *Average main: €18* ✉ *Via Evangelista Torricelli 2/12, Testaccio* ☎ *06/5746311* ⊕ *www.la-torricella.com* Ⓜ *Piramide* ✛ *3:D6.*

$$ ✕ **Porto Fluviale.** This massive structure is on a stretch of street that's
ITALIAN   gone from gritty clubland to popular night spot, thanks largely to Porto Fluviale, which has come to mean all things to all people: bar, caffè, pizzeria, lunch buffet, and lively evening restaurant. The food, too, is all-encompassing, featuring cuisine from all over Italy. As one might expect from such a cavernous, busy place, the service is not perfect, but it's a fun place to be and the food is tasty, from pizza made in wood-burning ovens to pasta and grilled meats and interesting salads. Cocktails at the

12

bar, if you can get a spot, are a fun option—accompany your drink with *cicchetti* (the Venetian word for tapas-style snacks). Ⓢ *Average main: €14* ☒ *Via del Porto Fluviale 22, Testaccio* ☏ *06/5743199* ⊕ *www.portofluviale.com* Ⓜ *Piramide* ✛ *3:D6.*

$ ✕**Pizzeria Remo.** Expect a line at this perennial-favorite pizzeria in
PIZZA Testaccio frequented by students and locals. It usually moves quickly, though, as the service inside is friendly and efficient. There are no tablecloths or other nonessentials, just excellent classic Roman pizza and boisterous conversation. Start with some fried delicacies like zucchini flowers stuffed with mozzarella and anchovy or a battered piece of baccalà, then order the justly renowned pizza: you can't go wrong with the simple margherita, especially if you opt for the buffalo mozzarella version. Ⓢ *Average main: €10* ☒ *Piazza Santa Maria Liberatrice 44, Testaccio* ☏ *06/5746270* ⊟ *No credit cards* ⊙ *Closed Sun., 3 weeks in Aug. No lunch* Ⓜ *Piramide* ✛ *3:C4.*

$$$ ✕**Stazione di Posta.** On the site of what was Rome's largest slaugh-
MODERN ITALIAN terhouse in the 1800s, Stazione di Posta manages to be both über-
Fodor's Choice modern—the Michelin-starred food is some of Rome's finest molecular
★ gastronomy—while retaining some of the feel of the historic cobblestones of the old building. For appetizers, expect deconstructed versions of Roman classics in miniature, such as carbonara sauce in an eggshell or an Asian-inspired pork bun filled, instead, with porchetta. Main courses might include tortelli pasta stuffed with mortadella mousse and served with pistachio and a pizza bianca. The "pre-dessert" course of a mini bonsai tree with cookies hanging from the branches is legendary. Ⓢ *Average main: €25* ☒ *Largo Dino Frisullo, Testaccio* ☏ *06/65743548* ⊕ *www.stazionediposta.eu* ⊙ *Closed Sun., and 2 wks in Aug.* Ⓜ *Piramide* ✛ *3:C5.*

$ ✕**Trapizzino.** Stefano Calegari is one of Rome's most famous pizza mak-
ROMAN ers, but at Trapizzino he's doing something a bit different. The name of
FAMILY the restaurant is derived from the Italian words for sandwich (tramezzino) and pizza, and the result is something like an upscale pizza pocket, stuffed on the spot with local specialties like chicken alla cacciatore, or trippa, or roast pumpkin, pecorino, and almonds. The genovese (with a slow-cooked beef sauce) and amatriciana "pizzas" are standouts. The supplì are also delicious. Ⓢ *Average main: €5* ☒ *Via Giovanni Branca 88, Testaccio* ☏ *06/43419624* ⊕ *www.trapizzino.it* ⊙ *Closed Mon., and 1 wk in Aug.* ⊟ *No credit cards* Ⓜ *Piramide* ✛ *3:C4.*

MONTI, ESQUILINO, AND SAN LORENZO

MONTI

Monti is a chic, bohemian neighborhood with an expanding food scene.

$$ ✕**Caffè Propaganda.** Black and white tiles create the atmosphere of a
CAFÉ Parisian brasserie, but the heart of the large food menu—printed on broadsheet like a newspaper—is still Italian. Signature dishes include red shrimp carpaccio, the justly popular artichokes cooked three ways, cacio e pepe–filled ravioli topped with crispy guanciale, and the house burger with fat chips. Desserts lean toward France, with colorful macarons, a decadent chocolate pudding, and several *crostate* (sweet pies

usually with jam or ricotta). This is one of the few places in the area open late: food is often served until 2 am. ⑤ *Average main: €18* ✉ *Via Claudia 15-19, Monti* ☎ *06/94534255* ⊕ *www.caffepropaganda.it* ⊘ *Closed Mon., and 2 wks in Aug.* Ⓜ *Colosseo* ✥ *3:G1.*

$$
WINE BAR
✕ **Cavour 313.** This long-popular wine bar a stone's throw from the Roman Forum has a tight seating area in the front, so you might want to head back to the larger, albeit darker, back room. The atmosphere is festive, almost like a rustic beer hall, though the focus is definitely on wine: there are about 25 options by the glass and more than 1,200 bottles. Food-wise, there is an excellent variety of cured meats, cheeses, and salads, chosen with a focus on locally grown, organic, and artisanal products. ⑤ *Average main: €14* ✉ *Via Cavour 313, Monti* ☎ *06/6785496* ⊕ *www.cavour313.it* ⊘ *Closed Sun. in July and Aug.* Ⓜ *Cavour* ✥ *2:B5.*

$$
MODERN ITALIAN
Fodor's Choice
★
✕ **Urbana 47.** This restaurant serving breakfast through dinner embodies the *kilometro zero* concept, highlighting hyper-local food from the surrounding Lazio region. The local boho crowd comes in the morning for a Continental or "American" breakfast (with free Wi-Fi); lunch means tasty "fast slow-food" options like grain salads and healthy panini. From 6 pm onward, there are tapas and drinks, then leisurely dinners like homemade pasta with broccoli, anchovies, and orange zest, or a local free-range chicken stuffed with potatoes and chicory. ⑤ *Average main: €15* ✉ *Via Urbana 47, Monti* ☎ *06/47884006* ⊕ *www.urbana47.it* Ⓜ *Cavour* ✥ *2:C5.*

ESQUILINO

Esquilino is Rome's main multicultural artery, with Mercato Esquilino, a great covered market for Italian, Asian, and African specialties. Tourist traps abound, but you can find some authentic Roman food.

$$
ETHIOPIAN
✕ **Africa.** For something very different from pizza and pasta, try this excellent Ethiopian restaurant where traditional food is served in a casual environment. Seating is at low tables, as is typical, and the spicy stews and salads are served with spongey *injera*bread, which also serves as a utensil—be prepared to eat with your hands. If you've never had Ethiopian food, this is a good place to try it; if you're familiar with the cuisine, you'll quickly realize that the food here is top-quality. ⑤ *Average main: €20* ✉ *Via Gaeta 26/28, Esquilino* ☎ *06/4941077* ▭ *No credit cards* ⊘ *Closed Mon.* Ⓜ *Castro Pretorio* ✥ *2:E2.*

$$
MODERN ITALIAN
Fodor's Choice
★
✕ **Agata e Romeo.** For the perfect combination of fine dining, creative cuisine, and rustic Roman tradition, this restaurant run by husband-and-wife team of Agata Parisella (in the kitchen) and Romeo Caraccio (in the front of the house) is a must. The intimate dining room and personal service make you feel as if you're dining in a friend's house; and the food is outstanding. Chef Agata was one of the first in the capital to put a gourmet spin on Roman ingredients and classic preparations, so even though the menu might look familiar, the quality of the food is several steps above. The cacio e pepe is particularly renowned. ⑤ *Average main: €20* ✉ *Via Carlo Alberto 45, Esquilino* ☎ *06/4466115* ⊕ *www.agataeromeo.it* ⊘ *Closed Sun., and 2 wks in Aug. No lunch Sat. and Mon.* ⚖ *Reservations essential* Ⓜ *Vittorio Emanuele* ✥ *2:E5.*

$$$
MODERN ITALIAN
✕ **Aroma.** The panoramas from the restaurant atop the Palazzo Manfredi Hotel are undeniably stunning; it's the best unobstructed view

12

of the Colosseum in Rome, so ask for a table on the terrace. When Executive Chef Giuseppe di Iorio was awarded a Michelin star, it was a convincing indication that the food was just as stellar. You can order off-menu, or opt for the chef's seven-course tasting menu: you might start withh bread-and-artichoke-crusted veal and roasted mackerel to start; move on to ravioli filled with white truffle and rice; a seafood course; a meat course; and then perhaps a chocolate and Sicilian pistachio delight to finish. Service is attentive without being obtrusive, and it all adds up to a dining experience not soon forgotten. ⑤ *Average main: €30* ⊠ *Via Labicana 125, Esquilino* ☎ *06/97615109* ⊕ *www.aromarestaurant.it* ⌒ *Reservations essential* Ⓜ *Colosseo* ✛ *3:G1*.

$ ✕ **Li Rioni.** This busy pizzeria conveniently close to the Colosseum has
PIZZA been serving real-deal Roman-style pizza—super thin and cooked to a
FAMILY crisp—since the mid-1980s. The magic might be due to the fact that they let their pizza dough rise 24–48 hours before baking to guarantee an extra-light pizza, said to be more easily digested than others. The Napoli and Margherita reign supreme here, as well as anything with buffalo mozzarella and pork sausage. Do as the Romans do, and start your meal with fritti; the olive ascolane are particularly good. ⑤ *Average main: €12* ⊠ *Via dei Santi Quattro 24, Esquilino* ☎ *06/70450605* ⊕ *www.lirioni.it* ⊘ *Closed 2 wks in Aug. No lunch.* Ⓜ *Colosseo* ✛ *3:H1*.

$ ✕ **Panella.** It's a little on the pricey side, but the baked goods here are
CAFÉ top-quality and the coffee drinks are excellent. Come in the morn-
FAMILY ing for a *cornetto* (it looks a lot like a croissant), or in the afternoon for a slice of pizza or one of the delicious mini tarts. Aperitivo time gets busy too, thanks to the savory pastry bites or croquettes you can sample at the pleasant outdoor tables. It's worth noting that although the food is top-notch, table service can be slow, so opt for the counter if you're in a hurry. ⑤ *Average main: €10* ⊠ *Via Merulana 54, Esquilino* ☎ *06/4872651* ⊕ *www.panellaroma.com* ⊘ *Closed Sun.* Ⓜ *Vittorio Emanuele* ✛ *2:E5*.

PIGNETO

Pigneto is Rome's up-and-coming *zona*: gritty caffè, artsy bars, and youth-driven, modern Italian restaurants are what you'll find.

$$ ✕ **Pigneto Quarantuno.** The busy pedestrian strip of Pigneto is full of
MODERN ITALIAN restaurants and bars, but this is the only spot not ushering in custom-
Fodor's Choice ers, because they simply don't need to. The top-quality food speaks
★ for itself and reservations are always a good idea (especially if you'd like to sit outside). The constantly changing menu reflects seasonal produce; start off with one of their many focaccie, such as thyme, goat cheese, and grilled zucchini. Then move on to a primo, like carbonara, a hearty ragù, or more delicate vegetarian pasta dishes in the summer. Main courses include superior meatballs, fillets of salted cod, or an excellent trippa alla romana. The wine list is impressive, with local and international labels. ⑤ *Average main: €15* ⊠ *Via del Pigneto 41-43, Pigneto* ☎ *06/70399483* ⊕ *www.pignetoquarantuno.it* ⊘ *Closed Mon. No lunch.* ✛ *2:H6*.

$$ ✕ **Primo al Pigneto.** One of the scene-setting restaurants in Pigneto, the
ITALIAN latest hip neighborhood in Rome, Primo puts a prime focus on quality ingredients, but the name might just as easily refer to the prime

people-watching. The young patrons sip from a selection of 250 wines and nibble hand-sliced prosciutto, anchovy-and-broccoli gratin, and salads with goat cheese and radicchio. Pastas include artichoke tortelli with marjoram and pecorino, and seafood secondi like grilled swordfish with a pistachio sauce. Those with more carnivorous desires can sink their teeth into dishes like the provolone-and-herb-stuffed veal. The neighborhood is a 10-minute bus ride from Termini station. $ *Average main: €18 ⊠ Via del Pigneto 46, Pigneto ☎ 06/7013827 ⊕ www. primoalpigneto.it ⊘ Closed Mon. and 1 wk in Aug. No lunch Mon.–Sat. ⚱ Reservations essential ✛ 2:H6.*

$$
ROMAN
✗ **Trattoria Pigneto.** This casual home-style trattoria follows the style of a fraschetta—a type of countryside restaurant where the menu focuses on porchetta in a relaxed and casual atmosphere. Ordering the porchetta here is an obvious must—the waiter will serve it on butcher's paper according to how many people are in your party—but your meal needn't start, or end, there. Accompany the main attraction with a cheese and charcuterie board, and follow with old-school classics such as pasta all'amatriciana, cacio e pepe, or chicken cacciatore. $ *Average main: €14 ⊠ Via del Pigneto 68, Pigneto ☎ 06/3888723723 ⊘ Closed 2 wks in Aug. No lunch. ✛ 2:H6.*

SAN LORENZO

San Lorenzo is a university quarter, where student budgets dictate low prices and good value. There are also a few hidden gems here.

$$
SOUTHERN
ITALIAN
✗ **I Fratelli.** The four owners of this proudly Southern Italian pizzeria and restaurant come from the deep south (Sicily, Calabria, Campania, and Puglia), and this influence can clearly be seen in the menu, especially in the pizza, which is of the thicker Neapolitan variety. There are classic pizzas and interesting combinations like pear and gorgonzola or brie and speck. Recommended primi include a classic filetto di baccalà served here with guanciale and honey; for secondi, look for cacio e pepe dressed up with black truffle. $ *Average main: €15 ⊠ Via degli Umbri 14, San Lorenzo ☎ 06/4469856 ⊕ www.ristoranteifratelli.it ⊘ Closed 10 days in Aug. No lunch Sun. ✛ 2:G4.*

$$
SOUTHERN
ITALIAN
✗ **Tram Tram.** The name refers to its proximity to the tram tracks, but could also describe the small, narrow interior of the restaurant, which is often packed with diners (in warmer weather there's a "side car" of tables along the sidewalk). The cuisine is mostly rooted in Puglia, with an emphasis on seafood and vegetables—prawns with saffron-kissed sautéed vegetables, for example—as well as pastas of very particular shapes. Try the homemade *orecchiette* (ear-shaped pasta), made here with clams and broccoli. $ *Average main: €20 ⊠ Via dei Reti 44/46, San Lorenzo ☎ 06/490416 ⊕ www.tramtram.it ⊘ Closed 1 wk in Aug. No lunch Sun. and Mon. ⚱ Reservations essential ✛ 2:H4.*

VIA APPIA ANTICA

$$$
ITALIAN
✗ **L'Archeologia.** In this farmhouse just beyond the catacombs, you can dine indoors beside the fireplace in cool weather or in the garden under age-old vines in summer. The atmosphere is friendly and intimate. Specialties include fettuccine *al finocchio salvatico* (with wild fennel), *abbacchio alla scottadito* (grilled lamb cutlets), and fresh seafood. $ *Average main: €26 ⊠ Via Appia Antica 139, Via Appia Antica ☎ 06/7880494 ⊕ www.larcheologia.it ✛ 2:E6.*

ROME DINING AND LODGING ATLAS

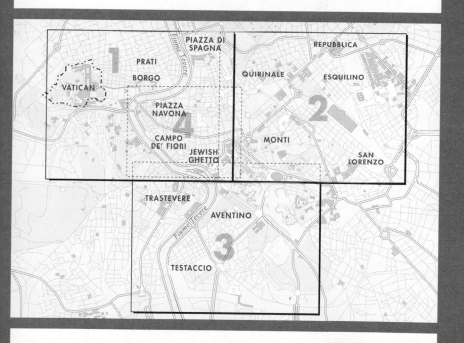

KEY

☐ *Hotels*
■ *Restaurants*
■ *Restaurant in Hotel*

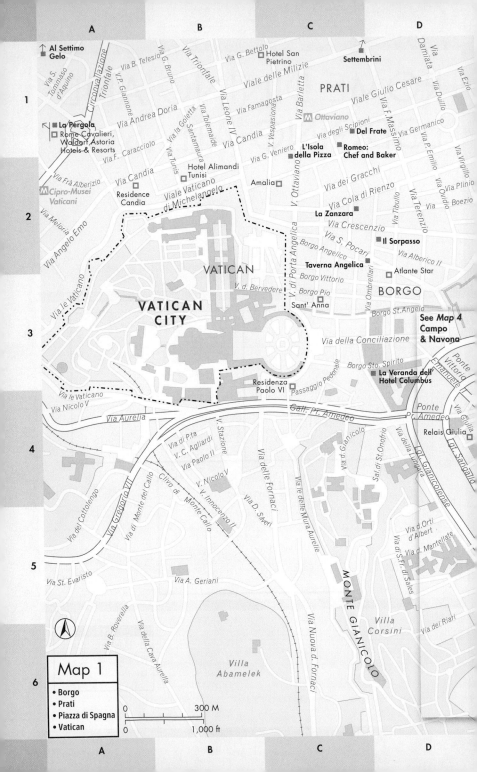

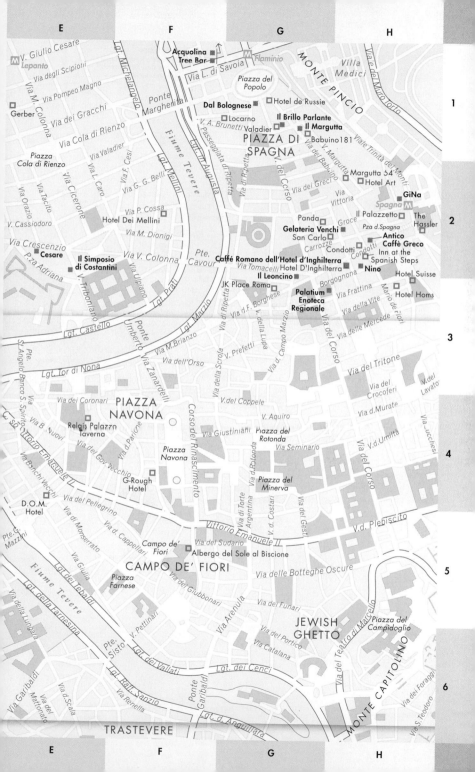

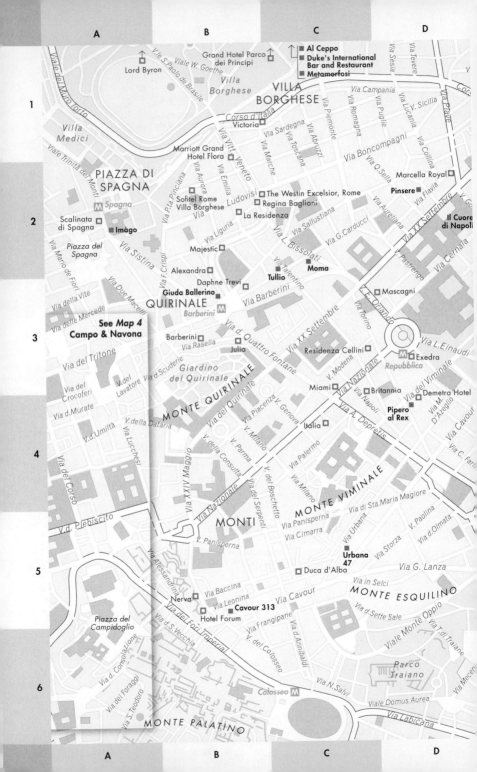

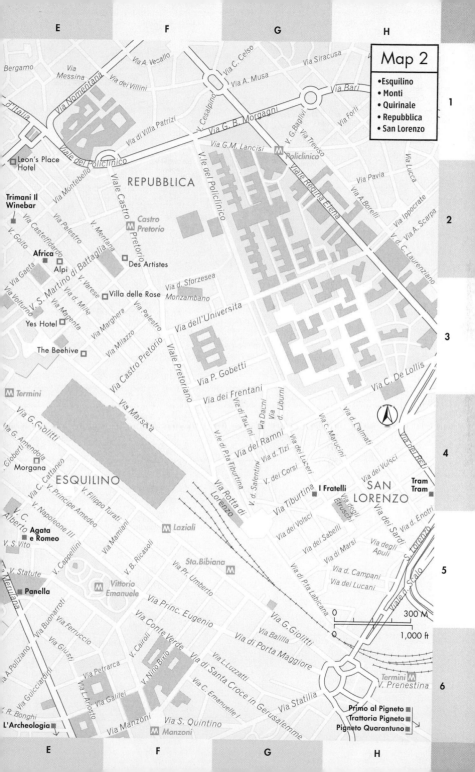

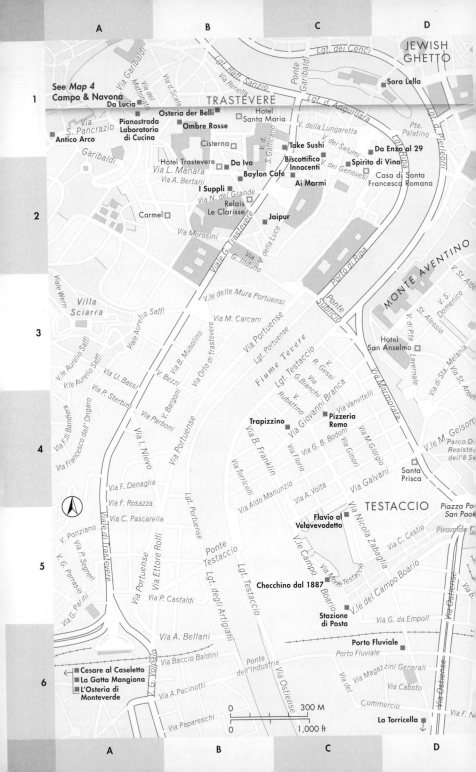

A   **B**   **C**   **D**

JEWISH
GHETTO

1

See Map 4
Campo & Navona

Da Lucia

Via S. Pancrazio

Antico Arco

Garibaldi

Sora Lella

TRASTEVERE

Osteria der Belli

Pianostrada
Laboratorio
di Cucina

Ombre Rosse

Hotel
Santa Maria

V. della Lungaretta

Pte.
Palatino

V. dei Salumi

Cisterna

Take Sushi

Da Enzo al 29

Hotel Trastevere

Da Ivo

Biscottificio
Innocenti

Spirito di Vino

Via L. Manara

Via A. Bertani

Baylon Café

Casa di Santa
Francesca Romana

I Suppli

Via N. del Grande

Ai Marmi

V. dei Genovesi

Relais
Le Clarisse

2

Carmel

Jaipur

Via Morosini

V. d. della Luce

Via G. Induno

V.le delle Mura Portuensi

MONTE AVENTINO

V. St. Albe

Villa
Sciarra

Via M. Carcani

Via Portuense

Via Aurelio Saffi

Lgt. Portuense

Porto di Ripa

Ponte
Subliccio

V. S.
Domenico

St. Alessio

3

V.le Aurelio Saffi

V. B. Musolino

Via Orto di Trastevere

Fiume Tevere

Lgt. Testaccio

R. Gessi

V. di P.ta
Lavernale

Hotel
San Anselmo

Via di Sta. Melania

V.le Aurelio Saffi

V. Bezzi

V. G.Bianchi. Branca

Via

Via Vanvitelli

V.le Aurelio Saffi

Via U. Bassi

Via P. Sterbini

Rubattino

Via di Sta. St. Melania

Via Fr.lli Bandiera

Via Francesco dall'Ongaro

Via P. Parboni

Via Bargoni

Via Parboni

Via Portuense

Trapizzino

Via Giovanni Branca

Pizzeria
Remo

Via M. Giorgio

V.le M. Gelson

Parco D
Resiste
dell'8 Se

4

Via I. Nievo

Via B. Franklin

Via Florio

Via G. B. Bodoni

Via Ginori

Via F. Denaglia

Via Torricelli

Santa
Prisca

Via F. Rosazza

Via Aldo Manunzio

Via A. Volta

Via Galvani

Via C. Pascarella

TESTACCIO

Piazza Po
San Pao

V. Ponziano

Flavio al
Velavevodetto

Via Nicola Zabaglia

Via C. Cestio

Piramide

5

V. P. Segneri

Viale di Trastevere

Via Portuense

Lgt. Portuense

Via Ettore Rolli

Ponte
Testaccio

Lgt. degli Artigiani

Lgt. Testaccio

Checchino dal 1887

V.le Campo Boario

Via Monte Testaccio

V.le del Campo Boario

Via Ostiense

V. G. Parasio

V. G. Parrasio

Via P. Castaldi

Stazione
di Posta

Via G. da Empoli

Via A. Bellani

Porto Fluviale

6

Via G. Volana

Via Baccio Baldini

Ponte
dell'Industria

Porto Fluviale

Via Ostiense

Via F. N

Cesare al Caseletto

La Gatta Mangiona

L'Osteria di
Monteverde

Via A.Pacinotti

Via Magazzini Generali

Via Caboto

Via Papareschi

Commercio

La Torricella

0   300 M

0   1,000 ft

A   **B**   **C**   **D**

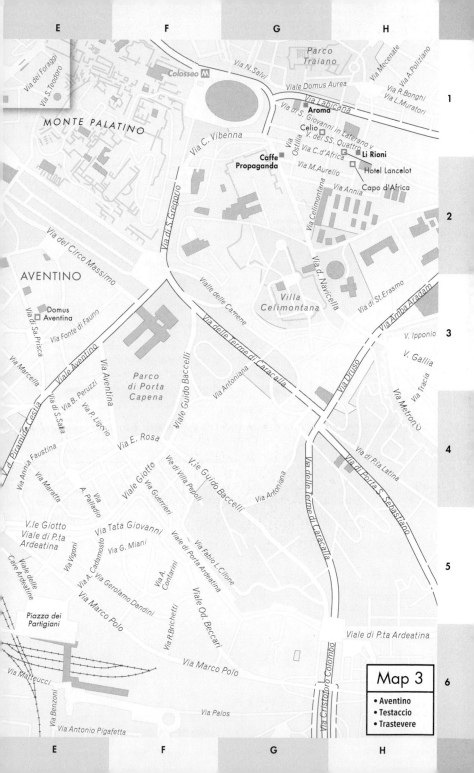

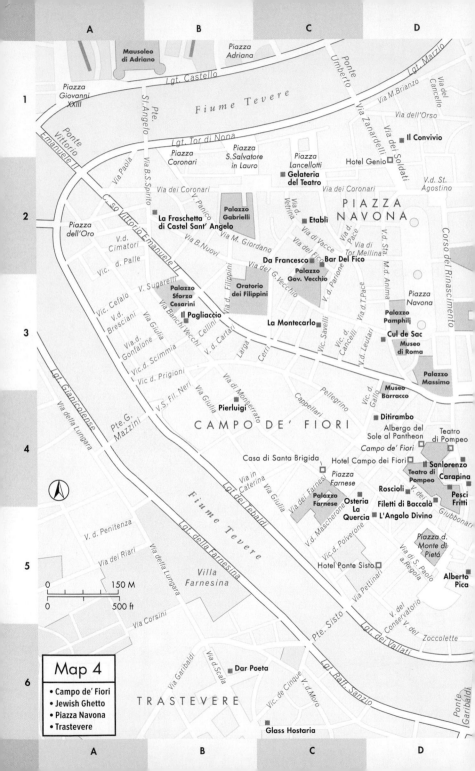

A   **B**   **C**   **D**

Mausoleo di Adriano

Piazza Adriana

Lgt. Castello

Fiume Tevere

1

Piazza Giovanni XXIII

Ponte S.Angelo

Ponte Vittorio Emanuele II

Lgt. Marzio

Ponte Umberto

Via M.Brianzo

Via del Cancello

Via dell'Orso

Lgt. Tor di Nona

Via Zanardelli

Via dei Soldati

■ Il Convivio

Piazza Coronari

Piazza S.Salvatore in Lauro

Piazza Lancellotti

Hotel Genio

V.d. St. Agostino

Via Paola

Via di B.S.Spirito

Via dei Coronari

■ Gelateria del Teatro

Via dei Coronari

PIAZZA NAVONA

Piazza dell'Oro

Corso Vittorio Emanuele II

V. Panico

Palazzo Gabrielli

Via d. Vetrina

■ Etabli

Via M. Giordano

2

■ La Fraschetta di Castel Sant' Angelo

Via di Vacce

Via di Pace

V.d. Sta.

V.d. M.d. Anima

Corso del Rinascimento

V.d. Cimatori

Via B.Nuovi

Via del Fico

Via di Tor Mellina

■ Da Francesco   Bar Del Fico ■

Via d. G.Vecchio

Palazzo Gov. Vecchio

V. d. Parione

Via d. T.Pace

Piazza Navona

Vic. d. Palle

V.d. Bresciani

V. Sugaretti

Palazzo Sforza Cesarini

Oratorio dei Filippini

Via d. Filippini

Palazzo Pamphili

Vic. Cefalo

Via di Giulia

Via Banchi Vecchi

■ Il Pagliaccio

Cellini

■ La Montecarlo

Vic. Savelli

Vic. d. Cancelli

V.d. Leutari

Cul de Sac ■

Museo di Roma

3

Lgt. Gianicolense

Via d. Gonfalone

Vic.d. Scimmia

V. d. Cartari

Larga

Cerri

Pellegrino

Vic. d. Gallo

Museo Barracco ■

Palazzo Massimo

Vic. d. Prigioni

V.S. Fil. Neri

Via di Giulia

Via di Monserrato

■ Pierluigi

Cappellari

■ Ditirambo

Albergo del Sole al Pantheon

Teatro di Pompeo

4

Pte.G. Mazzini

CAMPO DE' FIORI

Casa di Santa Brigida

Via in Caterina

Via di Giulia

Hotel Campo dei Fiori □

Campo de' Fiori □

Teatro di Pompeo

■ Il Sanlorenzo

Carapina ■

Fiume Tevere

Piazza Farnese

■ Roscioli

V. del

■ Pesci Fritti

Via dei Farnesi

Palazzo Farnese

Osteria La Quercia

Filetti di Baccalà ■

■ L'Angolo Divino

Giubbonari

Lgt. dei Tebaldi

Via Mascherone

Vic.d. Polverone

Piazza d. Monte di Pietá

Via di S.Paolo a.Regola

5

V. d. Penitenza

Via dei Riari

Via della Lungara

Lgt. della Farnesina

Villa Farnesina

Hotel Ponte Sisto □

Via Pettinari

■ Alberto Pica

0   150 M

0   500 ft

Via Corsini

Pte. Sisto

Lgt. dei Vallati

V. del Conservatorio

V. dei Zoccolette

Lgt. Farn. Sanzio

Ponte Garibaldi

Lgt. Garibaldi

Map 4

- Campo de' Fiori
- Jewish Ghetto
- Piazza Navona
- Trastevere

Via Garibaldi

Via d.Scala

■ Dar Poeta

T R A S T E V E R E

Vic. de Cinque   V. d'Moro

6

■ Glass Hostaria

A   **B**   **C**   **D**

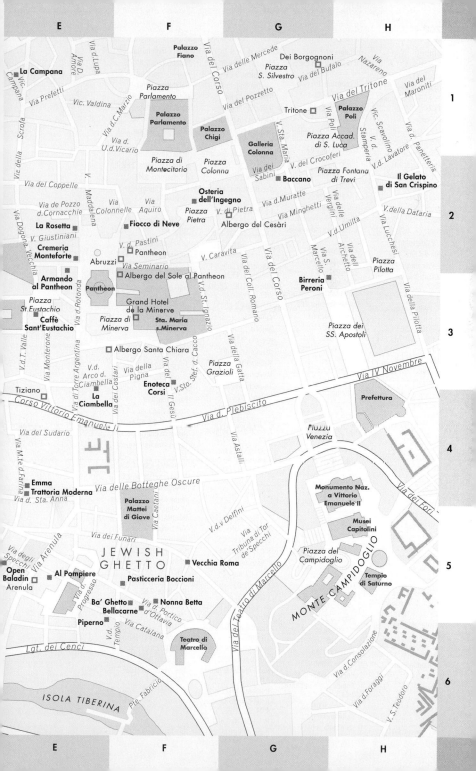

WHERE TO STAY

Updated by Nicole Arriaga

It's the click of your heels on inlaid marble, the whisper of 600-thread-count Frette sheets, the murmured *buongiorno* of a coat-tailed porter bowing low as you pass. It's a rustic attic room with a wood-beam ceiling, a white umbrella on a roof terrace, a 400-year-old palazzo. Maybe it's birdsong pouring into your room as you swing open French windows to a sun-kissed view of the Colosseum, a timeworn piazza, or a flower-filled marketplace.

When it comes to accommodations, Rome offers a wide selection of high-end hotels, bed-and-breakfasts, designer boutique hotels—options that run the gamut from whimsical to luxurious. Whether you want a simple place to rest your head or a complete cache of exclusive amenities, you have plenty to choose from.

Luxury hotels like the Eden, the Hotel Hassler, and the Hotel de Russie are justly renowned for sybaritic comfort: postcard views over Roman rooftops, silver flatware on white linen atop a groaning breakfast-buffet table, and the fluffiest towels. But in more modest categories, very often Rome's hotels are not up to the standards of space, comfort, quiet, and service taken for granted in the United States: you'll still find places with tiny rooms, lumpy beds, and anemic air-conditioning. The good news: if you're flexible, there are happy mediums aplenty.

One thing to figure out before you arrive is which neighborhood you want to stay in. There are obvious advantages to staying in a hotel within easy walking distance of the main sights. If a picturesque location is your main concern, stay in one of the small hotels around Piazza Navona or Campo de' Fiori. If luxury is a high priority, head for Piazza di Spagna or beyond the city center, where quality/price ratios are higher and some hotels have swimming pools. Most of Rome's good budget hotels are concentrated around Termini station, but here accommodations can vary widely, from fine to downright seedy, and you'll have to use public transportation to get to the *centro storico* (historic center). The popularity of Pope Francis has drawn hundreds of thousands of

WHERE SHOULD I STAY?

	Neighborhood Vibe	Pros	Cons
Around the Vatican: Borgo and Prati	Touristy near the Vatican but also with some upmarket restaurants and caffè; not especially atmospheric.	Close to the Vatican; pretty quiet at night.	Far from other tourist attractions and nightlife.
Piazza Navona, Campo de' Fiori, and Jewish Ghetto	Surrounding areas are filled with good restaurants and most of Rome's major attractions; the Jewish Ghetto is quieter.	Everything you need is within walking distance: good eats, shopping, and many of Rome's museums and monuments.	This is the height of hustle and bustle in Rome—convenient, but often pricey; street noise may be an issue.
Piazza di Spagna	Home to Rome's crème de la crème for lodging and shopping.	Where all the high rollers and A-listers like to reside.	Everything is expensive; not very close to central hot spots.
Repubblica	Repubblica, with its beautiful piazza, is near Termini station without the grungy feel.	Hotels are much cheaper than elsewhere in Rome; convenient to Termini station; great restaurants and hip bars.	Cheap, basic accommodations; the area surrounding Termini station can be iffy.
Villa Borghese and Piazza del Popolo, Monte Mario, and Parioli	Somewhat removed from the hubbub, this area is a bit more refined, with fancy boutiques and hotels.	Close to the Piazza di Spagna and shopping; lots of dining options nearby.	Pricey and a bit remote from Piazza Navona and Campo de' Fiori.
Trastevere	Villagelike Trastevere has winding cobblestone alleys, beautiful churches, and authentic mom-and-pop trattorias.	Fun area with great restaurants and caffè.	General area gets busy at night; can be rowdy and rambunctious on the weekends; full of students.
Aventino and Testaccio	Aventino is a relaxing hilltop retreat. Working-class Testaccio is the heart of Rome's nightlife.	Tranquility, amazing views, and spacious rooms await you in Aventino. Party like a rock star in Rome's famous nightlife district, Testaccio.	Transportation difficult on the Aventine Hill; Testaccio is crowded on weekends.
Monti and Esquilino	These are some of the more chic and funky neighborhoods in Rome.	Hotels are cheaper here than elsewhere in Rome; close to Termini station.	Far from main tourist attractions.

13

new tourists to the papal mass and blessings since his appointment in 2013; this has naturally been good business for hotels in the Vatican and surrounding areas.

PLANNING

RESERVATIONS

Unless you don't mind rolling the dice on your accommodations, it's best to book ahead. This is especially true for May and June, when the Eternal City is virtually bursting at the seams; the same goes for major

Catholic holidays such as Easter and Christmas. Rome is never really empty, but July–August and January–February are slower months—and the best times of year to find rock-bottom rates as well.

CHECKING IN

As soon as you get to Rome, you'll notice the leisurely pace of life here, which extends to hotel check-in times. If you arrive early in the morning (as is often the case with North American flights), you may find that your room is not ready yet (after 2 pm is pretty standard for hotels both big and small). In this case, most hotels will store your luggage and encourage you to go out sightseeing. If you think you'll arrive later in the day, mention this before booking to make sure someone will be on hand to check you in. Some smaller hotels don't have a round-the-clock staff, and it's best to avoid unpleasant surprises. Check-out times are a little stricter, between 10 am and noon. If you need more time that day, the hotel may try to charge you for an extra night; however, if you just want to store your luggage for a few hours on your last day, most hotels will accommodate this request.

FACILITIES

The most expensive hotels have all the amenities you would expect at top levels and rates, with a full range of services, spacious lounges, bars, restaurants, and some fitness facilities. Midrange hotels may have refrigerators, in-room safes, and double-glazed windows to keep out street noise. Budget hotels will have in-room direct-dial telephones and TVs, and most will have air-conditioning. In less expensive places, you may have to pay extra for air-conditioning, and the shower may be the drain-in-the-floor type that hovers over the toilet and drenches the whole bathroom.

Unless stated in the review, hotels are equipped with elevators, and all guest rooms have air-conditioning, TVs, and telephones.

WITH KIDS

Italians love kids, and many hotels go out of their way to accommodate families, with programming, special games, and other perks. Although hotels often allow children to stay in their parents' room for free, keep in mind that hotel rooms in Italy tend to be very small by American standards. It's a good idea to inquire about triples, connecting rooms, or suites, or to consider taking a short-term apartment rental or residence hotel for the duration of your stay.

PRICES

In 2011, the city of Rome implemented a new tax for all overnight stays. Guests in bed-and-breakfasts, vacation apartment rentals, and one-, two-, and three-star hotels will incur an additional €2 surcharge per person per night for a maximum of 10 nights. In four- and five-star hotels, the surcharge is €3 per person per night for a maximum of 10 nights. In the off-season months of late January, February, July, and August, prices can be considerably discounted (sometimes up to half off the regular rate). Inquire about specials and weekend deals, and you may be able to get a better rate per night if you are staying a week or longer. Rates are inclusive of service, but it's customary to tip porters, waiters, maids, and concierges.

WHAT IT COSTS IN EUROS			
$	$$	$$$	$$$$
FOR TWO PEOPLE	under €125	€125–€200	€201–€300	over €300

Prices are for a standard double room in high season.

HOTEL REVIEWS

Hotel reviews have been shortened. For full information, visit Fodors. com. The following reviews are listed alphabetically within neighborhoods. Use the coordinate (✛ 1:B2) at the end of each listing to locate a property on the dining and lodging atlas in the previous chapter.

AROUND THE VATICAN

BORGO

Just east of the Vatican, the Borgo area has a certain medieval charm but can be overwhelming with tourists (and the tourist traps who love them). That said, there are a few appealing and atmospheric hotels here, and you can't beat the location for soaking up the Vatican sights.

$$$
HOTEL

Atlante Star. The lush rooftop-garden terrace with a center-stage view of St. Peter's Basilica is just one reason to stay here; you'll also enjoy the proximity to the Vatican and superb shopping and dining nearby. **Pros:** close to St. Peter's; impressive view from the restaurant and some of the rooms. **Cons:** some rooms are nicer than others; the area can feel a bit residential; bathrooms in some rooms are a little outdated. $ *Rooms from: €280* ⌕ *Via Vitelleschi 34, Borgo* ☎ *06/686386* ⊕ *www.atlante-hotels.com* ⇆ *65 rooms* ⎆ *Breakfast* Ⓜ *Ottaviano* ✛ 1:D3.

$$$$
HOTEL
Fodor's Choice
★

Residenza Paolo VI. Set in a former monastery—still an extraterritorial part of the Vatican—magnificently abutting Bernini's colonnade of St. Peter's Square, the Paolo VI (pronounced "Sesto," a reference to Pope Paul VI) is unbeatably close to St. Peter's, with guest rooms that are luxurious, comfortable, and amazingly quiet. **Pros:** unparalleled views of St. Peter's from the rooftop terrace; quiet rooms; huge breakfast spread. **Cons:** small rooms are really small; bathrooms are small; atmosphere at night is a little too quiet. $ *Rooms from: €350* ⌕ *Via Paolo VI 29, Borgo* ☎ *06/684870* ⊕ *www.residenzapaolovi.com* ⇆ *35 rooms* ⎆ *Breakfast* Ⓜ *Ottaviano* ✛ 1:C4.

$$
HOTEL

Sant'Anna. In the picturesque, medieval Borgo neighborhood in the shadow of St. Peter's, this small, fashionable hotel is good value. **Pros:** Borgo Pio is a pedestrian-only zone during the day; beds are comfy; staff are friendly. **Cons:** no on-site bar or restaurant, and many nearby restaurants are tourist traps; the neighborhood is dead at night. $ *Rooms from: €180* ⌕ *Borgo Pio 134, Borgo* ☎ *06/68801602* ⊕ *www.santanna-hotel.net* ⇆ *20 rooms, 2 apartments* ⎆ *Breakfast* Ⓜ *Ottaviano* ✛ 1:C3.

13

PRATI

This calm residential neighborhood north of the Vatican is convenient to sightseeing and shopping but removed from the chaotic centro storico. Here you'll find small, friendly hotels that don't break the bank.

$$
HOTEL

Amalia. Convenient to St. Peter's, the Vatican, and Prati's Cola di Rienzo shopping district (and just a block from the Ottaviano stop of Metro line A), this small, family-run hotel is crisp and smart. **Pros:** good location for both visiting the Vatican and shopping; 24-hour turnaround on laundry services; large beds; late check-out at noon if you book directly through their website. **Cons:** Wi-Fi is free only when you book directly through their website. $ *Rooms from: €150* ⊠ *Via Germanico 66, Prati* ☎ *06/39723356* ⊕ *www.hotelamalia.com* ⊅ *34 rooms (27 with bath)* ⊚ *Breakfast* Ⓜ *Cipro, Lepanto* ✢ 1:C2.

$$
HOTEL

Gerber. Across the river from Piazza del Popolo on a quiet side street in the Prati neighborhood, this intimate, unpretentious hotel offers friendly service and simple, pleasant rooms. **Pros:** good value; great service; comfortable beds and big bathrooms. **Cons:** elevator is tiny; you'll probably need to take a taxi or public transport for sightseeing. $ *Rooms from: €175* ⊠ *Via degli Scipioni 241, Prati* ☎ *06/3216485* ⊕ *www.hotelgerber.it* ⊅ *27 rooms* ⊚ *Breakfast* Ⓜ *Lepanto* ✢ 1:E1.

$$
HOTEL

Hotel Alimandi Tunisi. A stone's throw from the Musei Vaticani, this family-run hotel offers good service and rates, with all sorts of perks. **Pros:** friendly staff; rooftop terrace; reasonably priced restaurants and shops nearby. **Cons:** breakfast is a good spread but goes quickly; rooms are small; not much of interest besides the Vatican nearby. $ *Rooms from: €200* ⊠ *Via Tunisi 8, Prati* ☎ *06/39723941* ⊕ *www.alimanditunisi.com* ⊅ *35 rooms* ⊚ *Breakfast* Ⓜ *Ottaviano, Cipro* ✢ 1:B2.

$$$
HOTEL

Hotel Dei Mellini. On the west bank of the Tiber between the Spanish Steps and St. Peter's Basilica (a five-minute stroll from Piazza del Popolo), this modern luxury hotel is tucked away from the chaos of the centro storico but still close enough for convenient sightseeing. **Pros:** spacious and spotless rooms; breakfast served until 11 am; quiet neighborhood means a good night's rest. **Cons:** not for those who want to be in the center of the action; few dining options right nearby. $ *Rooms from: €300* ⊠ *Via Muzio Clementi 81, Prati* ☎ *06/324771* ⊕ *www. hotelmellini.com* ⊅ *80 rooms* ⊚ *Breakfast* Ⓜ *Lepanto* ✢ 1:F2.

$
HOTEL
Fodor's Choice
★

Hotel San Pietrino. This cute, simple hotel on the third floor of a 19th-century palazzo offers rock-bottom rates at a five-minute walk from the Vatican. **Pros:** heavenly rates near the Vatican; free Wi-Fi; close to Rome's famous farmers' market, Mercato Trionfale. **Cons:** a couple of Metro stops from the centro storico; no breakfast (coffee/tea machine for guest use); no bar. $ *Rooms from: €110* ⊠ *Via Giovanni Bettolo 43, Prati* ☎ *06/3700132* ⊕ *www.sanpietrino.it* ⊅ *12 rooms* ⊚ *No meals* Ⓜ *Ottaviano* ✢ 1:C1.

$
RESORT
FAMILY

Residence Candia. Located in the Prati area just behind the Musei Vaticani, this place, offering both hotel-style studio and two- and three-bedroom apartments with kitchenettes, is the perfect solution for those looking to stay just outside the chaotic centro storico but close enough to major sights. **Pros:** Wi-Fi in all rooms; owner sometimes hosts free dinners for his guests and provides free papal mass tickets. **Cons:**

residence tends to be noisy when student groups are staying
breakfast not included. $ *Rooms from: €120* ✉ *Via Candia* ⸺
Prati ☎ *06/39721046* 🌐 *www.residencecandia.it* ⤳ *100 apartments*
🍴 *Breakfast* Ⓜ *Cipro or Ottaviano* ✠ *1:A2.*

PIAZZA NAVONA, CAMPO DE' FIORI, AND THE JEWISH GHETTO

PIAZZA NAVONA

Thanks to its Baroque palazzi, Bernini fountains, and outdoor caffè,
Piazza Navona is one of Rome's most popular squares. The nearby
Pantheon area, equally as beautiful but not as lively, offers great restaurants and shops. Hotels in this area offer postcard views of Rome
and personalized service.

$$$
HOTEL
Abruzzi. This friendly, comfortable, family-run hotel has magnificent
views of the Pantheon at relatively gentle rates, given the location. **Pros:**
views of the Pantheon; sizable bathrooms; the piazza is a hot spot.
Cons: area can be somewhat noisy; about a 10-minute walk from the
Spagna Metro stop. $ *Rooms from: €245* ✉ *Piazza della Rotonda 69,
Piazza Navona* ☎ *06/97841351* 🌐 *www.hotelabruzzi.it* ⤳ *26 rooms*
🍴 *Breakfast* Ⓜ *Spagna* ✠ *4:F2.*

$$$
HOTEL
Albergo Cesàri. On a pedestrian-only street near the Pantheon, this
lovely little hotel has an air of warmth and serenity, and a rooftop
bar with great views. **Pros:** prime location; free Wi-Fi throughout the
hotel; friendly staff. **Cons:** some rooms need a little updating; the area
can be a bit noisy. $ *Rooms from: €270* ✉ *Via di Pietra 89/a, Piazza
Navona* ☎ *06/6749701* 🌐 *www.albergocesari.it* ⤳ *48 rooms* 🍴 *Breakfast* Ⓜ *Barberini* ✠ *4:F2.*

$$$
HOTEL
Albergo del Sole al Pantheon. The granddaddy of Roman hotels and
one of the oldest in the world—the doors first opened in 1467—this
charming hotel is adjacent to the Pantheon and right in the middle
of the lovely Piazza della Rotonda. **Pros:** complimentary newspaper
delivered to your room daily; rich breakfast buffet. **Cons:** rooms are
a bit small and some need a little updating; despite the double-glazed
windows, street noise can be an issue. $ *Rooms from: €300* ✉ *Piazza
della Rotonda 63, Piazza Navona* ☎ *06/6780441* 🌐 *www.hotelsoleal-
pantheon.com* ⤳ *32 rooms* 🍴 *Breakfast* Ⓜ *Barberini* ✠ *4:F4.*

$$$
HOTEL
Fodor's Choice
★
Albergo Santa Chiara. If you're looking for a good location and top-
notch service at great rates—not to mention comfortable beds and a
quiet stay—look no further than this historic hotel, run by the same
family for some 200 years. **Pros:** great location; free Wi-Fi; lovely ter-
race/sitting area in front, overlooking the piazza. **Cons:** some rooms are
on the small side and need updating; breakfast selection isn't always the
best; Wi-Fi can be slow. $ *Rooms from: €270* ✉ *Via Santa Chiara 21,
Piazza Navona* ☎ *06/6872979* 🌐 *www.albergosantachiara.com* ⤳ *99
rooms, 3 apartments* 🍴 *Breakfast* Ⓜ *Spagna* ✠ *4:E3.*

$$$$
HOTEL
G-Rough Hotel. Rome's new cool cat of a hotel is strategically located
around the corner from the lively Piazza Navona, inside a 17th-cen-
tury palazzo. **Pros:** organic continental breakfast; free Wi-Fi; free soft
mini-bar that includes soda, juice, and water. **Cons:** rooms facing

13

Piazza Pasquino can be noisy; no real reception desk area. $\boxed{\$}$ *Rooms from: €350* ✉ *Piazza Pasquino, 69, Piazza Navona* ☎ *06/6880–1085* ⊕ *www.g-rough.com* ⟿ *10 rooms* ⧯ *Breakfast* ✛ *1:F4.*

$$$$ ⛭ **Grand Hotel de la Minerve.** Once one of Rome's landmark fixtures,
HOTEL this 17th-century palazzo used to be a favorite address for everyone from Stendhal to Sartre, along with a bevy of the crowned (and the uncrowned—Carlotta, the deposed empress of Mexico, resided here for a while). **Pros:** right by the Pantheon yet set on quiet Piazza della Minerva; staff are friendly and accommodating; some rooms have terraces. **Cons:** some rooms need updating and lack common five-star-hotel amenities; Internet can be spotty; plumbing problems in some of the rooms. $\boxed{\$}$ *Rooms from: €450* ✉ *Piazza della Minerva 69, Piazza Navona* ☎ *06/695201* ⊕ *www.grandhoteldelaminerve.com* ⟿ *135 rooms* ⧯ *No meals* Ⓜ *Spagna* ✛ *4:F3.*

$$ ⛭ **Hotel Genio.** Just outside one of Rome's most beautiful piazzas—
HOTEL Piazza Navona—this pleasant hotel has a lovely rooftop terrace perfect for enjoying a cappuccino or a glass of wine while taking in the view. **Pros:** friendly staff; breakfast buffet is abundant; free Wi-Fi; spacious, elegant bathrooms. **Cons:** rooms facing the street can be noisy; spotty Internet; beds can be too firm for some. $\boxed{\$}$ *Rooms from: €160* ✉ *Via Giuseppe Zanardelli 28, Piazza Navona* ☎ *06/6833781* ⊕ *www.hotelgenioroma.it* ⟿ *60 rooms* ⧯ *Breakfast* Ⓜ *Spagna* ✛ *4:D2.*

$$$ ⛭ **Pantheon.** On a quiet street around the corner from the Pantheon,
HOTEL this little hotel is warm and inviting, with trompe-l'oeil frescoes, Liberty-style staircase and terra-cotta floors. **Pros:** proximity to the Pantheon; big, clean bathrooms; friendly staff. **Cons:** some rooms are on the small side and need restyling; credit-card machine isn't always reliable. $\boxed{\$}$ *Rooms from: €280* ✉ *Via dei Pastini 131, Piazza Navona* ☎ *06/6787746* ⊕ *www.hotelpantheon.com* ⟿ *13 rooms* ⧯ *Breakfast* Ⓜ *Spagna* ✛ *4:F2.*

$$$ ⛭ **Relais Palazzo Taverna.** This little hidden gem on a side street behind
HOTEL the lovely Via dei Coronari is a good compromise for those looking for boutique-style accommodations on a budget. **Pros:** centrally located; boutique-style accommodations at moderate prices; free Wi-Fi; friendly, responsive staff; spacious rooms. **Cons:** staff on duty until 11 pm (can be contacted after-hours in an emergency); some rooms are starting to show some wear and tear. $\boxed{\$}$ *Rooms from: €210* ✉ *Via dei Gabrielli 92, Piazza Navona* ☎ *06/20398064* ⊕ *www.relaispalazzotaverna.com* ⟿ *11 rooms* ⧯ *Breakfast* Ⓜ *Spagna* ✛ *1:E4.*

CAMPO DE' FIORI

If you're looking to be in the *cuore of Roma vecchia* (or "heart of Old Rome"), there's no better place than Campo de' Fiori, a gorgeous piazza with lively merchants, outdoor caffè, and bars. The hotels here are not generally as lovely as their surroundings, however: many are cramped and could use updating.

$$ ⛭ **Albergo del Sole al Biscione.** This affordable and comfortable hotel,
HOTEL centrally located in the heart of Campo de' Fiori and built atop the ruins of the ancient Theatre of Pompey, has warm, cozy decor and a rooftop terrace with a stunning view of Sant'Andrea delle Valle. **Pros:** parking garage in the hotel; reasonable rates for the location; nice

rooftop terrace. **Cons:** some rooms are small and lack a/c; no elevator at the entrance of hotel; area can be a bit noisy. $ *Rooms from: €130* ⊠ *Via del Biscione 76, Campo de' Fiori* ☎ *06/68806873* ⊕ *www.sole-albiscione.it* ⤙ *59 rooms* ⍟ *No meals* Ⓜ *Barberini* ⊹ 1:F5.

$$$
B&B/INN
Fodor'sChoice
★

🖾 **Casa di Santa Brigida.** The friendly sisters of Santa Brigida oversee simple, straightforward, and centrally located accommodations in one of Rome's loveliest convents, with a rooftop terrace overlooking Palazzo Farnese. **Pros:** no curfew in this historic convent; insider papal tickets; location in the Piazza Farnese; large library and sunroof; free Wi-Fi. **Cons:** weak a/c; no TVs in the rooms (though there is a common TV room); not equipped for guests with disabilities. $ *Rooms from: €210* ⊠ *Piazza Farnese 96, entrance around the corner at Via Monserrato 54, Campo de' Fiori* ☎ *06/68892596* ⊕ *www.brigidine.org* ⤙ *20 rooms* ⍟ *Breakfast; All meals* ⊹ 4:C4.

$$$$
HOTEL

🖾 **D.O.M. Hotel.** In an old convent on Via Giulia, one of Rome's romantic ivy-covered streets, the D.O.M. (Deo Optimo Maximo) is an ultra-chic luxury hotel that resembles an aristocratic *casa nobile*. **Pros:** complimentary Aqua di Parma toiletries; heated towel racks; hip decor. **Cons:** pricey breakfast; delicious but expensive cocktails; rooms are small for a five-star standard. $ *Rooms from: €380* ⊠ *Via Giulia, 131, Campo de' Fiori* ☎ *06/683–2144* ⊕ *www.domhotelroma.com* ⤙ *18 rooms* ⍟ *Breakfast* ⊹ 1:E4.

$$$
HOTEL

🖾 **Hotel Campo de' Fiori.** This handsome, ivy-draped hotel is a romantic refuge located right in the heart of Campo de' Fiori. **Pros:** free Wi-Fi; rooftop terrace; a wonderfully stocked library where one can relax and read. **Cons:** rooms are on the small side; some apartments are too close to the area's noisy bar scene. $ *Rooms from: €275* ⊠ *Via del Biscione 6, Campo de' Fiori* ☎ *06/68806865* ⊕ *www.hotelcampodefiori.it* ⤙ *25 rooms* ⍟ *Breakfast* ⊹ 4:D4.

$$$
HOTEL
Fodor'sChoice
★

🖾 **Hotel Ponte Sisto.** Situated in a restored Renaissance palazzo with one of the prettiest patio-courtyards in Rome, this hotel is a relaxing retreat close to Trastevere and Campo de' Fiori. **Pros:** friendly staff; rooms with views (and some with balconies and terraces); luxury bathrooms; beautiful courtyard garden. **Cons:** streetside rooms can be a bit noisy; some upgraded rooms are small and not worth the price difference; carpets starting to show signs of wear; aside from breakfast, restaurant caters only to groups and must be booked in advance. $ *Rooms from: €260* ⊠ *Via dei Pettinari 64, Campo de' Fiori* ☎ *06/6863100* ⊕ *www.hotelpontesisto.it* ⤙ *107 rooms* ⍟ *Breakfast* ⊹ 4:D5.

$$$
HOTEL

🖾 **Relais Giulia.** In a 15th-century palazzo on one of Rome's oldest streets, Relais Giulia is a classic Roman Renaissance boutique hotel with sophisticated modern furnishings and fixtures. **Pros:** quiet area; great location in between Campo de' Fiori and Trastevere. **Cons:** many of the restaurants near Campo de' Fiori are tourist traps. $ *Rooms from: €220* ⊠ *Via Giulia, 93, Campo de' Fiori* ☎ *06/9558–1300* ⊕ *www.relaisgiulia.it* ⤙ *14 rooms* ⍟ *Breakfast* ⊹ 1:D4.

$$$
HOTEL

🖾 **Teatro di Pompeo.** Have breakfast under the ancient stone vaults of Theatre of Pompey, close to the site of Julius Caesar's assassination, and sleep under restored wood-beam ceilings that date to the days of Michelangelo at this hotel with simple (and perhaps slightly dated) rooms and wonderful, genuinely helpful staff. **Pros:** great location near Campo de' Fiori; helpful staff; an old-school Roman feel. **Cons:** rooms can be a bit noisy; rooms are small, and some are a bit musty; Wi-Fi is very spotty. $ *Rooms from:* €220 ⊠ *Largo del Pallaro 8, Campo de' Fiori* ☎ *06/6872812* ⊕ *www.hotelteatrodipompeo.it* ⟋ *12 rooms* ⦿*Breakfast* ✛ *4:D4.*

$$$
HOTEL

⊞ **Tiziano.** With Campo de' Fiori, Piazza Navona, and the Pantheon all at your doorstep, this 18th-century hotel in a former palace—the once-grand Palazzo Pacelli—makes an ideal base from which to explore. **Pros:** a very "European" feel; excellent value and location; Wi-Fi is free and fast. **Cons:** some rooms are noisy especially when university groups visit; single rooms the size of a closet; breakfast offerings are modest; not exactly four-star quality; decor could use an update. $ *Rooms from:* €205 ⊠ *Campo Vittorio Emanuele II 110, Campo de' Fiori* ☎ *06/6865019* ⊕ *www.tizianohotel.it* ⟋ *51 rooms* ⦿*Breakfast* ✛ *4:E4.*

JEWISH GHETTO

Next to Campo de' Fiori and across the river from Trastevere, the Jewish Ghetto is filled with shops, kosher restaurants and bakeries, and the city's biggest synagogue.

$$
HOTEL

⊞ **Arenula.** If you're looking for no-frills bargain accommodations in the center of Rome, this budget hotel is a good option with an almost unbeatable location. **Pros:** a real bargain; conveniently located, near Campo de' Fiori and Trastevere; spotless. **Cons:** totally no-frills accommodations; no elevator; breakfast is nothing to write home about. $ *Rooms from:* €145 ⊠ *Via Santa Maria dei Calderari 47, off Via Arenula, Jewish Ghetto* ☎ *06/6879454* ⊕ *www.hotelarenula.com* ⟋ *50 rooms* ⦿*Breakfast* ✛ *4:E5.*

PIAZZA DI SPAGNA

If being right in the heart of Rome's shopping district and within walking distance of major sights is a priority, this is the place to stay. You'll find a wide range of accommodations here—exclusive boutique hotels with over-the-top amenities as well as moderately priced urban B&Bs and *pensioni* with clean, comfortable rooms.

$$$
HOTEL

⊞ **Alexandra.** For nearly a century the hotel Alexandra has been a family affair, and distinguished style and moderate prices have allowed it to hold its own against its flashier big brothers and sisters on the Via Veneto. **Pros:** great location near Piazza Barberini for sightseeing, restaurants, and transportation; decorated with authentic antiques; free Wi-Fi. **Cons:** mostly tiny rooms and tinier bathrooms; breakfast is standard fare. $ *Rooms from:* €280 ⊠ *Via Veneto 18, Piazza di Spagna* ☎ *06/4881943* ⊕ *www.hotelalexandraroma.com* ⟋ *60 rooms* ⦿*Breakfast* Ⓜ *Barberini* ✛ *2:B2.*

$$$
HOTEL

⊞ **Barberini.** This elegant four-star hotel, housed in a 19th-century palazzo near Piazza Barberini, has old-world luxury and charm an easy distance from the Metro, the Trevi Fountain, and plenty of good restaurants. **Pros:** beautiful view from the rooftop terrace; located on a quiet side street close to several important attractions; attentive staff with deals for theater tickets and other events; spa facilities. **Cons:** some rooms are on the small side; not all rooms have bathtubs. ⑤ *Rooms from: €250* ✉ *Via Rasella 3, Piazza di Spagna* ☎ *06/4814993* ⊕ *www. hotelbarberini.com* ⤳ *39 rooms* ⦿❙ *Breakfast* Ⓜ *Barberini* ✛ *2:B3.*

$$$$ ⊞ **Babuino 181.** Named for the street it's on, which is also known
HOTEL for high-end boutiques and antiques shops, this stylish hotel, spread through two historic buildings, has spacious rooms and personalized service. **Pros:** spacious suites; luxury Frette linens; iPhone docks and other handy in-room amenities. **Cons:** rooms can be a bit noisy; breakfast is nothing special. ⑤ *Rooms from: €350* ✉ *Via Babuino 181, Piazza di Spagna* ☎ *06/32295295* ⊕ *www.romeluxurysuites.com/babuino* ⤳ *24 rooms* ⦿❙ *No meals* Ⓜ *Flaminio, Spagna* ✛ *1:G1.*

$$$ ⊞ **Condotti.** Near the most expensive shopping street in Rome, Via dei
B&B/INN Condotti, and one block from the Spanish Steps, this delightful little hotel is all about peace, comfort, and location. **Pros:** soundproof rooms with terraces; individual climate control. **Cons:** small rooms; tiny elevator. ⑤ *Rooms from: €240* ✉ *Via Mario de' Fiori 37, Piazza di Spagna* ☎ *06/6794661* ⊕ *www.hotelcondotti.com* ⤳ *18 rooms* ⦿❙ *Breakfast* Ⓜ *Spagna* ✛ *1:H2.*

$ ⊞ **Daphne Trevi.** This urban B&B is run by people who love Rome and
B&B/INN want to make sure you do, too—the staff will happily act as your personal travel planners, helping you map out destinations, plan day trips, choose restaurants, and organize transportation. **Pros:** kosher, gluten-free, and vegetarian breakfast options; friendly, helpful staff; beds have Simmons mattresses and fluffy comforters; free Wi-Fi. **Cons:** no TVs; two rooms share a bathroom. ⑤ *Rooms from: €115* ✉ *Via degli Avignonesi 20, Piazza di Spagna* ☎ *06/89345781* ⊕ *www.daphne-rome. com* ⤳ *10 rooms* ⦿❙ *Breakfast* Ⓜ *Barberini* ✛ *2:B3.*

$$$ ⊞ **Dei Borgognoni.** Travelers who love peace and tranquility appreciate
HOTEL the position of this quietly chic hotel set in a prestigious palazzo from the 1800s. **Pros:** free in-room Wi-Fi; some rooms have private balconies or terraces; small pets (13 pounds [6 kgs]) are permitted. **Cons:** some rooms are small for the price; breakfast lacks variety. ⑤ *Rooms from: €280* ✉ *Via del Bufalo 126, Piazza di Spagna* ☎ *06/69941505* ⊕ *www. hotelborgognoni.it* ⤳ *51 rooms* ⦿❙ *Breakfast* Ⓜ *Barberini* ✛ *4:G1.*

$$$ ⊞ **Hotel Art.** High Fashion Rome meets Chic Contemporary Art Gallery
HOTEL at this hotel that sits on Via Margutta, "the street of painters." As you glide through the stylish lobby, the smart furnishings and fixtures in the public spaces of the hotel will build up your urge to bid on one of them as if at a Christie's auction, but the color-coordinated guest rooms have been done in a more standard contemporary style (sleek wood headboards accented with handmade Florentine leather, puffy white comforters, bathrobes, and high-speed Internet). **Pros:** hotel has an ultrahip art-gallery feel; free access to the fitness center with sauna and Turkish baths; comfortable beds. **Cons:** glass floors are noisy at night; courtyard bar crowd may keep you awake; staff can be iffy. ⑤ *Rooms from: €260* ✉ *Via Margutta 56, Piazza di Spagna* ☎ *06/328711* ⊕ *www. hotelart.it* ⤳ *46 rooms* ⦿❙ *Breakfast* Ⓜ *Spagna* ✛ *1:H2.*

$$$$ ⊞ **Hotel d'Inghilterra.** Situated in a 17th-century guesthouse and founded
HOTEL in 1845, Hotel D'Inghilterra has a long, storied history. **Pros:** distinct

13

character and opulence; turndown service (with chocolates); genuinely friendly and attentive staff; excellent in-house restaurant. **Cons:** elevator is small and slow; the location, despite soundproofing, is still noisy; bathrooms are surprisingly petite; some rooms badly in need of renovations and maintenance. ⑤ *Rooms from: €400 ⊠ Via Bocca di Leone 14, Piazza di Spagna* ☎ *06/699811* ⊕ *www.hoteldinghilterrarome.com* ⇘ *88 rooms* ⌑⃝ *Breakfast* Ⓜ *Spagna* ✢ *1:H2.*

$$$$
HOTEL
Fodor'sChoice
★

⌖⃞ **The Hassler.** When it comes to million-dollar views, the best place to stay in the whole city is the Hassler. **Pros:** exclusive toiletries from hotel Amorvero SPA; prime location and panoramic views; stunning rooms. **Cons:** VIP rates (10% V.A.T. not included); breakfast not included (continental option is €29 plus 10% V.A.T. per person). ⑤ *Rooms from: €600 ⊠ Piazza Trinità dei Monti 6, Piazza di Spagna* ☎ *06/699340, 800/223–6800 from the U.S. (toll-free)* ⊕ *www.hotelhasslerroma.com* ⇘ *96 rooms* ⌑⃝ *No meals* Ⓜ *Spagna* ✢ *1:H2.*

$$
HOTEL

⌖⃞ **Hotel Homs.** Tucked away on a quiet street near the Spanish Steps, this midsize hotel is convenient to great caffè, serious shopping, and all the sights. **Pros:** walking distance to Piazza di Spagna; steps away from a big bus hub and close to the Metro; helpful staff. **Cons:** breakfast not included; small rooms and bathrooms. ⑤ *Rooms from: €170 ⊠ Via della Vite 71–72, Piazza di Spagna* ☎ *06/6792976* ⊕ *www.hotelhoms. it* ⇘ *58 rooms, 1 apartment* ⌑⃝ *No meals* Ⓜ *Barberini, Spagna* ✢ *1:H3.*

$$
HOTEL

⌖⃞ **Hotel Suisse.** Located on a picturesque street around the corner from the Spanish Steps, this warm and inviting hotel has been run by the same family for three generations. **Pros:** a good value; rooms are obviously cared for; great location. **Cons:** breakfast selection isn't that ample and is served in your room; bathrooms are on the small side. ⑤ *Rooms from: €175 ⊠ Via Gregoriana 54, Piazza di Spagna* ☎ *06/6783649* ⊕ *www. hotelsuisserome.com* ⇘ *12 rooms* ⌑⃝ *Breakfast* Ⓜ *Barberini, Spagna* ✢ *1:H3.*

$$$$
B&B/INN
Fodor'sChoice
★

⌖⃞ **Il Palazzetto.** This 15th-century house, once a retreat for one of Rome's richest noble families, is one of the most intimate and luxurious hotels in Rome, with gorgeous terraces where you can watch the never-ending theater of the Scalinatella. **Pros:** location and view; free Wi-Fi; guests have full access to the Hassler's services; Continental breakfast included (served at the Hassler). **Cons:** restaurant often rented out for crowded special events; bedrooms do not access communal terraces; with just four bedrooms, often books up far in advance, particularly in high season; only three rooms have a view of Piazza di Spagna. ⑤ *Rooms from: €350 ⊠ Vicolo del Bottino 8, Piazza di Spagna* ☎ *06/699341000* ⊕ *www.ilpalazzettoroma.com* ⇘ *4 rooms* ⌑⃝ *No meals* Ⓜ *Spagna* ✢ *1:H2.*

$$$$
B&B/INN

⌖⃞ **Inn at the Spanish Steps.** Occupying the upper floors of a centuries-old townhouse it shares with Antico Caffè Greco (Casanova's old haunt), this quaint yet cushy hotel wins a gold star for its smart design and sharp decor. **Pros:** pet-friendly hotel; rooms with superb views of the Spanish Steps; afternoon snacks and outstanding breakfast buffet. **Cons:** interior rooms are claustrophobic; the area can be noisy due to crowds at the Spanish Steps; rooms located in the annex don't always receive the same attention as those located directly in the hotel. ⑤ *Rooms from:*

€420 ☒ *Via dei Condotti 85, Piazza di Spagna* ☎ *06/69925657* ⊕ *www. atspanishsteps.com* ⤴ *22 suites, 7 apartments* ⦿ *Breakfast* Ⓜ *Spagna* ✛ *1:H2.*

$$$$
HOTEL
▥ **J.K. Place Roma.** Following in the footsteps of its sister hotels in Capri and Florence, this intimate boutique hotel is located a stone's throw from the mausoleum of Augustus, not far from the Spanish Steps. **Pros:** staff are eager to please; excellent meals at rooftop lounge; complimentary minibar. **Cons:** no fitness center; not all rooms have a balcony; some rooms are on the small side. Ⓢ *Rooms from: €700* ☒ *Via Monte d'Oro, 30, Piazza di Spagna* ☎ *06/982634* ⊕ *www.jkroma.com* ⤴ *30 rooms* ⦿ *Breakfast* Ⓜ *Spagna* ✛ *1:G3.*

$$
HOTEL
▥ **Julia.** This small three-star hotel, situated on a small cobblestone street just behind Piazza Barberini and a short walk to the Trevi Fountain, offers clean, comfortable rooms in the center of Rome that won't break the bank. **Pros:** safe neighborhood; convenient to sights and transportation; quiet location. **Cons:** no frills; very basic accommodations; some of the rooms are dark. Ⓢ *Rooms from: €180* ☒ *Via Rasella 29, Piazza di Spagna* ☎ *06/4881637* ⊕ *www.hoteljulia.it* ⤴ *35 rooms (32 with bath), 3 apartments* ⦿ *Breakfast* Ⓜ *Barberini* ✛ *2:B3.*

$$
HOTEL
▥ **La Residenza.** This cozy hotel in a converted townhouse near Via Veneto is widely popular among American travelers thanks to its American-style breakfast and helpful staff. **Pros:** big American breakfast with eggs, pancakes, and sausage; spacious rooms with balconies; friendly staff. **Cons:** the building's exterior doesn't compare to its interior; located on a street with some "gentlemen's clubs"; rooms are in need of restyling. Ⓢ *Rooms from: €180* ☒ *Via Emilia 22/24, Piazza di Spagna* ☎ *06/4880789* ⊕ *www.hotel-la-residenza.com* ⤴ *29 rooms* ⦿ *Breakfast* Ⓜ *Spagna* ✛ *2:B2.*

$$$$
HOTEL
▥ **Majestic.** The first luxury hotel built on the Via Veneto, in 1889, the luxurious Majestic was long a favorite among Roman nobility and high society (it served as a backdrop in Fellini's *La Dolce Vita*). **Pros:** silky linens on big, plush beds; some rooms have private balconies overlooking Via Veneto; 24-hour fitness center. **Cons:** breakfast is especially expensive; not all rooms are spacious. Ⓢ *Rooms from: €400* ☒ *Via Veneto 50, Piazza di Spagna* ☎ *06/421441* ⊕ *www.hotelmajestic.com* ⤴ *111 rooms* ⦿ *No meals* Ⓜ *Spagna* ✛ *2:B2.*

$$$$
B&B/INN
Fodor's Choice
★
▥ **Margutta 54.** Tucked away on a quiet, leafy street known for its art galleries, this four-suite property is like your very own hip, New York– style loft in the center of old-world Rome, with top-drawer amenities, contemporary design, and an ivy-draped courtyard. **Pros:** studio-loft feel in center of town; complete privacy; deluxe furnishings. **Cons:** breakfast not included (€20 per person), served at sister hotel Babuino 181; no staff available on-site after 8 pm. Ⓢ *Rooms from: €380* ☒ *Via Margutta 54, Piazza di Spagna* ☎ *06/69921907* ⊕ *www.romeluxurysuites.com/margutta* ⤴ *4 suites* ⦿ *No meals* Ⓜ *Spagna* ✛ *1:H2.*

$$$$
HOTEL
▥ **Marriott Grand Hotel Flora.** This handsome hotel at the top of Via Veneto next to the Villa Borghese park is something of a beacon on the Rome landscape. **Pros:** convenient location and pleasant staff; spectacular view from the terrace; free Internet. **Cons:** breakfast finishes fast; sometimes the noise from Via Veneto drifts in; crowded

with businessmen and big tour groups. $ *Rooms from: €415* ⊠ *Via Veneto 191, Piazza di Spagna* ☎ *06/489929* ⊕ *www.hotelfloraroma. com* ⇥ *176 rooms* ⍭ *Breakfast* Ⓜ *Barberini, Spagna* ✛ *2:B1.*

$$ ⛯ **Panda.** Located near the Spanish Steps, this little gem of a hotel has
HOTEL excellent service that gives you more bang for your buck. **Pros:** 10% discount if you pay in cash; free Wi-Fi; on a quiet street, but still close to the Spanish Steps; very high ceilings. **Cons:** dim lighting; no elevator directly to floor; breakfast not included. $ *Rooms from: €130* ⊠ *Via della Croce 35, Piazza di Spagna* ☎ *06/6780179* ⊕ *www.hotelpanda.it* ⇥ *28 rooms (20 with bath)* ⍭ *No meals* Ⓜ *Spagna* ✛ *1:G2.*

$$$$ ⛯ **Regina Baglioni.** The former playground of kings and poets, the Regina
HOTEL Baglioni, which enjoys a prime spot on the Via Veneto, is a favorite among today's international jetsetters. **Pros:** nice decor; luxury on-site spa; excellent onsite restaurant and bar. **Cons:** some rooms are noisy; staff are hit-or-miss; spotty Internet. $ *Rooms from: €380* ⊠ *Via Veneto 72, Piazza di Spagna* ☎ *06/421111* ⊕ *www.reginabaglioni.com* ⇥ *143 rooms* ⍭ *Breakfast* Ⓜ *Barberini* ✛ *2:B2.*

$$ ⛯ **San Carlo.** This renovated 17th-century-mansion-turned-hotel offers
HOTEL modern comforts at reasonable rates, right around the corner from the Spanish Steps and the best shopping in Rome. **Pros:** some rooms have terraces with views of historic Rome; rooftop garden; attentive staff. **Cons:** some rooms are on the small side; rooms can be noisy. $ *Rooms from: €200* ⊠ *Via delle Carrozze 92–93, Piazza di Spagna* ☎ *06/6784548* ⊕ *www.hotelsancarloroma.com* ⇥ *52 rooms* ⍭ *Breakfast* Ⓜ *Spagna* ✛ *1:G2.*

$$ ⛯ **Scalinata di Spagna.** Perched atop the Spanish Steps, this charming
B&B/INN boutique hotel makes guests fall in love over and over again—so popu-
Fodor's Choice lar, in fact, it's often booked far in advance. **Pros:** friendly and helpful
★ concierge; fresh fruit in the rooms; free Wi-Fi throughout. **Cons:** it's a hike up the hill to the hotel; small rooms; no porter and no elevator. $ *Rooms from: €190* ⊠ *Piazza Trinità dei Monti 17, Piazza di Spagna* ☎ *06/45686150* ⊕ *www.hotelscalinata.com* ⇥ *16 rooms* ⍭ *Breakfast* Ⓜ *Spagna* ✛ *2:A2.*

$$$ ⛯ **Sofitel Rome Villa Borghese.** Set in a refurbished 1902 Victorian pal-
HOTEL ace, the Hotel Sofitel—which has a long-standing good reputation with business travelers—exudes old-world elegance with modern-design sensibility. **Pros:** luxury lodging off the main drag (but not far from it); first-rate concierge and porter; fitness center. **Cons:** luxury chain with business clientele could feel a little stuffy; some say the a/c could be stronger; showers are a bit leaky. $ *Rooms from: €300* ⊠ *Via Lombardia 47, Piazza di Spagna* ☎ *06/478021* ⊕ *www.sofitel.com* ⇥ *104 rooms* ⍭ *Breakfast* Ⓜ *Spagna* ✛ *2:B2.*

$$$ ⛯ **Tritone.** This trusty hotel offers modern accommodations in a great
HOTEL location, steps from Rome's majestic Trevi Fountain. **Pros:** walking distance to major attractions; modern decor; friendly staff. **Cons:** rooms can be noisy despite soundproofing; breakfast is standard fare. $ *Rooms from: €220* ⊠ *Via del Tritone 210, Piazza di Spagna* ☎ *06/69922575* ⊕ *www.tritonehotel.com* ⇥ *43 rooms* ⍭ *Breakfast* Ⓜ *Barberini* ✛ *4:G1.*

$$$ ⬚ **Victoria.** Just across the street from Villa Borghese, this four-star bou-
HOTEL tique hotel, built in 1889, is popular with American business travelers.
Pros: view of the gardens; quiet and comfortable; rooftop bar and res-
taurant; great personalized service. **Cons:** it's a schlep to most sights;
rooms are small. ⑤ *Rooms from: €230 ✉ Via Campania 41, Piazza
di Spagna ☎ 06/423701 ⊕ www.hotelvictoriaroma.com ↩ 110 rooms
⎺⦶⎺ No meals ✣ 2:C1.*

$$$$ ⬚ **The Westin Excelsior, Rome.** Ablaze with lights at night, this seven-layer-
HOTEL cake hotel—topped off by its famous cupola, a landmark nearly as
FAMILY famous as the American Embassy palazzo across the street—is popular
with visiting diplomats, celebrities, and American conference groups.
Pros: elegant period furnishings and decor; health club and indoor pool.
Cons: some rooms need updating; expensive Wi-Fi. ⑤ *Rooms from:
€435 ✉ Via Veneto 125, Piazza di Spagna ☎ 06/47081 ⊕ www.westin-
rome.com ↩ 316 rooms ⎺⦶⎺ No meals Ⓜ Barberini, Spagna ✣ 2:C2.*

13

REPUBLICA

With its beautiful piazza and fountain, Republica is the place to stay
if you want to be near but not *too near* Termini station, Rome's central
train hub. You'll find lodging here in all price ranges, along with caffè
and shops. Rooms tend to be a better value in this part of town.

$$ ⬚ **Alpi.** You'll feel right at home from the moment you waltz into Hotel
HOTEL Alpi, where high ceilings with elegant chandeliers, white walls, and
marble floors lend it both elegance and warmth—right around the corner from Termini station. **Pros:** clean and comfortable; lovely terraces
and restaurant for dining and relaxing. **Cons:** not all rooms are created equal; location is not very picturesque; you'll need to take transportation to most sights. ⑤ *Rooms from: €180 ✉ Via Castelfidardo
84, Republica ☎ 06/4441235 ⊕ www.hotelalpi.com ↩ 48 rooms
⎺⦶⎺ Breakfast Ⓜ Castro Pretorio, Termini ✣ 2:E2.*

$$ ⬚ **The Beehive.** Living the American dream *dolce vita*–style is exactly
B&B/INN what one Los Angeles couple started to do in 1999, when they opened
Fodor's Choice the Beehive, a hip, alternative budget hotel near Termini station. **Pros:**
★ massage and other therapies offered on-site; convenient to Termini
station; very good prices, even in high season. **Cons:** some rooms do
not have private baths; standard rooms lack TV and a/c; breakfast
not included. ⑤ *Rooms from: €180 ✉ Via Marghera 8, Republica
☎ 06/44704553 ⊕ www.the-beehive.com ↩ 8 rooms, 1 dormitory
⎺⦶⎺ No meals Ⓜ Termini ✣ 2:E3.*

$$ ⬚ **Demetra Hotel.** This hotel near the glorious Santa Maria Maggiore
HOTEL Basilica is also close to Termini station, and has modern comforts and
a great concierge—all at moderate rates. **Pros:** free Wi-Fi if you book
directly through hotel website; convenient to Termini station; soundproof rooms. **Cons:** basic breakfast buffet; some rooms are on the small
side; no in-hotel bars or restaurants. ⑤ *Rooms from: €180 ✉ Via del
Viminale 8, Republica ☎ 06/45494943 ⊕ www.demetrahotelrome.
com ↩ 28 rooms ⎺⦶⎺ Some meals Ⓜ Republica ✣ 2:D4.*

$ ⬚ **Des Artistes.** This lovely hotel near Termini station (really in Cas-
HOTEL tro Pretorio rather than Republica) is a perfect example of a family

establishment: the three Riccioni brothers put their hearts and souls into running the place, while their parents oversee housekeeping and maintenance. **Pros:** a good value; decent-size rooms; relaxing rooftop garden. **Cons:** breakfast is nothing to write home about; some rooms charge a small fee for Wi-Fi. $ *Rooms from: €120* ⊠ *Via Villafranca 20, Repubblica* ☎ *06/4454365* ⊕ *www.hoteldesartistes.com* ⟿ *48 rooms* ❯❮| *Breakfast* Ⓜ *Castro Pretorio* ✛ 2:F2.

$$$$
HOTEL
Fodor'sChoice
★

Exedra. Located in one of the most spectacular piazzas in the city, this is the "it girl" of Rome's hotel scene, where high-rollers come to party by the rooftop pool—you'll experience exquisite service and pampering from the minute you waltz through the door. **Pros:** top-notch concierge and staff; great spa and pool overlooking one of the most beautiful piazzas in Rome; terrace with cocktail service; free Wi-Fi; close to Termini station. **Cons:** food and beverages are expensive; beyond the immediate vicinity of many sights. $ *Rooms from: €400* ⊠ *Piazza della Repubblica 47, Repubblica* ☎ *06/489381* ⊕ *www.exedra-roma.boscolohotels.com* ⟿ *238 rooms* ❯❮| *Breakfast* Ⓜ *Repubblica, Termini* ✛ 2:D3.

$$
HOTEL

Leon's Place Hotel. If you like a lot of bling for your buck, this stylish design hotel straight from the pages of Italian *Vogue* magazine is the place for you. **Pros:** gourmet minibar; free Wi-Fi; top-quality toiletries; affordable rates. **Cons:** not very central; some rooms face the courtyard; spotty Wi-Fi in rooms. $ *Rooms from: €160* ⊠ *Via XX Settembre 90/94, Repubblica* ☎ *06/890871* ⊕ *www.leonsplacehotel.it* ⟿ *54 rooms* ❯❮| *Breakfast* Ⓜ *Barberini, Repubblica* ✛ 2:E2.

$$
HOTEL

Marcella Royal. You can do your sightseeing from the rooftop terrace of the Marcella, a midsize hotel with the feel of a smaller, more intimate establishment, where staff go the extra mile to make your stay pleasant. **Pros:** breakfast in the rooftop garden; aperitivo at the piano bar; staff go the extra mile for guests. **Cons:** some of the rooms are in need of restyling; spotty Internet; not very close to major attractions. $ *Rooms from: €200* ⊠ *Via Flavia 106, Repubblica* ☎ *06/42014591* ⊕ *www.marcellaroyalhotel.com* ⟿ *87 rooms* ❯❮| *Breakfast* Ⓜ *Repubblica* ✛ 2:D2.

$$$
HOTEL
FAMILY

Mascagni. Situated on a side street around the corner from one of Rome's most impressive piazzas, this friendly hotel has staff that go out of their way to make you feel at home, public spaces cleverly styled with contemporary art pieces, and wood fixtures and furnishings accentuated by warm colors and handsome fabrics in the guest rooms. **Pros:** staff are friendly and attentive; evening lounge serves light fare; great for families with kids. **Cons:** elevator is too small and takes a while; free Wi-Fi in common areas only; some bathrooms are smallish. $ *Rooms from: €300* ⊠ *Via Vittorio Emanuele Orlando 90, Repubblica* ☎ *06/48904040* ⊕ *www.mascagnihotelrome.it* ⟿ *40 rooms* ❯❮| *Breakfast* Ⓜ *Repubblica* ✛ 2:C3.

$
HOTEL

Miami. Time spent at this comfy, low-key hotel, located in a dignified 19th-century building on Rome's busy Via Nazionale, is like staying at a friend's house. **Pros:** pleasant staff; soundproof windows; strong a/c; free Wi-Fi throughout the hotel. **Cons:** bathrooms on the small side; small breakfast room; single rooms are like a closet. $ *Rooms from: €100* ⊠ *Via Nazionale 230, Repubblica* ☎ *06/4817180* ⊕ *www.*

hotelmiami.com ⌁ *45 rooms, 1 apartment* |○| *Breakfast* Ⓜ *Barberini, Termini, Repubblica* ✛ 2:C3.

$$$
B&B/INN
⌗ **Residenza Cellini.** Fresh flowers in the foyer and personal attention from the staff help make this small, family-run residence close to Termini station feel like a gracious home. **Pros:** close to Termini station; Jacuzzi bathtubs and Hydrojet showers; personalized care from the staff. **Cons:** not close to the main attractions; rooms could use a bit of restyling; breakfast is standard Continental fare. Ⓢ *Rooms from: €205* ✉ *Via Modena 5, Repubblica* ☎ *06/47825204* ⊕ *www.residenzacellini.it* ⌁ *6 rooms, 1 apartment* |○| *Breakfast* Ⓜ *Repubblica, Termini* ✛ 2:C3.

13

$$
HOTEL
⌗ **Villa delle Rose.** When the Eternal City becomes too chaotic for you, head to this relaxing 19th-century palazzo retreat in a charming Roman villa just minutes from Termini station. **Pros:** delightful garden with blooming roses and jasmine; free parking; 24-hour reception; free Wi-Fi. **Cons:** some of the rooms are small (ask for a larger one); the elevator is small. Ⓢ *Rooms from: €130* ✉ *Via Vicenza 5, Repubblica* ☎ *06/4451788* ⊕ *www.villadellerose.it* ⌁ *37 rooms* |○| *No meals* Ⓜ *Termini* ✛ 2:E3.

$$
HOTEL
Fodor's Choice
★
⌗ **Yes Hotel.** This chic hotel may fool you into thinking the digs are expensive, but the contemporary coolness of Yes Hotel, located around the corner from Termini station, actually comes at a bargain. **Pros:** around the corner from Termini station; discount if you pay in cash; a great value without the budget feel. **Cons:** small rooms; fee for in-room Wi-Fi. Ⓢ *Rooms from: €140* ✉ *Via Magenta 15, Repubblica* ☎ *06/44363836* ⊕ *www.yeshotelrome.com* ⌁ *40 rooms* |○| *Breakfast* Ⓜ *Termini, Castro Pretorio* ✛ 2:E3.

VILLA BORGHESE, PIAZZA DEL POPOLO, MONTE MARIO, AND PARIOLI

VILLA BORGHESE

The area around the Villa Borghese gardens is a relaxing retreat from the hustle and bustle of the Eternal City. You won't get tired of waking up to views of the park.

$$$
HOTEL
⌗ **Grand Hotel Parco dei Principi.** The 1960s-era facade of this large, seven-story hotel contrasts with the turn-of-the-20th-century Italian court decor and the extensive botanical garden outside, resulting in a combination of traditional elegance and contemporary pleasure. **Pros:** quiet location on Villa Borghese; nice pool. **Cons:** beyond the city center; private events held at hotel some weekends can be noisy; a bit of a hike to caffè and restaurants. Ⓢ *Rooms from: €300* ✉ *Via G. Frescobaldi 5, Villa Borghese* ☎ *06/854421* ⊕ *www.parcodeiprincipi. com* ⌁ *203 rooms, 1 apartment* |○| *Breakfast* ✛ 2:C1.

PIAZZA DEL POPOLO

While Piazza del Popolo is still quite close to the centro action, it's just removed enough to feel relaxing after a day of sightseeing. Here, amidst high-end boutiques and galleries, you'll find several smart, stylish hotels.

$$$$ HOTEL FAMILY Fodor'sChoice ★ **Hotel de Russie.** A ritzy retreat for government bigwigs and Hollywood high rollers, the Hotel de Russie is just steps from the famed Piazza del Popolo and occupies a 19th-century hotel that once hosted royalty, Picasso, and Cocteau. **Pros:** big potential for celebrity sightings; extensive gardens (including a butterfly reserve); first-rate luxury spa; Wi-Fi included. **Cons:** some rooms need updating; breakfast not included. $ *Rooms from: €700* ⊠ *Via del Babuino 9, Piazza del Popolo* ☎ *06/328881* ⊕ *www.roccofortehotels.com* ➟ *122 rooms* ⦿| *No meals* Ⓜ *Flaminio* ✛ *1:G1.*

$$$ HOTEL **Locarno.** This hotel has been a longtime choice for art and cinema aficionados (it even inspired Bernard Weber's 1978 film *Hotel Locarno*), but everyone can appreciate its charm, intimate feel, and central location off Piazza del Popolo. **Pros:** spacious rooms; free bicycles; free Wi-Fi. **Cons:** some rooms are dark; annex doesn't compare to main hotel; staff may not go out of their way to help you. $ *Rooms from: €240* ⊠ *Via della Penna 22, Piazza del Popolo* ☎ *06/3610841* ⊕ *www.hotellocarno.com* ➟ *66 rooms* ⦿| *Breakfast* Ⓜ *Flaminio* ✛ *1:G1.*

$$$ HOTEL **Valadier.** Located in the heart of the centro storico, just steps from the prominent Piazza del Popolo and a few minutes' walk from the Spanish Steps, this luxury hotel—known for comfortable rooms with marble and travertine bathrooms and a superb location—has captured the hearts of elite travelers over the years. **Pros:** excellent American-style breakfast buffet; piano bar; 15% discount if you book directly through hotel website; good a/c. **Cons:** cocktails don't come cheap; rooms smaller than you'd expect for a luxury hotel; lighting in rooms is very dim. $ *Rooms from: €250* ⊠ *Via della Fontanella 15, Piazza del Popolo* ☎ *06/3611998* ⊕ *www.hotelvaladier.com* ➟ *60 rooms* ⦿| *Breakfast* Ⓜ *Flaminio* ✛ *1:G1.*

MONTE MARIO

Travelers looking for a relaxing getaway at a distance from the city center will appreciate staying in Monte Mario, but beware: public transportation is sparse in this area. It's a 20- to 30-minute drive to the centro storico—as much as an hour on public transport. Some hotels offer shuttles, but if you'd rather not have to rely on them or on taxi service, consider renting a car.

$$$$ RESORT **Rome Cavalieri, Waldorf Astoria Hotels & Resorts.** One of Rome's ritziest resorts, the Rome Cavalieri is a hilltop oasis far from the hustle and bustle of the centro storico, with magnificent views, an Olympic-size pool, and a palatial spa. **Pros:** beautiful bird's-eye view of Rome; complimentary shuttle to city center; three–Michelin star dining. **Cons:** you definitely pay for the luxury of staying here—everything is expensive; outside the city center; not all rooms have the view. $ *Rooms from: €600* ⊠ *Via Cadlolo 101, Monte Mario* ☎ *06/35091* ⊕ *www.romecavalieri.com* ➟ *370 rooms* ⦿| *Breakfast* ✛ *1:A1.*

PARIOLI

Rome's poshest residential neighborhood attracts a well-heeled international crowd who are happy to be away from the centro storico hubbub. Luxurious lodgings and a great night's sleep might make you feel like you're in an elegant country home. Public transportation is limited in this area, but some hotels offer shuttles to major attractions.

$$$ 🖽 Lord Byron. Rome's first boutique hotel, this Art Deco retreat has a
HOTEL jewelry-box charm inside and feels like a small country manor of which you are the lord. **Pros:** luxury bathrobes and slippers; friendly and helpful staff; free shuttle to some of the major tourist attractions. **Cons:** too far to walk to sights; not many caffè and shops in the area; cabs to the city center are expensive. $ Rooms from: €300$ ⊠ Via Giuseppe de Notaris 5, Parioli 🕾 06/3220404 ⊕ www.lordbyronhotel.com ⇄ 32 rooms ⊙ Breakfast ✛ 2:A1.

TRASTEVERE

This former working-class neighborhood, once the stomping ground of artists and artisans, is now home to many of Rome's expats and exchange students. Its villagelike charm makes it an appealing place to stay, and you'll find plenty of moderately priced accommodations here, including converted convents and small family-run hotels.

$ 🖽 Carmel. In the heart of Trastevere and across the Tiber from the
HOTEL main synagogue is Rome's only kosher hotel, a friendly and budget-friendly place to stay. **Pros:** good budget choice; kosher-friendly; short walk to Jewish Ghetto; free Wi-Fi; lovely garden terrace for guests to use. **Cons:** no frills; a/c is noisy; unexciting breakfast; reception closes after 8 pm. $ Rooms from: €100$ ⊠ Via Goffredo Mameli 11, Trastevere 🕾 06/5809921 ⊕ www.hotelcarmel.it ⇄ 11 rooms (9 with bath) ⊙ Breakfast ✛ 3:B2.

$$ 🖽 Casa di Santa Francesca Romana. In the heart of Trastevere but tucked
HOTEL away from the hustle and bustle of the medieval quarter, this cheap,
Fodor's Choice clean, comfortable hotel in a former monastery is centered on a lovely
★ green courtyard. **Pros:** rates can't be beat; excellent restaurants nearby; away from rowdy side of Trastevere. **Cons:** thin walls; interior is a bit bland; spotty Wi-Fi. $ Rooms from: €130$ ⊠ Via dei Vasceillari 61, Trastevere 🕾 06/5812125 ⊕ www.sfromana.it ⇄ 37 rooms ⊙ Breakfast Ⓜ Piramide, Circo Massimo ✛ 3:C2.

$ 🖽 Cisterna. On a quiet street in the very heart of medieval Trastevere,
HOTEL this basic but comfortable hotel is ideally situated for getting to know Rome's most authentic neighborhood, a favorite of artists and bohemians for decades. **Pros:** simple accommodations for budget travelers; good location in trendy Trastevere. **Cons:** staff can be iffy; occasional hot water and plumbing issues. $ Rooms from: €120$ ⊠ Via della Cisterna 7–8–9, Trastevere 🕾 06/5817212 ⊕ www.hotelcisternarome.com ⇄ 20 rooms ⊙ Breakfast Ⓜ Trastevere, Mastai ✛ 3:B1.

$$$ 🖽 Hotel Santa Maria. A Trastevere treasure with a pedigree going back
HOTEL four centuries, this ivy-covered, mansard-roof, rosy-brick-red, erstwhile
Fodor's Choice Renaissance-era convent—just steps away from the glorious Santa
★ Maria in Trastevere church and a few blocks from the Tiber—has sweet and simple guest rooms: a mix of brick walls, "cotto" tile floors, modern oak furniture, and matching bedspreads and curtains. **Pros:** a quaint and pretty oasis in a central location; relaxing courtyard; fully stocked wine bar; free bicycles to use during your stay; kettle for tea and coffee

in room. **Cons:** tricky to find; some of the showers drain slowly; finding a cab is not always easy in Trastevere. $ *Rooms from: €230* ⊠ *Vicolo del Piede 2, Trastevere* ☎ *06/5894626* ⊕ *www.hotelsantamariatrastevere.it* ⬎ *20 rooms* ⏀ *Breakfast* ✢ *3:B1.*

$ ⊞ **Hotel Trastevere.** This tiny hotel captures the village-like charm of
HOTEL the Trastevere district and offers basic, clean, comfortable rooms in a great location. **Pros:** good rates for location; convenient to tram and bus; free Wi-Fi; friendly staff. **Cons:** no frills; rooms are a little worn on the edges; few amenities. $ *Rooms from: €103* ⊠ *Via Luciano Manara 24/a–25, Trastevere* ☎ *06/5814713* ⊕ *www.hoteltrastevere.net* ⬎ *18 rooms* ⏀ *Breakfast* Ⓜ *Trastevere, Mastai* ✢ *3:B2.*

$$ ⊞ **Relais Le Clarisse.** Set within the former cloister grounds of the Santa
B&B/INN Chiara order, with beautiful gardens, Le Clarisse makes you feel like a
Fodor's Choice personal guest at a friend's villa, thanks to the comfortable size of the
★ guest rooms and personalized service. **Pros:** spacious rooms with comfy beds; high-tech showers/tubs with good water pressure; complimentary Wi-Fi. **Cons:** this part of Trastevere can be noisy at night; rooms fill up quickly; reception unavailable after 10:30 pm. $ *Rooms from: €180* ⊠ *Via Cardinale Merry del Val 20, Trastevere* ☎ *06/58334437* ⊕ *www.leclarissetrastevere.com* ⬎ *16 rooms, 1 apartment* ⏀ *Breakfast* ✢ *3:B2.*

AVENTINO AND TESTACCIO

AVENTINO

This affluent neighborhood full of trees, set on the Aventine Hill, attracts travelers looking for a green oasis removed from the centro storico. Hotels take advantage of the extra space, with gardens and courtyards where you can enjoy a little R&R alfresco, and where the only noise you'll hear in the morning is birdsong.

$$ ⊞ **Domus Aventina.** The best part of this quaint, friendly hotel is that
HOTEL it's between two of Rome's loveliest gardens—the municipal rose garden and the Orange Garden by Santa Sabina—in the heart of historic Aventino, not far from the Temple to Mithras and the House of Aquila and Priscilla. **Pros:** quiet location; within walking distance of tourist attractions; free Wi-Fi throughout hotel. **Cons:** no elevator; walls can be thin; small showers; some rooms are very dark. $ *Rooms from: €170* ⊠ *Via di Santa Prisca 11/b, Aventino* ☎ *06/5746135* ⊕ *www.hoteldomusaventina.com* ⬎ *26 rooms* ⏀ *Breakfast* Ⓜ *Circo Massimo* ✢ *3:E3.*

$$ ⊞ **Hotel San Anselmo.** This refurbished 19th-century villa is a romantic
HOTEL retreat from the city, set in a *molto* charming garden atop the Aventine Hill. **Pros:** free Wi-Fi; historic building with artful interior; great showers with jets; a garden where you can enjoy breakfast. **Cons:** a bit of a hike to sights; limited public transportation. $ *Rooms from: €160* ⊠ *Piazza San Anselmo 2, Aventino* ☎ *06/570057* ⊕ *www.aventinohotels.com* ⬎ *35 rooms* ⏀ *Breakfast* Ⓜ *Circo Massimo* ✢ *3:D3.*

TESTACCIO

Next to Aventino is this lively working-class neighborhood, filled with great Roman trattorias, *mercati all'aperto* (open-air markets), and gourmet food shops. The buzzing nightlife makes it attractive to budget-conscious travelers looking for a bit more action after dinner.

$ 🖭 **Santa Prisca.** Off the beaten path, this clean and comfortable hotel
HOTEL has been welcoming guests for more than 50 years. **Pros:** near public
transportation (trams and Metro); free Wi-Fi; terrace with chairs and
tables for relaxing. **Cons:** some say the breakfast is mediocre; the school
next door can be a little noisy on weekdays; a bit of a trek from the
main sights. ⑤ *Rooms from: €100* ⊠ *Largo M. Gelsomini 25, Testaccio*
☎ *06/5741917* ⊕ *www.hotelsantaprisca.it* ⏎ *51 rooms* ⏏️ *Breakfast*
Ⓜ *Piramide* ✛ 3:D4.

MONTI AND ESQUILINO

MONTI

A charming neighborhood with winding cobblestone streets, Monti
attracts an artsy, boho-chic crowd thanks to its abundance of funky
bars, good Roman and ethnic eateries, and cool vintage shops and
boutiques. The area around the Colosseum makes a fine base for exploring the sights of the ancient city, but many of the restaurants here are
tourist traps. Hotels here tend to be better value than in swankier parts
of town, whether budget or luxury.

$$$ 🖭 **Capo d'Africa.** Hotels in Rome come a dime a dozen, but the posh
HOTEL contemporary design of Capo d'Africa combined with modern ame-
nities and outstanding customer service make your stay worth every
centesimo. **Pros:** quiet, comfortable rooms; fitness center; great food
served at the hotel. **Cons:** hotel lacks a great view of Colosseum despite
proximity; not a lot of restaurants in the immediate neighborhood;
Wi-Fi is only free in the common areas. ⑤ *Rooms from: €250* ⊠ *Via
Capo d'Africa 54, Monti* ☎ *06/772801* ⊕ *www.hotelcapodafrica.com*
⏎ *65 rooms* ⏏️ *Breakfast* Ⓜ *Colosseo* ✛ 3:H2.

$$ 🖭 **Celio.** There's much more to brag about than proximity to the Col-
HOTEL osseum at this chic boutique hotel. **Pros:** rooftop garden; nice decor;
comfortable beds; gym. **Cons:** very small bathrooms; service can be
iffy. ⑤ *Rooms from: €170* ⊠ *Via dei Santissimi Quattro 35/c, Monti*
☎ *06/70495333* ⊕ *www.hotelcelio.com* ⏎ *22 rooms* ⏏️ *Breakfast*
Ⓜ *Colosseo* ✛ 3:G1.

$$$ 🖭 **Duca d'Alba.** In Italy, it's all about the *bella figura* (making a good
HOTEL impression), so when you step into this lovely little boutique hotel near
the Colosseum, you'll know you've hit the jackpot. **Pros:** great breakfast
selection; deep discounts if you book directly through hotel website.
Cons: some rooms are cramped and worn around the edges; the Irish
pub across the way tends to attract late-night revelers. ⑤ *Rooms from:
€220* ⊠ *Via Leonina 14, Monti* ☎ *06/484471* ⊕ *www.hotelducadalba.
com* ⏎ *27 rooms, 1 suite* ⏏️ *Breakfast* Ⓜ *Cavour* ✛ 2:C5.

$$$$ 🖭 **Hotel Forum.** A longtime favorite, this converted 18th-century convent
HOTEL has a truly unique setting on one side of the Fori Imperiali, with cin-
ematic views of ancient Rome across the avenue so impressive that it's
drawn celebrities and socialites, like Jackie Kennedy, Elizabeth Taylor,
and Brigitte Bardot. **Pros:** bird's-eye view of ancient Rome; "American"
bar on rooftop terrace. **Cons:** small rooms; noisy pub-crawlers con-
gregate on the street below; food and drinks are expensive. ⑤ *Rooms*

13

from: €320 ✉ *Via Tor de' Conti 25–30, Monti* ☎ *06/6792446* ⊕ *www. hotelforum.com* ↪ *80 rooms* ⧉ *Breakfast* Ⓜ *Cavour, Colosseo* ✛ *2:B5.*

$$$
HOTEL
FAMILY

⊡ **Hotel Lancelot.** This friendly home-away-from-home in a quiet residential area close to the Colosseum has been run by the same family since 1970. **Pros:** hospitable staff; secluded and quiet; very family-friendly. **Cons:** some bathrooms are on the small side; no refrigerators in the rooms; rooms are in need of restyling. Ⓢ *Rooms from: €220* ✉ *Via Capo d'Africa 47, Monti* ☎ *06/70450615* ⊕ *www.lancelothotel.com* ↪ *60 rooms* ⧉ *Breakfast* Ⓜ *Colosseo* ✛ *3:H1.*

$$
HOTEL

⊡ **Italia.** Just one block from bustling Via Nazionale and some of Rome's great shopping, this friendly, family-run hotel feels like a classic pensione: low budget with a lot of heart. **Pros:** free Wi-Fi; great price; individual attention and personal care. **Cons:** can be a bit noisy; Wi-Fi can be hit or miss. Ⓢ *Rooms from: €140* ✉ *Via Venezia 18, Termini* ☎ *06/4828355* ⊕ *www.hotelitaliaroma.com* ↪ *35 rooms, 1 apartment* ⧉ *Breakfast* Ⓜ *Repubblica* ✛ *2:C4.*

$$$
HOTEL

⊡ **Nerva.** Step out of this charming, clean, well-run hotel and you'll feel like you've landed in the middle of an ancient imperial stomping ground; a stone's throw from the Forum, it's surrounded by the breathtaking splendor of ancient Roman ruins. **Pros:** close to the Forum and the lovely Monti neighborhood; friendly staff; free Wi-Fi. **Cons:** some showers are tiny; single rooms are slightly bigger than a closet. Ⓢ *Rooms from: €230* ✉ *Via Tor de' Conti 3/4, Monti* ☎ *06/6781835* ⊕ *www.hotelnerva.com* ↪ *19 rooms* ⧉ *Breakfast* Ⓜ *Cavour, Colosseo* ✛ *2:B5.*

ESQUILINO

Budget-conscious travelers who want to be near Rome's major transport hub, Termini station, often stay here. There are a number of cheap, clean, no-frills hotels and pensioni, as well as a few more stylish options.

$$$
HOTEL
Fodor's Choice
★

⊡ **Britannia.** Situated in an elegant Art Nouveau palazzo dating back to 1876, this charming hotel feels like a luxurious private home, with all the modern amenities. **Pros:** spacious, comfortable rooms; free Wi-Fi; small dogs allowed upon request. **Cons:** rooms can be noisy for light sleepers; not very close to the city's main attractions. Ⓢ *Rooms from: €250* ✉ *Via Napoli 64, Esquilino* ☎ *06/4883153* ⊕ *www.hotelbritannia.it* ↪ *34 rooms* ⧉ *Breakfast* Ⓜ *Repubblica* ✛ *2:C4.*

$$
HOTEL

⊡ **Morgana.** A nice, cozy hotel just a stone's throw from Termini station sounds like some sort of a miracle, and yet the Morgana welcomes guests with elegant classically designed rooms and top amenities at unbeatable rates. **Pros:** practical base for public transportation; breakfast is abundant; pet-friendly. **Cons:** run-down neighborhood; removed from most sightseeing; some bathrooms are on the small side. Ⓢ *Rooms from: €180* ✉ *Via Filippo Turati 33/37, Esquilino* ☎ *06/4467230* ⊕ *www. hotelmorgana.com* ↪ *123 rooms* ⧉ *Breakfast* Ⓜ *Termini* ✛ *2:E4.*

NIGHTLIFE AND PERFORMING ARTS

Updated
by Ariston
Anderson

Rome has always been Italy's go-to city for epic evening adventures. Whether it's a romantic rooftop drink, dinner in a boisterous restaurant, or dancing into the wee hours, Roman nightlife has always been a scene set for a movie.

Director Federico Fellini immortalized nocturnal Rome in his many films about life in the Eternal City. *Satyricon* showcased the all-night Lucullan banquets (and some naughtier entertainments) of the days of the emperors, while *La Dolce Vita* flaunted the nightclubs and *paparazzi* of the Hollywood-on-the-Tiber era. And as the director lovingly showed in *Roma*, the city's streets and piazzas offered the best place for parties and alfresco dinners. More recently, Paolo Sorrentino's *The Great Beauty* captured both the stunning beauty and the seductive decadence of this double-edged city. Many visitors would agree with these Oscar-winning directors: Rome, the city, is a character all its own. The city's piazze, fountains, and delicately colored palazzi make impressive backdrops for a living theater. And Rome is a flirt, taking advantage of its spectacular cityscape, transforming ancient, Renaissance, and contemporary monuments into settings for the performing arts, whether outdoors in summer or in splendid palaces and churches in winter. Held at locations such as Villa Celimontana, Teatro dell'Opera, the Terme di Caracalla, or the church of Sant'Ignazio, the venue often steals the show.

Of all the performing arts, music is what Rome does best to entertain people, whether it's opera, jazz, or disco. The cinema is also a big draw (mostly for Italian-speakers), and there's a fantastic array of other options. Toast the sunset with prosecco while overlooking a 1st-century temple. Enjoy an evening reading in the Roman Forum or a live performance of Shakespeare in the Globe Theatre in Villa Borghese Gardens. Top off the night in your choice of Rome's many bars and dance clubs. When all else fails, there's always late-night caffè-sitting, watching the colorful crowds parade by on a gorgeous piazza—it's great fun, even if you don't speak the language. Little wonder Rome inspired the likes of Fellini and Sorrentino to make people-watching an art form.

PLANNING

HOW TO FIND EVENTS

With its foot firmly in the 21st century, Rome has a pantheon of publications heralding its cultural events. For city-sponsored events, Rome's official website ⊕ *www.comune.roma.it* tries to remain as *au courant* as any governmental entity can. A broader range of event listings can be found in the Cronaca and Cultura section of Italian newspapers, including *Metro,* the free newspaper found at Metro stops and on trams.

On the Internet, check out these websites written exclusively for the English-speaking community: ⊕ *www.rome.angloinfo.com* and ⊕ *rome.eventful.com.* Their Italian-language counterpart Roma 2night (⊕ *www.2night.it*) has an even more robust selection of nightlife, along with food spots. The monthly English-language periodical *Wanted in Rome* (⊕ *www.wantedinrome.com*) is available at many newsstands and has good coverage of arts events. For directory information, like addresses, *060608* (⊕ *www.060608.it*) has listings of every cultural site (monument, church, museum, art space, etc.) in the city.

TIMING

Discoteche open after 10 pm, but punctuality isn't important. The scene doesn't really heat up until later, so don't bother arriving much before midnight.

For early evening outings, *aperitivo* (the Italian version of happy hour, about 6:30–9 pm) at *enoteche* (wine bars) is the quintessential scene of Roman life where Italians and non-Italians mix for drinks and appetizers.

FEES AND TICKETS

Most clubs charge a cover (usually €10 €20), which often includes the first drink.

Depending on the venue, concert tickets can cost €7–€50, or as much as several hundred euros for an exclusive, sold-out event.

Often, you can find seating that is unreserved (identified in Italian as *posti non numerati*), or even last-minute tickets. Inquire about this option when ticket shopping; you may have to arrive early to get a good seat.

Purchase opera and concert tickets in advance at the box office, or just before the performance.

Orbis. An in-person, cash-only ticket vendor, Orbis stocks a wide array of tickets for music, cultural, and performance events. ⊠ *Piazza dell'Esquilino 37, Repubblica* ☎ *06/4827403* ⊕ *www.boxofficelazio.it.*

Ticketone. Ticketone is the go-to spot for all cultural event listings—from archaeological sites and museums to stand-alone events—in Rome. Online reservations require tenacity. ⊕ *www.ticketone.it.*

VivaTicket. One of Italy's largest ticket vendors (both online and at ticket offices), VivaTicket covers major musical performances and cultural events in Rome and throughout Italy. ⊕ *www.vivaticket.it.*

NIGHTLIFE

"*E mo' che fammo?*" ("And now what do we do?" in local dialect) ... For a great night out in Rome, all you need to do is to wander, because ready entertainment is sure to find you on every corner. It's important to follow Rome's rule of thumb: if you see an enoteca, stop in. Though most enoteche are tiny and offer a limited antipasti menu, they cover more ground in their wine lists and often have a charming gang of regulars. For the linguistically timid, there are also several stereotypical English and Irish pubs peppered around the city, complete with a steady stream of Guinness, darts, and rugby on their satellite televisions. Those oversize flat-screen TVs also show American football, baseball, and basketball—ideal for those who don't want to miss a playoff game.

Although Rome offers a cornucopia of evening bacchanalia, from ultra-chic to super-cheap, all that glitters is not gold. Insiders and visitors alike understand that finding "the scene" in Rome is the proverbial needle in the haystack: it requires patience and pursuit. Your best asset will be your ability to talk, since word-of-mouth is the most accurate source. Entertainment guides like Roma 2night provide great logistical information including up-to-date listings of bars and clubs. Most visitors head out in the centro storico to find some fun; Piazza Navona, Pantheon, Campo de' Fiori, and even Trastevere may be filled with tourists, but more recently, several niche and boutique bars have opened. (In contrast, the Spanish Steps area is a ghost town by 9 pm.) If you want to get out of the comfort zone, head to the Testaccio and San Lorenzo areas. And wherever you go, remember: Romans love an after-party, so plenty of nightlife doesn't start until midnight.

When it comes to clubs, discos, and DJs in Rome, Testaccio is considered a mecca. Testaccio's Via Galvani is Rome's Sunset Strip, where hybrid restaurant-clubs, largely identical in music and crowd, jockey for top ranking. On average, drinks range between €10 and €15, and one is often included with the entrance (€10–€20). In summer, many clubs relocate to the beach or the Tiber, so call ahead to confirm location and hours.

PRATI

The Prati area, right outside the Vatican, is best known for the high saturation of clergy and families, so expect the evening scene to be tamer here than in other neighborhoods. Nevertheless, it's possible to find some of the city's best jazz clubs here.

LIVE MUSIC

Alexanderplatz. The black-and-white-checker floors of Alexanderplatz, Rome's most important live jazz and blues club, are reminiscent of Harlem's 1930s jazz halls; and Alexanderplatz loves to promote this image with excellent jazz programming featuring both Italian and international performers. The bar and restaurant are always busy, so reservations are suggested. ⊠ *Via Ostia 9, Prati* ☎ *06/39721867* ⊕ *www.alexanderplatzjazzclub.com.*

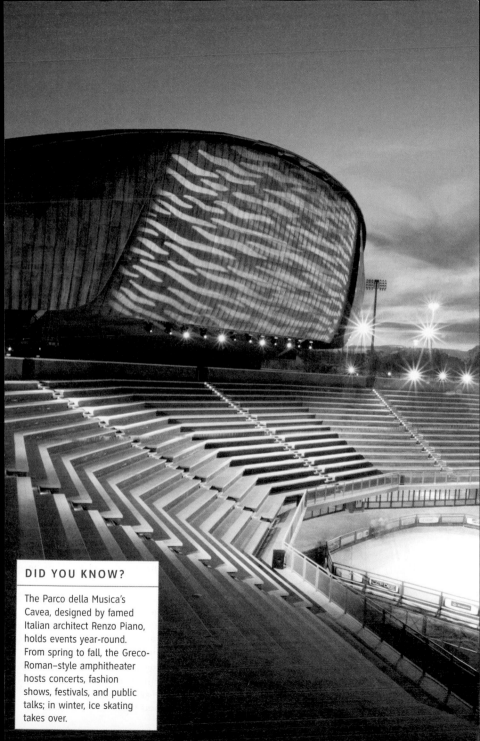

DID YOU KNOW?

The Parco della Musica's Cavea, designed by famed Italian architect Renzo Piano, holds events year-round. From spring to fall, the Greco-Roman–style amphitheater hosts concerts, fashion shows, festivals, and public talks; in winter, ice skating takes over.

Fonclea. Conveniently just around the corner from Castel Sant'Angelo, Fonclea jams with live music every night of the week—from jazz and Latin American to R&B and '60s cover bands. ⊠ *Via Crescenzio 82/a, Prati* ☎ *06/6896302* ⊕ *www.fonclea.it.*

PIAZZA NAVONA AND CAMPO DE' FIORI

PIAZZA NAVONA

Piazza Navona is where you can find just about anything, from sophisticated caffè life and flirty cocktail bars to dance clubs and chess games. Expect to be easily understood, as there is a high concentration of English-speaking establishments.

BARS

Fodor'sChoice
★ **Bar del Fico.** Bar del Fico looks a lot different from the days of yore when raucous outdoor chess matches accompanied cocktails at the once-barebones local hangout. Though the chess tables are still sitting in the shade of the historic fig tree, Bar del Fico is now a happening bar, restaurant, evening cocktail spot and late-night hangout. ⊠ *Piazza del Fico 26, Piazza Navona* ☎ *06/68891373* ⊕ *www.bardelfico.com/en/bar.*

Fodor'sChoice
★ **Etablì.** If you set up a wine bar in your living room, it'd feel a lot like Etablì. This is the perfect spot for meeting friends before a night out on the town. ⊠ *Vicolo delle Vacche 9, Piazza Navona* ☎ *06/97616694* ⊕ *www.etabli.it.*

Fluid. Fluid's looking-glass front window lures in the crowds for creative aperitivi and great music. ⊠ *Via del Governo Vecchio 46/47, Piazza Navona* ☎ *06/6832361* ⊕ *www.fluideventi.com.*

Fodor'sChoice
★ **Roof Garden Bar at Grand Hotel della Minerve.** During warm months, this lofty perch offers perhaps the most inspiring view in Rome—directly over the Pantheon's dome. The Roof Garden has an equally impressive cocktail menu. Take advantage of summer sunsets and park yourself in a front-row seat as the dome glows. ⊠ *Grand Hotel della Minerve, Piazza della Minerve 69, Piazza Navona* ☎ *06/695201* ⊕ *www.grand-hoteldelaminerve.com.*

Shari Vari. Shari Vari has reinvented itself as a sumptuous supper club, lounge, and disco. Its bistro and champagnerie are stocked with delicious delicacies and sought-after vintages. Its nightclub covers every genre of music from electronic and underground, to hip-hop, lounge, and international. ⊠ *Via di Torre Argentina 78, Piazza Navona* ☎ *06/68806936* ⊕ *www.sharivari.it.*

Terrace Bar of the Hotel Raphaël. Want to sneak a peek at Rome's rooftops? Head to the small terrace bar at the Hotel Raphaël, noted for its bird's-eye view of the campaniles and palazzi of Piazza Navona. This is one of Rome's most romantic spots for a proposal. ⊠ *Largo Febo 2, Piazza Navona* ☎ *06/682831* ⊕ *www.raphaelhotel.com.*

Vinoteca Novecento. A lovely, tiny enoteca with a very old-fashioned vibe, Vinoteca Novecento has a seemingly unlimited selection of wines, proseccos, vini santi, and grappe, along with salami-and-cheese tasting menus. Inside is standing-room only; in good weather, sit outside on one of the oak barriques. ⊠ *Piazza delle Coppelle 47, Piazza Navona* ☏ *06/6833078.*

DANCE CLUBS

La Cabala. Atop the medieval Hostaria dell'Orso, La Cabala is an after-dinner club and late-night dance party whose VIP room hosts wannabe models. Depending on the evening, the vibe can be chic, hipster, or clubby. Rome's version of a supper club, La Cabala is part of the Hostaria dell'Orso trio of restaurant, disco, and piano bar. Dress code is stylish. ⊠ *Hostaria dell'Orso, Via dei Soldati 23, Piazza Navona* ☏ *06/68301192* ⊕ *www.hdo.it.*

> ### GAY VILLAGE
>
> From the end of May through mid-September, Gay Village (⊕ *www.gayvillage.it*) hosts an outdoor mega-party held in a different central location each year. Each one more amazing than the last, Gay Village is larger than life with great bars, clubs, pop-up shops, and an international lineup of DJs and performance artists.

14

CAMPO DE' FIORI

With plenty of college bars, Campo de' Fiori is Rome's magnet for the study-abroad scene.

BARS

Il Goccetto. A rustic wine bar with a copious amount of elusive vintages, Il Goccetto specializes in wines from smaller vineyards from Sicily to Venice. Stay for a snack—its carefully chosen menu of Italian delicacies (meats and cheeses) represents the entire Italian peninsula. Il Goccetto is always busy and never accepts reservations. ⊠ *Via dei Banchi Vecchi 14, Campo de' Fiori* ☏ *06/6864268* ⊕ *www.ilgoccetto.com.*

L'Angolo Divino. Nestled on a quiet side street around the corner from the ever vivacious Campo de' Fiori, this wood paneled enoteca is a hidden treasure of wines. Its extensive selection lists more than 1,000 labels to go along quite nicely with its quaint menu of delicious homemade pastas and local antipasti. And since it's open every night until 1:30 am, it's the ideal place for a late-night tipple. ⊠ *Via dei Balestrari 12, Campo de' Fiori* ☏ *06/6864413* ⊕ *www.angolodivino.it.*

The Sofa Bar & Roof Terrace Restaurant. The romantic rooftop terrace at Sofa has a 360-degree view of the Eternal City, so it's no surprise that it's a prime spot for a late-afternoon cocktail (weather permitting). Head downstairs in the cooler months for a wide selection of craft beers on tap. ⊠ *Via Giulia 62, Campo de' Fiori* ☏ *06/686611* ⊕ *www. hotelindigorome.com.*

PIAZZA DI SPAGNA

After 9 pm, Piazza di Spagna holds the title for being the quietest area in the centro storico. Don't expect a party here, but do come to seek out some lovely enotecas.

BARS

Fodor's Choice ★ **Antica Birreria Peroni.** For beer lovers, the art nouveau–style halls of Antica Birreria Peroni will enchant you with their turn-of-the-century atmosphere, not to mention the always-flowing taps. Expect filling canteen-style meals and big steins, with several taps featuring Peroni favorites. It's also the best place for hot dogs in Rome, however tasteless their presentation. ✉ *Via di San Marcello 19, Piazza di Spagna* ☎ *06/6795310* ⊕ *www.anticabirreriaperoni.net.*

Antica Enoteca. Piazza di Spagna's staple wine bar literally corners the market on prime people-watching. In addition to a vast selection of wine, Antica Enoteca has delectable antipasti, perfect for a snack or a light lunch. ✉ *Via della Croce 76/b, Piazza di Spagna* ☎ *06/6790896* ⊕ *www.anticaenoteca.com.*

Café Doney at the Westin Excelsior. Nattily dressed businesspeople and harried tourists enjoy signature martinis at the streetside Café Doney, Via Veneto's grand dame, in front of the Westin Excelsior. The Italian design is impeccable, and the café also offers fresh fruit juices and smoothies for a healthy option. ✉ *Westin Excelsior, Via Vittorio Veneto 125, Piazza di Spagna* ☎ *06/47081* ⊕ *www.westinrome.com/en/cafe-doney.*

Fodor's Choice
★
Enoteca Regionale Palatium. Just down the street from the Piazza di Spagna hub is this modern gem run by Lazio's Regional Food Authority as a chic showcase for the best of Lazio's pantry and wine cellar. You can sample fine wines, olive oils, cheeses, and meats, and also a full seasonal menu of Lazio cuisine, including classics from top-notch ingredients (think gnocchi with ragù of mutton) and dishes with a twist (like lentil and calamari soup, or durum wheat rigatoni with zucchini sauce). Located where famed aesthete and poet Gabriele d'Annunzio once lived, this is not your garden-variety corner wine bar. ■TIP→ Stop by during aperitivo, from 6:30 pm onward (reservations recommended), to enjoy this burst of local flavor. ✉ *Via Frattina 94, Piazza di Spagna* ☎ *06/69202132* ⊕ *www.enotecaregionalepalatium.it.*

Wine Bar at the Palazzetto. The prize for perfect aperitivo spot goes to the Palazzetto, with excellent drinks and appetizers, as well as a breathtaking view of Rome's domes and rooftops—all from its fifth-floor rooftop overlooking Piazza di Spagna. Keep an eye on the sky, as any chance for a rainy day will close the terrace (as do special events). ✉ *Vicolo del Bottino 8, Piazza di Spagna* ☎ *06/69934711* ⊕ *www.ilpalazzettoroma. com* Ⓜ *Spagna.*

DANCE CLUBS
Gilda. Every year, historic disco Gilda reinvents herself to continue the never-ending party near the Spanish Steps. Recent incarnations have added a piano bar and a restaurant just off the dance floors. Expect a younger crowd. ✉ *Via Mario de' Fiori 97, Piazza di Spagna* ☎ *06/6784838* ⊕ *www.gildabar.it* Ⓜ *Spagna.*

REPUBBLICA

Piazza della Repubblica is by far one of Rome's prettiest and largest piazzas, but its proximity to Termini station means the nightlife scene can be a bit scruffy. There are a few spots worth visiting, though.

BARS

Fodor's Choice ★ **Champagnerie Tazio.** A chic champagne bar named after the original Italian *paparazzo* Tazio Secchiaroli, this spot brings a very dolce vita vibe with its red, black, and white lacquered interior with crystal chandeliers. The favorite pastime at Tazio is sipping champagne while watching people parade through the colonnade of the lobby. In summer, the hotel's rooftop Posh bar is the place to be, with its infinity pool and terrace view overlooking downtown. ⊠ *Hotel Exedra, Piazza della Repubblica 47, Repubblica* ☎ *06/489381* ⊕ *exedra-roma.boscolohotels.com/restaurant-and-bar/champagnerie-tazio* Ⓜ *Repubblica.*

SUMMER LOVIN'

From June through August, many of Rome's bars and clubs shut down and the owners get out of town to avoid the summer heat. Other hangouts open temporary clubs on the beaches of Ostia and Fregene, about 45 minutes outside the city center. More conveniently, *Estate Romana* (Roman Summer) ⊕ *www.estateromana.comune. roma.it* brings beach nightlife to the banks of the Tiber River, with mini-versions of familiar bars, restaurants, and clubs along the Tiber banks.

14

Eataly Roma Repubblica. If food is a religion in Italy, Eataly is its temple of worship. Although not as large as its Ostiense outpost, this new location is much easier to reach. It's a great spot for a glass of wine and plate of prosciutto on the piazza. ⊠ *Piazza della Repubblica 41, Repubblica* ☎ *06/45509130* ⊕ *www.eataly.net.*

Trimani Il Winebar. One of Rome's best-stocked enotecas, this never-ending cantina proudly boasts over 4,000 labels and is the offspring of Rome's oldest wine merchant next door. There is a menu of small plates to accompany your aperitif, or a wide selection of digestifs for an after-dinner tipple. ⊠ *Via Cernaia 37/b, Repubblica* ☎ *06/4469630* ⊕ *www.trimani.com.*

VILLA BORGHESE AND PIAZZA DEL POPOLO

Like nearby Piazza di Spagna, Piazza del Popolo takes a turn for quiet once the sun sets.

BARS

Stravinskij Bar at the Hotel de Russie. The Stravinskij Bar, in the Hotel de Russie's gorgeous garden, is the best place to catch a glimpse of la dolce vita. Celebrities, blue bloods, and VIPs hang out in the private courtyard garden where mixed drinks and cocktails are well above par. ⊠ *Hotel de Russie, Via del Babuino 9, Piazza del Popolo* ☎ *06/328881* ⊕ *www. roccofortehotels.com/hotels-and-resorts/hotel-de-russie/restaurant-and-bar/stravinskij-bar* Ⓜ *Flaminio.*

TRASTEVERE

Trastevere is no longer the rough-around-the-edges neighborhood where visitors used to come to get a glimpse of "real" Rome. Years of gentrification have made this medieval "country within a town" a mecca for tourists and for Americans studying abroad. Its nightlife is a fun mix of overflowing piazzas filled with creative buskers, busy pubs, and great hole-in-the-wall restaurants.

BARS

Fodor'sChoice **Freni e Frizioni.** This hipster hangout has a cute artist vibe, and is great
★ for an afternoon coffee, tea, or aperitivo, or for late-night socializing. In warmer weather, the crowd overflows the large terrazzo overlooking the Tiber and the side streets of Trastevere. ⊠ *Via del Politeama 4, Trastevere* ☎ *06/45497499* ⊕ *www.freniefrizioni.com.*

Grazia e Graziella. A charming wine bar and restaurant, "G e G" has an at-home atmosphere, from the relaxed vibe to the shabby chic decor. ⊠ *Largo F. Biondi 5, Trastevere* ☎ *06/5880398* ⊕ *www.graziaegraziella. it.*

LIVE MUSIC

Big Mama. Big Mama is Trastevere's homegrown institution for live music, including jazz, blues, rhythm and blues, international, and rock. ⊠ *Vicolo San Francesco a Ripa 18, Trastevere* ☎ *06/5812551* ⊕ *www. bigmama.it.*

TESTACCIO

Even if a bit isolated from the city, Testaccio is the usual go-to neighborhood for nightlife, in particular for discos and clubs. The Via Galvani is chock-a-block with clubs featuring every genre of music, which means weekends are congested with partygoers. More recently, the neighborhood has evolved as a hotbed for the restaurant and bar scene with some of Rome's newest hangouts.

DANCE CLUBS

Ketum Bar. One of Rome's few "organic" happy hours, the price of a drink will buy you a spread of healthy and organic vegetarian appetizers. It also serves up a great weekend brunch. Aperitivo starts at 6:30 pm. ⊠ *Via Galvani 24, Testaccio* ☎ *06/57305338* ⊕ *www.ketumbar.it.*

l'Alibi. One of Testaccio's longest-running clubs, l'Alibi hosts parties daily including its much anticipated Thursday Gloss Party. The crowd crosses all boundaries, and the music knows no limits at what is often considered Rome's most famous gay disco. In summer, the open terrace becomes a large dance floor. ⊠ *Via di Monte Testaccio 40, Testaccio* ☎ *06/5743448* ⊕ *www.lalibi.it.*

MONTI, ESQUILINO, AND SAN LORENZO

MONTI

Lately, Monti has been wearing the crown as the "it" neighborhood, reigning supreme as an all-ages hipster hang with trendy bars, top-notch restaurants, and artisan shops, as well as picturesque piazze.

BARS

Fodor'sChoice **Ai Tre Scalini.** An ivy-covered wine bar in the center of Monti, Rome's
★ trendiest 'hood, Ai Tre Scalini has a warm and cozy menu of delicious antipasti and light entrées to go along with its enticing wine list.

After about 8 pm, if you haven't booked, be prepared to wait—this is one extremely popular spot with locals. ⊠ *Via Panisperna 251, Monti* ☎ *06/48907495* ⊕ *www.aitrescalini.org* Ⓜ *Cavour*.

Caffè Propaganda. Propaganda is reminiscent of Parisian brasseries of the 1930s, with charming bar design, sultry music, a clever cocktail menu, and creative Italian/French cuisine—not to mention the delicious desserts. For a glimpse of Rome's super-stylish, park yourself at Propaganda's bar for a few hours. ⊠ *Via Claudia 15, Monti* ☎ *06/94534255* ⊕ *www.caffepropaganda.it*.

JAZZ CLUB

Charity Café. An intimate jazz club with live music performances nightly, Charity hosts local and international jazz musicians in a relaxed atmosphere. ⊠ *Via Panisperna 68, Monti* ☎ *06/47825881* ⊕ *www.charitycafe.it*.

ESQUILINO

Monti's neighbor Esquilino is lined up and ready for the next urban renaissance. Although not as pretty as neighboring Monti, Rome's top film directors and other artists have made Esquilino their home.

BARS

Fiddler's Elbow. The oldest Irish pub in Rome, the proud Fiddler's Elbow is a rustic, traditional pub that probably hasn't changed since it first installed its wood panels in 1976. Expect raucous nights of beer and singing. ⊠ *Via dell'Olmata 43, Esquilino* ☎ *06/4872110* ⊕ *www.thefiddlerselbow.com*.

SAN LORENZO

Literally the other side of the tracks, just beyond Termini train station, San Lorenzo is a traditional university area with lots of inexpensive bars and restaurants, as well as art spaces. Evenings are always brimming with people and activity.

BARS

Black Market. This bare-bones speakeasy-style bar offers top-notch cocktails expertly mixed with bitters or fruit, artisanal beer, organic wine, and a full spread of delicious appetizers. ⊠ *Via dei Sardi 50, Esquilino* ☎ *3398227541* ⊕ *www.blackmarketartgallery.it/san-lorenzo*.

Co.So. The name stands for Cocktail Social, and when you walk into this sleek and modern spot, you'll quickly feel that you've been whisked away from the working-class neighborhood of Pigneto. Owner Massimo d'Addezio used to be the barman at Stravinskij Bar, in Rome's luxury Hotel De Russie, so he knows a thing or two about making cocktails. He opened Co.So. in 2013, and it's been a hot spot ever since, serving bar snacks as well as dinner plates like sandwiches, nachos, as well as mouthwatering pulled-pork and deconstructed-porchetta burgers. The cocktail list itself is playful—one specialty is the Carbonara Sour, made with guanciale-infused vodka, though the bar staff are happy to mix traditional cocktails as well. ⊠ *Via Braccio da Montone 80, Pigneto* ☎ *06/45435428* ⊙ *Closed Sun. and 3 wks in Aug*.

PERFORMING ARTS

One of the pleasures of Rome is seeing a performance in one of the city's stunning venues, ancient or modern. This is the city where you might experience classical opera performed in the 3rd-century-AD Terme di Caracalla, or enjoy an experimental dance show in the postindustrial detergent factory Teatro India, or see a contemporary performance at the Renzo Piano–designed Auditorium Parco della Musica.

In summertime, most of the performing arts events move outdoors—any public space is fair game. Keep an eye on the Estate Romana ⊕ *www. estateromana.comune.roma.it* to find out what's happening in Rome on any night of the week. There is enough entertainment in Rome to take your breath away, in any season and in any location.

DANCE

Rome's classical and modern dance scene may play understudy to Milan and Bologna, but dance is flourishing in the Eternal City. Teatro dell'Opera and the Auditorium Parco della Musica, as well as other theaters, have enriched their programming to include more performances, feature international performers, and showcase contemporary along with classical dance. Each fall, the city hosts the six-week RomaEuropa Festival (⊕ *www.romaeuropa.net*), which includes various performance artists. RomaEuropa also continues with select programming throughout the year. Once a year, the Accademia Filarmonica Romana, together with the Teatro Olimpico, organizes the Festival Internazionale della Danza, another top event focused on contemporary dance and live music performances. The French Academy at Villa Medici is also a great source for contemporary dance performances.

Fodor'sChoice
★ **Corps de Ballet, Teatro dell'Opera.** Rome's Corps de Ballet perform throughout the year at the lovely Belle Epoque opera house, with leading international guest stars. During the summer season, ballet performances are held under the stars at the Terme di Caracalla, mixing innovative set design with classic structure. ⊠ *Teatro dell'Opera, Piazza Beniamino Gigli 7, Esquilino* ☎ *06/48160255* ⊕ *www.operaroma.it.*

Teatro Greco. As part of Rome's rich and intense performance circuit, the Teatro Greco features international contemporary dance performances. Its own dance company, established in 1973, has performed all over the world. ⊠ *Via Ruggero Leoncavallo 10, Parioli* ☎ *06/8607513* ⊕ *www. teatrogreco.it.*

Teatro Olimpico. Part of Rome's theater circuit, the 1930s-era Teatro Olimpico is one of the main venues for cabaret, contemporary dance companies, visiting international ballet companies, touring Broadway shows, and TEDxRoma. ⊠ *Piazza Gentile da Fabriano 17, Flaminio* ☎ *06/3265991* ⊕ *www.teatroolimpico.it.*

FILM

Andiamo al cinema! Rome has dozens of movie houses, where you'll find both blockbuster and art house films. All films are shown in Italian, unless noted "V.O." in the listing, which means *versione originale* (original version or original language).

Most international films are dubbed in Italian, *grazie a Mussolini,* who insisted on this approach in order to instill pride in the native language. Dubbing has since become an art form—voiceover actors receive recognition and awards and consistently dub their silver screen counterparts. During the Estate Romana summer arts festival, several squares and gardens in Rome also screen films, sometimes showing the original version.

For showtimes, see the entertainment pages of daily newspapers or Rome's English-language publications. Check out ⊕ *www.inromenow.com* for the most up-to-date reviews of all English-language films or visit ⊕ *www.trovacinema.repubblica.it* for a list of current features and theaters. Tickets range in price from €4.50 for matinees and some weekdays, up to €10 for weekend evenings.

Casa del Cinema. Casa del Cinema is Rome's hub for all things film, with multiple screening rooms, a resource center with DVD library, laptops for private viewings, plus a caffè and restaurant. Yearly programming includes new and retro films from its vast archives; original language films are often showcased from several festivals, including Venice Film Festival and Roma Cinema Fest (*www.romacinemafest.it*). In summer, the cinema heads outdoors to show a wide array of movies, sometimes in the original language. ⊠ *Largo Marcello Mastroianni 1, Villa Borghese* ☎ *06/423601* ⊕ *www.casadelcinema.it.*

Cinema Barberini. One of the most commercial and central theaters in the city, Barberini is guaranteed to have at least one film on offer in its original language. It's the best place to see the latest blockbuster without dubbing. ⊠ *Piazza Barberini 24/26, Piazza di Spagna* ☎ *06/86391361* ⊕ *www.cinemadiroma.it/programmazione-multisalabarberini* Ⓜ *Barberini.*

Nuovo Olimpia. Just off Rome's Via del Corso in the center of the city, Nuovo Olimpia is *the* cinema for Rome's international community, showing new-release films in original language with Italian subtitles. ⊠ *Via in Lucina 16/b, Piazza Navona* ☎ *06/6861068* ⊕ *nuovoolimpia. ccroma.circuitocinema.com.*

MUSIC

CLASSICAL

Since 2002, Rome has had its very own state-of-the-art auditorium a 10-minute tram ride north of Piazza del Popolo—the Parco della Musica (or Music Park)—splashed over the pages of glossy magazines everywhere. There's also a classical music program of Tempietto concerts (⊕ *www.amicimusicasacra.com*) performed in the beautiful open-air Teatro di Marcello. However, if you prefer smaller venues, Rome does not disappoint. Classical music concerts take place at numerous venues throughout the city, and you're very likely to see memorable performances in smaller halls and churches, often for free. This is true particularly at Christmas and Easter, both especially busy concert seasons in Rome. Some churches that frequently host afternoon and evening concerts are Sant'Ivo alla Sapienza, San Francesco a Ripa, and San Paolo entro le Mura. Look for posters outside churches announcing free performances, particularly at Sant'Ignazio (⊠ *Piazza Sant'Ignazio, Pantheon*; ☎ *06/6794560* ⊕ *www.amicimusicasacra.com*), which hosts concerts in a spectacular setting. Or try the summertime concerts at the ancient Teatro di Marcello (⊠ *Via del Teatro Marcello, Ghetto*; ☎ *06/488991*). Also look for the schedule of the Oratorio del Gonfalone (⊕ *www.oratoriogonfalone.com*), a concert hall that boasts a dizzying wealth of 16th-century frescoes that have often been compared to the Sistine Chapel.

One of the charming things about Rome is that, with all the little sidestreets tucked behind quiet piazze, not to mention the nearly 1,000 churches throughout the Eternal City, it's quite easy to stumble upon a choir rehearsing or a chorus performing for just a few churchgoers. Sometimes all it takes is some wandering around, and a little luck, to stumble upon a memorable concert experience.

Accademia di Santa Cecilia. One of the oldest conservatories in the world (founded 1585), this venue has a program of performances ranging from classical to contemporary and a lineup of world-renowned artists. The Renzo Piano-designed Auditorium Parco della Musica hosts many of Santa Cecilia's concerts, while others are at the concert hall on via della Conciliazione, close to the Vatican. ⊠ *Via Pietro de Coubertin 34, Flaminio* ☎ *06/8082058* ⊕ *www.santacecilia.it*.

Accademia Filarmonica Romana. Nearly two centuries old, this is one of Rome's historic concert venues featuring both symphonic and chamber-music presentations. The garden hosts occasional outdoor performances. ⊠ *Via Flaminia 118, Flaminio* ☎ *06/3201752* ⊕ *www.filarmonicaromana.org*.

Il Tempietto. Music festivals and concerts are organized throughout the year in otherwise inaccessible sites, such as the Teatro di Marcello, the Church of San Nicola in Carcere, and Villa Torlonia. Music covers the entire scope from classical to contemporary. ⊠ *Piazza Campitelli 9, Jewish Ghetto* ☎ *06/45615180* ⊕ *www.tempietto.it*.

Fodor'sChoice **Oratorio del Gonfalone.** A small concert hall with an internationally
★ recognized series of Baroque classics, the Oratorio del Gonfalone's mid-16th century frescoed walls are painted in high Mannerist style—a beautiful accompaniment to the music. ⊠ *Via del Gonfalone 32/a, Campo de' Fiori* ☎ *06/6875952* ⊕ *www.oratoriogonfalone.com*.

Teatro Eliseo. Hosting musical performances and the work of historical and contemporary playwrights throughout the year, Teatro Eliseo also offers innovative programming for children, including occasional English-language programs. ⊠ *Via Nazionale 183, Repubblica* ☎ *06/83510216,* ⊕ *www.teatroeliseo.com*.

AUDITORIUM PARCO DELLA MUSICA

✉ *Viale Pietro de Coubertin 30, Flaminio* ☎ *06/80241281,* ⊕ *www.auditorium.com.*

14

TIPS

■ To get to the Auditorium from Rome's Termini station, take Bus No. 910, which stops directly in front of the complex at Viale Pietro de Coubertin. If you're coming from the city center, walk to Piazzale Flaminio (the other side of Piazza del Popolo) and hop on Tram No. 2 for six stops. Using the Metro, take Linea A to Flaminio, and walk aboveground to Tram No. 2 (again, for six stops). Access the Auditorium's underground parking using Viale Maresciallo Pilsudski and Via Giulio Gaudini.

■ To book guided tours, email *visiteguidate@musicaperroma.it.*

■ If you're here in summer, there will be outdoor concerts and festivals.

Rome became a world-class arts contender when world-renowned architect Renzo Piano conceived and constructed the Parco della Musica, fondly known as "the Auditorium." The futuristic music complex is made up of three enormous, pod-shaped concert halls, which have heard the live melodies of Luciano Pavarotti, Philip Glass, Tracy Chapman, Peter Gabriel, Burt Bacharach, Woody Allen, and many more.

Likened to anything from beetles to computer "mice," the musical pods are consistently jammed with people: the Sala Santa Cecilia is a massive hall for grand orchestra and choral concerts; the Sala Sinopoli is more intimately scaled for smaller troupes; and the Sala Petrassi was designed for alternative events. All three are arrayed around the Cavea, a vast Greco-Roman–style theater.

The auditorium is more than just music. The music park also hosts seasonal festivals—including the Rome Film Fest, a Christmas Village, and a springtime science, math, and philosophy festival. The grounds also have restaurants, a charming caffe, a bookstore, an outdoor amphitheater, an archaeological site, and an outstanding children's playground. Located in the Flaminio neighborhood, the Auditorium is just 10 minutes from the city center, reachable by local tram transport.

ROCK, POP, AND JAZZ

Local and smaller-act rock, pop, and jazz concerts are frequent in Rome, with big-name acts coming through less frequently—and almost exclusively during warmer weather—and even these performances may not be well advertised. Some locales are outside the city center, and sometimes as far as Tivoli, so it's worth asking about transportation before you buy your tickets. Casa del Jazz ⊕ *www.casajazz.it*, hosted in a three-story 1920s villa, became a landmark for all lovers of the genre. The Estate Romana (Roman Summer) program, organized by the local and regional governments, has been growing every year. The program now includes a diverse offering of well-publicized and well-organized cultural events, most set outdoors and all free or reasonably priced. In addition to Estate Romana, both Rock in Roma and Fiesta! are cultural series with a heavy focus on music in places such as the Stadio Olimpico, the Ippodromo, and even on the banks of the Tiber.

Events spread from the center of town to the periphery and usually run early June–early September. They include music of every sort, as well as outdoor cinema, theater, and other events, such as book fairs and guided tours of some of Rome's monuments by night. The city administration has really made the push for important music acts to give free concerts, and the crowds at these gigs prove that music is, in fact, an international language. James Taylor gave a heartfelt free performance in lovely Piazza del Popolo. Record crowds once filled the Via dei Fori Imperiali, from Piazza Venezia down to the stage in front of a brightly lighted Colosseum, for free concerts by no less than Paul McCartney and Simon & Garfunkel, respectively.

PalaLottomatica. Built for the 1960 Rome Olympics for basketball and boxing events, the PalaLottamatica is now a concert venue for big names like Italian favorites Zucchero and Renato Zero, as well international superstars like Bruce Springsteen and Elton John. It's in the EUR neighborhood (about 15 minutes outside the city center), so bring extra cab fare. ⊠ *Piazzale Pier Luigi Nervi 1, Flaminio* ☏ *06/540901* ⊕ *www.palalottomatica.it.*

OPERA

Rome may be a tiny star in Italy's opera constellation, but with an increasing emphasis on quality productions, along with its never-ending supply of performances, this little star is twinkling. The historic Teatro dell'Opera, Rome's center for lyrical performance, has upped its brilliance by adding famed maestro Riccardo Muti as music director for select productions. Its season runs from late fall through spring, and showcases summertime alfresco performances at the Terme di Caracalla. There are also several churches and smaller venues that host operas, often for free.

Fodor's Choice
★

Teatro dell'Opera. Long considered a far younger sibling of La Scala in Milan and La Fenice in Venice, the company commands an audience during its mid-November–May season. In the hot summer months, the company moves to the Terme di Caracalla for its outdoor opera series. As can be expected, the oft-preferred performance is *Aida,*

CLOSE UP

Opera Alfresco

Opera buffs know that the best performances and most exquisite surroundings for opera are to be found at Milan's Scala, Venice's newly reconstructed Fenice, and at Verona's Arena (outdoor amphitheater). But Rome is Italy's capital, and so, even though its opera company does not have the renown of the aforementioned landmarks, it does have a healthy following. Rome's spring opera season runs from November or December to May. During the summertime exodus of many of the city's pubs, restaurants, and discos to outdoor venues, opera, too, heads outside for its summer season.

Rome's many opera companies commandeer church courtyards, ancient villas, and soccer *campi* (fields) with performances that range from mom-and-poperas to full-scale, big-budget extravaganzas. Quality is generally quite high, even for smaller, low-budget productions. Tickets cost €15–€40. To find these productions, listen closely or look for the old-fashioned posters advertising classic operas like *Tosca* and *La Traviata*. The weekly *Roma c'è*, the monthly *Wanted in Rome*, and the website ⊕ *www.inromenow.com* also have complete lists of performances.

14

for its spectacle, which once included real elephants. The company has lately taken a new direction, using projections atop the ancient ruins to create cutting-edge sets. ⊠ *Piazza Beniamino Gigli 8, Repubblica* ☏ *06/481601, 06/48160255 for tickets* ⊕ *www.operaroma.it* Ⓜ *Repubblica.*

Terme di Caracalla ballet and opera. The 3rd-century-AD baths of Caracalla are the spectacular backdrop for summer performances of the Teatro dell'Opera's ballet and opera series. *Aida* is the most sought-after performance, for its melodramatic flair and amazing props. Along with traditional pieces, many classical performances have contemporary elements, such as the stage design, which uses projections atop the ancient ruins. ⊠ *Via Antoniniana 14, Aventino* ☏ *06/481601* ⊕ *www.operaroma.it.*

THEATER

Romans are passionate about their theater and invest greatly in keeping the scene alive. On offer are a wide variety of performances, from the more rich and institutional productions of the Teatro Argentina, to the more experimental approach of the Teatro India. For Shakespeare, no one does it better than the Silvano Toti Globe Theatre, which often hosts performances in English. The Teatro Sistina focuses on larger Broadway hits, sometimes in English. For your best bet in understanding the production, head to the English Theatre of Rome.

English Theatre of Rome. The oldest English-language theater group in town, English Theatre of Rome has a repertoire of original and celebrated plays. Performances are held at John Cabot University and Teatro

Arciliuto. ⊠ *Piazza Montevecchio, 5, Piazza Navona* ☎ *06/4441375* ⊕ *www.rometheatre.com.*

Miracle Players. Looking for a bit of English humor? With an obvious penchant for Monty Python, the Miracle Players are Rome's most vocal English-language comedy troupe performing original plays. Head to the Roman Forum on Friday afternoons in summer for their free, live performances. ⊠ *Largo Romolo e Remo, Monti* ☎ *06/70393427* ⊕ *www. miracleplayers.org.*

Silvano Toti Globe Theatre. This oak-and-thatch theater is a replica of the Elizabethan landmark in London. It stages Shakespeare in the middle of Villa Borghese, occasionally in English. ⊠ *Largo Aqua Felix, Piazza di Siena, Villa Borghese* ☎ *060608* ⊕ *www.globetheatreroma.com.*

Fodor's Choice ★ **Teatro Argentina.** A gorgeous 18th-century theater, the Teatro Argentina evokes glamour and sophistication with its velvet upholstery, large crystal chandeliers and beautifully dressed theatergoers, who come to see international productions of stage and dance performances. ⊠ *Largo di Torre Argentina 52, Campo de' Fiori* ☎ *06/684000311* ⊕ *www.teatrodiroma.net.*

Teatro India. Hosting productions in English as well as in Italian, Teatro India occupies a former soap factory, showcasing the best in contemporary theater from local and visiting artists. ⊠ *Lungotevere Vittorio Gassman 1, Trastevere* ☎ *06/684000314* ⊕ *www.teatrodiroma.net.*

SHOPPING

WHAT TO SHOP FOR IN ROME

There's so much to shop for in Rome. Handmade leather goods are worth the splurge: excellent workmanship and attention to detail are the norm, and you'll find beautifully constructed jackets, shoes, gloves, handbags, and more.

ANTIQUES AND PRINTS

Rome is one of Italy's happiest hunting grounds for antiques and bric-a-brac. You'll find streets lined with shops groaning under the weight of gilded Rococo tables, charming Grand Tour memorabilia, fetching 17th-century engravings of realistic scenes, and curios—perhaps even Lord Byron's snuff spoon.

CERAMICS AND DECORATIVE ARTS

Unique pottery, beautiful ceramics, and other decorative arts are at the top of a shopper's list when searching for that special souvenir. The best finds are at Rome's many artisan shops tucked away on winding cobblestone streets.

Whether you fancy a quasi-authentic Roman mask or a copy of that popular Roman relic, *La Bocca della Verità*, you definitely won't go home empty-handed.

CLOTHING

Italians know fashion: that much is indisputable. There are plenty of upmarket flagship stores in Rome, if you're up to Prada, Fendi, or Valentino, but make sure to browse the smaller boutiques, too. You're sure to find a piece or two to liven up your wardrobe.

VINTAGE CLOTHING

Looking good needn't mean looking like everyone else. Rome has a wide range of vintage shops (mainly in the Monti and Navona areas), where you can find some great couture from the *Dolce Vita* days and other classic time periods. Spend some time going through the racks—you never know what treasures you might find.

FLEA MARKET FINDS

Treasure-seekers and bargain-hunters alike will appreciate Rome's *mercati all'aperto* (open-air markets). Flea markets are great spots to unearth some really good finds, whether you're hunting for something borrowed or something new. Every Sunday, all of Rome tends to gravitate to Trastevere for the Porta Portese flea market, where tents overflow with cheap luggage, new and used clothes, vintage World War II memorabilia, and everything else (but the kitchen sink). ⚠ **Be aware of your belongings at markets like these, as pickpockets abound.**

GLOVES

You just wouldn't be an Italian signora without a pair of fashionable handmade gloves, and you'll find plenty to choose from in Rome. Whether you're looking for cashmere, silk, lambskin, or other types of leather, there is a sea of colors to choose from. Gloves make wonderful presents, too.

HANDBAGS, LUGGAGE, AND LEATHER GOODS

Really good, top-quality bags—the classic kind you can carry for years—don't

15

come cheap. Whether you're in the market for something high-fashion the Hollywood A-listers are wearing or a one-of-a-kind travel bag, you'll find plenty of splurge-inducing shops. You'll also find other types of well-made leather goods in Rome, like wallets, belts, and jackets.

JEWELRY

Over the last few years, an array of delightful boutiques featuring unique handmade jewelry have made their debut in the Eternal City. Whether you're in the market for a sparkly something to wear for that special occasion or a practical but priceless piece that looks good for everyday use, don't leave Rome without stepping foot in a specialized *oreficeria*.

SHOES

When it comes to sexy stilettos, strappy sandals, or stylish *stivali* (boots), Rome has a *scarpa* (shoe) for every Cinderella. The best place to get your feet wet is in the swanky Piazza di Spagna area, but other *belle* boutiques can be found around the Piazza Navona and Campo de' Fiori areas as well. *Scarpe Diem!*

Updated
by Nicole
Arriaga

In Rome, shopping is an art form. Perhaps it's the fashionably bespectacled commuter wearing Giorgio Armani as he deftly zips through traffic on his Vespa, or all those Anita Ekberg, Audrey Hepburn, and Julia Roberts films that make us long to be Roman for a day. But with limited time and no Hollywood studio backing you, the trick is to find what you're looking for and still not miss out on the city's museums and monuments—and, of course, leave yourself plenty of euros to enjoy the rest of your trip.

Since you may be pressed for time, knowing how and where to put your best fashion foot forward is crucial. Luckily for shop-till-you-droppers, you can still fit your shopping sprees in between sights. A visit to the Trevi Fountain means not only reliving the movie classic *Three Coins in a Fountain,* but puts you within striking distance of some of the city's best shopping. Pose for a picture-perfect snapshot at Piazza di Spagna, as you keep your eye on that delicious handbag in the window at Dolce & Gabbana.

There may be no city that takes shopping quite as seriously as Rome, and no district more worthy of your time than Piazza di Spagna, with its abundance of shops and designer powerhouses like Fendi and Armani. The best of them are clumped tightly together along the city's three primary fashion arteries: Via dei Condotti, Via Borgognona, and Via Frattina. From Piazza di Spagna to Piazza Navona and on to Campo de' Fiori, shoppers will find an explosive array of shops within walking distance of one another: a shop for fine handmade Amalfi paper looks out upon the Pantheon, while slick boutiques anchor the corners of 18th-century Piazza di Spagna. Across town in the colorful hive that is Monti, a second-generation mosaic artist creates Italian masterpieces on a street named for a pope who died before America was even discovered. Even in Trastevere, one can find one of Rome's rising shoe designers creating next-century *nuovo chic* shoes nestled on a side street beside one of the city's oldest churches.

This chapter will help shopaholics choose the perfect souvenir for someone back home, find a vintage poster, choose a boutique for those *molto* chic Versace sandals, or rustle up some truffles. When you're done filling your bags with memories of Mamma Roma, you can be sure of two things: that you'll be nostalgic for Caput Mundi long after you arrive back home, and that you've saved a few coins to throw into that fabulous, famous fountain.

PLANNING

OPENING HOURS

Shopping escapades in Rome definitely require flexibility and a certain degree of *pazienza*. Small mom-and-pop shops may observe the traditional siesta and close down for lunch (1–1:30 pm until 4–4:30 pm), whereas larger retailers and chains will open around 10 am and keep continuous hours until 7:30–8 pm. ■TIP➡ **Most shops (unless located in one of Rome's malls) are typically closed on Sunday and on Monday morning.** Banks are generally open weekdays 8:30–1:30 and 2:30–3:30. Summer travelers should be aware that most small shops close for two to three weeks just before or after August's "Ferragosto" holiday.

COUNTERFEITS

Piracy, in any form, is a serious offense that could cost you a pretty penny during your trip in Italy. According to Italian law, anyone (citizens and tourists alike) caught buying counterfeit goods—DVDs, CDs, sunglasses, or those impossibly discounted "Fendi" and "Gucci" bags—sold by illegal sidewalk vendors is subject to a fine of no less than €1,000. While the police in Rome enforce this law to varying degrees, travelers are advised to purchase products only from stores and licensed retailers that give a receipt, to avoid buying counterfeit goods or committing tax evasion.

DUTY-FREE SHOPPING

Value-added tax (IVA) is 23% on clothing and luxury goods, but is already included in the amount on the price tag for consumer goods. All non–EU citizens visiting Italy are entitled to a reimbursement of this tax when purchasing nonperishable goods that total more than €180 in a single transaction. If you buy goods in a store that does not participate in the "Tax-Free Italy" program, ask the cashier to issue you a special invoice known as a *fattura*, which must be made out to you and includes the phrase *Esente IVA ai sensi della legge 38 quarter*. The bill should indicate the amount of IVA included in the purchase price. Present this invoice and the goods purchased to the Customs Office on your departure from Italy to obtain your tax reimbursement.

ITALIAN SIZES

Unfortunately, Italian sizes are not standard—it is therefore always best to try things on. If you wear a "small," you may be surprised to learn that in Italy, you are a medium. Children's sizes are just as complicated; they are typically based on Italian children's ages. Check labels on all garments, as many are dry clean–only or non–tumble dry. When in doubt about the proper size, ask the shop attendant—most will have an international size chart handy. At open-air markets, where there often isn't any place to try on garments, you'll have to take your best guess: if you're wrong, you may or may not be able to find the vendor the next day to exchange.

SALES

Italians wait year-round for the infamous *saldi* (end-of-season sales), which typically mean big bargains in clothing and accessories. Rome's main sale periods run twice a year: January 7–February and late July–mid-September. Unlike in many other countries, most stores adopt a no-exchange, all-sales-final policy on applicable goods. Others might even go as far as not allowing you to try on items on the "sales" rack. At other times of year, a *liquidazione* sign indicates a close-out sale, but take a hard look at the goods; they're often bottom-of-the-barrel scraps you often can't exchange.

■TIP➜ If your trip is truly a shopping holiday or if time is of the essence, consider scheduling your own personal shopping assistant through Context Rome (☎06/96727371 ⊕ *www.contexttravel.com*).

AROUND THE VATICAN

BORGO

Just outside the Vatican walls and around the corner from Prati, Borgo is your destination for religious relics.

Savelli Arte e Tradizione. Here you'll find a fully stocked selection of holier-than-thou gifts and sacred trinkets for you to take home. This family business has been around for more than 100 years and specializes in everything from rosaries, crosses, religious artwork, statues, and Pope Francis memorabilia. The family name, Savelli, dates back to an old Roman family that boasts four popes in its bloodline: Benedict II, Gregory II, Honorius III, and Honorius IV. The store has three other locations: Galleria Savelli in St. Peter's Square; Savelli Gift in Via della Concilliazione; and Art Studio Cafè in Via dei Gracchi. ⊠ *Via Paolo VI 27, Borgo* ☎06/68307017 ⊕ *www.savellireligious.com* Ⓜ *Ottaviano*.

PRATI

Just a hop, skip, and jump from the Vatican, you'll find an array of religious relic shops, department stores, and gourmet food and wine shops.

DEPARTMENT STORES

FAMILY **Coin.** Department stores aren't the norm in Italy, but one store that comes close is Coin. It's the perfect place for upscale merchandise including accessories, handbags, cosmetics, and clothing for men, women, and children. Searching for a pressure-driven espresso machine, a simpler stovetop Bialetti model, or a mezzaluna? You can find these and other high-quality, stylish cookware items that are difficult to find back home. If you are hopping a train from Termini station, be sure to check out the smaller version of this store, which has a fabulous emphasis on fashions. ⊠ *Via Cola di Rienzo 173, Prati* ☎ *06/36004298* ⊕ *www. coin.it* Ⓜ *Lepanto, Ottaviano.*

FOOD AND WINE

Fodor'sChoice **Castroni.** The legend over the door reads "Castroni Droghe Coloniali,"
★ but for years this international food emporium has been known by a single moniker: Castroni. Opening its flagship shop near the Vatican in 1932, this gastronomic paradise has long been Rome's port-of-call for decadent delicacies from around the globe; there are now more than 10 locations throughout the city. Jonesing expats and study-abroad students pop in for Twinings teas, exotic spices from Spain, and even some good old-fashioned Kraft Macaroni & Cheese. Even Italians stop by to check out the vast assortment of coffee and tea, decadent candies, and other sweets. If you're just doing a little window-shopping, be sure to try their in-house roasted espresso, some of the best coffee in Rome. Just be sure to bring an extra suitcase: you will want to buy everything. ⊠ *Via Cola di Rienzo 196, Prati* ☎ *06/6874383* ⊕ *www. castroni.it* Ⓜ *Lepanto, Ottaviano.*

SHOES AND ACCESSORIES

Il Sellaio Serafini Pelletteria. For more than 70 years, artisan Ferruccio Serafini has been churning out some of the best handmade leather bags, shoes, and belts in Rome. Only a handful of these true saddler artisans still exist today. Marlon Brando, Elizabeth Taylor, and the Kennedy brothers were all faithful followers of Serafini's design and work in the 1960s. Today, the family business is run by Francesca, Ferruccio Serafini's youngest daughter. Choose from their premade stock or select your own style and accompanying leathers. ⊠ *Via Caio Mario 14, Prati* ☎ *06/3211719* ⊕ *www.serafinipelletteria.it* ۩ *Closed Sun.* Ⓜ *Ottaviano.*

PIAZZA NAVONA AND CAMPO DE' FIORI

PIAZZA NAVONA

The area around Piazza Navona is filled with vintage boutiques and tiny artisan shops; unique gifts such as delicate Florentine stationery or hand-blown Murano glass can be found here. Near the Pantheon, you'll also find some classic Italian toys like wooden Pinocchios and cuckoo clocks.

ANTIQUES

Galleria Biagiarelli. Rome's leading antiques dealer of 18th- and 19th-century Russian icons and religious artifacts resides in a superb setting in the former chapel of the Pre-Renaissance Palazzo Capranica. The shop also features an exquisite array of English watercolors, Eastern European antique china figurines, and a vast collection of Soviet-era artwork. ⊠ *Piazza Capranica 97, Piazza Navona* ☎ *06/69940728* ⊕ *www. biagiarelli.it* ۩ *Closed on Sun. and Mon..*

Nardecchia. Since the 1950s, the Nardecchia family has been in the business of selling beautiful 19th-century prints, old photographs, and

15

watercolors that depict Rome in centuries past. Can't afford an 18th-century etching? They have beautiful postcards too. ⊠ *Via del Monserrato 106, Piazza Navona* ☎ *06/6869318.*

BEAUTY

Fodor's Choice **Ai Monasteri.** Among dark-wood paneling, choirlike alcoves, and painted
★ angels, at Ai Monasteri you'll find traditional products made by Italy's diligent friars and monks. Following century-old recipes, the herbal decoctions, liqueurs, beauty aids, and toiletries offer a look into the time-honored tradition of monastic trade. The Elixir dell'Amore (Love Potion) is perfect for any well-deserving valentine, or, if it isn't true love, you can opt for a bottle of the popular Elixir of Happiness. Other popular items include colognes for children to quince-apple and Cistercian jams, made exclusively with organic produce and Royal Jelly honey. ⊠ *Corso del Rinascimento 72a, Piazza Navona* ☎ *06/68802783* ⊕ *www.aimonasteri.it.*

Antica Erboristeria Romana. Complete with hand-labeled wooden drawers holding more than 200 varieties of herbs, flowers, and tinctures, Antica Erboristeria Romana has maintained its old-world apothecary feel (it's the oldest shop of its kind in Rome, dating back to 1752). The shop stocks an impressive array of teas and herbal infusions, more than 700 essential oils, bud derivatives, and powdered extracts. ⊠ *Via Torre Argentina 15, Piazza Navona* ☎ *06/6879493* ⊕ *www.anticaerboristeriaromana.it.*

CERAMICS AND DECORATIVE ARTS

Fodor's Choice **IN.OR. dal 1952.** For more than 50 years, IN.OR. dal 1952 has served
★ as a trusty friend for Romans in desperate need of an exclusive wedding gift or those oh-so-perfect china place settings for a fancy Sunday dinner. With seven rooms for browsing, the shop specializes in work handcrafted by the silversmiths of Pampaloni in Florence and Bellotto of Padua. ⊠ *Via della Stelletta 23, Piazza Navona* ☎ *06/6878579* ⊕ *www.inor.it.*

Murano Più. If you can't make it to Venice during your visit to the "Bel Paese," your next best option is to visit Murano Più for famous hand-blown Venetian glass pieces, including Murano jewelry (necklaces and pendants), tableware, vases, and extravagant chandeliers. Each individual piece is handcrafted from the furnaces of master glassblowers using ancient techniques kept alive by the island's artisans since 1291. ⊠ *Corso Rinascimento 53/55, Piazza Navona* ☎ *06/68301170* ⊕ *www.muranopiumadeinitaly.com.*

CLOTHING

Arsenale. Roman designer Patrizia Pieroni's sleek, unique, high-end fashion items stand out no matter the season. Her store, Arsenale, features everything from cleverly cut, stylish overcoats and seductive bustiers to sexy, flowing dresses perfect for the summer. ⊠ *Via del Pellegrino 172, Piazza Navona* ☎ *06/68802424* ⊕ *www.patriziapieroni.it.*

Davide Cenci. Thanks to immaculate tailoring and custom-designed clothing, Davide Cenci is an Italian fashion powerhouse. The store features high-quality men's and women's clothing for every occasion. Cenci's clothiers will tailor most anything to fit your body like a glove and have it delivered to your hotel within three days. The label is famous for its opulent cashmere, sailing sportswear, and trench coats, and you will appreciate their customer service and attention to detail. ⊠ *Via Campo Marzio 1–7, Piazza Navona* ☎ *06/6990681* ⊕ *www.davidecenci.com.*

Le Tartarughe. A familiar face on the catwalk of Rome's fashion shows, designer Susanna Liso, a Rome native, adds suggestive elements of playful experimentation to her haute couture and ready-to-wear lines, which are much loved by Rome's aristocracy and intelligentsia. With intense, enveloping designs, she mixes raw silks or cashmere and fine merino wool together to form captivating garments that mix seduction and linear form. ⊠ *Via Piè di Marmo 17, Piazza Navona* ☎ *06/6792240* ⊕ *www.letartarughe.eu.*

Mado. A leader in nostalgia styling, often appearing on the pages of *Vogue Italia* and *Vanity Fair,* Mado has been vintage cool in Rome since 1969. The shop is funky, glamorous, and often over-the-top wacky. Whether you are looking for a robin's egg–blue empire-waist dress or a 1950s gown evocative of a Lindy Hop, Mado understands the challenges of incorporating vintage pieces into a modern wardrobe. ⊠ *Via del Governo Vecchio 89/a, Piazza Navona* ☎ *06/6798660.*

15

Replay. A typical example of young Italians' passion for American trends, Replay has jeans and T-shirts with American sports teams emblazoned on them—with that little extra Italian kiss that transforms sloppy hip into fashionable casual-chic. Styles range from punk to hip-hop. Strictly for those under 30, with cash to spare. ⊠ *Via della Rotonda 24, Piazza Navona* ☎ *06/68301212* ⊕ *www.replay.it.*

SBU. SBU stands for Strategic Business Unit, a hip menswear fashion label created by the Perfetti brothers in 1993. Just as their last name suggests, the jeans, casual clothing, shoes and other sportswear sold here are just plain *perfetti.* In a 19th-century former draper's workshop, it's the place where Rome's VIPs buy their soft and supple vintage low-cut Japanese denims. The label also does well with its clothes among A-listers in Paris, London, and Los Angeles. ⊠ *Via di San Pantaleo 68–69, Piazza Navona* ☎ *06/68802547.*

Taro. Designed by owners Marisa Pignataro and Enrico Natoli, Taro's chic handmade knitwear in unusual yarns and striking colors is handmade in Rome. Selections from their casual, easy-to-wear line include luxuriously textured tunics, loose sleeveless jackets, and shawls and pants. ⊠ *Via di Ripetta 144, Piazza Navona* ☎ *06/6896476.*

Vestiti Usati Cinzia. Vintage clothes hunters, costume designers, and stylists alike love browsing through the racks at Vestiti Usati Cinzia. The shop is fun and very inviting and stocked with wall-to-wall funky '60s and '70s apparel and loads of goofy sunglasses. There's definitely no shortage of flower power bell bottoms and hippie shirts, embroidered tops, trippy and psychedelic boots, and other awesome accessories that will take you back to the days of peace and love. ⊠ *Via del Governo Vecchio 45, Piazza Navona* ☎ *06/6832945.*

FOOD AND WINE

Enoteca al Parlamento Achilli. The proximity of this traditional enoteca to Montecitorio, the Italian Parliament building, makes it a favorite with journalists and politicos, who often stop in for a glass of wine after work. But it's the tantalizing smell of truffles from the snack counter, where a sommelier waits to organize your tasting, that will probably lure you into Enoteca al Parlamento Achilli. There's also a lovely little restaurant where you can book a table and munch on a lovely array of cheese, salumi, and other cured meats. Don't forget to check out their wine shop to take home a bottle of your favorite wine. ⊠ *Via dei Prefetti 15, Piazza Navona* ☎ *06/6873446* ⊕ *www.enotecaalparlamento.it.*

Moriondo e Gariglio. Not exactly Willy Wonka (but in the same vein), Moriondo e Gariglio is a chocolate lover's paradise, churning out some of the finest chocolate delicacies in town. The shop dates back to 1850 and adheres strictly to family recipes passed on from generation to generation. In 2009, the shop partnered with Bulgari and placed 300 pieces of jewelry in their Easter eggs to benefit cancer research. While you may not find diamonds in your bonbons, marrons glacés, or dark-chocolate truffles, you'll still delight in choosing from more than 80 delicacies. ⊠ *Via Piè di Marmo 21, Piazza Navona* ☎ *06/6990856.*

HOME DECOR

Society. Have decorator envy? Everything you need for do-it-yourself Italian home couture can be found at Society, the flagship store for Limonta, one of the most prestigious and historic textile brands made in Italy. Centering on the rarest and most sought-after fabrics, their designs give the appearance they come from a different era (the 18th, 19th, and 20th centuries). You'll find everything from plush striped duvet covers and fancy table linens to comfy robes and other clothing perfect for lounging around the house. ⊠ *Piazza di Pasquino 4, Piazza Navona* ☎ *06/6832480* ⊕ *www.societylimonta.com.*

Tebro. First opened in 1867 and listed with the Associazione Negozi Storici di Roma (Association of Historic Shops of Rome), Tebro is a classic Roman department store that epitomizes quality. It specializes in household linens and sleepwear, and you can even find those 100-percent cotton, Italian waffle-weave bath sheets that are synonymous with Italian hotels. ⊠ *Via dei Prefetti 48, Piazza Navona* ☎ *06/6873441* ⊕ *www.tebro.it.*

JEWELRY

Delfina Delettrez. When your great grandmother is Adele Fendi, it's not surprising that creativity runs in your genes. Young Roman designer Delfina Delettrez creates edgy, glam-rock accessories using human body–inspired pieces that blend skulls, wild animals, and botanical elements in her jewelry. Delettrez also daringly merges gold, silver, bone and glass, crystals and diamonds to create gothic styles worthy of Fritz Lang's *Metropolis,*or *Blade Runner.* ⊠ *Via del Governo Vecchio 67, Piazza Navona* ☎ *06/68136362* ⊕ *www.delfinadelettrez.com.*

MMM—Massimo Maria Melis. Drawing heavily on ancient Roman and Etruscan designs, Massimo Maria Melis jewelry will carry you back in time. Working with 21-carat gold, he often incorporates antique coins in many of his exquisite bracelets and necklaces. Some of his pieces are done with an ancient technique, much-loved by the Etruscans, in which tiny gold droplets are soldered together to create intricately patterned designs. ⊠ *Via dell'Orso 57, Piazza Navona* ☎ *06/6869188* ⊕ *www. massimomariamelis.com.*

Quattrocolo. This historic shop dating to 1938 showcases exquisite antique micro-mosaic jewelry painstakingly crafted in the style perfected by the masters at the Vatican mosaic studio. You'll also find 18th- and 19th-century cameos and beautiful engraved stones. Their small works were beloved by cosmopolitan clientele of the Grand Tour age and offer modern-day shoppers a taste of yesteryear's grandeur. ⊠ *Via della Scrofa 48, Piazza Navona* ☎ *06/68801367* ⊕ *www.quat-trocolo.com.*

SHOES AND ACCESSORIES

Spazio IF. In a tiny piazza alongside Rome's historic Via dei Coronari, designers Irene and Carla Ferrara have created a tantalizing hybrid between fashion paradise and art gallery. Working with unconventional designers and artists who emphasize Sicilian design, the shop has more to say about the style of Sicily and the creativity of the island's inhabitants than flat caps, puppets, and rich pastries. Perennial favorites include handbags cut by hand in a shop in Palermo, swimsuits, designer textiles, jewelry, and sportswear. ⊠ *Via dei Coronari 44a, Piazza Navona* ☎ *06/64760639* ⊕ *www.spazioif.it.*

Superga. In business for over 100 years, Superga sells those timeless sneakers that every Italian wears at some point, in classic white or—yum—a rainbow of colors. Their 2750 model has been worn by every one from Kelly Brook to Katie Holmes. If you are a sneakerhead stuck on Converse, give these Italian brethren a look. ⊠ *Via delle Vite 86, Piazza Navona* ☎ *06/6787654* ⊕ *www.superga.com* Ⓜ *Spagna.*

STATIONERY

Cartoleria Pantheon dal 1910. Instead of sending a postcard home, head to the simply sumptuous Cartoleria Pantheon dal 1910 for fine handmade paper to write that special letter. In addition to simple, stock paper and artisanal sheets of handcrafted Amalfi paper, there are hand-bound leather journals in an extraordinary array of colors and sizes. The store has two other locations in the neighborhood. ⊠ *Via della Rotonda 15, Piazza Navona* ☎ *06/6875313* ⊕ *www.pantheon-roma.it* Ⓜ *Barberini.*

Il Papiro. One of Rome's preferred shops for those who appreciate exquisite writing materials and papermaking techniques that are almost extinct, Il Papiro sells hand-decorated papers made using the 17th-century marbleized technique called *à la cuve.* Their stationery and card-stock are printed with great care using exacting standards. Whether you are searching for unique lithography, engraving, or delicate water-marked paper, you'll find some indulgence here. They also carry a fine selection of wax seals, presses for paper embossing, Venetian glass pens, and ink stamps. ⊠ *Via del Pantheon 50, Piazza Navona* ☎ *06/6795597.*

15

TOYS

FAMILY **Al Sogno.** If you're looking for quality toys that encourage imaginative play and learning, look no further than Al Sogno. With an emphasis on the artistic as well as the multisensory, the shop has a selection of toys that are both discerning and individual, making them perfect for children of all ages. Carrying an exquisite collection of fanciful puppets, collectible dolls, masks, stuffed animals, and illustrated books, this Navona jewel, around since 1945, is crammed top-to-bottom with beautiful, well-crafted playthings. If you believe that children's toys don't have to be high-tech, you will adore reliving some of your best childhood memories here. ⊠ *Piazza Navona 53, corner of Via Agonale, Piazza Navona* ☎ *06/6864198* ⊕ *www.alsogno.net.*

FAMILY **Bartolucci.** For more than 60 years and three generations, the Bartolucci

Fodor's Choice family has been making whimsical, handmade curiosities out of pine,

★ including cuckoo clocks, bookends, bedside lamps, and wall hangings. You can even buy a child-size vintage car entirely made of wood (wheels, too!). Don't miss the life-size Pinocchio pedaling furiously on a wooden bike ⊠ *Via dei Pastini 98, Piazza Navona* ☎ *06/69190894* ⊕ *www.bartolucci.com.*

FAMILY **Bertè.** One of the oldest toy shops in Rome, Bertè carries a large selection of dolls, stuffed animals, Legos, and other collectibles. Located right in the heart of Piazza Navona, it's truly a paradise for children of all ages. ⊠ *Piazza Navona 108, Piazza Navona* ☎ *06/6875011.*

FAMILY **La Città del Sole.** Chock-full of fair-trade and eco-friendly toys that share shelf space with retro and vintage favorites, La Città del Sole is the perfect place for parents looking to stock up on educational toys. The store, which arranges toys by age group, is a child-friendly browser's delight crammed with puzzles, gadgets, books, and toys in safe plastics and sustainable wood. The knowledgeable sales staff can help you choose the perfect age-appropriate gift. ⊠ *Via della Scrofa 65, Piazza Navona* ☎ *06/68803805* ⊕ *www.cittadelsole.it.*

CAMPO DE' FIORI

Campo de' Fiori, one of Rome's most captivating piazzas, comes to life early in the morning, when merchants theatrically sell their best tomatoes, salumi, artichokes, blood oranges, herbs, and spices. Around the piazza, labyrinthine streets are crowded with small shops to suit any budget.

BOOKS AND STATIONERY

Libreria del Viaggiatore. *Viaggiatore* means "traveler" in Italian, and this lovely little bookstore, which recently moved to a larger location on the same quaint side street off Campo de' Fiori, welcomes wandering, curious travelers. The shop stocks guidebooks, maps, travel journals, and poetry from all over the world, in English as well as French and Italian. ⊠ *Via del Pellegrino 165, Campo de' Fiori* ☎ *06/68801048.*

CHILDREN'S CLOTHING

FAMILY **Rachele.** Rachele is a small, charming shop near the Piazza Campo de' Fiori that sells original and whimsical handmade children's clothing. If you're looking for something truly unique, Rachele (the Swedish owner and designer) makes only two of everything for tykes up to age 12. Your children can make a statement with any of her cute pants, skirts or rainbow-color tops. ⊠ *Vicolo del Bollo 6–7, Campo de' Fiori* ☎ *06/6864975.*

SHOES, HANDBAGS, AND LEATHER GOODS

Ibiz–Artigianato in Cuoio. In business since 1970, this father-and-daughter team creates colorful, stylish leather handbags, belts, and sandals near Piazza Campo de' Fiori. Choose from the premade collection or order something made to measure; their workshop is right next door to the boutique. ⊠ *Via dei Chiavari 39, Campo de' Fiori* ☎ *06/68307297.*

PIAZZA DI SPAGNA

15

The Piazza di Spagna area is considered to be the heart and soul of shopping in Rome, with all the international chains, as well as independent shops. If your budget isn't big enough to binge at the high-end fashion houses along Via dei Condotti, try the more moderate shops down Via del Corso, where young Romans come to shop for jeans and inexpensive, trendy clothes. As you move toward Piazza del Popolo, at one end of Via del Corso, you'll find more antiques shops and galleries.

ANTIQUES

FAMILY **Antica Farmacia Pesci dal 1552.** In business since 1552, the Antica Farmacia—likely Rome's oldest pharmacy—is run by a family of pharmacists. The shop's 18th-century furnishings, herbs, and vases evoke Harry Potter's Diagon Alley; and while they don't carry Polyjuice Potion, the pharmacists can whip up a just-for-you batch of composite powders, syrups, capsules, gels, and creams to soothe what ails you. ⊠ *Piazza di Trevi 89, Piazza di Spagna* ☎ *06/6792210* ⊕ *www.anticafarmaciapesci. it* Ⓜ *Barberini.*

Galleria Benucci. With carved and gilded late Baroque and Empire period furniture and paintings culled from the noble houses of Italy's past, Galleria Benucci is a literal treasure trove. An establishment favored by professionals from Europe and abroad, this elegant gallery has an astonishing selection of objects in a hushed atmosphere where connoisseurs will find the proprietors only too happy to discuss their latest finds. ⊠ *Via del Babuino 150/C, Piazza di Spagna* ☎ *06/36002190* ⊕ *www. galleriabenucci.it* Ⓜ *Spagna.*

BEAUTY

Castelli Profumerie. This straightforward Italian perfume shop has one distinct advantage: besides being a perfumed paradise offering an array of labels like Acqua di Parma, Bois 1920, Bond No. 9, and Comme de Garçons, their precise and courteous staff speak multiple languages and know their merchandise, making the experience a lot more pleasant than a dash through duty-free. There are four other locations around the city: two on Via Frattina, one on Via dei Condotti, and another on Via Oslavia in the Prati neighborhood. ⊠ *Via Frattina 18 and 54, Piazza di Spagna* ☎ *06/6790339* ⊕ *www.profumeriecastelli.com* Ⓜ *Spagna.*

Pro Fvmvm. Started in 1996 by the grandchildren of Celestino Durante, Pro Fvmvm is fast on its way to becoming a new cult classic in Italian fragrance design. Each of the 20 scents is designed to be unisex and comes complete with a poem that describes the intention of the artisans. Pricey but worth it, some of their top-selling perfumes are Acqva e Zvcchero, Fiore d'Ambra, Thvndra, Volo Az 686 (named after a direct flight from Rome to the Caribbean), and Ichnvsa. ⊠ *Via Ripetta 10, Piazza di Spagna* ☎ *06/3200306* ⊕ *www.profumum.com* Ⓜ *Spagna.*

BOOKS AND STATIONERY

Anglo-American Book Co. A large and friendly English-language bookstore with more than 45,000 books, Anglo-American Book has been a mecca for English-language reading material in Rome for more than 25 years. Whether you are a study-abroad student in need of an art history or archaeology textbook, or a visitor searching for a light read for the train, there is something for everyone here. Among shelves stuffed from floor to ceiling and sometimes several rows deep, book lovers can find British and American editions and easily spend hours just looking. The bilingual staff always go the extra mile to find what you need. ⊠ *Via della Vite 102, Piazza di Spagna* ☎ *06/6795222* ⊕ *www. aab.it* Ⓜ *Spagna.*

Ex Libris. Founded in 1931 and one of the oldest antiquarian bookshops in Rome, Ex Libris has a distinctive selection of scholarly and collectible books from the 16th to 21st century that will make bookworms drool. The selection includes rare editions on art and architecture, music and theater, and literature and humanities, as well as maps and prints. ⊠ *Via dell' Umiltà 77/a, Piazza di Spagna* ☎ *06/6791540* ⊕ *www.exlibrisroma.it* Ⓜ *Barberini.*

La Feltrinelli. On any given day, you're sure to walk in on a special reading or a meet-and-greet with a famous Italian bestselling author at La Feltrinell's flagship store. Situated in a prime location, the elegant 19th-century Galleria Alberto Sordi, this megabookstore fills three floors with books (including a selection in English), music, postcards, holiday items, and small gifts. A great place to explore Italian-style book shopping, there are 12 branches peppered throughout the city. The Torre Argentina shop also has a ticketing office for music and cultural events and a caffè tucked upstairs with refreshing snacks and good coffee. The Repubblica branch carries the largest section of English language titles. ⊠ *Piazza Colonna 31/35, Piazza di Spagna* ☎ *06/69755001* ⊕ *www. lafeltrinelli.it* Ⓜ *Barberini.*

CERAMICS AND DECORATIVE ARTS

Ceramiche Musa. Musa is the place to shop if you want to transform your home into a fancy Italian villa. The store is full of decorative ceramic accents and extravagant hand-painted ceramic tiles from Vietri, a region renowned for the quality of its clays and artisanal ceramic tradition. Want to take some home but don't have enough room in your suitcase? No problem: shipping can be arranged. ⊠ *Via di Campo Marzio 39, Piazza di Spagna* ☎ *06/6871202* ⊕ *www.ceramichemusa.it* Ⓜ *Spagna.*

Le IV Stagioni. If you're looking to purchase some traditional Italian pottery, Le IV Stagioni has a colorful selection of glazed pots, vases, and charming ceramic-flower wall ornaments made by well-known manufacturers such as Faenza, Capodimonte, Vietri, and Deruta. ⊠ *Via dell'Umiltà 30/b, Piazza di Spagna* ☎ *06/69941029* Ⓜ *Barberini.*

Marmi Line Gifts. For a wide variety of marble and alabaster objets d'art, Marmi Line offers three locations in central Rome (the other two are in Trastevere). Beautifully worked into familiar shapes, their mesmerizing pieces of fruit form centerpieces that would make Caravaggio proud. If you want something distinctly Roman, choose a practical or whimsical item made from travertine, the stone used to build the Colosseum and Bernini's St. Peter's Colonnade. ⊠ *Via dei Pastini 113, Piazza di Spagna* ☎ *06/69200711* Ⓜ *Barberini.*

15

CHILDREN'S CLOTHING

FAMILY **Pinco Pallino.** Recently relocated to a larger location, Pinco Pallino has extraordinary clothing for boys and girls, be it a sedate tulle petal jumper or savvy sailor wear. Moms will find their latest lines for babies and tots absolutely delicious. ⊠ *Via Vittoria 35, Piazza di Spagna* ☎ *06 /3212741* ⊕ *www.pincopallino.it* Ⓜ *Spagna.*

FAMILY **Pùre Sermoneta.** Well-heeled moms shop for their budding fashionistas at Pùre Sermoneta where you'll find garments straight off the catwalk. High-end designer labels include Fendi, Diesel, Dior, Juicy Couture, Nolita, and Miss Blumarine. The store has plush carpet to crawl on and children's clothes for newborns to age 12. ⊠ *Via Frattina 111, Piazza di Spagna* ☎ *06/6794555* ⊕ *www.puresermoneta.it.*

CLOTHING

Fodor'sChoice **Brioni.** Founded in 1945 and hailed for its impeccable craftsmanship
★ and flawless execution, the Brioni label is known for attracting and keeping the best men's tailors in Italy, where the exacting standards require that custom-made suits are designed from scratch and measured to the millimeter. For this personalized line, the menswear icon has 5,000 spectacular fabrics to select from. As thoughtful as expensive, one bespoke suit made from wool will take a minimum of 32 hours to create. Their prêt-à-porter line is also praised for peerless cutting and stitching. Past and present clients include Clark Gable, Barack Obama and, of course, James Bond. ⊠ *Via del Babuino 38/40, Piazza di Spagna* ☎ *06/484517* ⊕ *www.brioni.com* Ⓜ *Spagna.*

Dolce & Gabbana. Dolce and Gabbana met in 1980 when both were assistants at a Milan fashion atelier, and they opened their first store in 1982. With a modern aesthetic that screams sex appeal, the brand has always thrived on excess. The Rome store can be more than a little overwhelming, with its glossy decor and blaring music, but at least there's plenty of eye candy—masculine and feminine alike. There is a second location on Via dei Condotti. ⊠ *Piazza di Spagna 94–95, Piazza di Spagna* ☎ *06/6991592* ⊕ *www.dolcegabbana.it* Ⓜ *Spagna.*

Eddy Monetti. Eddy Monetti is a conservative but upscale men's store featuring jackets, sweaters, slacks, and ties made out of wool, cotton, and cashmere. Sophisticated and pricey, the store carries a range of stylish British- and Italian-made pieces. ⊠ *Via Borgognona 36, Piazza di Spagna* ☎ *06/6794117* ⊕ *www.eddymonetti.com* Ⓜ *Spagna.*

Elena Mirò. Elena Mirò is a high-end brand that specializes in sophisticated, beautifully sexy clothes for curvy, European-styled women size 46 (U.S. size 12, U.K. size 14) and up. There are several locations in Rome, including one in Prati and one in the San Giovanni neighborhood. ⊠ *Via Frattina 11–12, Piazza di Spagna* ☎ *06/6784367* ⊕ *www. elenamiro.it* Ⓜ *Spagna.*

Ermenegildo Zegna. For more than 100 years, Ermenegildo Zegna, has been a powerhouse of men's clothing. Believing that construction and fabric are the key, Zegna is the master of both. Suits here start from €1,500, with the top of the line, known as "Couture," costing considerably more. ⊠ *Via dei Condotti 58, Piazza di Spagna* ☎ *06/69940678* ⊕ *www.zegna.com* Ⓜ *Spagna.*

Fodor's Choice
★ **Fendi.** Fendi has been a fixture of the Roman fashion landscape since "Mamma" Fendi first opened shop with her husband in 1925. With an eye for crazy genius, she hired Karl Lagerfeld, who began working with the group at the start of his career. His furs and runway antics have made him worldwide one of the most influential designers of the 20th century and brought international acclaim to Fendi along the way. Recent Lagerfeld triumphs include new collections marrying innovative textures and fabrics (cashmere, felt, and duchesse satin) with exotic skins like crocodile. Keeping up with technology, they even have an iPad case that will surely win a fashionista's seal of approval. The atelier, now owned by the Louis Vuitton group, continues to symbolize Italian glamour at its finest, though the difference in ownership is noticeable. It's also gotten new life in the Italian press for its "Fendi for Fountains" campaign, which recently included funding the restoration of Rome's Trevi Fountain. ⊠ *Largo Carlo Goldoni 419–421, Piazza di Spagna* ☎ *06/3344501* ⊕ *www.fendi.com* Ⓜ *Spagna.*

Galassia. Classy, avant-garde women's styles by A-list designers including Gaultier, Westwood, Issey Miyake, and Yamamoto can be found at Galassia. If you're the type who dares to be different and you're in need of some closet therapy, you will love the extravagant selection, which gives the store a look that cannot be found elsewhere. ⊠ *Via Frattina 20, Piazza di Spagna* ☎ *06/6797896* ⊕ *www.galassiaroma.com* Ⓜ *Spagna.*

Giorgio Armani. One of the most influential designers of Italian haute couture, Giorgio Armani creates fluid silhouettes and dazzling evening gowns with décolletage so deep they'd make a grown man blush; his signature cuts are made with the clever-handedness and flawless technique achievable only by working with tracing paper and Italy's finest fabrics over the course of a lifetime. His menswear collection uses traditional textiles like wide-ribbed corduroy and stretch jersey in nontraditional ways while staying true to a clean, masculine aesthetic. It's true that exotic runway ideas and glamorous celebrities give Armani strong selling points, but his staying power is casual Italian elegance with just the right touch of whimsy and sexiness. ⊠ *Via dei Condotti 77–79, Piazza di Spagna* ☎ *06/6991460* ⊕ *www.giorgioarmani.com* Ⓜ *Spagna.*

Fodor's Choice
★ **Gucci.** As the glamorous fashion label approaches its centennial, the success of the double-G trademark is unquestionable. The fashion house is still seeking to maintain the label's trendiness while bringing in a breath of fresh air. Tom Ford may have made Gucci the sexiest label in the world, but it's today's reinterpreted horsebit styles and Jackie Kennedy scarves that keep the design house on top. And while Gucci remains a fashion must for virtually every A-list celebrity, their designs have moved from heart-stopping sexy rock star to something classically subdued and retrospectively feminine. There's another store on Via Borgognona. ⊠ *Via dei Condotti 8, Piazza di Spagna* ☎ *06/6790405* ⊕ *www.gucci.com* Ⓜ *Spagna.*

15

Krizia. Designer Mariuccia Mandelli borrowed the name "Krizia" from the title of Plato's unfinished dialogue on women's vanity. Born in 1933, she began designing dresses for her dolls at age 8. The designer's collections have gone through many top stylists and have recently returned to their original stylized roots. The current prêt-à-porter line emphasizes the use of black and dove gray, mixed with animal prints: it's dramatic, yet classy—wearing Krizia will get you noticed. ⊠ *Piazza di Spagna 87, Piazza di Spagna* ☎ *06/6793772* ⊕ *www.krizia.it* Ⓜ *Spagna.*

Fodor's Choice
★ **Laura Biagiotti.** For 40 years Laura Biagiotti has been a worldwide ambassador of Italian fashion. Considered the Queen of Cashmere, her soft-as-velvet pullovers have been worn by Sophia Loren, and her snow-white cardigans were said to be a favorite of the late pope John Paul II. Princess Diana even sported one of Biagiotti's cashmere maternity dresses. Be sure to indulge in sampling her line of his-and-her perfumes. ⊠ *Via Mario de' Fiori 26, Piazza di Spagna* ☎ *06/6791205* ⊕ *www.laurabiagiotti.it* Ⓜ *Spagna.*

Missoni. Notable for its bohemian knitwear designs with now-legendary patterns of zigzags, waves, and stripes (some of which are influenced by folk art), as well as elegant eveningwear and must-have swimsuits, Missoni is unlike other Italian fashion families: in three generations there have been neither vendettas nor buyouts by huge multinational conglomerates to stain their colorful history. ⊠ *Piazza di Spagna 78, Piazza di Spagna* ☎ *06/6792555* ⊕ *www.missoni.it* Ⓜ *Spagna.*

Fodor's Choice
★ **Patrizia Pepe.** One of Florence's best-kept secrets for up-and-coming fashions, Patrizia Pepe first emerged on the scene in 1993 with designs both minimalist and bold, combining classic styles with low-slung jeans and jackets with oversize lapels that are bound to draw attention. Her line of shoes are hot-hot-hot for those who can walk on stilts. It's still

not huge on the fashion scene as a stand-alone brand, but take a look at this shop before the line becomes the next fast-tracked craze. ⊠ *Via Frattina 44, Piazza di Spagna* ☏ *06/6781851* ⊕ *www.patriziapepe.com* Ⓜ *Spagna.*

Fodor's Choice **Prada.** Besides the devil, plenty of serious shoppers wear Prada season
★ after season, especially those willing to sell their souls for one of their ubiquitous handbags. If you are looking for that blend of old-world luxury with a touch of fashion-forward finesse, you'll hit pay dirt here. Recent handbag designs have a bit of a 1960s Jackie Kennedy feel, and whether you like them will hinge largely on whether you find Prada's signature retro-modernism enchanting. You'll find the Rome store more service-oriented than the New York City branches—a roomy elevator delivers you to a series of thickly carpeted rooms where a flock of discreet assistants will help you pick out dresses, shoes, lingerie, and fashion accessories. The men's store is located at Via dei Condotti 88/90, women's down the street at 92/95. ⊠ *Via dei Condotti 88/90 and 92/95, Piazza di Spagna* ☏ *06/6790897* ⊕ *www.prada.com* Ⓜ *Spagna.*

Renard. A leather boutique that scrupulously selects from superior quality leather hides, Renard carries leathers tanned with natural extracts, not chemicals, a slow process that maintains the hides' original properties. Choose from classic leather blazers, trench coats, and skirts in various colors and styles. Be sure to eye their racy motorcycle styles, perfect for gutsy, windswept Ducati rides. ⊠ *Via dei Due Macelli 53, Piazza di Spagna* ☏ *06/6797004* Ⓜ *Spagna.*

Salvatore Ferragamo. A major fashion player when it comes to footwear, Hollywood's gliteratti and social butterflies trust their pretty little feet with one brand: Salvatore Ferragamo. Fans will think they have died and followed the white light when they enter this store. The Florentine design house also specializes in handbags, small leather goods, men's and women's ready-to-wear, and scarves and ties. Men's styles are found at Via dei Condotti 65, women's at 73/74. Want to sleep in Ferragamo style? Their splendid luxury Portrait Suites Hotel is on the upper floors. ⊠ *Via dei Condotti 65 and 73/74, Piazza di Spagna* ☏ *06/6781130* ⊕ *www.ferragamo.com* Ⓜ *Spagna.*

Save the Queen! A hot Florentine design house with exotic and creative pieces for women with artistic and eccentric frills, cutouts, and textures, Save the Queen! has one of the most beautiful shops in the city, with window displays that are works of art unto themselves. The store is chock-full of baroque-inspired dresses, shirts, and skirts that are ultra-feminine and not the least bit discreet. Pieces radiate charming excess, presenting a portrait of youthful chic. ⊠ *Via del Babuino 49, Piazza di Spagna* ☏ *06/36003039* ⊕ *www.savethequeen.com* Ⓜ *Spagna.*

Fodor's Choice **Valentino.** Since taking the Valentino reins nearly 10 years ago, cre-
★ ative directors Maria Grazia Chiuri and Pierpaolo Piccioli have faced numerous challenges, the most basic of which is keeping Valentino true to Valentino after the designer's retirement in 2008. Both served as accessories designers under Valentino for more than a decade and understand exactly how to make the next generation of Hollywood stars swoon. Valentino has taken over most of Piazza di Spagna, where

multiple boutiques showcase designs with a romantic edginess; think kitten heels or a show-stopping prêt-à-porter evening gown worthy of the Oscars. ⊠ *Via dei Condotti 15, Piazza di Spagna* ☎ *06/6739420* ⊕ *www.valentino.com* Ⓜ *Spagna.*

Versace. Versace's new Rome flagship, which opened in a palazzo at the Piazza di Spagna in fall 2013, is a gem of architecture and design, with Byzantine-inspired mosaic floors and futuristic interiors, not to mention, of course, fashion: here shoppers will find apparel, jewelry, watches, fragrances, cosmetics, and home furnishings in designs every bit as flamboyant as Donatella and Allegra (Gianni's niece), drawing heavily on the sexy rocker gothic underground vibe. There's also a smaller boutique on the Via Veneto with prêt-à-porter and jewelry. ⊠ *Piazza di Spagna 12, Piazza di Spagna* ☎ *06/6691773* ⊕ *www.versace.com* Ⓜ *Spagna.*

DEPARTMENT STORES

15

La Rinascente. Located inside the chic Galleria Alberto Sordi, La Rinascente is Italy's best-known department store. It's also the store where Italian fashion genius Giorgio Armani got his start as a window dresser. Here, one can find oodles of cosmetics on the ground floor, as well as a phalanx of ready-to-wear designer sportswear and blockbuster handbags and accessories. The Piazza Fiume location has more floor space and a wider range of goods, including a homeware department. ⊠ *Galleria Alberto Sordi, Piazza Colonna, Piazza di Spagna* ☎ *06/6784209* ⊕ *www.rinascente.it* Ⓜ *Spagna.*

FOOD AND WINE

Buccone. A landmark wine shop inside the former coach house of the Marquese Cavalcabo, Buccone has 10 layers of shelves packed with quality wines and spirits ranging in price from a few euros to several hundred for rare vintages. The old atmosphere has been preserved in the original wood-beam ceiling and an antique till. You can also buy sweets, biscuits, and packaged candy perfect for inexpensive gifts. Lunch is available daily, and dinner is served Friday and Saturday (reservations required for dinner). Book a week in advance, and they can also give you a guided wine tasting, with highlights from many of Italy's important wine-producing regions. ⊠ *Via di Ripetta 19/20, Piazza di Spagna* ☎ *06/3612154* ⊕ *www.enotecabuccone.com* Ⓜ *Piazza del Popolo.*

HATS

Borsalino Boutique. Considered by many to be the Cadillac of fedoras, the dashing Borsolino fedora has been a staple of the fashionable Italian man since 1857. Adorning the heads of many silver-screen icons, including Humphrey Bogart and Gary Cooper, Borsalino retains its unmistakable class, style, and elegance. Few hats are made with such exacting care and attention, and the company's milliners still use machines that are more than 100 years old. Borsalino also has boutiques near the

Pantheon and Piazza di Spagna. ⊠ *Piazza del Popolo 20, Piazza di Spagna* ☎ *06/32650838* ⊕ *www.borsalino.it* Ⓜ *Flaminio.*

HOME DECOR

Cesari. Since 1946, Cesari is where Italian brides traditionally buy their trousseaux. Precious velvets, silks, cottons, damasks, and taffeta abound and are shippable internationally. Famous for their personalized line of bedspreads, tablecloths, lingerie, and embroidered linens, they supply their goods to high-end hotels and old-fashioned girls of all ages. Be sure to check their seashell-inspired Nettuno collection for a beach vibe, or its royal Palazzo Ducale collection if you want to add some new fancy Italian decor to your home. ⊠ *Via del Babuino 193, Piazza di Spagna* ☎ *06/3613456* ⊕ *www.cesari.com* Ⓜ *Spagna, Flaminio.*

Frette. Classic, luxurious, colorful, timeless, and fun, there is nothing like Frette's bed collections. A leader in luxurious linens and towels for the home and hotel industry since 1860, their sophisticated bed linens in cotton satin, percale, and silk are just what the doctor ordered for a great night's sleep. There is a second location nearby on Via del Corso near Piazza Colonna. ⊠ *Piazza di Spagna 11, Piazza di Spagna* ☎ *06/6790673* ⊕ *www.frette.com* Ⓜ *Spagna.*

JEWELRY

Bulgari. Every capital city has its famous jeweler, and Bulgari is to Rome what Tiffany is to New York and Cartier to Paris. The jewelry giant has developed a reputation for meticulous craftsmanship melding noble metals with precious gems. In the middle of the 19th century, the great-grandfather of the current Bulgari brothers began working as a silver jeweler in his native Greece and is said to have moved to Rome with less than 1,000 lire in his pocket. Today the megabrand emphasizes colorful and playful jewelry as the principal cornerstone of its aesthetic. Popular collections include Parentesi, Bulgari-Bulgari, and B.zero1. The Rome flagship store was refurbished in honor of the 130th anniversary, in 2015, and the restoration was hailed by critics for its savvy update that also stayed true to its 1930s modernist style. ⊠ *Via dei Condotti 10, Piazza di Spagna* ☎ *06/696261* ⊕ *www.bulgari.com* Ⓜ *Spagna.*

LINGERIE

Brighenti. Brighenti looks like what it is: a traditional Roman shop from a gentler era, replete with a marble floor and a huge crystal chandelier suspended overhead. Sexy silk nightgowns and classic sleepwear are available, as are sumptuous vintage-inspired swimsuits that will make you feel like Marlene Dietrich. There's a second location nearby on Via Borgognona. ⊠ *Via Frattina 7/8, Piazza di Spagna* ☎ *06/6791484* ⊕ *www.brighentiroma.it* Ⓜ *Barberini, Spagna.*

La Perla. La Perla is the go-to for beautifully crafted lingerie and glamorous underwear for that special night, a bridal trousseau, or just to spoil yourself on your Roman holiday. If you like decadent finery that is both stylish and romantic, you will find something here to make you feel like a goddess. There are silk boxers for gents here, too. ⊠ *Via Bocca di Leone 28, Piazza di Spagna* ☎ *06/69941934* ⊕ *www.laperla. com* Ⓜ *Spagna.*

Marisa Padovan. The place to go for exclusive, made-to-order lingerie and bathing suits, Marisa Padovan has been sewing for Hollywood starlets like Audrey Hepburn and the well-heeled women of Rome for more than 40 years. Whether you want to purchase a ready-made style trimmed with Swarovski crystals and polished turquoise stones or to design your own bespoke bikini or one-piece, their made-to-measure precision will have you looking like Rita Hayworth. ⊠ *Via delle Carrozze 81–82, Piazza di Spagna* ☎ *06/6793946* ⊕ *www.marisapadovan. it* Ⓜ *Spagna.*

MALLS

Galleria Alberto Sordi. This gorgeous covered shopping arcade on the Piazza Colonna was envisioned in the late 19th century but not built until the 20th, and finally opened to the public in 1922. It's worth a visit as much to marvel at the unique building as for its selection of classy shops. There are a couple of pleasant caffè on the concourse too. ⊠ *Via del Corso 79, Piazza di Spagna* ⊕ *www.galleriaalbertosordi.it* Ⓜ *Barberini.*

MARKETS

La Soffitta Sotto i Portici. For an interesting display of antique jewelry, furniture, artwork, and other collectibles, check out this colorful vintage market held on the first and third Sunday of every month. It's open from 9 am until sunset. ⊠ *Piazza Augusto Imperatore, Piazza di Spagna* ☎ *06/36005345* ⊕ *www.collezionando.org* Ⓜ *Spagna.*

SHOES, HANDBAGS, AND LEATHER GOODS

A. Testoni. Amedeo Testoni, the brand's founder and original designer, was born in 1905 in Bologna, the heart of Italy's shoemaking territory. In 1929, he opened his first shop and began producing shoes as artistic as the Cubist and Art Deco artwork of the period. His shoes have adorned the feet of Fred Astaire, proving that lightweight shoes can be comfortable and luxurious and still turn heads. Today the Testoni brand includes an extraordinary women's collection and a sports line that is relaxed without losing its artistic heritage. The soft, calfskin sneakers are a dream, as are the matching messenger bags. ⊠ *Via del Babuino 152, Piazza di Spagna* ☎ *06/6788944* ⊕ *www.testoni.com* Ⓜ *Spagna.*

Fodor's Choice ★ Braccialini. Founded in 1954 by Florentine stylist Carla Braccialini and her husband, Braccialini—currently managed by their sons—makes bags that are authentic works of art in delightful shapes, such as little gold taxis or Santa Fe stagecoaches. The delightfully quirky beach bags have picture-postcard scenes of Italian resorts made of brightly colored appliquéd leather: be sure to check out their eccentric Temi (Theme) creature bags; the opossum-shape handbag made out of crocodile skin makes a richly whimsical fashion statement. There's a second location at

15

the Galleria Alberto Sordi. ⊠ *Via Mario De' Fiori 73, Piazza di Spagna* ☎ *06/6785750* ⊕ *www.braccialini.it* Ⓜ *Spagna.*

Di Cori. A woman just isn't a signora without a good pair of gloves. With that in mind, head to Di Cori, which packs a lot of gloves into a tiny space, offering a rainbow of color choices. Made of the softest lambskin, and lined with silk, cashmere, rabbit fur, or wool, a pair of these gloves will ensure warm and fashionable hands. They also carry a smaller selection of unlined, washable versions. ⊠ *Piazza di Spagna 53, Piazza di Spagna* ☎ *06/6784439* ⊕ *www.dicorigloves.it* Ⓜ *Spagna.*

Fausto Santini. Shoe lovers with a passion for minimalist design flock to Fausto Santini to get their hands on his preppy-hipster/nerdy-chic shoes. Santini has been in business since 1970 and caters to a sophisticated, avant-garde clientele looking for elegant, classic shoes with a kick. An outlet at Via Cavour 106 sells last season's shoes at a deep discount. ⊠ *Via Frattina 120, Piazza di Spagna* ☎ *06/6784114* ⊕ *www. faustosantini.it* Ⓜ *Spagna.*

Fratelli Rossetti. An old-world company with modern aspirations, Fratelli Rossetti is the epitome of sophisticated, classic men's and women's leather shoes, loafers, and pumps. While their focus has always revolved around sheer classic elegance with an emphasis on quality and luxurious craftsmanship, their new line is a bit more playful and whimsical—think blue suede shoes, green plaid tweed fabric, and Hobo sparkling shoes. ⊠ *Via Borgognona 5/a, Piazza di Spagna* ☎ *06/6782676* ⊕ *www.rossetti.it* Ⓜ *Spagna.*

Furla. Furla sells high-end quality handbags and purses at affordable prices. There are multiple locations throughout the Eternal City (including one at Fiumicino Airport), but its flagship store can be found in the heart of Piazza di Spagna. Be prepared to fight your way through crowds of passionate handbag lovers, all anxious to possess one of the delectable bags, wallets, or watch straps in ice-cream colors. ⊠ *Piazza di Spagna 22, Piazza di Spagna* ☎ *06/69200363* ⊕ *www.furla. com* Ⓜ *Spagna.*

Gherardini. In business since 1885, Gherardini has taken over a deconsecrated church and slickly transformed it into a showplace for their label. Gherardini's leather totes, sling bags, and soft luggage have become classics, and the quality of each piece is worth the investment. ⊠ *Via Belsiana 48, Piazza di Spagna* ☎ *06/6795501* ⊕ *www.gherardini. it* Ⓜ *Spagna.*

Fodor's Choice ★ **Saddlers Union.** Reborn on the mythical artisan's street, Via Margutta, across the street from Federico Fellini's old house, Saddlers Union first launched in 1957 and quickly gained a cult following among those who valued Italian artistry and a traditional aesthetic. Jacqueline Kennedy set the trend of classical elegance by sporting Saddlers Union's rich saddle-leather bucket bag. If you're searching for a sinfully fabulous handbag in a graceful, classic shape or that "I have arrived" attorney's briefcase, you will find something guaranteed to inspire envy. Items are made on-site with true artistry and under the watchful eye of Angelo Zaza, one of Saddlers Union's original master artisans. Prices are a bit steep, but the quality is definitely worth it. ⊠ *Via Margutta 11, Piazza* *di Spagna* ☎ *06/32120237* ⊕ *www.saddlersunion.com* Ⓜ *Flaminio, Spagna.*

Schostal. A Piazza di Spagna fixture since 1870, the shop was once the go-to place for women looking to stock up on corsets, bonnets, stockings and petticoats. Today, it's the place to stop for fine-quality shirts, underwear, and handkerchiefs made of wool and pure cashmere at affordable prices. There's a second location at Piazza Euclide. ✉ *Via Fontanella Borghese 29, Piazza di Spagna* ☎ *06/6791240* ⊕ *www.schostalroma.com* Ⓜ *Spagna.*

Sermoneta. Whether you're looking for some fancy gloves to wear to the opera or for a fashionable pair of warm leather gloves to get you through the winter, Sermoneta has a vast selection to choose from. Browse through stacks of nappa leather, deerskin, and pigskin hand-stitched gloves in all colors. You can even have your gloves personalized with your own initials, logos, or other designs. ✉ *Piazza di Spagna 61, Piazza di Spagna* ☎ *06/6791960* ⊕ *www.sermonetagloves.com* Ⓜ *Spagna.*

Fodor'sChoice ★ **Tod's.** With just 30 years under its belt, Tod's has grown from a small family brand into a global powerhouse so wealthy that its owner, Diego Della Valle, donated €20 million to the Colosseum restoration project. The shoe baron's trademark is his simple, classic, understated designs. Sure to please are his light and flexible slip-on Gommini driving shoes with rubber-bottomed soles for extra driving-pedal grip—now you just need a Ferrari. There are also locations on Via dei Condotti and Via Borgogona. ✉ *Via Fontanella di Borghese 56a–57, Piazza di Spagna* ☎ *06/68210066* ⊕ *www.tods.com* Ⓜ *Spagna.*

STATIONERY

Fodor'sChoice ★ **Pineider.** This shop, near Piazza di Spagna, has been making exclusive stationery in Italy since 1774; this is where Rome's aristocratic families have their wedding invitations engraved and their stationery personalized. They also use the best Florentine leather for their wallets, briefcases, and other desk accessories. There's a second location on Via dei Due Macelli. ✉ *Via di Fontanella Borghese 22, Piazza di Spagna* ☎ *06/6878369* ⊕ *www.pineider.com* Ⓜ *Spagna.*

REPUBBLICA

In this neighborhood you'll find bookstores, souvenir shops, and places to shop for decorative pieces like Roman masks or busts.

BOOKS AND STATIONERY

Libreria IBS. One of the best parts of Libreria IBS (formerly known as Mel Bookstore) is the lovely Art Deco–style caffè where you can sip on a cappuccino while flipping through the pages of your new purchase. Another perk is the discount the store dishes out on its stock of remainders and secondhand books. The shop also has a modest selection of

English-language paperbacks and DVDs. ✉ *Via Nazionale 254–255, Repubblica* ☎ *06/4885405* ⊕ *www.ibs.it* Ⓜ *Repubblica.*

CERAMICS AND DECORATIVE ARTS

Il Giardino di Domenico Persiani. At first glance, you might be surprised to find a shop tucked away in this cool courtyard garden. Those curious enough to step inside will find a lovely little open-air terra-cotta shop called Il Giardino di Domenico Persiani. The shop features a large selection of handmade Roman masks, busts, flower pots, and vases; there is something here for anyone with a green thumb. ✉ *Via Torino 92, Repubblica* ☎ *06/4883886* Ⓜ *Repubblica.*

FOOD AND WINE

Trimani Vinai a Roma dal 1821. In business since 1821, Trimani Vinai a Roma occupies an entire block near Termini station with one of the city's largest selection of wines from all over Italy, plus champagne, spumante, grappa, and sundry liqueurs. With more than 1,000 bottles to choose from and knowledgeable wine stewards to consult, Trimani will give you the opportunity to explore Europe's diverse wine regions without leaving the city. ✉ *Via Goito 20, Repubblica* ☎ *06/4469661* ⊕ *www.trimani.com* Ⓜ *Castro Pretorio.*

MALLS AND SHOPPING CENTERS

Il Forum Termini. Rome's handiest central shopping mall is Il Forum Termini, a cluster of shops that stay open until 10 pm (even on Sunday), conveniently located directly inside Rome's biggest train station, Stazione Termini. In a city not exactly known for its convenient shopping hours, this "shop before you hop, buy before you fly" hub is a good spot for last-minute goodies or a book for your train or airplane ride. There are more than 100 shops, including the ever-popular United Colors of Benetton, Nike, Mango, Intimissimi, L'Occitane, Sephora, and bookshops with a hearty selection of English-language classics and best sellers. ✉ *Stazione Temini, Repubblica* ⊕ *www.romatermini.com* Ⓜ *Termini.*

TRASTEVERE

Across the Tiber from the city center, Trastevere, one of Rome's most charming neighborhoods, is filled with authentic trattorias, ivy-draped buildings, funky boutiques, lively wine bars and pubs, and the biggest open-air flea market in Rome. The neighborhood attracts a lot of tourist traffic and an American college-student crowd thanks to the bustling nightlife, but it's also a local favorite.

BOOKSTORES

Almost Corner Bookshop. Busting at the seams, with not an ounce of space left on its shelves, this tiny little bookshop is a favorite meeting point for English speakers in Trastevere. Irish owner Dermot O'Connell goes out of his way to find what you're looking for, and if he doesn't have it in stock he'll make a special order for you. The shop carries everything from popular best sellers to translated Italian classics. ⊠ *Via del Moro 45, Trastevere* ☏ *06/5836942.*

CERAMICS AND DECORATIVE ARTS

Polvere di Tempo. Collectors with a passion for rare and decorative timepieces should consider taking a stroll over to Polvere di Tempo. The owner and craftsman, Adrian Rodriguez, has a deep adoration for decorative sundials, watches, and even hourglasses—all entirely made by hand. Stop in at his store, and he'll tell you a story about how monks used candles to tell time and other interesting anecdotes related to timepieces. ⊠ *Via del Moro 59, Trastevere* ☏ *06/05880704* ⊕ *www. polvereditempo.com.*

15

FOOD AND WINE

Antica Caciara Trasteverina. All of the Trasteverini come to this deli to get their hands on some of the freshest ricotta in town. Step inside and you'll encounter giant helpings of ham, salami, Sicilian anchovies, and burrata cheese from Puglia, as well as Parmigiano-Reggiano and local wines all served with polite joviality. ⊠ *Via San Francesco a Ripa 140a/b, Trastevere* ☏ *06/5812815* ⊕ *www.anticacaciara.it.*

MARKETS

Porta Portese. One of the biggest flea markets in Italy—even in Europe, perhaps—Porta Portese welcomes visitors in droves every Sunday 7 am–2 pm. One can literally find anything and everything under the kitchen sink. Treasure seekers and bargain hunters love scrounging around tents for new and used clothing, antique furniture, used books, accessories, and other odds 'n' ends—all at rock-bottom prices. Bring your haggling skills, and cash (preferably small bills—it'll work in your favor when driving a bargain); stallholders don't accept credit cards, and the nearest ATM is a hike. Keep your valuables close; pickpockets lurk nearby. Tram No. 8 is the best way to reach the market. ⊠ *Via Portuense and adjacent streets between Porta Portese and Via Ettore Rolli, Trastevere.*

SHOES AND ACCESSORIES

Fodor's Choice **Joseph DeBach.** The best-kept shoe secret in Rome and open only in the
★ evenings (or by appointment), Joseph DeBach has eccentric creations that are more art than footwear. Entirely handmade from wood, metal, and leather in his small and chaotic studio, his abacus wedge is worthy of a museum. Styles are outrageous "wow" and sometimes finished with

hand-painted strings, odd bits of comic books, newspapers, or other unexpected baubles. ⊠ *Piazza de' Renzi 21, Trastevere* ☎ *3460255265* ⊕ *www.josephdebach.it.*

TESTACCIO

The working-class neighborhood and nightlife hub, Testaccio is also home to foodies, with specialty food and wine shops, as well as an abundance of great Roman eateries.

FOOD AND WINE

Fodor'sChoice
★
Volpetti. A Roman institution, Volpetti sells excellent cured meats and salami. Its rich aromas and flavors are captivating from the moment you enter the store. The food selection also includes genuine buffalo-milk mozzarella, Roman pecorino, sauces, spreads, oils, balsamic vinegars, and desserts. It's also a great place for assembling gift baskets, and they offer a worldwide delivery service. ⊠ *Via Marmorata 47, Testaccio* ☎ *06/5742352* ⊕ *www.volpetti.com* Ⓜ *Piramide.*

MONTI, ESQUILINO, SAN LORENZO, AND SAN GIOVANNI

MONTI

Today, Rome's oldest quarter is a lively neighborhood for college students and the boho-chic thirtysomething crowd. You'll find fun, eclectic shops here selling homemade chocolate, tea, and other gourmet goodies, clothing, antique watches, and more.

CLOTHING

Anteprima. For African-style and Roma-chic inspired clothing, Anteprima has a delightful selection of eye-catching pieces that will have you turning heads. The store carries a large selection of both day and evening wear dresses and separates. The deliberate mismatching of colors and patterns makes the garments fun and refreshing. Another plus is that the store's friendly staff knows how to put together the perfect outfit from head to toe. ⊠ *Via delle Quattro Fontane 38–40, Monti* ☎ *06/4828445* ⊕ *www.anteprimadimoda.com* Ⓜ *Repubblica.*

Hydra 2. Italian teens and college students looking to make a bold statement are frequent shoppers at Hydra 2. The store stocks up on everything from Betty Boop dresses and indie underground wear to heavy-metal T-shirts that would make your *nonna's* hair stand up. ⊠ *Via Urbana 139, Monti* ☎ *06/48907773* Ⓜ *Cavour.*

Fodor'sChoice
★
Le Gallinelle. This tiny boutique may live in a former butcher's shop, but it houses some of the most sophisticated retro-inspired fashion garments around Rome. Its owner, Wilma Silvestri, cleverly combines ethnic and contemporary fabrics, evolving them into stylish clothing with a modern edge made for everyday wear. There is a second shop

at Via del Boschetto 22. ⊠ *Via Panisperna 61, Monti* ☎ *06/4881017* ⊕ *www.legallinelle.it* Ⓜ *Cavour.*

Mikiway. Fun and friendly clothing, jewelry, and accessories for the home are the focus of the eclectic collection here. Look for designs by up-and-coming Italian fashion designers. ⊠ *Via del Boschetto 40b, Monti* ☎ *06/4880914* ☺ *Closed Sun.* Ⓜ *Cavour or Repubblica.*

Mimmo Siviglia. For custom-made dress shirts, Rome's best-kept secret is 80-year-old master tailor Mimmo Siviglia. For more than 50 years, Siviglia has held the secret to making you look smooth: he cuts the pattern just right, accounting for the person's shoulder to ensure there are no wrinkles around the collarbone. If you know your textiles, you'll enjoy discussing the merits of high-end fabrics such as Alumo, Albini, or Riva. Dress-shirt aficionados will be impressed by his attention to each customer and assiduous dedication to each order. Once his daughter has your size in the computer, future orders can be shipped anywhere in the world. ⊠ *Via Urbana 14a, Monti* ☎ *06/48903310, 348/8710079 (English speaking)* ⊕ *www.mimmosiviglia.com* Ⓜ *Cavour.*

FOOD

La Bottega del Cioccolata. Follow the scent of decadent chocolate down this tiny, picturesque street, and you'll stumble upon this chocolate lover's *paradiso*. La Bottega del Cioccolato churns out beautiful, mouthwatering treats thanks to its master chocolate maker Maurizio Proietti and his father. There's a second location near Piazza del Popolo. ⊠ *Via Leonina 82, Monti* ☎ *06/4821473* ⊕ *www.labottegadelcioccolato.it* Ⓜ *Cavour.*

JEWELRY

Art Privé. Just off Monti's principal square is the small jewelry shop where Tiziana Salzano makes chunky, multistrand torsade necklaces using the finest silverwork and a combination of semiprecious gemstones. Each piece is unique, so if you feel something tug at your heart be sure to grab it. ⊠ *Via Leonina 8, Monti* ☎ *06/47826347* Ⓜ *Cavour.*

Artigianaio. Artigianaio (artisan) is the place to go for handmade watches and rare vintage timepieces. The store's expert watchmakers specialize in nostalgic mechanical watches and chronographs from the 1900s through the 1970s. Whether you are looking for a solid gold dress watch or a World War II military pilot's chronograph, chances are you'll find what you're looking for here. Have an heirloom piece that has stopped working or that needs a little fine-tuning? Bring it to the shop, and the owners will get it ticking again in no time. ⊠ *Via Urbana 103, Monti* ☎ *06/4742284* Ⓜ *Cavour.*

15

ESQUILINO

Home to a variety of ethnic communities, the shops in Esquilino feel very authentic. The market here is a fabulous place to explore.

MARKETS

Mercato Esquilino. This fabulous covered market is an excellent place to wander thanks to its sights and smells. There are plenty of Italian, Asian, and African specialties to be found, since the neighborhood is a mix of ethnicities. ⊠ *Via Gialotti, Esquilino* ⊗ *Closed Sun.* Ⓜ *Termini or Vittorio Emanuele.*

SAN LORENZO

This university district is a good place to hunt for unique boho-chic clothing and Roman pottery.

CLOTHING

L'Anatra all'Arancia. Repetto ballerinas, chunky handbags, and funky dresses make L'Anatra all'Arancia one of the best local secrets of boho San Lorenzo. The shop showcases innovative designer clothes from Marina Spadafora, Antik Batik, See by Chloé, and Donatella Baroni (the store's owner). Leaning toward the alternative with an eclectic selection of handpicked Italian and French labels, Donatella also carries luxurious perfumes and beautiful jewelry. ⊠ *Via Tiburtina 105, San Lorenzo* ☎ *06/4456293* Ⓜ *Termini, Castro Pretorio.*

Fodor'sChoice **Pifebo.** Vintage aficionados, university students, musicians, and the
★ occasional costume designer looking for something a little offbeat all love browsing through the racks of the hip vintage clothing emporium Pifebo. The clothes fly off the racks quite quickly thanks to its eclectic selection of '70s, '80s, and '90s apparel and shoes at hard-to-beat prices. The shop has two other locations farther up via dei Serpenti in Monti and in San Giovanni. ⊠ *Via dei Serpenti 141, Monti* ☎ *06/89015204* ⊕ *www.pifebo.com* Ⓜ *Cavour.*

Red Frame Shop. A small and somewhat hard-to-find boutique that is identified only by its redbrick-framed door, Red Frame Shop keeps odd hours, so don't be afraid to knock if the door seems locked. A favorite of TV personality Giada De Laurentiis, the shop is filled with wool and cotton sweaters and skirts, each handmade with attention to detail. ⊠ *Via degli Equi 70, San Lorenzo.*

SAN GIOVANNI

San Giovanni has a wide selection of department stores and chains, as well as a great street market.

MARKETS

Via Sannio. The *mercato* (market) on Via Sannio is the perfect place for flea-market junkies looking for something borrowed or something new. Rummage through piles of military surplus, leather jackets, cosmetics, and other bargains. Also expect great deals on shoes, handbags and accessories. It's open Monday–Saturday, 8 am–2 pm. ⊠ *Via Sannio, near San Giovanni in Laterano, San Giovanni* Ⓜ *San Giovanni.*

UNDERSTANDING ROME

ITALIAN VOCABULARY

ITALIAN VOCABULARY

ENGLISH	ITALIAN	PRONUNCIATION

BASICS

ENGLISH	ITALIAN	PRONUNCIATION
Yes/no	Sí/No	see/no
Please	Per favore	pear fa- **vo**-ray
Yes, please	Sí, grazie	see **grah**-tsee-ay
Thank you	Grazie	**grah**-tsee-ay
You're welcome	Prego	**pray**-go
Excuse me, sorry	Scusi	**skoo**-zee
Sorry!	Mi dispiace!	mee dis-spee- **ah**-chay
Good morning/ afternoon	Buongiorno	bwohn- **jor**-no
Good evening	Buona sera	**bwoh**-na **say**-ra
Good-bye	Arrivederci	a-ree-vah- **dare**-chee
Mr. (Sir)	Signore	see- **nyo**-ray
Mrs. (Ma'am)	Signora	see- **nyo**-ra
Miss	Signorina	see-nyo- **ree**-na
Pleased to meet you	Piacere	pee-ah- **chair**-ray
How are you?	Come sta?	**ko**-may **stah**
Very well, thanks	Bene, grazie	**ben**-ay **grah**-tsee-ay
Hello (phone)	Pronto?	**proan**-to

NUMBERS

ENGLISH	ITALIAN	PRONUNCIATION
one	uno	**oo**-no
two	due	**doo**-ay
three	tre	tray
four	quattro	**kwah**-tro
five	cinque	**cheen**-kway
six	sei	say
seven	sette	**set**-ay
eight	otto	**oh**-to
nine	nove	**no**-vay
ten	dieci	dee- **eh**-chee
twenty	venti	**vain**-tee
thirty	trenta	**train**-ta
forty	quaranta	kwa- **rahn**-ta

ENGLISH	ITALIAN	PRONUNCIATION
fifty	cinquanta	cheen-**kwahn**-ta
sixty	sessanta	seh-**sahn**-ta
seventy	settanta	seh-**tahn**-ta
eighty	ottanta	o-**tahn**-ta
ninety	novanta	no-**vahn**-ta
one hundred	cento	**chen**-to
one thousand	mille	**mee**-lay
ten thousand	diecimila	dee-eh-chee-**mee**-la

USEFUL PHRASES

Do you speak English?	Parla inglese?	**par**-la een-**glay**-zay
I don't speak Italian.	Non parlo italiano.	non **par**-lo ee-tal-**yah**-no
I don't understand.	Non capisco.	non ka-**peess**-ko
Can you please repeat?	Può ripetere?	pwo ree-**pet**-ay-ray
Slowly!	Lentamente!	**len**-ta-men-tay
I don't know.	Non lo so.	non lo **so**
I'm American.	Sono americano(a).	**so**-no a-may-ree-**kah**-no(a)
I'm British.	Sono inglese.	so-no een-**glay**-zay
What's your name?	Come si chiama?	**ko**-may see kee-**ah**-ma
My name is ...	Mi chiamo ...	mee kee-**ah**-mo
What time is it?	Che ore sono?	kay **o**-ray **so**-no
How?	Come?	**ko**-may
When?	Quando?	**kwan**-doe
Yesterday/today/ tomorrow	Ieri/oggi/domani	**yer**-ee/ **o**-jee/ do-**mah**-nee
This morning/	Stamattina/Oggi	sta-ma-**tee**-na/ **o**-jee
afternoon	pomeriggio	po-mer-**ee**-jo
Tonight	Stasera	sta-**ser**-a
What?	Che cosa?	kay **ko**-za
Why?	Perché?	pear-**kay**
Who?	Chi?	kee

ENGLISH	ITALIAN	PRONUNCIATION
Where is …	Dov'è …	doe- **veh**
the bus stop?	la fermata dell'autobus?	la fer- **mah**-ta del ow-toe- **booss**
the train station?	la stazione?	la sta-tsee- **oh**-nay
the subway	la metropolitana?	la may-tro-po-lee- **tah**-na
the terminal?	il terminale?	eel ter-mee- **nah**-lay
the post office?	l'ufficio postale?	loo- **fee**-cho po- **stah**-lay
the bank?	la banca?	la **bahn**-ka
the … hotel?	l'hotel …?	lo- **tel**
the store?	il negozio?	eel nay- **go**-tsee-o
the cashier?	la cassa?	la **kah**-sa
the … museum?	il museo …?	eel moo- **zay**-o
the hospital?	l'ospedale?	lo-spay- **dah**-lay
the elevator?	l'ascensore?	la-shen- **so**-ray
the restrooms?	il bagno?	eel **bahn**-yo
Here/there	Qui/là	kwee/la
Left/right	A sinistra/a destra	a see- **neess**-tra/a **des**-tra
Straight ahead	Avanti dritto	a- **vahn**-tee **dree**-to
Is it near/far?	È vicino/lontano?	ay vee- **chee**-no/ lon- **tah**-no
I'd like …	Vorrei …	vo- **ray**
a room	una camera	**oo**-na **kah**-may-ra
the key	la chiave	la kee- **ah**-vay
a newspaper	un giornale	oon jor- **nah**-lay
a stamp	un francobollo	oon frahn-ko- **bo**-lo
I'd like to buy …	Vorrei comprare …	vo- **ray** kom- **prah**-ray
How much is it?	Quanto costa?	**kwahn**-toe **coast**-a
It's expensive/cheap.	È caro/economico.	ay **car**-o/ ay-ko- **no**-mee-ko
A little/a lot	Poco/tanto	**po**-ko/ **tahn**-to
More/less	Più/meno	pee- **oo** / **may**-no
Enough/too (much)	Abbastanza/troppo	a-bas- **tahn**-sa/tro-po

ENGLISH	ITALIAN	PRONUNCIATION
I am sick.	Sto male.	sto **mah**-lay
Call a doctor.	Chiama un dottore.	kee- **ah**-mah oondoe- **toe**-ray
Help!	Aiuto!	a- **yoo**-toe
Stop!	Alt!	ahlt
Fire!	Al fuoco!	ahl **fwo**-ko
Caution/Look out!	Attenzione!	a-ten- **syon**-ay

DINING OUT

A bottle of ...	Una bottiglia di ...	**oo**-na bo- **tee**-lee-ah dee
A cup of ...	Una tazza di ...	**oo**-na **tah**-tsa dee
A glass of ...	Un bicchiere di ...	oon bee-key- **air**-ay dee
Bill/check	Il conto	eel **cone**-toe
Bread	Il pane	eel **pah**-nay
Breakfast	La prima colazione	la **pree**-ma ko-la- **tsee**-oh-nay
Cocktail/aperitif	L'aperitivo	la-pay-ree- **tee**-vo
Dinner	La cena	la **chen**-a
Fixed-price menu	Menù a prezzo fisso	may- **noo** a pret-so **fee**-so
Fork	La forchetta	la for- **ket**-a
I am diabetic.	Ho il diabete.	o eel dee-a- **bay**-tay
I am vegetarian.	Sono vegetariano/a.	**so**-no vay-jay-ta-ree- **ah**-no/a
I'd like ...	Vorrei ...	vo- **ray**
I'd like to order.	Vorrei ordinare.	vo- **ray** or-dee- **nah**-ray
Is service included?	Il servizio è incluso?	eel ser- **vee**-tzee-o ay een- **kloo**-zo
It's good/bad.	È buono/cattivo.	ay **bwo**-no/ka- **tee**-vo
It's hot/cold.	È caldo/freddo.	ay **kahl**-doe/ **fred**-o
Knife	Il coltello	eel kol- **tel**-o
Lunch	Il pranzo	eel **prahnt**-so
Menu	Il menù	eel may- **noo**
Napkin	Il tovagliolo	eel toe-va-lee- **oh**-lo

ENGLISH	ITALIAN	PRONUNCIATION
Please give me ...	Mi dia ...	mee **dee**-a
Salt	Il sale	eel **sah**-lay
Spoon	Il cucchiaio	eel koo-kee- **ah**-yo
Sugar	Lo zucchero	lo **tsoo**-ker-o
Waiter/Waitress	Cameriere/cameriera	ka-mare- **yer**-ay/ ka-mare- **yer**-a
Wine list	La lista dei vini	la **lee**-sta **day**-ee **vee**-nee

TRAVEL SMART
ROME

GETTING HERE AND AROUND

▌ AIR TRAVEL

Flying time to Rome is 7½–8½ hours from New York, 10–11 hours from Chicago, 12–13 hours from Los Angeles, and 2½ hours from London.

Although the trend with international flights is to drop reconfirmation requirements, many airlines still ask you to reconfirm each leg of your international itinerary. Failure to do so may result in your reservations being canceled. When flying out of Italian airports, always check with the airport or tourist agency about upcoming transport strikes (*scioperi*), which are frequent in Italy and can affect air travel.

Airlines and Airports Airline and Airport Links.com. ⊕ *www.airlineandairportlinks.com.*

Airline Security Issues Transportation Security Administration. ☎ *866/289–9673* ✎ *TSA-ContactCenter@dhs.gov* ⊕ *www.tsa.gov.*

AIRPORTS

The principal airport for flights to Rome is Leonardo da Vinci Airport, more commonly known as Fiumicino (FCO). It's 30 km (19 miles) southwest of the city. There is a direct train link with Rome's Termini station on the Leonardo Express train, and a local train to Trastevere and Ostiense stations. Rome's other airport is Ciampino (CIA), on Via Appia Nuova, 15 km (9 miles) south of downtown. Ciampino is a national and international hub for many low-cost airlines. There are no trains linking the Ciampino airport to downtown Rome, but there are a number of shuttle buses running daily.

Airport Information Ciampino. ☎ *06/65951* ⊕ *www.adr.it/ciampino.* **Leonardo da Vinci Airport/Fiumicino.** ☎ *06/65951* ⊕ *www.adr. it/fiumicino.*

TRANSFERS BETWEEN FIUMICINO AND DOWNTOWN

If you're driving into the city, follow the signs for Rome and the GRA (the ring road that circles Rome). The direction you take on the GRA depends on where your lodging is located. If you're staying in the *centro storico* (historic center), follow indications for Roma Centro. Get a map and directions from the car-rental service, and if you aren't using one on your phone, considering renting a GPS as well.

A new law implemented by the Comune di Roma requires all Rome taxi drivers to charge a fixed fare of €48 (including luggage handling) if your destination is within the Aurelian walls (this covers the centro storico, most of Trastevere, most of the Vatican area, and parts of San Giovanni). To make sure your hotel falls within the Aurelian walls, ask when you book your room. If your hotel is outside of the walls, the cab ride will run you about €60 plus *supplementi* (extra charges) for luggage. (Of course, this also depends on traffic.) The ride from the airport to the city center takes about 30–45 minutes. Private limousines can be booked at booths in the Arrivals hall; they charge more than taxis but can carry more passengers. The Comune di Roma now has a representative in place outside the International Arrivals hall (Terminal 2), where the taxi stand is located, to help tourists get into a taxi cab. Use only licensed white taxis. When in doubt, always ask for a receipt and write the cab company and taxi's license number down (it's written on a metal plate on the inside of the passenger door). Avoid drivers who may approach you in the Arrivals hall; they charge exorbitant, unmetered rates and are most often unauthorized taxi drivers.

Airport Connection charges €35 for one passenger, €39 for two, and €6 for each additional passenger. Booking is required. **Airport Shuttle Express** offers a daily service from/to FCO. The shuttles stop at all major hotels in the center of Rome. It costs €25 one-way for one passenger, €30 for two, and €10 for each additional passenger. (The rate includes two bags per person.) **Airport Shuttle** provides door-to-door shuttle service, at a cost of €25 for one person and €6 for each additional passenger (up to 8). Advance booking is recommended.

Two trains link downtown Rome with Fiumicino—a nonstop express and a local. Inquire at the APT tourist information counter in the International Arrivals hall (Terminal 2) or train information counter near the tracks to determine which takes you closest to your destination in Rome. The 32-minute nonstop Airport–Termini express (called the **Leonardo Express**) goes directly to Tracks 23 or 24 at Termini station, which is well served by taxis and is a hub of Metro and bus lines. Departures to Termini station run every half hour beginning at 6:23 am from the airport, with a final departure at 11:23 pm. Trains depart Termini station from Tracks 23 and 24 to the airport starting at 5:35 am and the last train leaves at 10:35 pm. Tickets cost €14.

Trenitalia's **FL1**, the commuter rail, leaves from the same tracks and runs to Rome and beyond. The main stops in Rome are at Trastevere (27 minutes), Ostiense (30 minutes), and Tiburtina (45 minutes); at each you can find taxis and public transport connections to other areas of Rome. FL1 trains run from Fiumicino between 5:57 am and 11:27 pm, with departures every 30 minutes; the schedule is similar going to the airport. Tickets cost €8. For either train, you can buy your ticket at a vending machine or at ticket counters at the airport and at some stations (Termini, Trastevere, Tiburtina). At the airport, stamp the ticket at the gate. Remember when using the train at other stations to stamp the ticket in the little yellow or red machine near the track before you board. If you fail to stamp your ticket before you board, you could receive a hefty fine, as much as €100 on top of the ticket price.

At night, take **COTRAL buses** from the airport to Tiburtina station in Rome (45 minutes); they depart from in front of the International Arrivals hall at 1:15, 2:15, 3:30, 5, 10:55 am, noon, and 3:30 pm. Buses leave Tiburtina station for the airport at 12:30, 1:15, 2:30, 3:45, 9:30, 10:30 am, 12:35 pm, and 5:30 pm. Tickets either way cost €5 (€7 if purchased onboard).

TRANSFERS BETWEEN CIAMPINO AND DOWNTOWN

By car, go north on the Via Appia Nuova into downtown Rome.

The new taxi fare law implemented by the Comune di Roma that affects Fiumicino applies to this airport, too. All taxi drivers are supposed to charge a fixed fare of €30 (including luggage handling) if your destination is within the Aurelian walls. If your hotel is outside the walls, the cab ride will run you about €60, plus supplementi for luggage. The ride takes about 30 minutes. Take only official white cabs with the "taxi" sign on top; unofficial cabs often overcharge disoriented travelers.

Airport Connection Services has shuttles that cost €39 for the first two passengers. **Airport Shuttle** charges €25 for the first person, and €5 for each additional passenger.

The **ATRAL bus** connects Ciampino airport with Termini station. Buses depart from in front of the airport terminal around 20 times a day 4 am–10:50 pm. The fare is €3.90, and tickets can be bought on the bus. Travel time is approximately 40 minutes.

TRANSFERS BETWEEN AIRPORTS

It's not easy to move from one airport to another in Rome—the airports aren't connected by a railway system or by the Metro. The only way to make the transfer is by car, taxi, or a combination of bus, Metro, and train. The latter option is not advisable because it would take you at least two to three hours to get from one airport to the other.

A taxi ride from Fiumicino Leonardo Da Vinci Airport to Ciampino Airport will take approximately 45 minutes and could cost roughly €50.

Contacts Airport Connection Services.
☏ 06/21116248, 353/16530992 emergency line (in case you cannot find the driver), 44/2035297228 from the UK ⊕ www.airportconnection.it. **Airport Shuttle.** ☏ 06/42013469, 06/4740451 ⊕ www.airportshuttle.it. **Airport Shuttle Express.** ☏ 06/65017448 ⊕ www.airportshuttleexpress.it.

GETTING FROM THE AIRPORT TO CENTRO HISTORICO

Mode of Transport	Duration	Price
Taxi	20 minutes from Ciampino, 30–40 minutes from Fiumicino	€30 from Ciampino, €48 from Fiumicino
Leonardo Express Train	30 minutes	€14
Car	20 minutes from Ciampino, 30–40 minutes from Fiumicino	N/A

▌ BUS TRAVEL

An extensive network of bus lines that covers all of Lazio (the surrounding geographical region of which Rome is the capital) is operated by **COTRAL** (Consorzio Trasporti Lazio). There are several main bus stations. Long-distance and suburban COTRAL bus routes terminate either near Tiburtina station or at outlying Metro stops, such as Rebibbia and Ponte Mammolo (Linea B) and Anagnina (Linea A).

ATAC, Rome's city transport service, offers reasonable fares for travel in and around Rome, especially with the BIRG (Biglietto Integrale Regionale Giornaliero), which allows you to travel on all the lines (and some railroad lines) up to midnight on the day of the ticket's first validation. The cost of a BIRG depends upon the distance to your destination and how many "zones" you travel through. Because of the extent and complexity of the system, it's a good idea to consult with your hotel concierge, review ATAC's website, or to telephone COTRAL's central office when planning a trip. COTRAL buses and other similar bus companies such as **SENA** are good options for taking short day trips from Rome. There are several buses that leave daily from Rome's Ponte Mammolo (Linea B) Metro station for the town of Tivoli, where Hadrian's Villa and Villa D'Este are located. SENA buses leave from Rome's Tiburtina Metro and train station (Linea B) and will take you to Siena and other towns in Tuscany.

While the bus may be an affordable way of moving around, keep in mind that buses can be crowded due to commuter traffic. Just because you've managed to purchase a ticket doesn't mean you're guaranteed a seat. Make sure to arrive early and stand your ground in line. If you are not able to procure a seat, you may be standing for the entire ride.

If you're taking a city bus, make sure the bus you're waiting for actually runs during that part of the day or on that particular day of the week. For example, *notturno* buses (late-night buses)—distinguished by the "N" sign just above the bus number—don't run until after midnight and then only a few times per hour. Tourists often get confused while waiting at the bus stop, since the notturno bus schedules are listed side-by-side with the regular day bus schedules. Also, be aware that *deviata* buses are those that have been rerouted due to road construction or public demonstrations. And *festivi* buses are ones that only run on Sunday and holidays. Neither notturno buses or festivi buses run as often as other buses do on weekdays and Saturday. Regular buses will either say *feriali*, which means "daily," or won't have any special distinction.

Bus Information ATAC. ⊕ *www.atac.roma.it.*
COTRAL. ☏ *800/174471 in Italy (from landline only), 06/7257205* ⊕ *www.cotralspa.it.* **SENA.**
☏ *0861/1991900* ⊕ *www.sena.it.*

▌ CAR TRAVEL

The main access routes from the north are the A1 (Autostrada del Sole) from Milan and Florence and the A12–E80 highway from Genoa. The principal route to or from points south, including Naples, is the A2. All highways connect with the Grande Raccordo Anulare Ring Road (GRA), which channels traffic into the city center. Markings on the GRA are confusing: take time to study the route you need. Be extremely careful of pedestrians and mopeds when driving: Romans are casual jaywalkers and pop out frequently from between parked cars. People on scooters tend to be the most careless drivers, as they weave in and out of traffic.

For driving directions, check out ⊕ *www. tuttocitta.it.*

GASOLINE

Only a few gas stations are open on Sunday, and most close for a couple of hours at lunchtime and then at 7 pm for the night. Many, however, have self-service pumps that accept both cash and credit cards and are operational 24 hours a day. After-hours at self-service stations, it is not uncommon to find someone who will pump your gas for you. While they're not official employees of the gas station, a small tip is usually expected (about €0.50 is acceptable). Gas stations on autostrade are open 24 hours. As of this writing, gas costs about €1.50 per liter; diesel costs about €1.30 per liter.

PARKING

Be warned: parking in Rome can be a nightmare. The situation is greatly compounded by the fact that private cars without permits are not allowed access to the centro storico on weekdays 6:30 am–6 pm, Saturday 2–6 pm, or Friday and Saturday nights (11 pm–3 am). Other areas, including Trastevere, Testaccio, and San Lorenzo, are closed to cars at various times. Check the **Agenzia Mobilità** website for the most up-to-date information. These areas, known as Zona Traffico Limitato (ZTL), are marked by electric signs, and bordering streets have video cameras for photographing license plates. Fines are sent directly to car rental companies and added to your bill. There is limited free parking in Rome; most parking is metered, on a pay-by-the-hour basis. Spaces with white lines are free parking; spaces with blue lines are paid parking; and spaces with yellow lines are for the handicapped only. All other color-coded spaces are usually reserved for residents or carpooling and require special permits. If you park in one of these spaces without a permit, your car could be ticketed or towed. Make sure to check with your hotel regarding appropriate places to park nearby. Meter parking costs €1–€1.20 per hour (depending on what area you're in) with a limit on total parking time allowed in many areas; however, if you pay for four consecutive hours, you will get eight hours of meter time for just €4. Parking facilities near historic sights exist at the Villa Borghese underground car park (entrance at Viale del Muro Torto) and the Vatican (entrance from Piazza della Rovere).

ROAD CONDITIONS

Italians drive fast and are impatient with those who don't, a tendency that can make driving on the congested streets of Rome a hair-raising experience. Traffic is heaviest during morning and late-afternoon commuter hours, and on weekends. Watch out for mopeds.

ROADSIDE EMERGENCIES

There are phone boxes on highways to report breakdowns. Major rental agencies often provide roadside assistance, so check your rental agreement if a problem arises. Also, **ACI** (Auto Club of Italy) offers 24-hour road service. Dial *803–116* from any phone anytime to reach the nearest ACI service station. When speaking to ACI, ask and you will be transferred to an English-speaking operator. Be prepared to tell the operator which road you're on, the direction you're going—for example, "*verso* (in the direction of) Pizzo"—and the *targa* (license plate number) of your car.

Contacts Agenzia Mobilità. ☎ *06/46951* ⊕ *www.agenziamobilita.roma.it/it/servizi/ orari-ztl.* **Auto Club of Italy (ACI).** ☎ *803–116, 39/06491115 from abroad* ✉ *infoturismo@aci. it* ⊕ *www.aci.it.*

RULES OF THE ROAD

Driving is on the right. Regulations are largely similar to those in Britain and the United States, except that the police have the power to levy on-the-spot fines. Although honking abounds, the use of horns is forbidden in many areas; a large sign, "*zona di silenzio,*" indicates where. Speed limits are 50 kph (31 mph) in Rome, 110 kph (70 mph) on state and provincial roads, and 130 kph (80 mph) on autostrade, unless otherwise marked. Talking on a mobile phone while driving is strictly prohibited, and if caught, the driver will be issued a fine. Not wearing a seat belt is also against the law. The blood-alcohol content limit for driving is 0.5 gr/l with fines up to €6,000 and the possibility of 12 months imprisonment for surpassing the limit. Fines for speeding are uniformly stiff: 10 kph (6 mph) over the speed limit can warrant a fine in the hundreds and even thousands of euros; over 10 kph, and your license could be taken away.

Whenever the city decides to implement an "Ecological Day" in order to reduce smog levels, commuters are prohibited from driving their cars during certain hours of the day and in certain areas of the city. These are usually organized and announced ahead of time; however, if you're planning to rent a car during your trip, make sure to ask the rental company and your hotel if there are any planned, because the traffic police won't cut you any breaks, even if you say you're a tourist.

CAR RENTAL

When you reserve a car, ask about cancellation penalties, taxes, drop-off charges (if you're planning to pick up the car in one city and leave it in another), and surcharges (for being under or over a certain age, for additional drivers, or for driving across regional or country borders or beyond a specific distance from your point of rental). All these things can add substantially to your costs. Request car seats and extras such as GPS when you book. Make sure to ask the rental car company if they require you to obtain an International Driver's Permit beforehand (most do). These can generally be obtained for a fee through AAA in the United States. Rates are sometimes—but not always—better if you book in advance or reserve through a rental agency's website. There are other reasons to book ahead, though: for popular destinations, during busy times of the year, or to ensure that you get certain types of cars (automatic transmission, vans, SUVs, exotic sports cars).

■TIP→ Make sure that a confirmed reservation guarantees you a car. Agencies sometimes overbook, particularly for busy weekends and holiday periods.

Rates in Rome begin at around $75 per day for an economy car with air-conditioning, a manual transmission, and unlimited mileage. This includes the 20% tax on car rentals. Note that Italian legislation now permits certain rental wholesalers, such as Auto Europe, to drop the value-added tax (V.A.T.). All international car-rental agencies in Rome have a number of locations.

It's usually cheaper to rent a car in advance through your local agency than to rent on location in Italy. Or book ahead online—you can save as much as $10 per day on your car rental. Within Italy, local and international rental agencies offer similar rates. Whether you're going with a local or international agency, note that most cars are manual; automatics are rarer, so inquire about those well in advance.

In Italy, your own driver's license is acceptable. But to be extra safe, an International Driver's Permit is a good idea; it's available from the American or Canadian Automobile Association and, in the United Kingdom, from the Automobile Association or Royal Automobile Club. These international permits are universally recognized, and having one in your wallet may save you a problem with the local authorities.

In Italy you must be 21 years of age to rent an economy or subcompact car, and most companies require customers under the age of 23 to pay by credit card. Upon rental, all companies require credit cards as a warranty; to rent bigger cars (2,000 cc or more), you must often show two credit cards. Debit or check cards are not accepted. Call local agents for details. There are no special restrictions on senior-citizen drivers.

Car seats are required for children under three and must be booked in advance. The rental cost is €5 and up, depending on the type of car.

The cost for an additional driver is about €5–€7 per day.

CAR INSURANCE

Everyone who rents a car wonders whether the insurance that the rental companies offer is worth the expense. No one—including us—has a simple answer. It all depends on how much regular insurance you have, how comfortable you are with risk, and whether or not money is an issue. Keep in mind that it's not uncommon for drivers in Italy to cruise the roads without insurance so it can be better to err on the side of caution to protect your own rental.

If you own a car, your personal auto insurance may cover a rental to some degree, though not all policies protect you abroad; always read your policy's fine print. If you don't have auto insurance,

then seriously consider buying the collision- or loss-damage waiver (CDW or LDW) from the car-rental company, which eliminates your liability for damage to the car. If you choose not to purchase the CDW coverage, you could be liable for the first €500 worth of damage. Some credit cards offer CDW coverage, but it's usually supplemental to your own insurance and rarely covers SUVs, minivans, luxury models, and the like. If your coverage is secondary, you may still be liable for loss-of-use costs from the car-rental company. But no credit-card insurance is valid unless you use that card for *all* transactions, from making the reservation to paying the final bill. All credit-card companies exclude coverage in some countries, so be sure to find out about the destination to which you are traveling.

Some rental agencies require you to purchase CDW coverage; many will even include it in quoted rates. All will strongly encourage you to buy CDW—possibly implying that it's required—so be sure to ask about such things before renting. In most cases it's cheaper to add a supplemental CDW plan to your comprehensive travel-insurance policy than to purchase it from a rental company. That said, you don't want to pay for a supplement if you're required to buy insurance from the rental company.

▌ PUBLIC TRANSPORTATION: BUS, TRAM, AND METROPOLITANA

Although most of Rome's sights are in a relatively circumscribed area, the city is too large to be seen solely on foot. Try to avoid rush hour when taking the Metro (subway) or a bus, as public transport can be extremely crowded. Midmorning or midday through early afternoon tends to be less busy. Otherwise, it's best to take a taxi to the area you plan to visit if it is across town. You should always expect to do a lot of walking in Rome, especially considering how little ground the subway actually covers, so plan on wearing a pair of comfortable, sturdy shoes to cushion the impact of the *sampietrini* (cobblestones). Get away from the noise and polluted air of heavily trafficked streets by taking parallel streets whenever possible. You can get free city and transit maps at municipal information booths.

Rome's integrated transportation system includes buses and trams (ATAC), the Metropolitana (the subway, or Metro), suburban trains and buses (COTRAL), and commuter rail run by the state railway (Trenitalia). A ticket (BIT), valid for 100 minutes on any combination of buses and trams and one entrance to the Metro, costs €1.50. Tickets are sold at tobacco shops, newsstands, some coffee bars, automatic ticket machines in Metro stations, some bus stops, in machines on some buses, and at ATAC ticket booths. You can purchase individual tickets or buy in quantity. It's always a good idea to have a few tickets handy so you don't have to hunt for a vendor when you need one. All tickets must be validated by time-stamping in the yellow meter boxes aboard buses and in underground stations, and immediately prior to boarding. Failure to validate your ticket will result in an on-the-spot fine of €50. Pay the ticket controllers on the spot; otherwise, it'll cost you €100 if you pay after five days.

A Roma24H ticket, or *biglietto integrato giornaliero* (integrated daily ticket), is valid for 24 hours (from the moment you stamp it) on all public transit and costs €7. You can also purchase a Roma48H (€12.50), a Roma72H (€18), and a CIS (Carta Integrata Settimanale), which is valid for one week (€24). Each option gives unlimited travel on ATAC buses, COTRAL urban bus services, trains for the Lido and Viterbo, and Metro. There's an ATAC kiosk at the bus terminal in front of Termini station.

If you're going farther afield, or planning to spend more than a week in Rome, think about getting a BIRG (daily regional ticket) or a CIRS (weekly regional ticket) from the railway station. These give you unlimited travel on all state transport throughout the region of Lazio. This can take you as far as the Etruscan city of Tarquinia or medieval Viterbo.

The Metro is the easiest and fastest way to get around Rome (*see our Metro map*). There are stops near most of the main tourist attractions; street entrances are marked with red "M" signs. The Metro has three lines: A and B, which intersect at Termini station, and also C. Linea A (red) runs from the eastern part of the city, with stops at San Giovanni in Laterano, Piazza Barberini, Piazza di Spagna, Piazzale Flaminio (Piazza del Popolo), and Ottaviano/San Pietro, near the Basilica di San Pietro and the Musei Vaticani. Linea B (blue) has stops near the Colosseum, the Circus Maximus, the Pyramid (Ostiense station and trains for Ostia Antica), and the Basilica di San Paolo Fuori le Mura. Linea C runs from the eastern outskirts of the city through Pigneto. The Metro opens at 5:30 am, and the last trains leave the last station at either end at 11:30 pm (on Friday and Saturday nights the last trains on the A and B lines leave at 1:30 am). We give Metro stops in our listings if the closest station is not more than about a 10-minute walk away.

Although not as fast as the Metro, bus and tram travel is more scenic. With reserved bus lanes and numerous tram lines, surface transportation is surprisingly efficient, given the volume of Roman traffic. At peak times, however, buses can be very crowded. If the distance you have to travel is not too great, walking can be a more comfortable alternative. ATAC city buses are orange, gray-and-red, or blue-and-orange; trams are orange or green. Remember to board at the rear and to exit at the middle: some bus drivers may refuse to let you out the front door, leaving you to scramble through the crowd to exit the middle or rear doors. Don't forget that you must buy your ticket before boarding, and be sure to stamp it in a machine as soon as you enter. If you find the bus too crowded to get to the ticket machine, write the date and time you boarded on the ticket where you would normally validate it. The ticket is good for a transfer and one Metro trip within the next 100 minutes. Buses and trams run 5:30 am–midnight, after which time there's an extensive network of night buses with service throughout the city.

The bus system is a bit complicated to navigate due to the number of lines, but ATAC has a website (⊕ *www.atac.roma. it*) that will help you calculate the number of stops and bus route needed, and even give you a map directing you to the appropriate stops. To navigate the site, look for the British flag in the upper right-hand corner to change the website into English.

TICKET/PASS	PRICE
Single Fare	€1.50
Weekly unlimited Pass	€24
Monthly unlimited Pass	€35

Information **ATAC urban buses.** ☎ *06/57003* ⊕ *www.atac.roma.it.* **COTRAL.** ☎ *800/174471, 06/72057205* ⊕ *www.cotralspu.it.* **Trenitalia** suburban trains. ☎ *892021, 06/68475475* from abroad ⊕ *www.trenitalia.it.*

∎ SCOOTER TRAVEL

After a few days in the city, you'll quickly notice that mopeds/scooters are everywhere. Riders are required to wear helmets, and traffic police are tough in enforcing this law. Producing your country's driver's license should be enough to convince most rental firms that they're not dealing with a complete beginner; but if you're unsure of exactly how to ride a moped, think twice, as driving a scooter in Rome is not like you see it in the movies. It can be very dangerous, and Roman drivers tend to be ruthless; at least ask the attendant for a detailed demonstration. If you don't feel up to braving the Roman traffic on a moped, you can hire a Segway or electric bicycle to explore the seven hills of Rome.

Rental Agencies **Bici & Baci.** ⊕ *www. bicibaci.com.* **Rolling Rome.** ⊠ *Piazza del Gesù 47* ☎ *320/8076437* ⊕ *www.rollingrome.com.* **Treno e Scooter.** ⊠ *Piazza dei Cinquecento, in the parking lot in front of the train station, Termini* ☎ *06/48905823* ⊕ *www. trenoescooter.com.*

∎ TAXI TRAVEL

The best way to find a taxi in Rome is generally to hire a taxi at a taxi stand. Taxis do not cruise, but if free they may stop if you flag them down. They wait at stands but can also be called by phone, in which case you're charged a supplement (the meter will already be running when you're picked up). The various taxi services are considered interchangeable and are referred to by their phone numbers rather than names. Taxicabs can be reserved the night before only if you're traveling to or from the airport or the train station. Only some taxis are equipped to take credit cards; inquire when you phone to make the booking.

The meter starts at €3 during the day, €6.50 10 pm–6 am, and €4.50 on Sunday and holidays.

Supplemental charges, such as for luggage or even for pick up at Termini station, are added to the meter fare. When in doubt, ask for a receipt (*ricevuta*). This will encourage the taxicab driver to be honest and charge you the correct amount. Women traveling alone via taxi 10 pm–6 am are entitled to a 10% discount; the same discount applies if your destination is a public hospital. (Make sure to ask for it.) Use only licensed, metered white cabs, identified by a numbered shield on the side, an illuminated taxi sign on the roof, and a plaque next to the license plate reading "*servizio pubblico.*" Avoid unmarked, unauthorized, unmetered gypsy cabs (numerous at Rome airports and train stations), whose drivers actively solicit your trade and may demand astronomical fares.

Taxi Companies Cab. ☎ *06/6645, 06/3570, 06/8822, 06/5551, 06/4157* ⊕ *www.3570.it.*

▌TRAIN TRAVEL

State-owned Trenitalia trains are part of the Metrebus system and also serve some destinations on side trips outside Rome. The main Trenitalia stations in Rome are Termini, Tiburtina, Ostiense, and Trastevere. Suburban trains use all of these stations. The Ferrovie COTRAL line departs from a terminal in Piazzale Flaminio, connecting Rome with Viterbo.

Only Trenitalia trains such as Frecciarossa, Frecciargento, Eurostar, and Intercity Plus have first- and second-class compartments. Local trains can be crowded early in the morning and in the evening as many people commute to and from the city, so try to avoid traveling at these times. Be ready to stand if you plan to take one of these trains and don't arrive early enough to secure a seat. On long-distance routes (to Florence and Venice, for instance), you can either travel by the cheap (but slow) *regionale* trains, or the fast, but more expensive, Intercity, Eurostar, Frecciarossa, or Frecciargento, which require seat reservations, available at the station when you buy your ticket, online, or through a travel agent.

For destinations within 200 km (124 miles) of Rome, you can buy a *kilometrico* ticket. Like bus tickets, they can be purchased at some newsstands and in ticketing machines, as well as at Trenitalia ticket windows. Buy them in advance so you won't waste time in line at station ticket booths. Like all train tickets, they must be date-stamped in the little yellow or red machines near the track before you board. Within a range of 200 km (124 miles) they're valid for six hours from the time they're stamped, and you can get on and off at will at stops in between for the duration of the ticket's validity.

The state railways' excellent and user-friendly site at ⊕ *www.trenitalia.it* will help you plan any rail trips in the country. Since 2012, Italy's rails have had a private competitor, Italo, whose gorgeous and very fast trains travel between large cities including Naples, Rome, Florence, Bologna, Milan, Venice, and Torino. In Rome, Italo trains stop at Termini and Tiburtina stations.

Information Italo Treno–Nuovo Trasporto Viaggiatori. ☎ *06/0708 within Italy, 06/89371892 from abroad* ⊕ *www.italotreno. it.* **Trenitalia.** ☎ *892/2021 within Italy, 199/892021 within Italy, 06/68475475 from abroad* ⊕ *www.trenitalia.it.*

ESSENTIALS

■ COMMUNICATIONS

INTERNET

There are various free Wi-Fi hotspots around the city through DigitRoma (⊕ *digitroma.nuvolaitpeoplelinked. it*), Romawireless (⊕ *www.romawireless.com*), and Provincia Wifi (⊕ *www. mappawifi.provincia.roma.it*), the latter of which also accepts a credit card for identity verification if you don't have an Italian phone number. After you register with one of these providers, your phone should recognize the company's free Wi-Fi hotspots, but you will be required to enter a login and password each time. However these public systems are often a bit hit-or-miss in terms of quality, so usually the easiest thing to do is take advantage of the Wi-Fi at bars and cafés, for the price of a beer or a cup of coffee.

Cafés with Wi-Fi Friends Café. ⊠ *Piazza Trilussa 34, Trastevere* ☎ *06/5816111.* **The Library.** ⊠ *Vicolo della Cancelleria 7, Piazza Navona* ☎ *333/3517581, 06/97275442* ⊕ *www.thelibrary.it*

PHONES

The good news is that you can now make a direct-dial telephone call from virtually any point on earth. The bad news? You can't always do so cheaply. Calling from a hotel is almost always the most expensive option; hotels usually add huge surcharges to all calls, particularly international ones. Calling cards usually keep costs to a minimum, but only if you purchase them locally. In Italy, you can also place international calls from call centers. And then there are mobile phones *(Mobile Phones)*—as expensive as mobile calls can be, they are still usually a much cheaper option than calling from your hotel.

The country code for Italy is 39. The area code for Rome is 06. When dialing an Italian number from abroad, do not drop the initial 0 from the local area code.

The country code is 1 for the United States and Canada, 61 for Australia, 64 for New Zealand, and 44 for the United Kingdom.

CALLING WITHIN ITALY

When calling within Italy to an Italian number, always include the city dialing code such as 06 for Rome, 02 for Milan, and 055 for Florence.

You'll notice that only mobile phones have a set number of digits, whereas landlines can range from 6 to 10 digits. Calls within Rome are preceded by the city code 06, with the exception of three-digit numbers (113 is for general emergencies) and mobile phone numbers. Emergency numbers can be called for free from pay phones. Calling to cities outside of Rome follows the same procedure: city dialing code plus number.

CALLING OUTSIDE ITALY

Avoid making international and long-distance calls from hotels as they tend to overcharge. If you do not have a mobile-phone with international mobile plan, purchase an international phone card, which supplies a local number to call and offers a low rate. You can make collect calls from any phone by dialing *800/172444*, which will get you an English-speaking AT&T operator. To make an international call, you must dial 00 and then the country code.

Access Codes AT&T Direct. ☎ *800/172444.* **MCI WorldPhone.** ☎ *800/905825.*

CALLING CARDS

The few surviving payphones now only accept *schede telefoniche* (phone cards), not coins. You can buy cards of varying values (€5, €10, and so forth) at post offices, newsstands (called *edicole*), and tobacconists. Tear off the corner of the card and insert it in the slot. When you dial, its value appears in the window. After you hang up, the card is returned so you can use it until its value runs out.

LOCAL CUSTOMS AND TABOOS

GREETINGS

Italians greet friends with a kiss, usually first on the right cheek, and then on the left. When you meet a new person, shake hands and say *piacere* (*pee*-ah- *cher*-ay).

SIGHTSEEING

Italy is teeming with churches, many containing significant works of art. Because they are places of worship, care should be taken with appropriate dress. Shorts, cropped tops, miniskirts, and bare midriffs are taboo at St. Peter's in Rome, and in many other churches throughout Italy. When touring churches—especially in summer, when it's hot and sleeves are undesirable—it's wise to carry a sweater or scarf, to wrap around your shoulders before entering the church. Do not enter a church while eating or drinking—keep all food items in a bag. Avoid entering altogether when a service is being held. All mobile phones must be on silent. If there are signs reading *No photography* or *No flash photography*, abide by these rules.

OUT ON THE TOWN

In Italy, almost nothing starts on time except for (sometimes) a theater, opera, or movie showing. Italians even joke about a "15-minute window" before actually being late somewhere.

LANGUAGE

You can always find someone who speaks at least a little English in Rome, albeit with an accent. Remember that the Italian language is pronounced exactly as it's written, so many Italians try to speak English as it's written—somtimes with bewildering results.

You may run into a language barrier outside big cities, but a phrasebook and close attention to the Italian use of expressive gestures will go a long way.

Try to master a few phrases for daily use, and familiarize yourself with the terms you'll need to decipher signs and museum labels,

although most museums have exhibits labeled in both English and Italian.

Most exhibitions have multilanguage headphones you can rent, and English-language guidebooks are generally available at museum shops.

Many newsstands and bookstores stock a useful guide called *Rome, Past & Present*. It has photos of the most famous ancient monuments, together with drawings of what they originally looked like, and is particularly useful to get children interested in the ancient sites.

Private language schools and U.S.– and U.K.–affiliated educational institutions offer a host of Italian-language-study programs in Rome.

Language Schools American University of Rome. ⊠ *Via Pietro Rosselli 4* ☎ *06/58330919* ⊕ *www.aur.edu.* **Berlitz.** ⊠ *Via Fabio Massimo 95, Prati* ☎ *06/6872561* ⊕ *www.berlitz.it.* **Club Italiano Dante Alighieri.** ⊠ *Piazza Bologna 1* ☎ *06/44231490* ⊕ *www.clidante.it.* **Ciao Italia.** ⊠ *Via delle Frasche 5, Repubblica* ☎ *06/4814084* ⊕ *www.ciao-italia.it.* **Dilit International House.** ⊠ *Via Marghera 22, Termini* ☎ *06/4462593* ⊕ *www.dilit.it.* **Scuola Leonardo da Vinci.** ⊠ *Piazza dell'Orologio 7, Piazza Navona* ☎ *06/68892513* ⊕ *www.scuolaleonardo.com.*

MOBILE PHONES

Depending on how much you want to use your phone, it may be best to add an international package with some combination of calls, texts, and data—consult your service provider before your trip. Otherwise, roaming fees can be steep. For those with unlocked phones, consider buying an Italian SIM card and prepaid service plan. Or else rent an Italian phone (via a domestic provider) with an unlimited plan. Look into rentals carefully though—there are often hidden fees, and if you're not planning to make a lot of calls, it may be cheaper and simpler to stick with your own mobile phone.

Contacts Cellular Abroad. ☎ 800/287–5072 in the U.S. (toll-free), 800/3623–3333 within Italy (toll-free) ⊕ www.cellularabroad.com. **Mobal.** ☎ 888/888–9162 ⊕ www.mobalrental. com.

■ CUSTOMS AND DUTIES

You're always allowed to bring goods of a certain value back home without having to pay any duty or import tax. But there's a limit on the amount of tobacco and liquor you can bring back duty-free, and some countries have separate limits for perfumes; for exact figures, check with your customs department. The values of so-called "duty-free" goods are included in these amounts. When you shop abroad, save all your receipts, as customs inspectors may ask to see them as well as the items you purchased. If the total value of your goods is more than the duty-free limit, you'll have to pay a tax (most often a flat percentage) on the value of everything beyond that limit.

Of goods obtained anywhere outside the European Union or goods purchased in a duty-free shop within an EU country, the allowances are as follows: (1) 200 cigarettes or 100 cigarillos or 50 cigars or 250 grams of tobacco; (2) 2 liters of still table wine or 1 liter of spirits over 22% volume or 2 liters of spirits under 22% volume or 2 liters of fortified and sparkling wines;

and (3) 50 ml of perfume and 250 ml of eau de toilette.

Of goods obtained (duty and tax paid) within another EU country, the allowances are (1) 800 cigarettes or 400 cigarillos (under 3 grams) or 200 cigars or 1 kilogram of tobacco; (2) 90 liters of still table wine or 10 liters of spirits over 22% volume or 20 liters of spirits under 22% volume or 110 liters of beer.

Information in Rome Italian Customs, Fiumicino Airport. ✉ Via Bragadin, Fiumicino ☎ 06/65956366.

U.S. Information U.S. Customs and Border Protection. ☎ 877/227–5511 in the U.S., 202/325-8000 from abroad ⊕ www.cbp.gov.

■ ELECTRICITY

The electrical current in Italy is 220 volts, 50 cycles alternating current (AC); wall outlets take Continental-type plugs, with two or three round prongs.

Consider making a small investment in a universal adapter, which has several types of plugs in one lightweight, compact unit. Most laptops and mobile phone chargers are dual voltage (i.e., they operate equally well on 110 and 220 volts), so require only an adapter. These days the same is true of small appliances such as hair dryers. Always check labels and manufacturer instructions to be sure. Don't use 110-volt outlets marked "for shavers only" for high-wattage appliances such as hair dryers.

Note that straightening irons from the United States don't heat up very well and tend to blow a fuse even with correct adapters—as do American hair dryers.

Contacts Walkabout Travel Gear. ☎ 800/852–7085 in the U.S. (toll-free) ⊕ www. walkabouttravelgear.com.

■ EMERGENCIES

No matter where you are in Italy, dial *113* for all emergencies, or ask somebody (your concierge, a passerby) to call for you, as not all 113 operators speak English. Key words to remember for emergency situations are *Aiuto!* (Help!, pronounced ah- *you*-toh) and *Pronto soccorso*, which means "first aid." When confronted with a health emergency, head straight for the Pronto Soccorso department of the nearest hospital or dial ☎*118*. To call a Red Cross ambulance (*ambulanza*), dial *06/5510*. If you just need a doctor, ask for *un medico*; most hotels will be able to refer you. Ask the physician for *una fattura* (an invoice) to present to your insurance company for reimbursement. Alternatively, the city of Rome has a medical clinic dedicated to sick tourists (flu, fever, minor aches and pains, etc.). The Nuovo Regina Margherita Hospital offers a 24-hour tourist medical service and is staffed by one medical doctor and two nurses. The tourist service is located at the Nuovo Regina Margherita Hospital on Via Morosini 30 (Trastevere); the phone number is *06/58441*.

Other useful Italian words to use are *Fuoco!* (Fire!, pronounced *fwoe*-co) and *Ladro!* (Thief!, pronounced *lah*-droh).

Italy has a national military police force (*carabinieri*) as well as local police (*polizia*). Both are armed and have the power to arrest and investigate crimes. Always report any theft or the loss of your passport to either the carabinieri or the police, as well as to your embassy. Local traffic officers are known as *vigili* (though their official name is Polizia Roma Capitale)—they are responsible for, among other things, giving out parking tickets and clamping cars. Should you find yourself involved in a minor car accident, you should contact the vigili (*06/67691*). Call the countrywide toll-free number *113* if you need the police.

Most pharmacies are open Monday–Saturday 8:30–1 and 4–8, though some are open later or even 24 hours. A schedule posted outside each pharmacy indicates the nearest pharmacy open during off-hours (afternoons, through the night, and Sunday). Farmacia Internazionale

Capranica, Farmacia Internazionale Barberini (open 24 hours), and Farmacia Cola di Rienzo are pharmacies that have some English-speaking staff. The hospitals listed here have English-speaking doctors. Rome American Hospital is about 30 minutes by cab from the center of town.

For a full listing of doctors and dentists in Rome who speak English, visit your embassy's webpage.

Doctors and Dentists Aventino Medical Group. ⊠ *Via Sant'Alberto Magno 5, Aventino* ☎ *06/57288349, 06/5780738* ⊕ *www.aventinomedicalgroup.com*. **Roma Medica.** ☎ *338/6224832 for 24-hr service* ⊕ *www.romamedica.com*.

General Emergency Contacts Ambulance. ☎*118*. **Carabinieri (Military and Civilian Police Force). Fire Department.** ☎ *115*. **Polizia (Police).** ☎ *113*.

Hospitals and Clinics Rome American Hospital. ⊠ *Via Emilio Longoni 69* ☎ *06/22551* ⊕ *www.rah.it*. **Salvator Mundi International Hospital.** ⊠ *Viale delle Mura Gianicolensi 67* ☎ *06/588961* ⊕ *www.salvatormundi.it*.

Hotlines Highway Police. ☎ *06/22101*. **Roadside Assistance (Automobile Club d'Italia).** ☎ *803116*.

Pharmacies Farmacia Cola di Rienzo. ⊠ *Via Cola di Rienzo 223, San Pietro* ☎ *06/3243130, 06/3244476* ⊕ *www.farmaciacoladirienzo.com*. **Farmacia Internazionale Barberini.** ⊠ *Piazza Barberini 49* ☎ *06/4825456, 06/4871195*. **Farmacia Internazionale Capranica.** ⊠ *Piazza Capranica 96, Piazza Navona* ☎ *06/6794680*.

▌ HEALTH

Smoking is banned in Italy in all public places. This includes trains, buses, offices, hospitals, and waiting rooms, as well as restaurants, pubs, and discotheques (unless the latter have separate smoking rooms). Fines for breaking the law are exorbitant. You'll find that most people skirt the law by sitting outside on the many outdoor restaurant terraces. Sit inside if the smoke in outdoor seating areas bothers you. Many restaurants are now equipped with air-conditioning.

It's always best to travel with your own trusted medications. Should you need medication while in Italy, you should speak with a physician to make sure it is the proper kind and in case a prescription is necessary. Aspirin (*l'aspirina*) can be purchased at any pharmacy, as can over-the-counter medicines such as ibuprofen or paracetamol. Other over-the-counter remedies, including cough syrup, antiseptic creams, and headache pills, are sold only in pharmacies. Pharmacists are happy to dispense advice and, in the city center especially, almost always speak English.

▌ HOURS OF OPERATION

Banks are typically open weekdays 8:30–1:30 and 2:45–3:45 or 3–4. Exchange offices are open all day, usually 8:30–8, although ATMs offer the most economical exchange rates.

Post offices are open Monday–Saturday 8–2; central and main district post offices stay open until 7 or 8 on weekdays for some operations. You can buy stamps (*francobolli*) at tobacconists (*tabacchi*).

Most gas stations are open Monday–Saturday, with only a few open on Sunday, and most close during weekday lunch hours and at 7 pm for the night. Many, however, have self-service pumps that are operational 24 hours a day, and gas stations on autostrade are open 24 hours.

Museum hours vary and may change with the seasons. Many important national museums are closed one day a week, often Monday. The Roman Forum, other sites, and some museums may be open until late in the evening during the summer. Always check before you go.

Most churches are open from early morning until noon or 12:30, when they close for two hours or more; they open again in the afternoon, generally around 4 pm, closing about 7 pm or later. Major cathedrals and basilicas, such as the Basilica di San Pietro, are open all day. Note that sightseeing in churches during religious rites is usually discouraged. Be sure to have some coins handy for the *luce* (light) machines that illuminate the works of art in the perpetual dusk of ecclesiastical interiors. A pair of binoculars will help you get a good look at painted ceilings and domes. Many churches do not allow you to take pictures inside. When permitted, use of flash is prohibited.

A tip for pilgrims and tourists keen to get a glimpse of the pope: avoid the weekly general audience on Wednesday morning in Piazza di San Pietro, and go to his Sunday Angelus instead. This midday prayer tends to be far less crowded (unless beatifications or canonizations are taking place) and is also shorter, which makes a difference when you're standing. He is, however, much further away.

Most pharmacies are open Monday–Saturday 8:30–1 and 4–8; some are open all night. A schedule posted outside each pharmacy indicates the nearest pharmacy open during off-hours (afternoons, through the night, and Sunday).

Shop hours vary. Many shops in downtown Rome are open all day during the week and also on Sunday, as are some department stores and supermarkets. Alternating city neighborhoods also have general once-a-month Sunday opening days. Otherwise, most shops throughout the city are closed on Sunday. Shops that take a lengthy lunch break are open 9:30–1 and 3:30–7:30 or 4–8. Many shops close for one half day during the week: generally Monday morning in winter and Saturday afternoon in summer.

Food shops are open 8–2 and 4–7:30, some until 8, and most are closed on Sunday. They also closed for one half day during the week, usually Thursday afternoon September–June and Saturday afternoon in July and August. Larger supermarket chains often stay open on Sundays.

Termini station has a large, modern shopping mall with more than a hundred stores, many of which are open late in the evening. Pharmacies, bookstores, and boutiques, as well as cafés, bathrooms, ATMs, and money-exchange services, a first-aid station, and an art gallery and exhibition center can all be found here. The Drug Store here (which oddly doesn't sell medicine) is open daily 6 am–midnight. It sells sandwiches, fresh fruit, gourmet snacks, toiletries, gifts, and things like cameras, electric razors, and bouquets of fresh flowers (useful if you get an unexpected invitation to someone's home).

HOLIDAYS

If you can avoid it, don't travel at all in Italy in mid-August, when much of the population is on the move, especially around Ferragosto, the August 15 national holiday, when cities such as Rome are deserted and many restaurants and shops are closed. If you've done the tourist circuit several times, though, you may enjoy a quieter, emptier version of the city during this time.

National holidays are New Year's Day (January 1); Epiphany (January 6); Easter Sunday and Monday; Liberation Day (April 25); Labor Day (May 1); Republic Day (June 2); Ferragosto (August 15); All Saint's Day (November 1); Immaculate Conception (December 8); Christmas Day and the feast of Saint Stephen (December 25 and 26). Rome-specific holidays are Rome's birthday (April 21) and St. Peter and Paul Day (June 29).

▌ MAIL

The Italian mail system has improved tremendously with the introduction of a two-tier postal system. A *posta prioritaria* (first-class) stamp within Italy costs €0.80; to EU destinations, it costs €0.95 and usually guarantees delivery within three days. Mailing a letter or a postcard from Italy to the United States costs €2.30, and delivery times unfortanately can vary widely. When you mail letters, pay attention to the mail slot on the mailbox. The red mailboxes have two slots: the slot on the left is for Rome mail, and the slot on the right is for all other destinations (*tutte le altre destinazioni*), including abroad. Blue mailboxes are for foreign (*estero*) mail only.

The Vatican postal service has a reputation for efficiency, and many foreigners prefer to send their mail from there, although recently this has proven to be more myth than fact. It's not advisable to send anything valuable through either service. Even Vatican stamps can't guarantee that your mail won't get lost. You can buy Vatican stamps in the post offices on either side of Piazza di San Pietro, one next to the information office and the other under the colonnade opposite. During peak tourist seasons a Vatican Post Office mobile unit is set up in Piazza di San Pietro. All letters with Vatican stamps can be mailed only from the Vatican Post Office or Vatican mailboxes located near San Pietro.

Letters and postcards to the United States and Canada cost €2.30 for up to 20 grams and automatically go airmail. Letters and postcards to the United Kingdom cost €0.95. You can buy stamps at tobacco shops.

If you can avoid it, try not to have packages sent to you while you're in Rome or in Italy. Packages sent from abroad are notorious for being stopped by the Italian Customs Office, or Ufficio Dogonale. If your package gets stuck in customs, not only will you likely have to pay hefty customs fees but it could also take weeks for you to receive it. Sending medicine and even vitamins through the mail is highly inadvisable, and, if discovered, your package will be held up in customs for inspection.

Main Branches **Poste Italiane (Main Post Office).** ✉ *Piazza San Silvestro 19, Piazza di Spagna* ☏ *06/69737216* ⊕ *www.poste.it.*

■ MONEY

Rome's prices are comparable to those in other major capitals, such as Paris and London. Dining out can be expensive, but doesn't need to be. Do your homework and you can eat very well without breaking the bank. Clothes and leather goods are generally less expensive in Rome than in northern Europe, but pricey compared to the U.S. Public transport is one of the few things in Rome that is relatively cheap.

A 3-km (1-mile) taxi ride in Rome costs €8. An inexpensive hotel room for two, including breakfast, is about €120; an inexpensive dinner for two is €55. A simple pasta item on the menu is about €8–€12, pizzas €6–€9, a ½-liter carafe of house wine is around €6, and a cappuccino at the bar can cost €1.20. A movie ticket is approximately €8.50, the cheapest seat at the opera is €17, and full-fare admission to the Musei Vaticani is €16.

Though most places accept credit cards, cash is still preferred. This holds especially true for street markets and small mom-and-pop stores and restaurants.

ITEM	AVERAGE COST
Cup of coffee	€0.80–€1
Glass of wine or beer	€3–€8
Sandwich	€2.50–€5
2-km (1-mile) taxi ride	€8
Museum admission	€8–€16

Prices throughout this guide are given for adults. Substantially reduced fees are almost always available for children, students, and senior citizens when it comes to entrances to monuments and museums.

■TIP→ Banks never have every foreign currency on hand, and it may take as long as a week to order. If you're planning to exchange funds before leaving home, don't wait until the last minute.

ATMS AND BANKS

Your own bank will probably charge a fee for using ATMs abroad; the foreign bank you use may also charge a fee. Some banks, such as Citibank, which has a branch in Rome (near Via Veneto), don't charge extra fees to customers who use the Citibank ATM. Other banks may have similar agreements with Italian or foreign banks in Rome where customers won't get charged a transaction fee. Check with your bank to see if they have any agreements before your trip. Nevertheless, you'll usually get a better rate of exchange at an ATM than you will at a currency-exchange office or even when changing money in a bank. And extracting funds as you need them is a safer option than carrying around a large amount of cash.

■TIP→ PIN numbers with more than five digits are not recognized at ATMs in many countries. If yours has five or more, remember to change it before you leave.

ATMs are common in Rome and are the easiest way to get euros. The word for ATM in Italian is *bancomat,* and *codice segreto* for PIN.

CREDIT CARDS

Always inform your credit card company and bank that you'll be traveling or spending some time abroad, especially if don't travel internationally very often. Otherwise, the credit-card company or even your bank might put a hold on your card owing to unusual activity—not a good thing halfway through your trip. Record all your credit-card numbers— as well as phone numbers to call if your cards are lost or stolen—in a safe place, so you're prepared should something go wrong. Both MasterCard and Visa have general numbers you can call (collect, if you're abroad) in the event your card is lost, but you're better off calling the number of your issuing bank, since MasterCard and Visa usually just transfer you anyway; your bank's number is usually printed on your card.

If you plan to use your credit card for cash advances, you'll need to apply for a PIN at least two weeks before your trip. Although it's usually cheaper (and safer) to use a credit card abroad for large purchases (so you can cancel payments or be reimbursed if there's a problem), note that some credit-card companies *and* the banks that issue them add substantial percentages to all foreign transactions, whether they're in a foreign currency or not. Check on these fees before leaving home, so there won't be any surprises when you get the bill.

Although increasingly common, credit cards aren't accepted at all establishments, and some require a minimum expenditure. If you want to pay with a card in a small hotel, store, or restaurant, it's a good idea to ask before conducting your business. Visa and MasterCard are preferred to American Express, but in tourist areas American Express is usually accepted. Diners Club is rarely accepted.

Some credit card companies require that you obtain a police report if your credit card was lost or stolen. In this case, you should go to the police station at Termini train station or at Rome's central police station on Via San Vitale 15.

Reporting Lost Cards American Express.
📠 *06/72900347 for lost or stolen cards, 06/72282* ⊕ *www.americanexpress.com.*
Diners Club. 📠 *800/393939 in Italy (toll-free), 02/32162656 from abroad* ⊕ *www.dinersclub. com.* **MasterCard.** 📠 *636/7227111 from abroad (collect), 800/870866 in Italy (toll-free)* ⊕ *www.mastercard.com.* **Visa.** 📠 *303/967–1096 from abroad (collect), 800/819-014 in Italy (toll-free)* ⊕ *www.visaeu.com.*

CURRENCY AND EXCHANGE
The euro is the main unit of currency in Italy, as well as in 18 other European countries. Under the euro system, there are eight coins: 1, 2, 5, 10, 20, and 50 *centesimi* (at 100 centesimi to the euro),

and 1 and 2 euros. There are seven notes: 5, 10, 20, 50, 100, 200, and 500 euros.

As of this writing the exchange rate is about €0.90 to the U.S. dollar; €0.69 to the Canadian dollar; €1.19 to the pound sterling; €0.68 to the Australian dollar; and €0.66 to the New Zealand dollar. But of course these rates flucuate constantly, so be sure to consult a currency converter right before your trip.

■TIP➔ Even if a currency-exchange booth has a sign promising no commission, rest assured that there's some kind of hidden fee, or a very poor exchange rate. You're almost always better off getting foreign currency at an ATM.

Currency Conversion Google. ⊕ *www. google.com.* **Oanda.com.** ⊕ *www.oanda.com.* **XE.com.** ⊕ *www.xe.com.*

■ PACKING

Plan your wardrobe in layers, no matter what the season. Rome generally has mild winters and hot, sticky summers. Heavy rain showers are common in spring and late fall, so bring some fashionable rain boots. Take a medium-weight coat for winter; a lightweight all-weather coat for spring and fall; and a lightweight jacket or sweater for summer evenings, which may be cool. Brief summer thunderstorms are common, so take a folding umbrella, and keep in mind that anything more than light cotton clothes is unbearable in the humid heat. Few public buildings in Rome, including museums, restaurants, and shops, are air-conditioned. Interiors can be cold and sometimes damp in the cooler months, so take woolens or flannels.

Dress codes are strict for visits to the Basilica di San Pietro, the Musei Vaticani, and some churches: for both men and women, shorts, scanty tops, bare midriffs, and sometimes even flip-flops are taboo. Shoulders must be covered. Women should carry a scarf or shawl to cover bare arms if the custodians insist.

Those who do not comply with the dress code are refused admittance. Although there are no specific dress rules for the huge outdoor papal audiences, you'll be turned away if you're in shorts or a revealing outfit. The Vatican Information Office in Piazza di San Pietro will tell you the dress requirements for smaller audiences.

Many public and private bathrooms are often short on toilet paper so it's best to carry a small packet of tissues with you.

■ PASSPORTS AND VISAS

All U.S., Canadian, U.K., Australian, and New Zealand citizens, even infants, need a valid passport to enter Italy for stays of up to 90 days. Visas are not required for stays under 90 days.

■TIP➔ Before your trip, make two copies of your passport's data page (one for someone at home and another for you to carry separately). Or scan the page and email it to someone at home and/or yourself.

U.S. Passport Information U.S. Department of State. ☎ 877/487–2778 ⊕ travel.state.gov/passport. U.S. Embassy Rome. ✉ Via Vittorio Veneto 121 ☎ 06/46741 ⊕ italy.usembassy.gov.

U.S. Passport and Visa Expediters A. Briggs Passport & Visa Expeditors. ☎ 800/806–0581 ⊕ www.abriggs.com. American Passport Express. ☎ 800/455–5166 ⊕ www.americanpassport.com. Passport Visas Express. ☎ 888/5966028 ⊕ www.passportvisasexpress.com. Travel Document Systems. ☎ 800/874–5100, 877/874–5104 ⊕ www.traveldocs.com. Travel the World Visas. ☎ 202/223–8822 ⊕ www.world-visa.com.

■ RESTROOMS

Public restrooms are a rare commodity in Rome, and when found, they are often undesirable. Although there are public toilets in Piazza San Pietro, Piazza di Spagna, on the Palatine Hill, and in a few other strategic locations (often with a token service charge €0.50–€0.70), consider making well-timed pit stops at local snack bars. Standards of cleanliness and comfort vary greatly. Restaurants, hotels, department stores like La Rinascente and Coin, and McDonald's tend to have the cleanest restrooms. It's a good idea to carry a packet of tissues with you. There are bathrooms in all museums, airports, train stations, and in some subway stations. In major train stations you'll also find well-kept pay toilets for €1. Carry a selection of coins, as some turnstiles do not give change. There are also facilities at highway rest stops and gas stations: a small tip to the cleaning person is always appreciated.

■ SAFETY

Rome is like any other major Western city: generally quite safe, but the occasional pick-pocketing does happen. Wear a bag or camera slung across your body bandolier-style, and don't rest your bag or camera on a table or underneath your chair at a sidewalk café or restaurant. If you have to bring a purse, make sure to keep it within sight by wearing it toward the front. Women should avoid wearing purses that don't have a zipper. Men should always keep their wallet in one of their front pockets, with their hand in the same pocket. In Rome, beware of pickpockets on buses, especially No. 64 (Termini–Stazione di San Pietro); the No. 40 Express, which takes a faster route; and No. 46, which takes you closer to St. Peter's Basilica; on subways and in subway stations; and on trains, when making your way through the corridors of crowded cars. Pickpockets often work in teams and zero in on tourists who look distracted or are in large groups. Pickpockets may be active wherever tourists gather, including the Roman Forum, the Spanish Steps, Piazza Navona, and Piazza di San Pietro. ■TIP➔ Distribute your cash, credit cards, IDs, and other valuables between a deep front pocket, an inside jacket or vest pocket, and a hidden money pouch. Don't reach for the money pouch once you're in public.

TAXES

The service charge and IVA, or value-added tax (V.A.T.), are included in the hotel rate except in five-star deluxe hotels, where the IVA (12% on luxury hotels) may be a separate item added to the bill at departure.

Many, but not all, Rome restaurants have eliminated extra charges for *pane e coperto* (a cover charge that includes bread, whether you eat it or not). If there is such a fee, it will be €1 or €2 per person. Unscrupulous places sometimes add a service charge—this is only ever written in English and is not legitimate; if you see this on the menu, it might be best to find another place to dine.

Always ask for an itemized bill and a *scontrino,* or receipt. Be advised that the vendors selling imitation knock-off purses, sunglasses, and other accessories are unauthorized street vendors. If caught buying from any of these street vendors, you could be served with a hefty fine by Italy's tax police (Guardia di Finanza).

Value-added tax (IVA in Italy, V.A.T. to English-speakers) is 22% on luxury goods, clothing, and wine. On most consumer goods, it's already included in the amount shown on the price tag; on services, such as car rentals, it's an extra item. If a store you shop in has a "euro tax free" sign outside and you make a purchase above €155 (before tax), present your passport and request a "Tax Free Shopping Check" when paying, or at least an invoice itemizing the article(s), price(s), and the amount of tax.

To get an IVA refund when you're leaving Italy, take the goods and the invoice to the customs office at the airport or other point of departure and have the invoice stamped. (If you return to the United States or Canada directly from Italy, go through the procedure at Italian customs; if your return is, say, via Britain, take the Italian goods and invoice to British customs.) Once back home—and within 90 days of the date of purchase—mail the stamped invoice to the store, which will forward the IVA rebate to you.

V.A.T. Refunds Global Blue. ☎ *866/706-6090, 800/32111111 within Italy (toll-free)* ⊕ *www.global-blue.com.*

TIME

Rome is one hour ahead of London, six ahead of New York, seven ahead of Chicago, and nine ahead of Los Angeles. Rome is nine hours behind Sydney and 11 behind Auckland. Like the rest of Europe, Italy uses the 24-hour (or "military-style") clock, which means that after 12 noon you continue counting forward: 13:00 is 1 pm, 23:30 is 11:30 pm.

TIPPING

In Italy, service is always included in the menu prices. It's customary to leave an additional 5%–10% tip, or a couple of euros, for the waiter, depending on the quality of service. Tip checkroom attendants €1 per person, restroom attendants €0.50. In both cases tip more in expensive hotels and restaurants. Tip €0.05–€0.10 for whatever you drink standing up at a coffee bar, €0.25 or more for table service in a café. At a hotel bar, tip €1 and up for a round or two of cocktails, more in the grander hotels.

For tipping taxi drivers, it is acceptable if you round up to the nearest euro. Tip an additional €0.50, more if the porter is very helpful. Give a barber €1–€1.50 and a hairdresser's assistant €1.50–€4 for a shampoo or cut, depending on the type of establishment and the final bill; 5%–10% is a fair guideline.

On sightseeing tours, tipping your guides will always be appreciated, but isn't required. In museums and other places of interest where admission is free, a contribution is expected; give anything from €0.50 to €1 for one or two people, more if the guardian has been especially helpful. Service station attendants are tipped only for special services.

In hotels, give the *portiere* (concierge) about 15% of his bill for services, or €2.50–€5 if he has been generally helpful. For two people in a double room, leave the chambermaid about €1 per day, or about €4–€6 a week, in a moderately priced hotel; tip a minimum of €1 for valet or room service. Increase these amounts by one half in an expensive hotel, and double them in a very expensive hotel. In very expensive hotels, tip doormen €0.50 for calling a cab and €1 for carrying bags to the check-in desk, bellhops €1.50–€2.50 for carrying your bags to the room, and €2–€2.50 for room service.

■ TOURS AND GUIDES

ORIENTATION TOURS

Some might consider them kitsch, but guided bus tours can prove a blissfully easy way to enjoy a quick introduction to the city's top sights—if you don't feel like being on your feet all day. Sitting in a bus, with friendly tour guide commentary (and even friendlier fellow sightseers, many of whom will be from every country under the sun), can make for a delightful and fun experience—so give one a whirl even if you're an old Rome hand. Of course, you'll want to savor these incredible sights at your own leisure later on.

Carrani, CitySightseeing Roma, Roma Opentour, and other operators offer half-day and full-day tours in air-conditioned buses with English-speaking guides. The four main itineraries are: "Ancient Rome," "Classic Rome," "Christian Rome," and "The Vatican Museums and Sistine Chapel." Half-day tours cost around €30 and full-day tours (including entrance fees) start at about €50. The Musei Vaticani tour costs €65, but offers the advantage of not having to line up (sometimes for an hour or more) at the museum doors, awaiting your turn for admission. All the companies can also pick you up from centrally located hotels.

All operators can provide a luxury car for up to three people, a limousine for up to seven, or a minibus for up to nine, all with an English-speaking driver, but guide service is extra. Almost all operators offer "Rome by Night" tours, with or without dinner and entertainment. You can book tours through travel agents.

Various sightseeing buses following a continuous circle route through the center of town operate daily. **Viator** does a hop-on, hop-off bus loop of Rome's key tourist sights.

The least expensive organized sightseeing tour of Rome is the one run by City-Sightseeing Roma. Double-decker buses leave from Via Marsala, beside Termini station, but you can pick them up at any of their nine stopping points. A day ticket costs €25 and allows you to get off and on as often as you like. The price includes an audio guide system in six languages. The total tour takes about two hours and covers the Colosseum, Piazza Navona, St. Peter's, the Trevi Fountain, and Via Veneto. Tickets can be bought on board. Two- and three-day tickets are also available. Tours leave from Termini station every 20 minutes 9–8:30.

Of course, you get a real bargain if you do your sightseeing "tours" of Rome by public transport. Many buses and trams pass major sights. With a single €1.50 ticket, you can get in 100 minutes of sightseeing (or an entire day, with a €7 *giornaliero* ticket). Time your ride to avoid rush hours. The little electric Bus No. 116 scoots through the heart of Old Rome, with stops near the Pantheon, the Spanish Steps, and Piazza del Popolo, among others. The route of Bus No. 117 takes in San Giovanni in Laterano, the Colosseum, and the Spanish Steps. With public transport, though, you won't get any accompanying guide.

Since certain parts of the historic center are open to pedestrians only, some walking is involved in most escorted bus tours of the city. Don't forget to dress appropriately for visits to churches.

Rex Tours. You can tour Rome by bike or by Segway, by day or at night, with Rex Tours. They also offer a popular culinary tour, with tastings around the city. ☎ *06/87690040* ⊕ *www.rex-tours.com* ✉ *From €39.*

Rome Open Tour. Double-decker buses make 10 stops around Rome, and ticketholders can jump on and off. Discount prices can often be found on their website. ✉ *Rome* ☎ *06/45555270* ⊕ *www.romeopentour.it* ✉ *From €20.*

SPECIAL-INTEREST TOURS

You can make your own arrangements (at no cost) to attend a public papal audience at the Vatican or at the Pope's summer residence at Castel Gandolfo. The easiest way is to request them online through the Santa Susanna Church, the American Catholic Church of Rome (⊕ *www.santasusanna.org*).

WALKING TOURS

In Rome, there are tours and there are *tours.* Why pay to be led around by someone who just memorizes some lines and gives you the run-of-the-mill tour, when you can learn firsthand from the experts? **Context Rome** is an organization formed by a group of architects, archaeologists, art historians, sommeliers, and professors that give specialized walking seminars to small intimate groups (no more than six people) in and around Rome. **Walks of Italy** also gives specialized tours of Rome in small, intimate groups.

Through Eternity offers various walking tours of the city and its sights. For a popular food tour that's off-the-beaten-path, check out **Eating Italy Food Tours.**

Those who want to see everything during their trip to Rome without eliminating their daily run or workout might consider hiring a guide from **Sight Jogging Tours.**

Context Rome. With more than 50 scholars in its ranks of tour leaders, the walks led by Context are top-of-the-line and groups are a maximum of six people. Every day of the week there are five or six themed walks, which might include Imperial Rome: Architecture and History of the Archaeological Center; Underground Rome: The Hidden City; Baroque Rome: The Age of Bernini; Vatican Collections; and even Rome Shopping. ✉ *Via Santa Maria Maggiore 145* ☎ *06/96727371 within Italy, 800/691–6036 in the U.S.* ⊕ *www.contexttravel.com* ✉ *From €75 per person.*

Eating Italy Food Tours. The expert guides at Eating Italy will take you behind the scenes at restaurants and specialty food shops around the city, with samples and tastings, on various city food tours. Guides can also delve into the history of different neighborhoods and the slow-food movement in Italy. ☎ *215/6885571 in the U.S. or Canada, 333/8479138 within Italy* ⊕ *www.eatingitalyfoodtours.com* ✉ *From €75.*

Sightjogging. For a tour of Rome on the run (literally), this company has highly experienced trainers that give tours based on the level of difficulty chosen by the client. Routes may take in Villa Borghese, Imperial Forum and Colosseum, St. Peter's Basilica, and many other sights. Trainers meet tourists at their hotel and take them back after the run is over. ✉ *Rome* ☎ *347/3353185* ⊕ *www.sightjogging.it* ✉ *From €85 per person.*

Through Eternity. Tours of the Sistine Chapel, the Musei Vaticani, and St. Peter's are the specialty of Through Eternity Tours. Exclusive tours to the sights before they open to the public are especially popular. ☎ *06/7009336* ⊕ *www.througheternity.com.*

Walks of Italy. Small group tours with exclusive access to sights are the focus of this tour company. They also offer a variety of food tours and cooking classes. ☎ *069/4804888 within Italy, 202/684–6916 in the U.S.* ⊕ *www.walksofitaly.com* ✉ *From €55.*

EXCURSIONS

Most operators offer half-day excursions to Tivoli to see the fountains and gardens of Villa d'Este. Argiletum's afternoon tour to Tivoli includes a visit to Hadrian's Villa, with its impressive ancient ruins, as well as the many-fountained Villa d'Este. Most operators also have full-day excursions to Assisi, Pompeii, Capri, and Florence.

Argiletum Tour. For tours outside of Rome, including half-day excursions to Tivoli, Argiletum is a good option. Their afternoon tour to Tivoli includes a visit to Hadrian's Villa, with its impressive ancient ruins, as well as the many-fountained Villa d'Este. ⊠ *Via Madonna dei Monti 49* ⊕ *www.argiletumtour.com.*

▍ VISITOR INFORMATION

In Rome 060608 (Tourist Information and Tickets). ☎ *06/0608* ⊕ *www.060608.it.* **TurismoRoma.** ☎ *06/0608* ⊕ *www.turismoroma. it/?lang=en.*

ONLINE RESOURCES

For information on Italy in general, visit ⊕ *www.italiantourism.com* or ⊕ *www. initaly.com.* The Turismo Roma website (⊕ *www.turismoroma.it*) is packed with information about events and places to visit in Rome. Another particularly useful site is ⊕ *www.romeguide.it,* which has an English-language version. Particularly provocative, fascinating, and up-to-date are the monthly online issues of *The American,* a popular English-language magazine based in Rome (⊕ *www. theamericanmag.com*). "Magnificent" is the only word to describe this passionate writer's ode to the city's treasures of art and architecture, replete with hundreds of photos and little-known facts: ⊕ *www. romeartlover.it.* The official website for many of Rome's most famous sights (⊕ *www.060608.it.*) is a good place for advance ticket sales and reservations. One of the richest site-specific resources is ⊕ *www.capitolium.org,* for the Fori Imperiali; it has a large amount of historical and archaeological information. If you're particularly curious about the history of food and where to get the best of it in Rome, check out food writer Katie Parla's comprehensive blog at ⊕ *www.parlafood. com.* And for negotiating the many bus lines threading Rome and its surrounding areas, check ⊕ *www.atac.roma.it* and ⊕ *www.cotralspa.it.*

INDEX

A

Abruzzi ▣, 267
Acquolina ✕, 241
Addresses, 14
Africa ✕, 248
Agata e Romeo ✕, 248
Ai Marmi ✕, 241–242
Ai Monasteri (shop), 308
Ai Tre Scalini, 292–293
Air travel, 336–338
Al Ceppo ✕, 239
Al Pompiere ✕, 233
Al Settimo Gelo ✕, 223
Albergo Cesàri ▣, 267
Albergo del Sole al Biscione ▣, 268–269
Albergo del Sole al Pantheon ▣, 267
Albergo Santa Chiara ▣, 267
Alberto Pica ✕, 230
Alexanderplatz (club), 286
Alexandra ▣, 270
Alpi ▣, 275
Altare della Patria, 143–145
Amalia ▣, 266
Ancient Rome, 12, 51–84
Ancient "stone prow", 38
Antica Birreria Peroni (bar), 289–290
Antico Arco ✕, 242
Antico Caffè del Brasile ✕, 203
Antico Caffè Greco ✕, 235
Antiques shops, 302, 307–308, 313
Appian Way, 12
Arch of Constantine, 46, 83
Arch of Septimium Severus, 49
Arch of Titus, 46
Arco di Costantino, 46, 83
Arco di Settimio Severo, 60
Arco di Tito, 60–61
Arenula ▣, 270
Armando al Pantheon ✕, 225
Aroma ✕, 248–249
Atlante Star ▣, 265
ATMs, 351
Auditorium-Parco della Musica, 297
Aventino, 12, 193–200
lodging, 280

B

Babington's Tea Rooms ✕, 141
Babuino 181 ▣, 271
Baccano ✕, 238
Ba' Ghetto ✕, 233
Baker's Tomb, 207
Banks, 351
Baptistery, 211
Bar del Fico ✕, 225, 288
Barberini ▣, 270–271
Baroque art, 161–167
Baroque Quarter, 29–36
Bars, 288, 289–290, 291, 292–293
Bartolucci (shop), 312
Basilica di Massenzio, 61
Basilica di San Pietro, 16, 19, 87, 89, 92–97
Basilica Emilia, 47, 63
Basilica Giulia, 63–64
Basilica Julia, 47–48
Basilica of Maxentius, 46–47
Baths of Caracalla, 74, 195, 198–199
Baths of Diocletian, 157
Baylon Cafe ✕, 242
Beauty shops, 308, 313–314
Beehive ▣, 275
Bellacarne ✕, 233–234
Benediction Loggia, 94
Bernini's Elephant Obelisk, 125
Bioparco, 180
Birreria Peroni ✕, 225
Biscottificio Innocenti ✕, 242
Bocca della Verità, 198
Bookstores, 312, 314, 323–324, 325
Borgia apartments, 100
Borgo, 101
dining, 222–223
lodging, 265
shopping, 306
Botanical Gardens, 43
Braccialini (shop), 321–322
Britannia ▣, 282
Brioni (shop), 315
Buccone (wine shop), 182
Bus travel, 14, 338–339, 341–342
Business hours, 15, 349–350
nightlife, 285
restaurants, 219–220
shopping, 305

C

Caesar's Altar, 47
Cafés, 21, 234–235
Caffè Canova-Tadolini ✕, 141
Caffè del Arti ✕, 175
Caffè di Marzio ✕, 187
Caffè Propaganda ✕, 247–248
Caffè Romano dell'Hotel Inghliterra ✕, 235
Caffè Sant'Eustachio ✕, 226
Campidoglio, 55–59, 68
Campo de' Fiori, 12, 127–136
dining, 230–232
lodging, 268–270
nightlife, 289
shopping, 312–313
Campus Borum, 74
Capitoline Hill, 55–59, 68
Capo d'Africa ▣, 281
Cappella Cornaro, 158
Cappella di San Zenone, 206
Cappella Paolina, 205
Cappella Sforza, 205–206
Cappella Sistina (Santa Maria Maggiore), 205
Cappella Sistina (Vatican), 96–97
Capuchin Crypt, 24, 155, 168
Car rental, 340–341
Car travel, 339–341
Carapina ✕, 230
Carcere Mamertino, 58
Carceri Nuove, 135
Carmel ▣, 279
Cartoleria Pantheon dal 1910 (shop), 311
Casa dei Mattei, 38, 192
Casa delle Vestali, 62
Casa di Augustus, 78
Casa di Livia, 78
Casa di Santa Brigida ▣, 269
Casa di Santa Francesca Romana ▣, 279
Case Romane del Celio, 207–208, 209
Casina delle Civette, 158
Casina Nobile, 158
Casino dell'Aurora, 160
Castel Sant'Angelo, 113
Castroni ✕, 98
Castroni (shop), 307
Catacombe di San Callisto, 24, 212–213
Catacombe di San Sebastianom, 213
Catacombs and Via Appia Antica, 12, 203, 212–213
Cavour 313 ✕, 248
Celio, 12, 207–209
Celio ▣, 281
Centrale Montemartini, 18, 197

PHOTO CREDITS

NOTES

NOTES

ABOUT OUR WRITERS

Writer **Ariston Anderson** updated the Experience, Best Walks, Nightlife and Performing Arts, and Travel Smart chapters this edtion.

After her first Italian coffee and her first Italian *bacio* in 1999, **Nicole Arriaga** just knew she'd have to find a way to make it back to Rome, and she moved to the Eternal City in 2003 to earn her master's in political science. Nicole's freelance work has appeared in various travel publications, including *Romeing, 10Best,* Eurocheapo, and *The American.* When not writing, Nicole works as a programs coordinator for an American Study Abroad organization based in Rome. For this edition, she updated our Shopping and Where to Stay chapters.

Writer **Agnes Crawford** updated all the neighborhood chapters this editon.

This edition, writer **Maria Pasquale** updated the Where to Eat chapter.

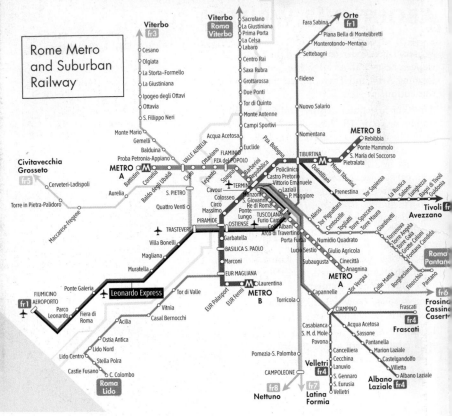

Rome Metro and Suburban Railway

Tickets

A ticket (BIT) valid for 100 minutes on any combination of buses and trams and one entrance to the metro costs €1.50. Tickets are sold at newsstands, some coffee bars, ticket machines in metro stations, and ATAC and COTRAL ticket booths. Time-stamp your ticket when boarding the first vehicle, and stamp it again when boarding for the last time within 75 minutes. You stamp the ticket at Metro sliding electronic doors, and in the little yellow machines on buses and trams.

Fare fees	Price
Single fare	€1.50
Biglietto integrato giornaliero (Integrated Daily Ticket) BIG	€6
Biglietto turistico integrato (Three-Day Pass) BTI	€16.50
Weekly pass	€24
Monthly unlimited pass	€35